W9-BIR-724

Noruegia

Tartaria

EVROPA

ASIA

Mongol

Mongul

Cathaio

Russia

Turcheltan

China

Natolia

Soria

Persia

Guzarate

India orien
talis

AFRICA.

Arabia

Aegyptus

Nubia

Tymba

Abissi
ni.

Manicon
go.

Mel
inde.

Gylam

Due Compagne

Don Garya

Poueula

Lantchido
mare

OCEANVS AE
THIOPICVS.

MAR DI INDIA

MALEVR

C. Bona Spes

Los Romeros

Pittacorum regio,
sic a Lusitanis appellata eo in
credibile tantas auium studem
magnitudinem.

ALIIS NONDVM COGNITA.

Texas DISCARDED

ADVENTURES IN TIME AND PLACE

James A. Banks

Barry K. Beyer

Gloria Contreras

Jean Craven

Gloria Ladson-Billings

Mary A. McFarland

Walter C. Parker

NATIONAL
GEOGRAPHIC
SOCIETY

"THE MUSTANGS OF LAS
COLINAS" IS A BRONZE
SCULPTURE OF NINE WILD
MUSTANGS CROSSING A
STREAM. SCULPTOR ROBERT
GLEN CREATED THIS
MONUMENT IN IRVING,
TEXAS, TO HONOR THE
PROUD PIONEER HERITAGE
OF OUR STATE.

 **Macmillan McGraw-Hill**

New York   Farmington

ACKNOWLEDGMENTS The Publisher gratefully acknowledges permission to reprint the following copyrighted material: Texas State Song, **"Texas, Our Texas"** © 1925 by William J. Marsh. Copyright renewed 1953 by William J. Marsh. Reprint granted by permission of Mary C. Hearne and Owen Edward Thomas, Copyright owners. Publisher, Southern Music Company. From **The Best Town in the World** by Byrd Baylor. © 1982 by Byrd Baylor, Charles Scribner's Sons, N.Y.; Macmillan/McGraw-Hill School Publishing, 1982. From **Leaves of Grass**, Edited by Harold W. Blodgett and Sculley Bradley. © 1965 by New York University. W.W. Norton & Company, Inc., N.Y. From **Life on the Mississippi** by Mark Twain (Samuel L. Clemens). ©1950 by Harper & Brothers. Harper & Brothers Publishers, N.Y. From **The Book of America; Inside 50 States Today** by Neal Peirce and Jerry Hagstrom, and **The Great Plains States of America** by Neal R. Peirce. Used by permission of W.W. Norton & Co. From **Anne of Green Gables** by Lucy Maud Montgomery. ©1908 by L.C. Page & Company, Inc., renewed 1935 by L.C. Page & Company, Inc., now Farrar, Straus & Giroux, Inc. A Bantam Book/published by arrangement with Farrar, Straus & Giroux, Inc. Anne of Green Gables is a registered trademark of the Anne of Green Gables Licensing Authority Inc. which is owned by the heirs of L.M. Montgomery and the Province of Prince Edward Island and located in Charlottetown, Prince Edward Island. From **Caddoan Mounds** by G. Elaine Acker. Used by permission of G. Elaine Acker. From **Aztec Thought and Culture; A Study of the Ancient Nahuatl Mind** by Miguel León-Portilla. ©1963 by the University of Oklahoma Press, Publishing Division of the University. From **The Indians of Texas; From Prehistoric to Modern Times** by William W. Newcomb, Jr . © 1961, renewed 1989. By permission of the University of Texas Press. From **Conquest of Mexico** by Hugh Thomas. ©1994 by Hugh Thomas. From **Lone Star: A History of Texas and the Texans**, by T.R. Fehrenbach, by permission of Author and Author's agents, Richard Curtis Associates, Inc. From **Travels and Adventures in Texas in the 1820's** by Mary Crownover Rabb. © 1962 by W.M. Morrison, Waco, Texas. From **Unknown Texas**, Edited by Jonathan Eisen and Harold Straughn. ©1988 by Macmillan Publishing Co. Collier Books, a division of Macmillan Publishing Company, N.Y. From **100 Days in Texas: The Alamo Letters** by Wallace O. Chariton. © 1990 Wordware Publishing, Inc. From **The Polish Texans** by T. Lindsay Baker. Used by permission of the University of Texas Institute of Texan Cultures, San Antonio. From **Anson Jones: The Last President of Texas** by Herbert Gambrell. © 1964, renewed 1992. By permission of the University of Texas Press. From **Black Texas Women: 150 years of Trial and Triumph** by Ruthe Winegarten. ©1995. by University of Texas Press, Austin. By permission of the author and the University of Texas Press. From **Governor Ann Richards & Other Texas Women: From Indians to Astronauts** by Ruthe Winegarten. ©1993 by Ruthe Winegarten. Eakin Press, a division of Sunbelt Media, Inc. Austin, Texas. From **American Cattle Trails East & West** by Marian T. Place. © 1967 by Marian T. Place. Reprinted by permission of Henry Holt and Co., Inc. From **Rails at the Pass of the North** by Edward A. Leonard. © 1981, reprinted by permission of Texas Western Press. From **The Texas Pecan** by Gene Fowler. Courtesy of Gene Fowler. From **Black Heroes of the Wild West** by Ruth Pelz, by permission of Open Hand Publishing Inc. © 1990 by Open Hand Publishing Inc. From **American Indian Leaders: Studies in Diversity**, edited by R. David Edmunds, by permission of the University of Nebraska Press. ©1980 by the University of Nebraska Press. From **Documents of Texas History**, Edited by E. Wallace, D. Vigness, G. Ward. ©1963 by The Steck Company; ©1994 by State House Press. State House Press, Austin, Texas. From **Women of theDepression: Caste and Culture in San Antonio, 1929-1939** by Julia Kirk Blackwelder. ©1984 by Julia Kirk Blackwelder. Texas A&M University Press, College Station. From **Citizens At Last: The Woman Suffrage Movement in Texas** by permission of Ellen C. Temple Publishing, Inc., Lufkin, Texas 75901. From **Straight From The Heart: My Life in Politics and Other Places** by Ann Richards with Peter Knobler. ©1989 by Ann Richards. Simon and Schuster, N.Y. From **The Loblolly Book II** edited by Thad Sitton and Lincoln King. ©1986 by Gulf Publishing Company, Houston, Texas. Used with permission. All rights reserved. **"Deep in the Heart of Texas"** printed in Texas: Great Songs of The Lone Star State, Words by June Hershey, Music by Don Swander. ©1941 by Melody Lane Publications, Inc. Melody Lane Publications, Inc. From **By George: The Autobiography of George Foreman** by George Foreman and Joel Engel. ©1995 by George Foreman. Villiard Books, a division of Random House, Inc., N.Y. From **Georgia O'Keeffe: Art and Letters** by Jack Cowart and Juan Hamilton. National Gallery of Art, Washington. © 1987 Board of Trustees, National Gallery of Art. Miss O'Keeffe's letters © 1987 by the Estate of Georgia O'Keeffe. From **The Art of the Woman: The Life and Work of Elisabet Ney** by Emily Fourmy Cutrer, by permission of the University of Nebraska Press. From **And As I Rode Out on the Morning** by Buck Ramsey. ©1993 by Texas Tech University Press. Texas Tech University Press. From "Attwater's Greater Prairie Chicken" in **The Official Wildlife Fund Guide to Endangered Species of North America, Vol. 2**, Originating Editor, John R. Matthews. ©1990 by Walton Beachum. Beachum Publishing, Inc., Washington, D.C. From **"Portland Passes Skateboarding, In-Line Skating Rules"** by Dan Parker. Article in the Corpus Christi Call Times on Feb. 8, 1995. From **Sea to Shining Sea** by Robert Leckie. ©1993 by Robert Leckie. Reprinted by permission of HarperCollins Publishers, Inc.

Macmillan/McGraw-Hill

A Division of The **McGraw·Hill** *Companies*

CONTENTS

UNIT TWO   *Settling the Western Hemisphere*
84

UNIT THREE *Independence and Statehood*
144

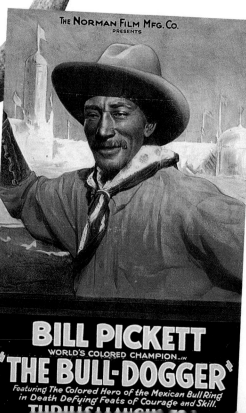

THE NORMAN FILM MFG. CO.
PRESENTS

BILL PICKETT
WORLD'S COLORED CHAMPION ...IN
'THE BULL-DOGGER'
*Featuring The Colored Hero of the Mexican Bull Ring
in Death Defying Feats of Courage and Skill.*

REFERENCE SECTION

FEATURES

MANY VOICES

CHARTS, GRAPHS, & DIAGRAMS

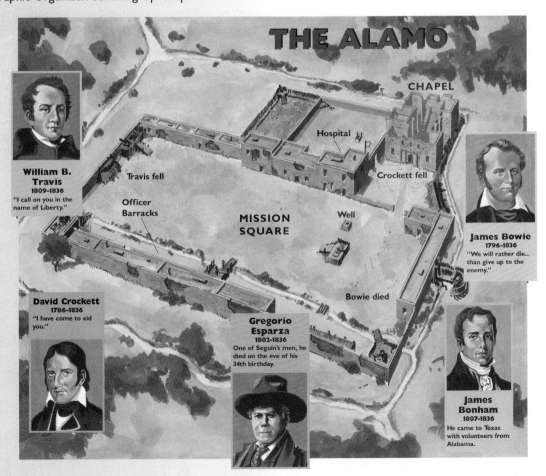

THE ALAMO

CHAPEL

Hospital

Crockett fell

William B. Travis
1809-1836
"I call on you in the name of Liberty."

Travis fell

Officer Barracks

MISSION SQUARE

Well

James Bowie
1796-1836
"We will rather die... than give up to the enemy."

Bowie died

David Crockett
1786-1836
"I have come to aid you."

Gregorio Esparza
1802-1836
One of Seguín's men, he died on the eve of his 34th birthday.

James Bonham
1807-1836
He came to Texas with volunteers from Alabama.

TIME LINES

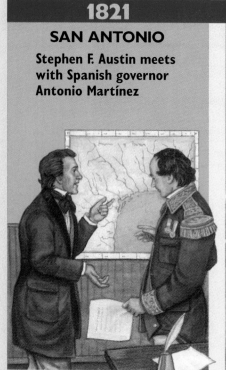

1821

SAN ANTONIO

Stephen F. Austin meets with Spanish governor Antonio Martínez

1823

LA GRANGE

Mary Crownover Rabb and other settlers begin moving to Texas

1832

SAN FELIPE DE AUSTIN

Texan settlers hold a convention on relations with Mexico

MAPS

YOUR TEXTBOOK at a glance

Your book is called *Texas: Adventures in Time and Place*. It has thirteen chapters, each with three or more lessons. There are also many special features for you to study and enjoy.

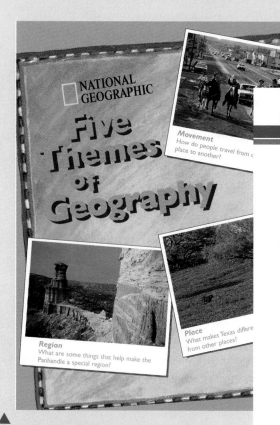

NATIONAL GEOGRAPHIC

Five Themes of Geography

Movement
How do people travel from one place to another?

Region
What are some things that help make the Panhandle a special region?

Place
What makes Texas different from other places?

▲ Special pages bring you ideas and **Adventures** in geography from **National Geographic**.

TEXAS, PART OF NORTH AMERICA

Texas is located on the very large body of land, or continent, known as North America. North America is one of seven continents in the world. Find North America on the map on this page. Which countries are to the north and south of the United States? Which country is Texas's closest neighbor?

The United States, Canada, Mexico, and the countries of Central America are all located on the continent of North America. You know that Texas is large compared to other states. But it is an entire continent that's even smaller, doesn't...

TEXAS POPULATION TODAY

In 1990 the United States government sent a letter and a list of questions to every home in our country. The letter was part of a census (SEN sus), a count of the people who live in a place. The United States census takes place every ten years. The census of 1990 asked people across the nation to give information about themselves. When Texans returned their letters, the government had learned a great deal about our state.

The census showed that 16,986,510 people were living in Texas in 1990. That's enough people to fill the Houston Astrodome 309 times! Population estimates since then show that Texas is now the second most populated state in the nation, after California. In the year 2000 the government will carry out another census. By then the population of Texas is predicted to be about 20 million.

DID YOU KNOW?

How big is Texas?
Texas is so large that the city of El Paso is closer to the state of California than it is to the city of Houston. And the city of Texarkana is closer to the state of Illinois than it is to El Paso!

Texas, Part of the Western Hemisphere

Links to LANGUAGE ARTS

Names with Meaning!

Have you ever been to Fredericksburg? What you might not know is that *burg* means "town" in German. You also read that Castroville was begun by Henri Castro. But did you know that *ville* means "town" in French?

Arroyo City got its name from a Spanish word. Look up the meaning of *arroyo* in the dictionary.

Learning About Texans

The 1990 census told us that only two out of every three Texans were born in our state. Every day, more than 400 newcomers move here from around the world. The census also told us that four out of five Texans live in cities.

◀ Some lessons have features called **Links** or **Did You Know—** activities to try and interesting information to share.

LESSON 3

A TRIP ACROSS TEXAS

READ ALOUD

Writer Dick Reavis knows the 72,000 miles of Texas highways better than almost anybody. He should. In 1987, he drove every mile of them! His trip took him through mountains, plains, coastal areas, and more. Along the way he learned that "the one thing Texans have in common is Texas."

THE BIG PICTURE

Geography (jee AHG ruh fee) is the study of Earth and all the different kinds of things on it. Land and water, plant and animal life, and human activities are a part of what geographers study.

One way to learn about our state's geography would be to travel across Texas. Suppose your class took a trip from the coast of the Gulf of Mexico to the Guadalupe (gwahd ul OOP ay) Mountains. Texas is about 770 miles across from east to west. If your school bus traveled 12 hours a day at 50 miles per hour, you would need more than 15 hours to make the trip. It would take even longer for your school bus to drive the 800 miles from the northern tip of the Panhandle to the south part of the Gulf coast.

Focus Activity

READ TO LEARN
What is the geography of Texas?

VOCABULARY
geography
landform
plain
plateau
basin
recreation
canyon
aquifer
spring

PLACES
Guadalupe Mountains
Coastal Plain
Balcones Escarpment
Guadalupe Peak
Rio Grande

Welcome to Texas
Drive Friendly - The Texas Way

20

Look for a variety of lessons and features. **Infographics** inform you with pictures and maps. You will build **Skills**, learn about **Legacies** that connect us to the past, and meet people who show what **Citizenship** is.

CITIZENSHIP
VIEWPOINTS
1800s: WHAT DID TEXANS THINK ABOUT JOINING THE UNITED STATES?

Three **DIFFERENT** Viewpoints

1 **SAM HOUSTON**
President of the Republic of Texas
Excerpt from Letter to United States President Andrew Jackson, written in 1836

My great desire is that our country Texas shall be annexed to the United States . . . It is [popular] to hold out the idea . . . that we are able to [support and protect] ourselves against any power . . . yet I am free to say to you that we cannot do it. . . . I look to you as [a] friend and . . . the [helper] of mankind to [get involved] in our behalf and save us.

Legacy
LINKING PAST AND PRESENT
Landmarks of TEXAS HISTORY

GEOGRAPHYSKILLS

Reading Elevation Maps

USING THE SKILL
Of course, elevation maps tell us about many things beside mountains and flat areas. For example, they give us important information about rivers.
Have you ever wondered why the water in a river flows? The answer is

and the country of Mexico. Then the Rio Grande empties into the Gulf of Mexico which is at sea level.

TRYING THE SKILL
You have just used the map to trace the path of

HELPING Yourself
• Elevation maps show you how high the land is above the sea level.
• Study the map key to see which colors stand for different

REVIEWING THE SKILL
Now use the elevation map to answer the following questions. Use the Helping Yourself box for hints.
1. What is elevation?

Infographic

Famous People and Places

Our state is filled with places that people find interesting and fun to visit. You can see why many Texans spend their vacations right in our own state. How many of these places have you visited?

Amarillo

Where else but at CADILLAC RANCH can you see 10 cars sticking out of

TOMMY TUNE was born here and studied at the University of Texas and the University of Houston, before moving to New York City to become one of our country's leading musical theater directors.

JOBETH WILLIAMS graduated from Jesse H. Jones High School before moving on to become a famous actress.

In 1981 **HAKEEM OLAJUWON** moved here from Nigeria to study and play at the University of Houston. He is now one of the world's best basketball players.

CATHERINE CRIER was a judge here before becoming a national television reporter.

Did you ever wonder who invented the first hamburger? According to the "HOME OF THE HAMBURGER" sign here, an Athens cook named Fletcher Davis achieved that honor back in 1895.

Dallas   Athens
Houston
Wharton

DAN RATHER was born here, then attended Sam Houston State College in Huntsville, before becoming one of our country's leading television reporters.

At the **TEXAS STATE AQUARIUM** you can see over 250 kinds of amazing sea creatures, including rare sea turtles that first came as injured "patients" and now call the aquarium home.

27

367

TEXAS'S LAND

Another way to see our state is by taking a plane ride. Before you begin your journey, you should know that landforms are the shapes that make up Earth's surface. Hills, for example, are one kind of landform. So is a plain, a large area of nearly flat land.

A View from Above

Now you are ready to begin your trip. Your plane is flying over the flat land of the Coastal Plain. Flying west, the land rises gently until you reach the Balcones Escarpment (bal KOH nus e SKAHRP munt), which cuts across part of Texas from north to south. An escarpment is a steep cliff. You are at the beginning of the "Hill Country."

Higher and Higher Land

Your pilot points out that the "Hill Country" is part of a plateau. A plateau is a high, flat area that rises steeply above the surrounding land. Read the words of the poet Byrd Baylor about the town of Fredericksburg, which is in the Hill Country. Fredericksburg is near Enchanted Rock, a well-known landmark. What landforms and other natural features does Baylor describe?

MANY VOICES LITERATURE

Excerpt from *The Best Town in the World*, written by Byrd Baylor in 1982.

All my life I've heard about
a little, dirt-road,
one-store,
country town
not far from a rocky **canyon**
way back
in the Texas hills.
This town had lots of space
     around it
          with caves to find
          and honey trees
          and giant rocks to
               climb.
          it had a creek
          and there were
          panther tracks
          to follow
          and you could swing
          on the wild grapevines.

_____
canyon: deep valley with steep sides

As you go west to the Panhandle, the land gets higher. Artist Georgia O'Keeffe once wrote to a friend about the Panhandle: "I am loving the plains more than ever it seems—and the SKY—Anita, you have never seen SKY—it is wonderful."

Farther west, mountains appear. You fly over Guadalupe Peak, the highest mountain in our state. Between the mountains are basins—low, bowl-shaped landforms surrounded by higher land.

21

The end of your book has a **Reference Section** with many types of information. Use it to look up words, people, and places.

Biographical Dictionary

The Biographical Dictionary tells you about the people you have learned about in this book.

Dictionary of GEOGRAPHIC TERMS

C

Cabeza de Vaca, Alvar Núñez (ka bā'sa da vä'kä), 1490?-1560? Spanish who was shipwrecked and enslaved by Indians in Texas. (p. 124)

Álvares (ka brāl', pä'dro äl'vä rēz) 1467? First Portuguese explorer to land in what is now Brazil. (p. 99)

nry (sis ne'rôs), 1947- In 1993, he ted States Secretary of Housing Development. (p. 340)

rd (clärk), 1815-1880 Governor of the Confederacy. (p. 229)

rah (kôk'rål), 1879-1892 Dallas man. (p. 257)

ristopher (ka lum'bas), 1451-1506 rer working on behalf of Spain in the Americas in 1492. (p. 118)

rancisco Vásquez de (kôr ô nä'dŏ, väs'kā väs'kāz da), 1510-1554 lorer who led an army into Texas r the Seven Cities of Gold. (p. 125)

ernando (kôr tes', er nän'dô), 1485- h conquistador who defeated the (p. 120)

Perfecto de (kôs, mär'tēn pär fek'tô), 1800-1854 Mexican general during evolution. (p. 164)

vid (krä'kät), 1786-1836 Led a unteers from Tennessee who e Alamo. (p. 167)

is Wright (kyu'nê), 1846-1897 erican businessman who served in tional governments. (p. 255)

nd J. (dā'vis), 1827-1883 Governor ring Reconstruction. (p. 240)

GULF (gulf)- Part of an ocean that extends into the land, larger than a bay.

PLATEAU (pla tō')- A high, flat area that rises steeply above the surrounding land.

DAM (dam)- A wall built across a river, creating a lake that stores water.

RESERVOIR (rez'ər vwär)- A natural or artificial lake that stores water.

ESCARPMENT (e skärp'mənt)- A steep cliff.

CANYON (kan'yən)- A deep, narrow valley with steep sides.

MESA (mā'sə)- A hill with a flat top, smaller than a plateau.

BUTTE (byūt)- A small, flat-topped hill with smaller than a mesa or a plateau.

VALLEY (val'ē)- An area of low land between hills or mountains.

DESERT (dez'ərt)- A dry, environment where few plants can grow.

COAST (kōst)- The land along an ocean.

BAY (bā)- Part of an ocean or lake that is partly surrounded by land.

Lessons begin with a **Read Aloud** selection and **The Big Picture**. Study with the **Read to Learn** question and a list of words, people, and places. Enjoy **Many Voices**—writings from many sources.

NATIONAL GEOGRAPHIC

Five Themes of Geography

Movement
How do people travel from one place to another?

Place
What makes Texas different from other places?

Region
What are some things that help make the Panhandle a special region?

Location
How do people know exactly where things are?

Human/Environment Interactions
What do people get from the Texas environment?

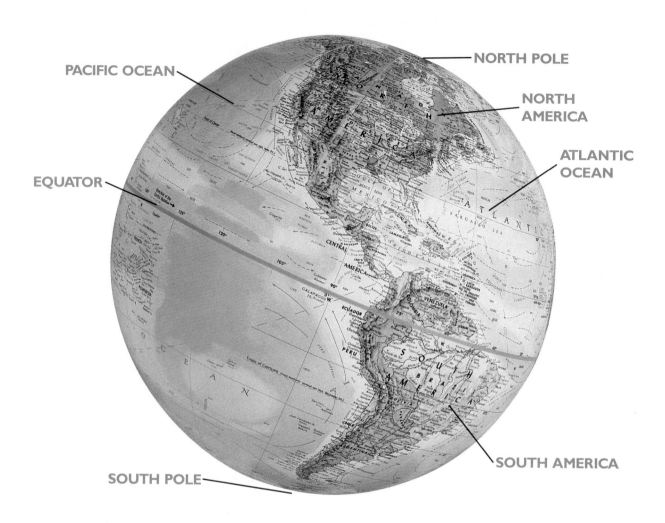

PACIFIC OCEAN

NORTH POLE

NORTH AMERICA

ATLANTIC OCEAN

EQUATOR

SOUTH AMERICA

SOUTH POLE

PART 1
Using Globes

VOCABULARY

ocean   hemisphere

continent   equator

What does a globe show?

- A globe is a small copy of Earth. Like Earth, a globe is a round object, or sphere. A globe is a useful tool for showing what Earth looks like.

- Globes show the parts of Earth that are land and the parts that are water.

- Earth's largest bodies of water are called oceans. There are four oceans—the Atlantic, Arctic, Indian, and Pacific. Look at the globe above. What color is used on the globe to show oceans?

- Globes also show the seven large bodies of land called continents. The continents are Africa, Antarctica, Asia, Australia, Europe, North America, and South America. Find North America and South America on the globe above. Which oceans do you see bordering these continents?

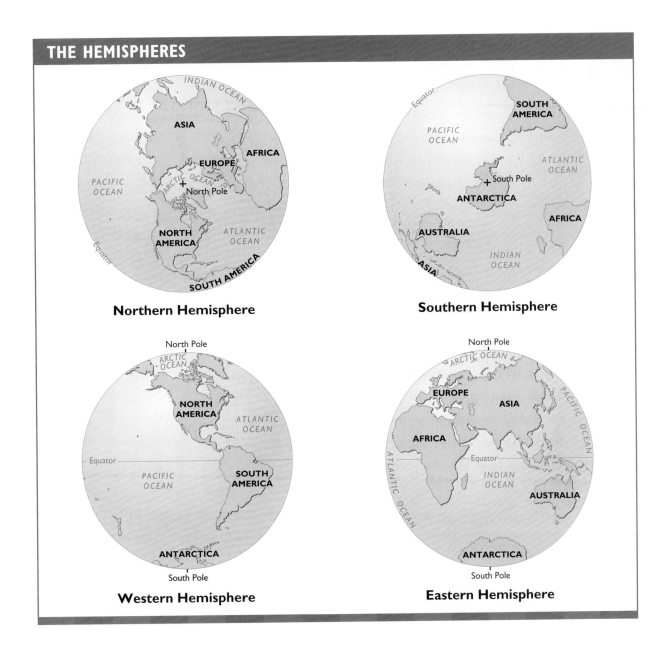

Northern Hemisphere

Southern Hemisphere

Western Hemisphere

Eastern Hemisphere

What are the four hemispheres?

- Look at the globe on page G4. Can you see the whole globe? You can see only half of a globe from any one direction. A word for half a globe or sphere is hemisphere. The word *hemi* means "half." Geographers divide Earth into four different hemispheres.

- Earth is divided into the Northern Hemisphere and Southern Hemisphere by the equator. The equator is an imaginary line that lies halfway between the North Pole and the South Pole. Look at the maps of the hemispheres, above. What continents are located on the equator? On which continent is the South Pole shown?

- Earth can also be divided into two other hemispheres. What are the names of these hemispheres? In which hemispheres do you live?

More Practice

There are more maps in this book that show the equator. For examples, see pages 60, 62, and 91.

PART 2
Using Maps

VOCABULARY
cardinal directions
compass rose
intermediate directions
symbol
map key
scale
locator

What are cardinal directions?

- Directions describe the way you face or move to get somewhere. North, east, south, and west are the main directions, or cardinal directions.

- If you face the North Pole, you are facing north. When you face north, south is directly behind you. West is to your left. What direction will be to your right?

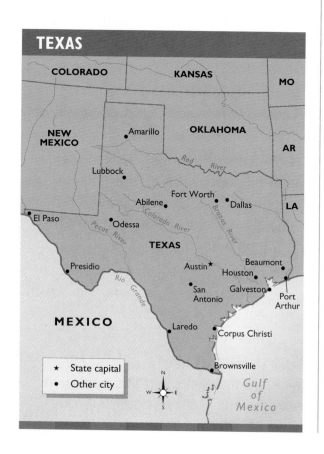

How do you use a compass rose?

- A compass rose is a small drawing on a map that can help you find directions.

- The cardinal directions are written as **N**, **E**, **S**, and **W**. Find the compass rose on the map below. In which direction is Lubbock from Amarillo?

What are intermediate directions?

- Notice the spikes between the cardinal directions on the compass rose. These show the intermediate directions, or in-between directions.

- The intermediate directions are northeast, southeast, southwest, and northwest. The direction northeast is often written as **NE**. What letters are used for the other intermediate directions? Which intermediate direction lies between south and east?

More Practice

You can practice finding directions using a compass rose on most maps in this book. For examples, see pages 27, 137, and 228.

TEXAS: Ports

COLORADO
KANSAS
MO
NEW MEXICO
OKLAHOMA
AR
Amarillo
Lubbock
Red River
Fort Worth
Abilene
Dallas
LA
El Paso
Odessa
Colorado River
Pecos River
Brazos River
TEXAS
Presidio
Austin ★
Beaumont
San Antonio
Houston
Galveston
Freeport
Port Arthur
Rio Grande
Port Lavaca
MEXICO
Laredo
Corpus Christi
Port Mansfield
Port Isabel
Brownsville
Gulf of Mexico

★ State capital
● Other city
■ Port

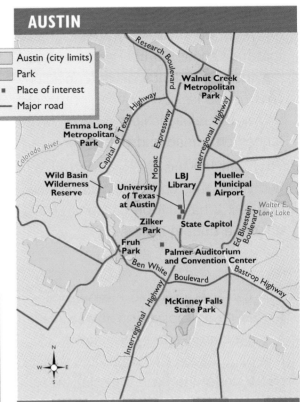

AUSTIN

Austin (city limits)
Park
■ Place of interest
— Major road

Research Boulevard
Walnut Creek Metropolitan Park
Emma Long Metropolitan Park
Capital of Texas Highway
Mopac Expressway
Interregional Highway
Wild Basin Wilderness Reserve
University of Texas at Austin
LBJ Library
Mueller Municipal Airport
Walter E. Long Lake
Zilker Park
State Capitol
Fruh Park
Ed Bluestein Boulevard
Palmer Auditorium and Convention Center
Ben White Boulevard
Bastrop Highway
Interregional Highway
Colorado River
McKinney Falls State Park

Why do maps have titles?

- When using a map, first look at the map title. The title names the area the map shows. It may also tell you the kind of information shown on the map. Look at the maps above. What is the title of each?

Why do maps include symbols?

- A symbol is something that stands for something else.

- On a map common symbols include dots, lines, triangles, and colors. Many maps use the color blue to stand for water, for example. What do dots sometimes stand for?

- Maps also often use symbols that are small drawings of the things they stand for. A drawing of a tree, for example, might stand for a forest. What might an airplane stand for?

How can you find out what map symbols stand for?

- Often the same symbol stands for different things on different maps. For this reason many maps include a map key. A map key gives the meaning of each symbol used on the map.

- When you look at a map, you should always study the map key. Look at the maps on this page. What symbol marks places of interest on the map of Austin? How many places of interest are shown on the map of Austin? What does the same symbol stand for on the map of Texas ports? How many ports do you see on the map?

More Practice

There are many maps with symbols and map keys in this book. For examples, see pages 29, 175, and 248.

What is a map scale?

- All maps are smaller than the real area that they show. So how can you figure out the real distance between places? Most maps include a scale. The scale shows the relationship between distances on a map and real distances.

- The scales in this book are drawn with two lines. The top line shows distance in miles. What unit of measurement does the bottom line use?

How do you use a map scale?

- You can use a ruler to measure distances on a map. You can also make a scale strip like the one shown on this page. Place the edge of a strip of paper under the scale lines on the map below. Mark the distances in miles.

- Use your scale strip to measure the distance between Castolon and Emory Peak. Place the edge of the strip

under the two points. Line the zero up under Castolon. What is the distance to Emory Peak in miles?

What do locators show?

- A locator is a small map set onto the main map. It shows where the area of the main map is located. Where on the map below is the locator?

- Most of the locators in this book show either the United States or the Western Hemisphere. Look at the map below. What area does this locator show?

More Practice

For examples of scales, see pages 22, 109, and 270. For examples of locators, see pages 10, 69, and 199.

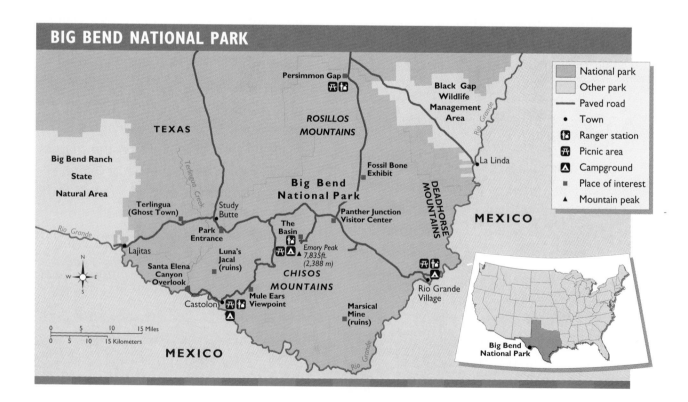

BIG BEND NATIONAL PARK

G8

PART 3
Different Kinds of Maps

VOCABULARY

political map
physical map
landform map
transportation map
historical map

What is a political map?

- A political map shows information such as cities, capital cities, states,

and countries. What symbol is used to show state capitals on the map below? What city is the capital of our state? What is the symbol for our national capital?

- Political maps use lines to show borders. The states or countries are also shown in different colors. Look at the map below. What color is used to show our state? How many different colors are used to show the states? What countries are shown?

More Practice

There are other political maps in this book. For examples, see pages 382 and R8.

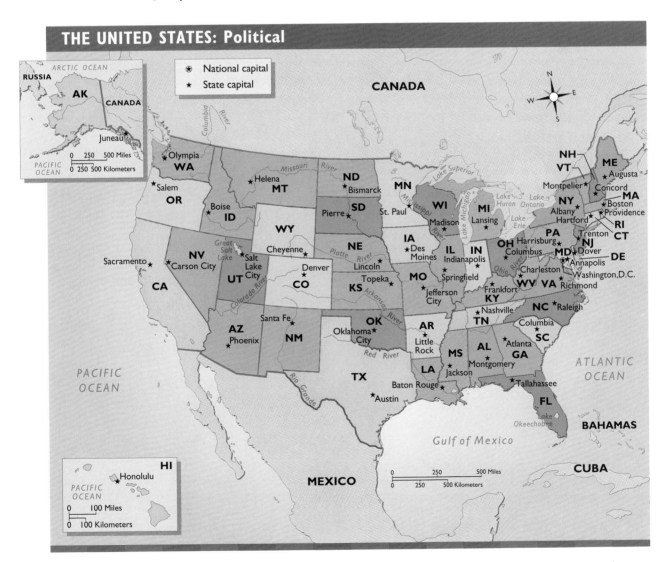

THE UNITED STATES: Political

⊛ National capital
★ State capital

G9

What are physical maps?

- Maps that show the natural features of Earth are called physical maps. There are different kinds of physical maps in this book.

- One kind of physical map shows landforms, or the shapes that make up Earth's surface. These maps are called landform maps. Mountains, hills, and plains are all examples of landforms. Landform maps also show bodies of water such as lakes, rivers, and oceans.

- Look at the map below. What kinds of landforms are found in Texas? What mountains are found in the western part of our state? What kinds of bodies of water are shown?

What is a transportation map?

- A transportation map is a kind of map that shows how you can travel from one place to another.

- Some transportation maps show roads for traveling by car, by bike, or on foot. Other transportation maps may show bus, train, ship, or airplane routes. What kinds of routes are shown on the map of Houston?

More Practice

There are other physical maps and transportation maps shown in this book. For examples of physical maps, see pages 22 and 45. For examples of transportation maps, see pages 248, 256, and 376.

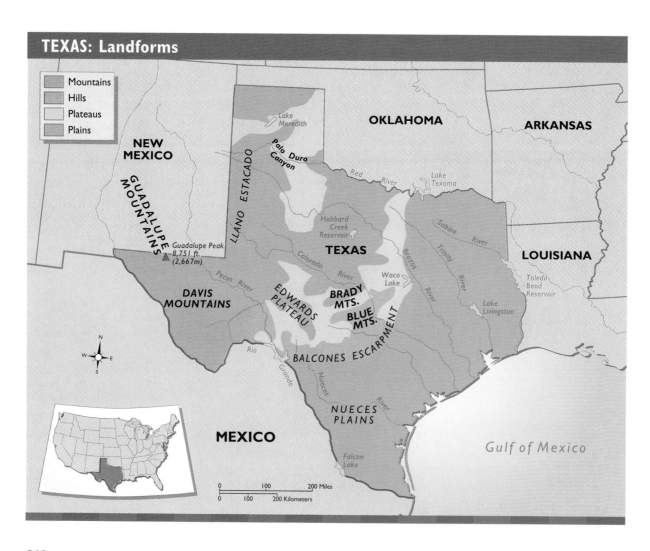

TEXAS: Landforms

- Mountains
- Hills
- Plateaus
- Plains

NEW MEXICO

OKLAHOMA

ARKANSAS

Lake Meredith

Palo Duro Canyon

GUADALUPE MOUNTAINS

LLANO ESTACADO

Red River

Lake Texoma

Guadalupe Peak 8,751 ft. (2,667m)

Hubbard Creek Reservoir

TEXAS

Sabine River

LOUISIANA

Pecos River

Colorado River

Waco Lake

Brazos River

Trinity River

Toledo Bend Reservoir

DAVIS MOUNTAINS

EDWARDS PLATEAU

BRADY MTS.

BLUE MTS.

Lake Livingston

Rio

BALCONES ESCARPMENT

Grande

Nueces River

NUECES PLAINS

MEXICO

Falcon Lake

Gulf of Mexico

0   100   200 Miles
0   100   200 Kilometers

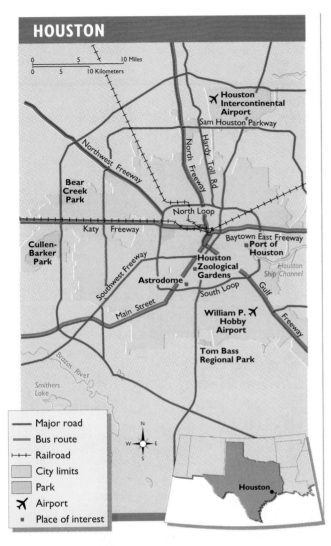

HOUSTON

Map Key:
- Major road
- Bus route
- Railroad
- City limits
- Park
- ✈ Airport
- ▪ Place of interest

Labels on map: Houston Intercontinental Airport, Sam Houston Parkway, Northwest Freeway, Hardy Toll Rd, North Freeway, Bear Creek Park, North Loop, Katy Freeway, Cullen-Barker Park, Baytown East Freeway, Port of Houston, Southwest Freeway, Houston Zoological Gardens, Houston Ship Channel, Astrodome, South Loop, Gulf Freeway, Main Street, William P. Hobby Airport, Tom Bass Regional Park, Brazos River, Smithers Lake, Houston

What is an historical map?

- An **historical map** is a map that shows information about past events and where they occurred.

- When you look at an historical map, first study the map title. What does the title tell you about the historical map below?

- Historical maps often show dates in the title or on the map. Study the map below. What historical date does it show?

- Next look at the map key. The map key tells you what the symbols stand for on the map. What is the symbol for the Texas colonies? In which country were the Texas colonies located? In which colony was the community of Victoria established?

More Practice

There are other historical maps in this book. For examples, see pages 165, 197, and 234.

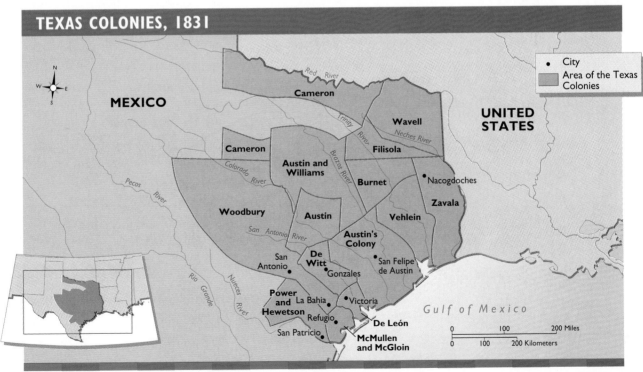

TEXAS COLONIES, 1831

Map Key:
- • City
- Area of the Texas Colonies

Labels on map: MEXICO, UNITED STATES, Red River, Cameron, Wavell, Trinity River, Neches River, Cameron, Filisola, Austin and Williams, Colorado River, Brazos River, Burnet, Nacogdoches, Pecos River, Zavala, Woodbury, Austin, Vehlein, San Antonio River, Austin's Colony, San Antonio, De Witt, San Felipe de Austin, Gonzales, Rio Grande, Nueces River, Power and Hewetson, La Bahia, Victoria, Refugio, Gulf of Mexico, San Patricio, De León, McMullen and McGloin

TEXAS STATE TREE: PECAN

TEXAS STATE FLAG
TEXAS STATE BIRD: MOCKINGBIRD
TEXAS STATE FISH: GUADALUPE BASS

2

Geography and People of Texas

" . . . wide and glorious . . ."

from "Texas, Our Texas"
See page 18.

WHY DOES IT MATTER?

"Honor the Texas Flag. I pledge allegiance to thee, Texas. One and indivisible." When we say this pledge to the Lone Star flag, we feel proud of our state.

Our state is like no other place in the world. It is huge. It reaches from the shore of the Gulf of Mexico to the high Guadalupe Mountains.

People from many different places have made Texas their home. What makes Texans different from one another? What do we have in common? Read on. Unit 1 will introduce the geography and people that make our state the special place that it is.

TEXAS STATE FLOWER: BLUEBONNET

Adventures
with
NATIONAL GEOGRAPHIC

★ Good Times in Texas

Feel like hiking? How about canoeing, tubing, beachcombing, or riding? You can do it all in Texas. The different landscapes and waterways of Texas create an outdoor playground. Start up north for horseback riding in the Panhandle. Head west to hike the Guadalupe Mountains. In the central part of the state, cool off in a tube on the Guadalupe River. Travel east to canoe in Big Thicket country. Amble south for a lazy day at the beach on Padre Island. As you explore, keep an eye out for bluebonnets, our state flower.

GEO JOURNAL

You only had time for one outdoor activity in Texas—but it was terrific! Describe your adventure.

A Place Called Texas

THINKING ABOUT
GEOGRAPHY AND CULTURE

Texas is a huge state. It has many different types of land, bodies of water, weather, and resources. It also has a great number of very special people—Texans. You will learn more about the land and people of our state as you read Chapter 1.

CANADA

UNITED
STATES

TEXAS

ATLANTIC
OCEAN

PACIFIC
OCEAN

MEXICO

THE LOCATION OF TEXAS

Focus Activity

READ TO LEARN
What is special about the location of Texas?

VOCABULARY
coast
natural feature
urban
rural
region
trade
interdependent

PLACES
Panhandle
Gulf of Mexico
Mexico
Houston
North America
Canada
Central America
South America
Western Hemisphere

READ ALOUD

Sam Houston was a Texas leader in the 1800s. In many of his letters he wrote about how much he loved Texas. He often called our state ". . . the finest country . . . upon the globe."

THE BIG PICTURE

Most Texans would agree with Sam Houston, for Texas is truly special. Our state is a place of golden fields, towering mountains, rolling hills, pine forests, and more. It is home to hundreds of unusual plants and animals.

Texas is BIG, too. A walk around the borders of our state would take longer than a walk across the United States. The Panhandle in northern Texas is so far from the Gulf of Mexico that Texans in the Panhandle can be shoveling snow while Texans along the Gulf are playing on the beach. That's BIG!

WHERE WE LIVE

Suppose you wanted to tell a pen pal in another country what Texas is like. You could talk about its location by looking at a map of the United States. You could say that it is in the southern part of the United States. You could mention that some of its borders follow straight lines. Others follow the course of winding rivers. Look at the map of Texas in the Southwest on page 10. Find the rivers that form some of Texas's borders. Another border, which is along the coast of Texas, is the Gulf of Mexico. A coast is the land along an ocean or sea.

You could also tell your pen pal that Texas's neighboring states are New Mexico to the west, Oklahoma to the north, and Arkansas and Louisiana to the east. Look again at the map on page 10. Find another neighbor of Texas that is not a part of the United States. The country of Mexico also has the the Gulf of Mexico as one of its borders.

Your pen pal might want to know some of the natural features found in Texas. A natural feature is any part of Earth's surface formed by nature. Texas has many different places, and they all have different features. Some of our state's natural features are sandy beaches, pine trees, rolling hills, tall mountains, and dry land.

Communities

You probably would tell your pen pal about your own community. A community is a group of people who live and work together in the same area. Maybe your community is just one neighborhood. Maybe it is made up of several neighborhoods near one another. Either way, it's "home."

Cities are made up of many communities. Have you ever visited or lived in Houston? Houston is our state's largest city. It also is one of the busiest urban areas in the United States. An urban area is a city and the communities that surround it. Most Texans live in large urban areas such as Dallas-Fort Worth, El Paso, Austin, and San Antonio.

Other Texans prefer rural life. Rural means living in the countryside. Many farm and ranch families have lived on the same land for a long time. Small towns are also found throughout rural Texas.

Houston is the fourth largest urban area in the United States. It was named for Sam Houston.

TEXAS, OUR HOME STATE

Texas has a special place among the fifty states of our country. It is the second largest state in the United States. Only Alaska is larger. Texas also has a special name. *Texas* comes from the Caddo Indian word *Tejas,* (TAY hahs) which means "friends." "Friendship" is the motto of our state.

Texas, Part of the United States

Look at the map of Texas in the Southwest on this page. If you are in central Texas and you travel north, which other state will you reach first?

The map shows you where in the United States Texas is located. Texas lies in the **region** of the United States called the Southwest. A region is an area with common features that set it apart from all other areas.

The four states of the Southwest are Texas, Arizona, New Mexico, and Oklahoma. A region is a little like a family. Each part of the region is different from the other parts. However, all the parts of the region share certain things. One thing that the states of the Southwest have in common is their location. Location is where a place can be found on Earth. You can find the states of the Southwest on the map below.

You have just read that Texas is part of the Southwest and part of the United States. Now let's find out what continent Texas is part of.

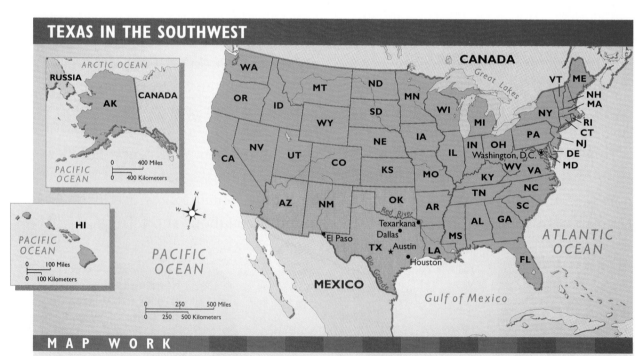

TEXAS IN THE SOUTHWEST

MAP WORK

Texas is one of the fifty states that make up the United States.

1. What states are Texas's neighbors?

2. What other states are also located along the Gulf of Mexico?

3. What bodies of water border our country?

TEXAS, PART OF NORTH AMERICA

Texas is located on the very large body of land, or continent, known as North America. North America is one of seven continents in the world. Find North America on the map on this page. Which countries are to the north and south of the United States? Which country is Texas's closest neighbor?

The United States, Canada, Mexico, and the countries of Central America are all located on the continent of North America. You know that Texas is big in size compared to other states. But as part of an entire continent Texas seems smaller, doesn't it?

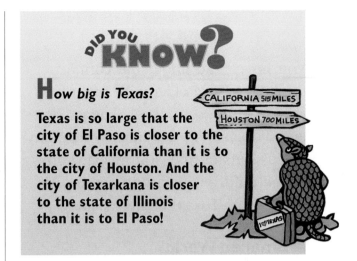

Texas, Part of the Western Hemisphere

Look again at the map. If a ship sailed from the tip of South America to Texas in North America, it would travel all that distance in just the Western Hemisphere.

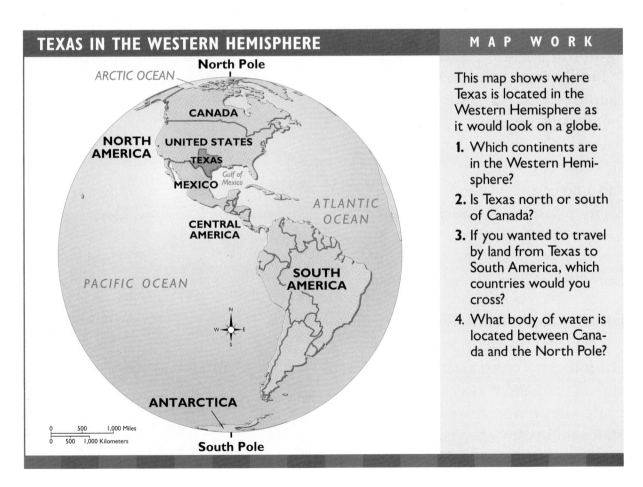

TEXAS IN THE WESTERN HEMISPHERE

North Pole
ARCTIC OCEAN
CANADA
NORTH AMERICA
UNITED STATES
TEXAS
Gulf of Mexico
MEXICO
CENTRAL AMERICA
ATLANTIC OCEAN
PACIFIC OCEAN
SOUTH AMERICA
ANTARCTICA
South Pole

0   500   1,000 Miles
0   500   1,000 Kilometers

MAP WORK

This map shows where Texas is located in the Western Hemisphere as it would look on a globe.

1. Which continents are in the Western Hemisphere?

2. Is Texas north or south of Canada?

3. If you wanted to travel by land from Texas to South America, which countries would you cross?

4. What body of water is located between Canada and the North Pole?

TEXAS, PART OF THE WORLD

You have read about the connections that Texas has with other states in the Southwest. Today, however, Texas also has links with many places outside the Southwest. Look at the diagram below to see the location of Texas in the world.

A Smaller World

Today people travel all over the world by airplane. Television, movies, computers, magazines, newspapers, and books all show us places that we might never see otherwise. These make the world seem like a "smaller" place because they connect Texans with many people around the world.

People from other countries visit our state for many different reasons. Some come for an education at colleges and universities. Others come to visit their families and friends who have moved here. Still others want to see the sights and enjoy the natural beauty of Texas.

Foreign Business in Texas

Texas is also an important center of business. Trains, planes, trucks, and ships make it easy for Texas to **trade** with other states in the United States and with other countries. To trade is to buy and sell goods.

In recent years Texas's trade has grown rapidly. Look at the picture of Julie Williams. Right now she is using her computer to do her home-

Texas is part of the Western Hemisphere and the world. The Port of Houston (bottom) is a center of international business. Ships docking here bring goods from around the world to people like Julie Williams (below).

WESTERN HEMISPHERE

UNITED STATES

TEXAS

LYKES LINES

work. Although Julie's parents bought the computer in a local store, the computer was made in California. They brought the computer home in a car that was made in Germany. The wheat crackers that Julie is eating were made in Illinois. The orange juice comes from oranges grown in her backyard.

Some of these goods came from places that are far away from Texas. No one place can meet all of the needs and wants of its people. Therefore, Texans trade with businesses around the world.

Today many companies and places around the world are becoming more and more **interdependent** (ihn tur dih PEN dunt). This word means people in each area are dependent on each other to meet their needs and wants.

The Sister Cities Program is a national program that helps people from the United States and around the world learn more about each other. There are many Sister Cities programs in Texas. One program in Fort Worth links local and foreign businesses together. It teaches people how to do business in each other's country. Fort Worth Sister Cities connects Texans with businesses in other countries such as Italy, Germany, Japan, and Indonesia.

WHY IT MATTERS

In this lesson you have read that Texas is part of the Southwestern region of the United States. You have seen that Texas is part of a growing, interdependent world in which other states and other countries have become closer neighbors. In the next lesson you will read about some of the ways in which Texans are connected to each other and to other places in the world.

✓✓ Reviewing Facts and Ideas

SUM IT UP

- Texas is part of the Southwest region of the United States, on the continent of North America, which is in the Western Hemisphere.
- Texas's trade is growing rapidly as it becomes more interdependent with other states and with countries around the world.

THINK ABOUT IT

1. What are urban and rural areas?

2. What is a region? In which United States region is Texas located?

3. **FOCUS** How would you describe the location of Texas? How would you describe the size of Texas?

4. **THINKING SKILL** List three _questions_ that you could ask to learn more about Texas's trade with other states and other countries.

5. **GEOGRAPHY** Suppose that you are explaining the diagram shown on page 12 to a third grader. What might you say?

TEXANS: PEOPLE OF MANY CULTURES

Focus Activity

READ TO LEARN
What do Texans share?

VOCABULARY
culture
custom
ancestor
immigrant
slavery
heritage
ethnic group

PLACES
San Antonio

READ ALOUD

In the magazine Texas Highways, writer Jack Lowry wrote about all the different people who call themselves Texans. He said, "At the root of Texas are its people. And though our roots reach deeply into soil from around the world, Texans form part of the same family tree."

THE BIG PICTURE

As you read in the last lesson, Texas has a special location in the United States, in the Western Hemisphere, and in the world. However, Texas is more than just a location on Earth. Even more important are the people who live in our state.

In order to understand Texas fully, we must study our people. We must study the cultures, or ways of life, of the many groups living in our state. Culture includes many things people share, such as beliefs, religion, languages, holidays, art and music. Culture even includes the foods people eat. People in Texas have many different cultures. All of these cultures have contributed to the Texan way of life that we all share. Our state has a rich culture because so many people have added to it.

PEOPLE AND CULTURE

"May I have a drumstick?" "Please pass the gravy!" On Thanksgiving many Americans eat a turkey dinner with all the trimmings.

Customs

Celebrating Thanksgiving is an example of an American custom. A custom is the special way a group of people does something. Customs are an important part of any culture. Giving birthday or Christmas gifts, for example, are customs in many cultures of the world.

Each culture has its own customs. When you sit down at the table, you may pick up a knife and fork. But some Texans will pick up chopsticks. These different ways of eating reflect the many cultures found in our state.

Foods from different cultures served at fairs and festivals can be tasty as well as fun to try.

At a Street Fair

Many Texan towns and cities hold street fairs. Perhaps you're in San Antonio during Fiesta, a ten-day, city-wide street fair in April. You can see a parade of beautiful floats. You can hear all kinds of music. High-school brass bands, Mexican mariachis (mah ree AH cheez), and African American blues can be heard, along with country music and rock 'n' roll.

While at Fiesta, you can watch a *charreada* (chahr ray AH dah), a Mexican rodeo. There are games of skill where you can win prizes. But your nose leads you away to the booths where you can try many different foods.

You might have some Texas barbecue. You could eat a *taco Polaco* (TAH koh puh LAK koh), a blend of a Mexican tortilla and a Polish sausage. Or the smell of German *bratwurst* (BRAHT werst) on a roll might tempt you. Or maybe you will try a San Antonio favorite, the corn chip. People are also serving Vietnamese egg rolls and French crêpes suzettes (KRAYP soo ZET).

These foods come from many cultures. But they are all served at Texan tables. A variety of cultures helps to make Texas an exciting place.

OUR ANCESTORS

Why do Texans have so many different customs and cultures? The answer has to do with our ancestors (AN ses turz). Beginning with your parents and grandparents, your ancestors are all those in your family who were born before you. Our ancestors came to our state from many lands and in many ways.

The First Americans

Some Texans can trace their roots in this state deep into the past. These are Native Americans, who are also called Indians. Their ancestors were the first people to live on this continent.

In addition to English, many Native Americans also speak the languages their ancestors spoke. As many as 250 different Native American languages are still spoken in the United States today.

New Americans

For thousands of years, Native Americans were the only people living in the land that is now the United States. Today people from almost every country of the world live here. What happened? Starting in the 1600s, immigrants (IHM ih gruntz) began to arrive. An immigrant is a person who comes to a new land from another place to live.

Our ancestors are an important part of who we are. Do you have pictures of your ancestors at home? In which countries were they born? Ask members of your family about your ancestors.

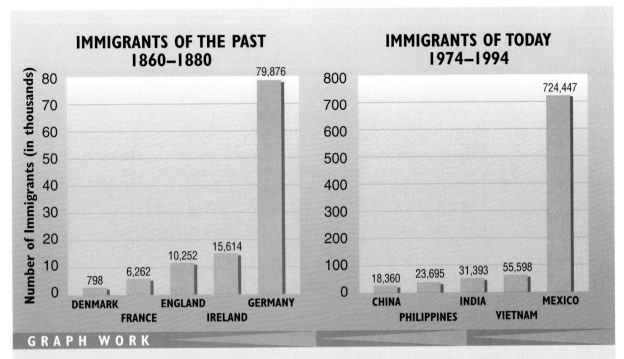

IMMIGRANTS OF THE PAST 1860–1880

Number of Immigrants (in thousands)

DENMARK 798
FRANCE 6,262
ENGLAND 10,252
IRELAND 15,614
GERMANY 79,876

IMMIGRANTS OF TODAY 1974–1994

CHINA 18,360
PHILIPPINES 23,695
INDIA 31,393
VIETNAM 55,598
MEXICO 724,447

GRAPH WORK

The graph shows immigration to Texas in the past and recently.

1. In which period did more immigrants arrive from Mexico? From Ireland?

2. Based on these graphs, did more immigrants arrive in Texas between 1860 and 1880 or between 1974 and 1994?

As with other states, most immigrants came to Texas to find a better life. However, in the 1800s, thousands of African Americans were brought to Texas against their will in slavery. Slavery is the practice of making one person the property of another. Enslaved people were forced to work for no pay and had no freedom. Slavery ended in the United States in 1865.

Our Heritages

Throughout history people have come to Texas from all over the world. Today many immigrants continue to come to Texas. Look at the graphs to compare the immigrants of today with those who came to our state in the past.

Many Texans value their Mexican heritage (HER ih tihj). Heritage is the history and culture a group of people share. People with a common heritage form an ethnic group. This is a group of people whose ancestors are from the same country. Our state's ethnic groups keep customs that may have started in other places. Honoring our ethnic heritage as well as our Texan heritage is part of what it means to be a Texan.

What Texans Share

Many Texans keep alive the cultures of their ethnic groups. Yet we all share many things as Texans. For example, we all share our state's song. The words and music to this song are on the next page.

17

Texas, Our Texas

MANY VOICES MUSIC

Not Fast

Words by Gladys Yoakum Wright and William J. Marsh

Music by William J. Marsh

1. Tex - as, our Tex - as! All hail the might - y State!
2. Tex - as, O Tex - as! Your free-born Sin - gle Star
3. Tex - as, dear Tex - as! From ty -rant grip now free;

mf

Tex - as, our Tex - as! So won - der - ful, so great!
Sends out its ra - diance To na - tions near and far.
Shines forth in splen - dor Your star of Des - ti - ny!

mf

Bold - est and grand - est, With - stand - ing ev - 'ry test; O
Em - blem of Free - dom! It sets our hearts a - glow, With
Moth - er of He - roes! We come, your chil - dren true, Pro -

f

Em - pire, wide and glo - rious, You stand su - preme - ly blest.
tho'ts of San Ja - cin - to And glo - rious A - la - mo.
claim - ing our al - le - giance, Our Faith, our Love for you.

Chorus *Repeat **ff***

p

God bless you Tex - as! And keep you brave and

2nd time

strong, That you may grow in pow'r and worth Thru -

1. out the a - ges long.

2. out the a - ges long.

SHARING CUSTOMS

When you step onto the football field, you are sharing a custom with all other Americans. When you dance in the Cinco de Mayo festival in Austin or another city, you are sharing a Texan custom that came from Mexico.

Texans also share important ideas with the rest of the United States. We obey the same laws. We respect the freedoms of other people. Respect for others is part of our country's heritage.

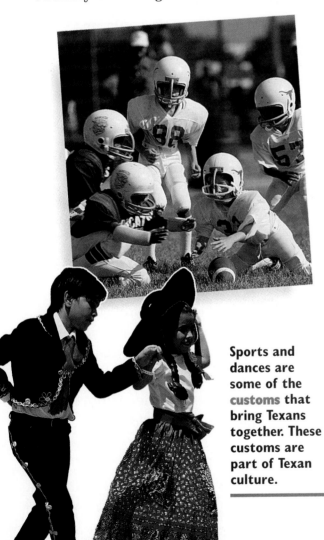

Sports and dances are some of the customs that bring Texans together. These customs are part of Texan culture.

WHY IT MATTERS

Texan culture began with Native Americans who lived here long before the first immigrants arrived. Immigrants from other countries continue to move to our state every day to find jobs and a better life. Today the Texan way of life is made up of many rich and interesting cultures. In the next lesson we'll learn about the land in which Texans live.

✓ Reviewing Facts and Ideas

SUM IT UP

- All people have a culture or way of life.
- Customs are an important part of a culture.
- Texans came to our state from many different lands and in many different ways.
- An ethnic group is made up of people with a common heritage.
- Texans include people of many ethnic groups.

THINK ABOUT IT

1. What is included in a group's culture?

2. What is an ancestor?

3. **FOCUS** What do all Texans share?

4. **THINKING SKILL** List two ways in which your life is the _same_ as it was for your ancestors. List two ways your life is _different_.

5. **WRITE** Suppose you are arriving in Texas for the first time. Write a letter to a friend describing your new home.

A TRIP ACROSS TEXAS

READ ALOUD

Writer Dick Reavis knows the 72,000 miles of Texas highways better than almost anybody. He should. In 1987, he drove every mile of them! His trip took him through mountains, plains, coastal areas, and more. Along the way he learned that "the one thing Texans have in common is Texas."

Focus Activity

READ TO LEARN
What is the geography of Texas?

VOCABULARY
geography
landform
plain
plateau
basin
recreation
canyon
aquifer
spring

PLACES
Guadalupe Mountains
Coastal Plain
Balcones Escarpment
Guadalupe Peak
Rio Grande

THE BIG PICTURE

Geography (jee AHG ruh fee) is the study of Earth and all the different kinds of things on it. Land and water, plant and animal life, and human activities are a part of what geographers study.

One way to learn about our state's geography would be to travel across Texas. Suppose your class took a trip from the coast of the Gulf of Mexico to the Guadalupe (gwahd ul OOP ay) Mountains. Texas is about 770 miles across from east to west. If your school bus traveled 12 hours a day at 50 miles per hour, you would need more than 15 hours to make the trip. It would take even longer for your school bus to drive the 800 miles from the northern tip of the Panhandle to the south part of the Gulf coast.

Welcome to Texas

Drive Friendly - The Texas Way

20

TEXAS'S LAND

Another way to see our state is by taking a plane ride. Before you begin your journey, you should know that landforms are the shapes that make up Earth's surface. Hills, for example, are one kind of land-form. So is a plain, a large area of nearly flat land.

A View from Above

Now you are ready to begin your trip. Your plane is flying over the flat land of the Coastal Plain. Flying west, the land rises gently until you reach the Balcones Escarpment (bal KOH nus e SKAHRP munt), which cuts across part of Texas from north to south. An escarpment is a steep cliff. You are at the beginning of the "Hill Country."

Higher and Higher Land

Your pilot points out that the "Hill Country" is part of a plateau. A plateau is a high, flat area that rises steeply above the surrounding land. Read the words of the poet Byrd Baylor about the town of Fredericks-burg, which is in the Hill Country. Fredericksburg is near Enchanted Rock, a well-known landmark. What landforms and other natural features does Baylor describe?

Excerpt from *The Best Town in the World*, written by Byrd Baylor in 1982.

*All my life I've heard about
a little, dirt-road,
one-store,
country town
not far from a rocky **canyon**
way back
in the Texas hills.*

*This town had lots of space
        around it
            with caves to find
            and honey trees
            and giant rocks to
            climb.
            It had a creek
            and there were
            panther tracks
            to follow
        and you could swing
        on the wild grapevines.*

canyon: deep valley with steep sides

As you go west to the Panhandle, the land gets higher. Artist Georgia O'Keeffe once wrote to a friend about the Panhandle: "I am loving the plains more than ever it seems—and the SKY—Anita, you have never seen SKY—it is wonderful."

Farther west, mountains appear. You fly over Guadalupe Peak, the highest mountain in our state. Between the mountains are basins— low, bowl-shaped landforms surrounded by higher land.

BODIES OF WATER

Rivers, streams, and lakes are sources of fresh water. Fresh water is important to every Texan. People, plants, and animals must have water to live and grow. Did you know that each Texan uses about 100 gallons of fresh water daily at home? That amount is enough to fill ten 10 gallon fish tanks!

Although most people travel by cars, buses, trains, and planes, water still provides an important form of transportation. Ships travel on rivers and across the Gulf of Mexico to transport goods and people to their destinations.

People use water for recreation. Recreation is what people do in order to relax and enjoy themselves. The variety of Texas's landscapes offers many opportunities for recreation. Do you like to swim, water-ski, sail, fish, or just float on a raft? You couldn't do any of these things without water.

The Gulf of Mexico

One of the most important bodies of water is the Gulf of Mexico. Ships from around the world dock along our 367 miles of coast. Fishing boats search the Gulf every day for oysters, shrimp, snapper, and other kinds of seafood.

All of our state's major rivers empty into the Gulf of Mexico. Look at the landforms map of our state. Name three of the rivers that empty into the Gulf of Mexico.

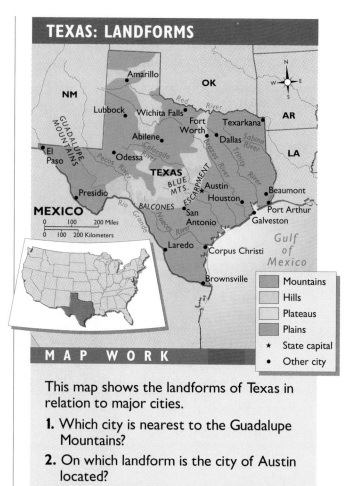

TEXAS: LANDFORMS

Mountains
Hills
Plateaus
Plains
★ State capital
• Other city

MAP WORK

This map shows the landforms of Texas in relation to major cities.

1. Which city is nearest to the Guadalupe Mountains?
2. On which landform is the city of Austin located?
3. Is Amarillo surrounded by plateaus or hills?

Our state's longest river is the Rio Grande (REE oh GRAHN dee). This river forms part of the border between the United States and the country of Mexico. *Rio Grande* means "big river" in Spanish. Part of the Rio Grande flows through deep canyons. A canyon is a deep valley with steep sides.

If you found a map of Texas in 1800, you would see only a few large lakes. Today, however, our state has about 212 major lakes. Most of these lakes were made by people.

Lakes play a big role in our state. Some lake water is used to water crops on farms. It is also used to make electric power for homes and businesses. But most lake water supplies our state's cities with drinking water. By the year 2000, lakes will be the source of more than half the water used in Texas.

Texas Aquifers

Some of Texas's water resources do not appear on the map and cannot be seen. They flow underground throughout our state. Look at the diagram below. Underneath a large portion of Texas's soil is a layer of limestone, a soft rock that absorbs rainfall like a sponge. This layer is called an **aquifer** (AHK wih fer). The Edwards Aquifer and the Ogallala (OH guhl lah lah) Aquifer are major sources of water for many areas of our state. Both of these aquifers supply water to millions of people in our state.

Aquifers are major sources of water in our state. What are the different ways in which water is being used in the diagram below?

A Texas Aquifer

Spring

Lake

Earth's Surface

Limestone

Limestone

Underground River

AQUIFERS SUPPLY WATER

One way to obtain water from an aquifer is to find a natural spring. A spring is a place where underground water comes to the surface. The other way is to drill down to the water and pump it out. Water that has been pumped out of the state's aquifers can not always be easily replaced.

Even when rain falls, it cannot always replace the water as quickly as it is removed. Some people think that by the year 2020 there may not be enough water in the Edwards Aquifer and the Ogallala Aquifer to supply the areas they do today. Tom Fox, a Texas water manager from San Antonio says, "If we hope to save these aquifers, now is our chance." Today Texans are working to make sure that we don't run out of water.

Links to SCIENCE

Ice is Nice!

Most of Earth's water is salt water. Very little of Earth's water is fresh water. People, plants, and animals need fresh water to stay alive. Most of the fresh water on Earth is in sheets of ice called glaciers (GLAY shurze). Look up the word glacier in an encyclopedia and find out where on Earth they can be found.

WHY IT MATTERS

Our state has a great variety of landforms. It has mountains that seem to touch the sky. It has plains that never seem to end. It has winding rivers and many lakes. Our state also has many people. In studying geography, we study the way people interact with Earth.

As you read "Saving Our Wildflowers" on the next page think about how it involves geography.

Reviewing Facts and Ideas

SUM IT UP

- Geography is the study of Earth and everything on it.
- The shapes that make up Earth's surface are called landforms.
- Texas has important bodies of water including the Gulf of Mexico, rivers, lakes, and aquifers.

THINK ABOUT IT

1. What is geography? In what ways can studying geography help you learn about our state?

2. What is a landform? Name four examples found in Texas.

3. **FOCUS** Name one plain, one river, and one mountain range that can be found in our state.

4. **THINKING SKILL** *Compare* and *contrast* the Coastal Plain to the mountain areas of our state.

5. **GEOGRAPHY** Locate the nearest city to where you live on the Texas landforms map on page 22. On what kind of landform is this city located?

Saving Our Wildflowers

AUSTIN, TEXAS—Driving down a state highway in the springtime, Texans can enjoy a rainbow of wildflowers, grasses, shrubs, and trees. There are millions of bluebonnets, reddish-orange Indian paintbrush and purple sage wildflowers.

Texans can thank Claudia Taylor "Lady Bird" Johnson for lining our roadsides with native plants. We call these plants *native* because nobody planted them here—they were a natural part of our state's environment in the past. As cities grew and new highways were built, however, many of these native plants died. Some were in danger of being lost forever. This was a problem not only in our state, but all over our country. These flowers, trees, and bushes provide food and homes for wild birds and animals. They also help prevent soil from washing away.

In the 1960s Lady Bird Johnson began to make people in our state and all over the United States more aware of native plants. At that time her husband, Lyndon Baines Johnson, was President of the United States. It was Lady Bird Johnson's idea to place native plants along roadsides and on public lands. When Lyndon Johnson's term as President was over in 1969, they returned to our state where Lady Bird Johnson continued her work.

In 1995 Lady Bird Johnson opened the National Wildflower Research Center near Austin. At the Center visitors can learn how to make their own gardens with native plants.

Why has Lady Bird Johnson worked so hard to make our environment beautiful for everyone? "Whatever its condition," she said, "the environment is a reflection of ourselves—our hopes, our successes and our failures." Lady Bird Johnson believes that making native plants a part of our state's landscape is one of the best ways to make sure that Texans have a healthy environment today and always.

"... a reflection of ourselves ..."

Lady Bird Johnson

GEOGRAPHYSKILLS

Reading Elevation Maps

VOCABULARY
elevation

WHY THE SKILL MATTERS

On your trip across Texas, you flew over many different landforms. Suppose you wanted to land near some mountains and go hiking. How would you find a flat place to land the plane? How would you know which mountain would be easy to hike? The landforms map on page 22 would have shown you some things. It shows the location of the Guadalupe Mountains and the Blue Mountains. But it would not have shown you other things, such as the fact that the Guadalupe Mountains are four times higher than the Blue Mountains!

For this kind of information, you would need an **elevation** (el uh VAY shun) map. Elevation is the height of the land above sea level. Elevation at sea level is 0 feet.

An elevation map uses colors to show elevations. You can see the map key on this page. For example, all the places shown on the map in gold are between 1,000 feet and 2,000 feet above sea level.

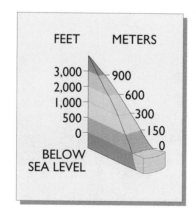

USING THE SKILL

Of course, elevation maps tell us about many things beside mountains and flat areas. For example, they give us important information about rivers.

Have you ever wondered why the water in a river flows? The answer is simple: water runs downhill. The elevation is higher where a river begins than where it ends. Gravity pulls the water downhill toward a lower elevation. Let's say the land slopes downhill toward the east. Then the river will flow from west to east. If the land slopes downhill toward the south, the river will flow south. That's why an elevation map can help you understand a river's course.

Let's try using an elevation map to trace the path of a Texas river. The Rio Grande begins in western Colorado. This is high in the Rocky Mountains. Locate the Rio Grande on the map on the opposite page. What color is the area where the Rio Grande enters Texas? Check the map key to find out what elevation this color represents. You can see that the Rio Grande enters Texas at an elevation of 3,000 feet above sea level.

Follow the river's path. You can see that the Rio Grande flows through areas of lower and lower elevation moving from west to east. For several hundred miles the Rio Grande forms the border between the state of Texas and the country of Mexico. Then the Rio Grande empties into the Gulf of Mexico which is at sea level.

TRYING THE SKILL

You have just used the map to trace the path of the Rio Grande. Now use the elevation map to trace the path of the Brazos River.

Does the Brazos River enter Texas at a higher, lower, or the same elevation as the Rio Grande? In which direction does the Brazos River flow? What does that show you about the elevations in that direction? Into what other body of water does the Brazos River flow?

REVIEWING THE SKILL

Now use the elevation map to answer the following questions. Use the Helping Yourself box for hints.

1. What is elevation?

2. How does an elevation map tell us which way a river flows?

3. What is the elevation of the highest point in Texas? What is the elevation along the Gulf of Mexico?

4. In what color would this map show a plateau that is 2,000 feet above sea level?

5. How does an elevation map help us learn about geography?

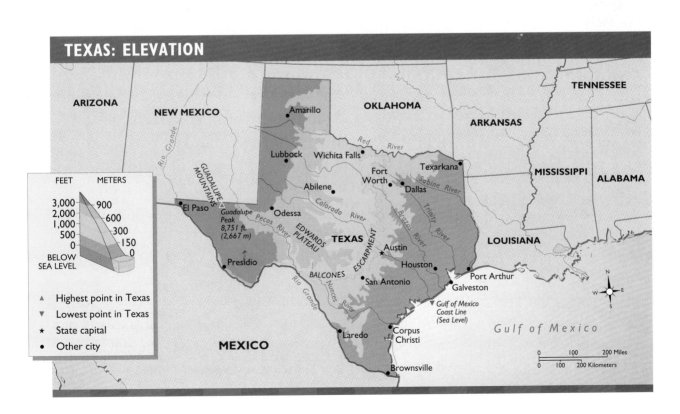

TEXAS: ELEVATION

OUR STATE'S CLIMATE

READ ALOUD

On a day in January, the temperature can be as low as 10°F in Amarillo. On the same day, 765 miles to the south, the people of Brownsville can be enjoying a temperature of 70°F. That's 60° higher! Can both of these places really be in our state?

THE BIG PICTURE

These differences are part of weather. Weather describes the air at a certain time and place. It may be hot or cold, rainy or dry, windy or calm. The weather may change very quickly in some parts of our state. In fact, there's an old Texas saying that "only fools and strangers predict weather in Texas."

Every place has a pattern of weather over many years. This is its climate (KLI mit). What's the difference between weather and climate? Weather affects how you live day to day. Will you bring an umbrella to school today? Climate affects long-range plans. Will you buy a light jacket or a heavy coat for the winter?

Different parts of our state have very different climates. Today many people have heating or air conditioners in their homes. These keep them comfortable in every season. Yet climate still plays a big role in our lives. It affects what foods we eat, how we enjoy ourselves, and the type of work we do.

Focus Activity

READ TO LEARN
Why do different parts of our state have different climates?

VOCABULARY
climate
temperature
precipitation
hurricane
tornado

PLACES
El Paso
Port Arthur
Amarillo
San Antonio
Corpus Christi
Pearsall
Galveston

TWO PARTS OF CLIMATE

What questions would you ask to find out about the climate of a certain place in Texas? You might start by asking, "How hot is the summer? How cold is the winter?" These questions ask about temperature (TEM pur uh chur). Temperature is how hot or cold the air is. The map below tells you what temperatures you might expect in January.

Another question you would want to ask is, "How much precipitation (prih sihp ih TAY shun) falls?" Precipitation is the moisture that falls to the ground in the form of rain, snow, sleet, or hail. The precipitation map below shows you how much precipitation to expect during one year. In El Paso, in the western part of our state, rainfall averages less than 10 inches per year. But in Port Arthur it averages more than 50 inches per year.

Investigating Climate

You have read about a plane trip across Texas. Temperatures would be cooler when you arrived in the Guadalupe Mountains than when you started out along the Gulf coast. Let's find out why.

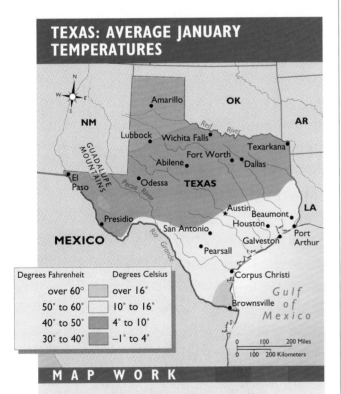

TEXAS: AVERAGE JANUARY TEMPERATURES

Degrees Fahrenheit	Degrees Celsius
over 60°	over 16°
50° to 60°	10° to 16°
40° to 50°	4° to 10°
30° to 40°	–1° to 4°

MAP WORK

January temperatures vary in Texas.

1. Which city is warmer in January, Houston or Presidio?
2. As you travel from Dallas to El Paso, would you notice a change? Why?

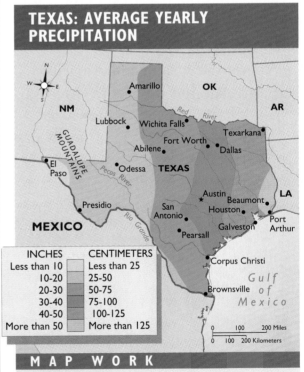

TEXAS: AVERAGE YEARLY PRECIPITATION

INCHES	CENTIMETERS
Less than 10	Less than 25
10–20	25–50
20–30	50–75
30–40	75–100
40–50	100–125
More than 50	More than 125

MAP WORK

Precipitation in our state varies greatly.

1. Which cities on the map receive the most precipitation?
2. In which direction does Texas get more precipitation?

WHAT AFFECTS CLIMATE?

Why is it cooler in the Guadalupe Mountains? In the last skill, you learned about elevation. Did you realize that it also plays a role in climate? The higher a place is above sea level, the colder its climate tends to be. That's why you might feel chilly if you are hiking in the Guadalupe Mountains.

How Far from the Equator?

What if your plane flew from north to south instead of from east to west? In May, in Amarillo, the temperature might be a cool 55°F. The trees would just be starting to bud. When you arrive in San Antonio, the temperature might be 80°F. And the trees here would have their leaves already.

Why is the weather in Amarillo and San Antonio different? One reason is that Amarillo is north of San Antonio. This means Amarillo is farther from the equator. The farther from the equator you go, the cooler the climate tends to be.

How Far from the Gulf?

Did you ever go swimming on a hot summer day and find your teeth chattering? Water heats up during the spring and summer more slowly than air. As a result, the Gulf of Mexico stays cooler than the land all through summer. Breezes from the Gulf cool the land near the coast. The Gulf also stays warmer during fall and winter than the land. In winter, Gulf breezes bring warmer air to the land.

Places far from the Gulf, however, do not feel these breezes. They tend to get hotter in the summer. They also get colder in the winter. The coastal city of Corpus Christi enjoys summer breezes from the Gulf. But the town of Pearsall, 138 miles inland, is too far away to be cooled by Gulf breezes.

The Panhandle (above) and the Gulf Coast (right) have very different kinds of weather. Tornadoes (far right) can occur all over our state.

Severe Weather

Sometimes our state gets violent storms with very strong winds and heavy rains known as **hurricanes** (HUR ih kaynz). In 1900 **Galveston** was destroyed by a hurricane. Many people died, and homes and businesses were lost. Today Galveston is protected by a 17-foot sea wall. And scientists know how to track hurricanes and warn people.

In some parts of our state, weather can change very quickly. A clear sky can turn suddenly dark. The Panhandle is in the part of our country known as **Tornado** (tawr NAY doh) Alley because there are more tornado warnings here than any other place on Earth. A tornado is a swirling funnel of wind that moves quickly. Tornadoes can occur in any part of our state. A tornado can destroy anything in its path.

WHY IT MATTERS

Our state is very large and has a variety of climates. Elevation, distance from the equator, and distance from the Gulf of Mexico affect the climate in different parts of our state in very different ways. As you continue to read about our state, think about how people learn to live in their surroundings.

Reviewing Facts and Ideas

SUM IT UP

- Climate is the pattern of weather a place has over a long period of time. Temperature and precipitation are the two key parts of climate.
- Elevation, distance from the equator, and distance from the Gulf of Mexico affect the climate of our state.
- Severe weather in Texas may include hurricanes and tornadoes.

THINK ABOUT IT

1. What is the difference between climate and weather?
2. As you move away from the equator, what happens to the climate?
3. **FOCUS** Why do different parts of our state have different climates?
4. **THINKING SKILL** _Predict_ whether or not El Paso will get snow next winter. Explain your prediction.
5. **WRITE** Write a description of the climate of your area. Include how the elevation, distance from the equator, and distance from the Gulf of Mexico affect it.

OUR STATE'S RESOURCES

READ ALOUD

Between the years 1918 and 1919, the number of people living in Ranger, Texas, jumped from 800 to 30,000. What happened? The answer is oil. The well at Nanny Walker's farm gushed oil. But the oil flow in Ranger lasted only about 20 years. Writer A. C. Greene says, "the boom had no place to go, so it left."

THE BIG PICTURE

You have already read about the climate and land-forms of our state. They are important parts of our environment (en VĪ run munt). Environment is the surroundings in which people, plants, or animals live. You can read about the environment in which some of our state's animals live in the Infographic on page 36.

Our lives are shaped by the environment in many ways. We also use and shape our environment. The people in Ranger, for example, pumped oil out of the ground for energy. Something in the environment that people can use is called a natural resource (REE sors). We depend on our environment for countless natural resources. But the most important resource in Texas is its people. Farmers, doctors, and teachers are just a few of the people we need to keep things running.

Focus Activity

READ TO LEARN

In what ways are natural resources important to Texans?

VOCABULARY
environment
natural resource
renewable resource
nonrenewable resource
fuel
petroleum
mineral
pollution
conservation
recycle

PLACES
Ranger
El Paso

RENEWABLE RESOURCES

Many different natural resources are found in our environment. Some of these are renewable resources. We can renew them. That is, we can replace them.

Forests

Trees, for example, are renewable resources because they can be replanted. About 100 kinds of trees grow in the Sabine National Forest, in eastern Texas. When a lumber company cuts down an area of forest, workers often plant new trees. Still, some trees take many years to grow. Because forests take time to be replaced, we need to use our forest resources carefully.

Soil

Texas farmers plant crops such as cotton, wheat, corn, and peanuts in the same soil over and over. But soil can be worn out from growing too many crops. Farmers renew soil by adding the fertilizer that plants use up as they grow. So soil is also a renewable resource. Parts of our state have rich soil that can produce plenty of food for Texans. Farmers must be careful that the soil does not get worn out.

Water

No one can live without water. Think about all the things you use it for. Drinking and washing, watering crops, and making electricity are all necessary to our lives. Every time it rains, water is returned to our state's land, rivers, lakes, and aquifers. That means water also is a renewable resource.

What renewable resource is each person in these photographs making use of?

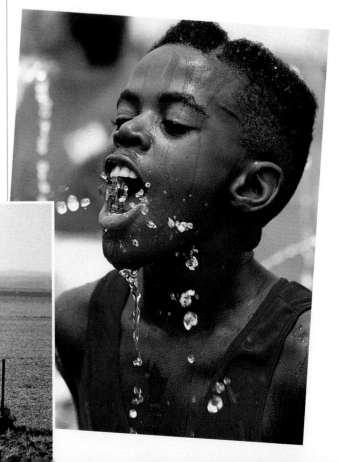

NONRENEWABLE RESOURCES

Some resources are nonrenewable resources. They are available in a limited supply. When we have used them up, they will be gone from our state forever.

Fuels

If you could look underground in Texas, you would see deposits of

various kinds of fuels (FYOO ulz), such as oil, coal, and natural gas. These fuels are nonrenewable resources. We use fuels to make heat or energy. With fuels we heat our houses, power machinery that plows fields, and

Gasoline is a fuel that is used to power cars.

cook meals. They power buses, cars, trucks, and airplanes.

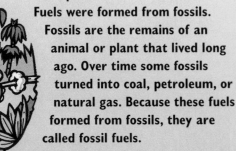

How did fuels get in the ground in the first place?

Fuels were formed from fossils. Fossils are the remains of an animal or plant that lived long ago. Over time some fossils turned into coal, petroleum, or natural gas. Because these fuels formed from fossils, they are called fossil fuels.

Fuels for the Future

Fuel resources affect the way cities grow in Texas. Like Ranger, many cities are built near oil wells. The thick, black oily liquid found underground is called petroleum (pih TROH lee um). Petroleum, or oil, as it is often called, is more valuable than gold. Without it, our country and others would come to a stop. Petroleum is used to make gasoline, plastic, and even some fabrics used to make clothing.

Scientists know that someday nonrenewable fuels will be gone. So they are looking for new sources of energy. Solar power is one possibility. Solar power is the use of the sun's rays to make energy. Wind power and water power are other possible sources.

Nuclear power is a source for electricity. There are two nuclear power plants in Texas. Some people have raised questions about the safety of nuclear power. Because of these questions, fewer nuclear power plants are being built today.

Minerals

Minerals are another kind of nonrenewable resource. A mineral is a natural substance found in the ground that does not come from plants or animals. Sulfur, limestone, uranium, and gypsum are minerals found in our state. Much of our country's sulfur is found in Texas. It is used to make matches, shampoo, and even some medicines.

POLLUTION AND CONSERVATION

As you have read, nonrenewable resources can be used up. Renewable resources need to be used wisely. **Pollution** (puh LOO shun) is the result of careless use of resources. Air, soil, or water become polluted as a result.

Let's see how the people in one Texas city are practicing methods of **conservation** (kahn sur VAY shun). Conservation is the careful use of our natural resources.

Conserving Water in El Paso

Like people in other parts of Texas, the people of **El Paso** have found ways to control water use. El Paso is very dry and needs to conserve its water.

Rules limit how often people can water lawns and how they wash their cars. Many people's gardens contain plants that need little water.

Recycling in El Paso

Another way to use our resources wisely is to **recycle** (ree SĪ kul). To recycle something is to use it again. Many people in El Paso and other Texas cities recycle newspaper, aluminum, tin and steel cans, paper, glass, and some plastics.

What are some other ways that you can recycle? Instead of using a fresh sheet of paper, why not write your list of chores on the back of a used envelope? You can decorate a cardboard box and store your games in it. What other ways can you recycle?

Recycling, conserving water, and growing plants that need little water are examples of using our resources wisely.

Infographic

Animal Life of Texas

Animals, too, are a natural resource. And Texas is crawling, hopping, and soaring with some truly amazing animals! What are just a few of the animals you might find outside your window?

4. RATTLESNAKES have a warning rattle that grows each time they shed their skin. Ten different kinds of rattlesnakes live in Texas.

5. GUADALUPE BASS are our state fish. You'll find this freshwater fish in many lakes and streams on the Edwards Plateau.

6. ARMADILLOS are bony-plated animals found just about everywhere in Texas. The name is Spanish for "little armored one."

7. MOCKINGBIRDS are the state bird of Texas. The mockingbird can imitate the sounds of many different birds. It can even imitate the sounds of street noises and machinery!

1. PRAIRIE DOGS live in groups called "towns," in places such as Big Bend and Guadalupe Mountains National Parks. If you visit you might hear their barking "yip."

2. JAVELINAS, or peccaries, are pig-like animals. They eat prickly-pear cactuses as well as grasses, fruit, and insects.

3. MOUNTAIN LIONS— also called pumas, panthers, or cougars—are endangered, or in danger of disappearing forever. People have killed mountain lions and built on the land where these animals used to roam.

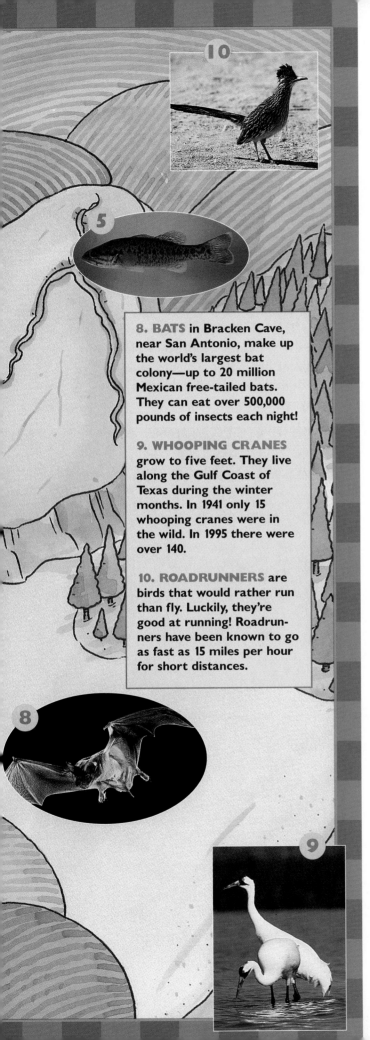

8. BATS in Bracken Cave, near San Antonio, make up the world's largest bat colony—up to 20 million Mexican free-tailed bats. They can eat over 500,000 pounds of insects each night!

9. WHOOPING CRANES grow to five feet. They live along the Gulf Coast of Texas during the winter months. In 1941 only 15 whooping cranes were in the wild. In 1995 there were over 140.

10. ROADRUNNERS are birds that would rather run than fly. Luckily, they're good at running! Roadrunners have been known to go as fast as 15 miles per hour for short distances.

WHY IT MATTERS

People are our most important resource. We must continue to develop our human resources through education so that our state and country can continue to grow. Our human resources are finding ways to use and conserve all the other resources.

✓✓ Reviewing Facts and Ideas

SUM IT UP

- Natural resources are things in the environment that are useful to people. People are our state's most important resource.
- Renewable resources in Texas include forests, soil, and water.
- Nonrenewable resources include fuels and minerals.
- Conservation helps to protect our state's resources.

THINK ABOUT IT

1. List three examples of natural resources. Are they renewable or nonrenewable?

2. How do farmers renew soil when they plant crops?

3. **FOCUS** Why is it important for Texans to protect the natural resources found in our state?

4. **THINKING SKILL** *Classify* solar power as a resource. Is it renewable or nonrenewable? Why?

5. **GEOGRAPHY** Name one natural resource that is important to the area in which you live. What do people use this resource for?

National Parklands in Texas

Have you ever visited one of the National Parklands in Texas? Maybe you have seen some of the scenery shown on these pages. National Parks and other protected places such as Seashores and Preserves are lands the United States government has set aside to protect wildlife and plant life. They are a legacy for all Americans to enjoy. A legacy is something we have received from the past that we want to pass on to the future.

National Parklands are a source of wonder. Some artists have captured that sense of wonder in paintings and photographs. Others have written about the natural beauty of the land that is Texas.

As you read the words and look at the pictures, think about what nature means to you. Thanks to our National Parklands, you may have the chance to visit some of these special places yourself!

Big Thicket National Preserve is a huge forest set aside to protect plant and animal life. Some visitors enjoy paddling canoes or fishing in the bayous.

One of our highest mountains is El Capitan in Guadalupe Mountains National Park. It is topped by a hunk of bare rock that rises 8,085 feet into the sky. Hike it for a beautiful view. But go slow, because the trail is very steep.

Padre Island National Seashore is one of the last natural seashores in the United States. Visitors swim or comb the beaches for shells. Or they can climb to the top of the Port Isabel Lighthouse.

CHAPTER 1 REVIEW

THINKING ABOUT VOCABULARY

Number a sheet of paper from 1 to 10. Next to each number write the word or phrase from the list that best completes the sentence.

ancestor
climate
conservation
culture
environment

geography
landform
natural resource
rural
region

1. A _____ is an area with common features that set it apart from other areas.

2. If you live in a small town or in the countryside, you live in a _____ area.

3. The way of life of a group of people is called its _____.

4. An _____ is any person in your family who was born before you.

5. _____ is the study of Earth and all the different kinds of things on it.

6. A _____ is any of the shapes that make up the surface of Earth.

7. The _____ of your area is the pattern of weather over a long time.

8. Your _____ is the surroundings in which you and other people, plants, and animals live.

9. Something found in the environment that people can use is called a _____.

10. _____ is the careful use of natural resources.

THINKING ABOUT FACTS

1. What is the motto of our state? Where did the motto come from?

2. In what region of the United States is our state located?

3. Who were the first Americans?

4. Name four different landforms that are found in Texas.

5. Name two large bodies of water that are important in our state.

6. What is the difference between climate and weather?

7. How does the Gulf of Mexico affect the climate of our state?

8. What is a tornado?

9. Name some examples of renewable resources found in our state.

10. Why is conservation important in our state?

THINK AND WRITE

WRITING AN EXPLANATION

You have read how climate is affected by three factors. Write an explanation of how the climate in your area is affected by those three factors.

WRITING A DESCRIPTION

Write a paragraph about a custom you are familiar with. Describe the clothing, food, dance, or activities that are part of the custom.

WRITING A POSTER

Suppose you wanted to start a conservation project in your school. Write and design a poster about conserving water or some other resource.

APPLYING GEOGRAPHY SKILLS

ELEVATION MAPS

Answer the following questions about the map on this page to practice your skill of reading elevation maps.

1. How do you know that this is an elevation map?

2. What landform in Texas has the lowest elevation?

3. What is the approximate elevation of the city of Lubbock?

4. In what color would this map show a mountain that is 2,000 feet above sea level?

5. Why might it be useful to have an elevation map on a trip across Texas?

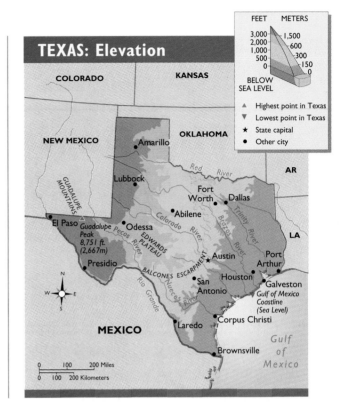

TEXAS: Elevation

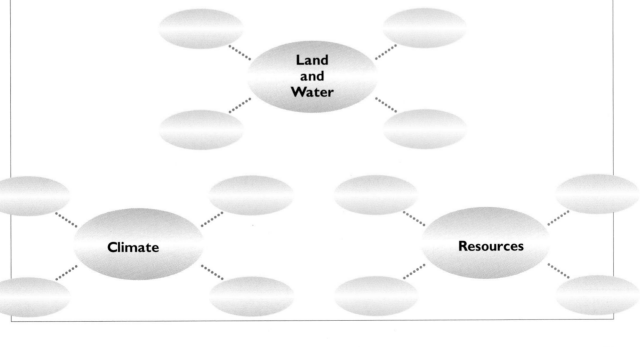

Summing Up the Chapter

Use the following word map to organize information from the chapter. Copy the word map on a sheet of paper. Then write at least one piece of information in each blank circle. When you have filled in the maps, use them to write a paragraph that answers the question "How does your environment affect how you live?"

Land and Water

Climate

Resources

CHAPTER 2

The Regions of the United States and Texas

THINKING ABOUT GEOGRAPHY AND CULTURE

You know that Texas is in the Southwestern region of the United States. Texas is so big that we break it into four regions of its own. What makes each region of the United States special? What makes each region of our state special? Find out as you read Chapter 2.

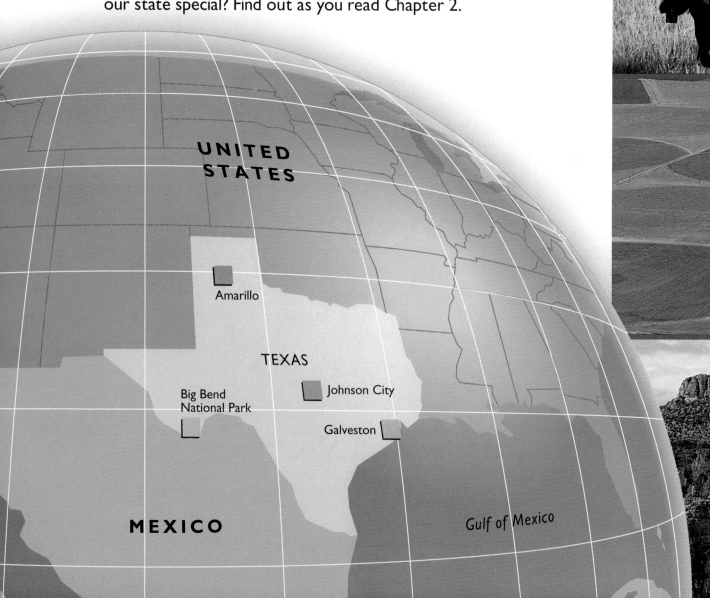

UNITED STATES

Amarillo

TEXAS

Big Bend
National Park

Johnson City

Galveston

MEXICO

Gulf of Mexico

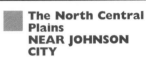 **The Coastal Plain
NEAR GALVESTON**

These boats are docked near Galveston, which is located in the Coastal Plain region of our state. As you will learn in this chapter, two out of three Texans live in this region of our state.

 **The North Central Plains
NEAR JOHNSON CITY**

As you will learn, the North Central Plains region of our state is mostly a sea of grass. It is a good place for raising cattle and for growing crops such as cotton, corn, and peanuts.

**The Great Plains
NEAR AMARILLO**

The Panhandle is part of the Great Plains region of Texas. This region has a very dry climate. How do these green fields survive without heavy rains? You will learn the answer to this question in Chapter 2.

**Mountains and Basins
BIG BEND NATIONAL PARK**

People from all over our state and country come to enjoy the natural beauty of Big Bend National Park. It is in the Mountains and Basins region of our state.

43

ONE COUNTRY, FIVE REGIONS

READ ALOUD

In the late 1800s, the poet Walt Whitman cele-brated America in a poem:

> *Land of coal and iron! land of gold! land of cotton, sugar, rice!*

> *Land of wheat, beef, pork! land of wool and hemp! land of the apple and the grape! . . .*

> *Land of the ocean shores!*

THE BIG PICTURE

As Walt Whitman wrote, the United States is a country of great variety. Geographers find it useful to divide our country into five main regions. You already know that Texas is in the Southwest. The other regions are the Northeast, the Southeast, the Middle West, and the West. Find these regions on the Atlas map on page R12.

The five regions of the United States are interdependent. The Infographic on page 50 shows how our country's people use our nation's resources to make the United States strong.

Geographers also divide our country into areas that have certain landforms in common. Look at the map on the next page. What familiar landforms do you see? In this lesson you will read about the regions and landforms of the United States. Later on in this chapter you will read how these landforms are used to divide our state into regions.

Focus Activity

READ TO LEARN
What is special about each region of the United States?

VOCABULARY
source
mouth
tributary
desert
rain shadow

PLACES
Appalachian Mountains
Mississippi River
Interior Plains
Central Plains
Great Plains
Rocky Mountains
Grand Canyon

THE NORTHEAST

One landform that can be found in the Northeast is the Coastal Plain, a flat strip of land along the edge of the Atlantic Ocean. Look at the map on this page and find the Coastal Plain. Many large cities in the Northeast are located on this plain.

Among the oldest mountains in the world are the Appalachian (ap uh LAY chee un) Mountains, another landform. They are found in almost every state in the Northeast. Some scientists think they once rose miles into the sky. Yet today the Appalachians are not very high. Over many years wind, water, and ice have worn them down.

Four Seasons

In the Northeast, winter, spring, summer, and autumn bring different kinds of weather. Autumn is the favorite season of many Northeasterners. In the fall the days grow shorter and the temperature drops. These changes have an effect on the colors of the leaves of many trees. For a few weeks, the leaves change from green to bright red, gold, and orange. Then the leaves drop off the branches. These trees are preparing for winter when there is less sunlight and lower temperatures.

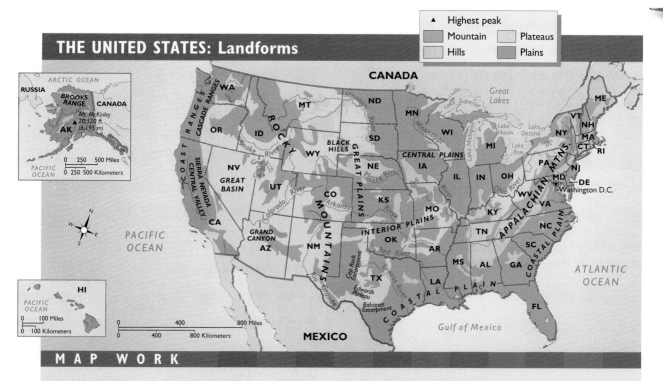

THE UNITED STATES: Landforms

Highest peak | Mountain | Plateaus | Hills | Plains

MAP WORK

This map shows some of the different landforms found in the United States.

1. Name one mountain range in Texas. Name one mountain range found in another part of the United States.

2. Name four states that are located on the Coastal Plain.

3. How do the landforms found in Texas make our state different from most other states?

THE SOUTHEAST

Like the Northeast, the Southeast is also part of the Coastal Plain of the United States. The Appalachian Mountains run through the Southeast too.

The Southeast is generally a warm region that is crisscrossed with rivers. Most rivers in the Southeast start in the Appalachian Mountains. The region's biggest river, though, is the Mississippi River. It begins in the Middle West.

The Mississippi River

Algonkian-speaking Native Americans named the Mississippi River. Their words *Misi Sipi* mean "big water" or "father of waters." The source, or starting point, of the Mississippi is Lake Itasca in Minnesota. A drop of water leaving this tiny lake takes 60 days to reach the river's mouth in Louisiana. The mouth of a river is the place where it empties into the ocean or another large body of water. Look at the map on page 45. Into which body of water does the Mississippi River empty?

At its source the Mississippi is hardly more than a shallow creek. The river grows broader and deeper as it flows south. Why? A major reason is that throughout its course the Mississippi is fed by smaller rivers called tributaries.

The writer Mark Twain worked on a Mississippi riverboat in the 1850s. What does Mark Twain mean when he writes about "reading" the river like a book?

MANY VOICES LITERATURE

Excerpt from *Life on the Mississippi*, written by Mark Twain in 1863.

*The face of the water . . . became a wonderful book. . . . And it was not a book to be read once and thrown aside, for it had a new story to tell every day. Throughout the long twelve hundred miles there was never a page that was **void** of interest . . . never one that you would want to skip.*

void: empty

Library of Congress

This paddleboat steamer is a modern version of the boat Mark Twain rode in the 1850s.

NATCHEZ

The corn grown on the Central Plains (left) and the wheat grown on the Great Plains (below) help feed our growing country.

THE MIDDLE WEST

The Middle West is part of a landform of the United States called the Interior Plains. There are really two parts to the Interior Plains. They are the Central Plains in the east and the Great Plains in the west. There is no sharp dividing line between them. Yet the geography of these two areas is different. Find them on the map on page 45.

Different Kinds of Plains

The Central Plains are low in elevation, not much higher than sea level in some places. Gently rolling hills cover much of the land. Corn is one of the main crops on the Central Plains. Farmers in Iowa can produce over 900 million bushels of corn in a year. This amount is enough to give each person in the United States more than 100 quarts of corn! Can you imagine eating that much corn? Some of the corn is shipped to markets across the country and around the world.

The climate of the Middle West can be extreme. Writer Neal Peirce called the Great Plains "a land of fiercely cold winters and furnace-like summers." This region also experiences harsh storms and tornadoes, and the wind is often blowing.

The Great Plains are mostly dry grassland. Not enough rain falls for most trees to survive there.

Wheat is the major crop on the Great Plains. In fact, the drier climate is perfect for growing it. The states of Kansas and North Dakota are the biggest wheat producers in the United States.

47

THE SOUTHWEST

As you have read, our state is part of the Southwest of the United States. Only three other states are part of this region—Oklahoma, Arizona, and New Mexico. Except for Arizona, the states of the Southwest all share the Great Plains of the Middle West.

Like the Northeast and the Southeast, the Southwest also is part of the Coastal Plain. But Texas is the only state of the Southwest that has this landform. Much of this region is made up of high plateaus and plains.

As you move farther west, the geography changes suddenly. The Rocky Mountains appear. This mountain range stretches from Canada through many states of the United States, including Texas, and into Mexico.

The climate of the Southwest is varied. The Coastal Plain in Texas is warm and rainy. High up in the Rocky Mountains, the temperature can drop far below the freezing mark. Much of the Southwest, however, is hot and dry. Many parts of the region are covered by deserts—dry land where little rain falls. A desert gets less than 10 inches of precipitation each year. As you learned in Chapter 1, the eastern part of our state gets more rain than the western part.

The Grand Canyon

One of the most famous landforms of the Southwest is the Grand Canyon. As you have read in Chapter 1, a canyon is a deep valley with steep sides.

The Grand Canyon was cut over centuries by the Colorado River and stretches 217 miles through northern Arizona. In some places this gigantic canyon is more than one mile deep! At its widest, the canyon measures 18 miles from one rim, or edge, to the other. If there were a footbridge across the canyon, it would take about six hours to walk across.

The Grand Canyon is vast—whether you are at the top looking down or riding into it.

THE WEST

Like the other regions of the United States, the West has many different landforms. Among them are mountains, plateaus, and valleys. The mountains, in particular, have a special effect on the climate.

The Rain Shadow

The high elevations of the West's mountains affect temperature and precipitation in the region. Winds from the Pacific Ocean bring warm, wet air to the West. As this air reaches the mountains, it rises upward, forming clouds.

Look at the diagram on this page. The winds push the clouds up one side of the mountains. As the clouds rise, the temperature decreases. As the clouds cool, they drop most of their moisture in the form of precipitation—rain, and if it is cold enough, snow. Once the clouds have reached the top, most of the moisture is gone. Little water is left when the wind-driven air reaches the other side of the mountains. This eastern side of the mountains will stay much drier. The dry side lies in the rain shadow.

Tallest Trees

As a result of the rain shadow, the western part of this region receives much more rainfall than the eastern part. Huge forests are found along parts of the Pacific Coast.

The redwood trees that grow here are among the tallest trees in the world. Many are over 300 feet tall.

4. Air becomes cooler at higher elevations, causing precipitation.

3. Warm winds push clouds up mountains.

2. Wet air rises to form clouds.

1. Ocean winds carry warm air westward.

5. Winds reach the other side of mountains with little moisture.

PACIFIC OCEAN

Some redwood trees on the western side of the mountains grow as tall as sixty people! Why aren't these trees in the rain shadow?

Infographic

Goods and Services of the United States

In this lesson you have learned about some of the most important natural resources in the United States. What are some other goods and services that are important to the economy?

Timber! More than half the lumber used in our country comes from forests of the West.

America's Dairyland Wisconsin is the top producer of milk and cheese in the United States. In 1992 it boasted 1,620,000 milk cows—about one for every three people in the state.

Nuts and Bolts Oklahoma and Texas manufacture all kinds of machinery, but Arizona specializes in electronic and communications devices.

Watch It! Entertainment may be California's best-known service industry. Over 300 movies are made in California every year.

Penny for Your Thoughts Arizona produces more than half of our country's copper, used for electrical wires and pennies.

Where To? The port of South Louisiana at the mouth of the Mississippi River handles more cargo than any other port in the nation. Around 200 million tons of cargo enter and leave this port every year.

Something's Fishy More than half the country's lobsters come from the cold Atlantic waters of Maine. Maryland's fishers haul in tons of crabs, oysters, and striped bass.

Start Your Engines! Detroit, Michigan, is the heart of the automobile industry.

Drink Up Soggy wetlands, called bogs, found in Massachusetts make this state the Cranberry Capital of America. It produces nearly 2 million barrels a year. That's a lot of juice and sauce!

Have A Bite Florida supplies about 4 out of 5 of our country's oranges. More rice is grown in Arkansas than in any other state. Georgia grows more than three times as many peanuts as any other state.

WHY IT MATTERS

Our country is one of the largest in the world, with a great variety of landforms. Geographers sometimes divide the United States into five regions because of the common features found in a region.

In this chapter you will read about the geography of the regions in our state—and how each region's geography affects the way people live and work.

✓ Reviewing Facts and Ideas

SUM IT UP

- The five regions of the United States are the Northeast, the Southeast, the Middle West, the Southwest, and the West.
- The Coastal Plain is found in the Northeast, the Southeast, and the Southwest.
- Corn and wheat are the main crops of the Middle West.
- The mountains of the West have an effect on rainfall.

THINK ABOUT IT

1. Name the major landforms of the United States.

2. Describe how the rain shadow affects the climate of the West.

3. **FOCUS** What is different about each of our country's regions?

4. **THINKING SKILL** What _questions_ would you ask someone to learn about his or her region?

5. **GEOGRAPHY** Look at the map on page 45. What landforms does Texas share with other states?

THE COASTAL PLAIN OF TEXAS

READ ALOUD

Texas writer Lewis C. Fay was fond of the land along the Gulf of Mexico. He described it as a place "of peace and the swoop of seagulls, and the soft purples of twilight plunging into east-dark sky."

Focus Activity

READ TO LEARN

What are some of the special features of the Coastal Plain region of Texas?

VOCABULARY
vegetation
barrier island
lowland
prairie
metropolitan area
industry
service industry
port

PLACES
Piney Woods
Padre Island
Corpus Christi Bay
Dallas
Austin
Houston Ship Channel

THE BIG PICTURE

You have read about the regions of the United States and the major landforms found in each of these regions. They include mountains, coastal plains, interior plains, and plateaus. Geographers use these same kinds of landforms to divide Texas into four geographic regions. They are the Coastal Plain, the North Central Plains, the Great Plains, and the Mountains and Basins regions. In the rest of this chapter, you'll learn about these Texas regions. We'll start with the Coastal Plain region.

Look at the Coastal Plain map on the next page. This is the largest region in Texas. The land here is mostly flat, but it rises gently as you go inland. The Coastal Plain has many different kinds of plant life, or vegetation, including forests and grassy areas. Geographers use these different types of vegetation to divide the Coastal Plain into five smaller areas. They are the Piney Woods, the Gulf Coast Plain, the South Texas Plain, the Post Oak Belt, and the Blackland Prairie. You can see these areas on the map on the next page.

THE LAND

The Coastal Plain region begins at the Gulf of Mexico. Off the coast are narrow **barrier** (BA ree er) **islands**. A barrier separates things, and barrier islands separate the mainland from the gulf. **Padre Island** is the largest of these barrier islands.

On the mainland you find beaches and then **lowlands**, which have an elevation just above sea level. In the wettest part of the lowlands is the Piney Woods, known for its many pine trees. To the west, the land rises gently and the trees are replaced by **prairie**. Prairies are flat or rolling land covered with tall grass. Farther inland is the Balcones Escarpment. It forms the border between the Coastal Plain region and the North Central Plains region.

Climate

The Coastal Plain gets a lot of rain because winds pick up moisture from the gulf and carry rain to the land. Crops need water to grow, so they do well on the Coastal Plain. A variety of fruits and vegetables are grown here.

Hurricanes and other storms can arrive suddenly. Ruth West fishes for shrimp in **Corpus Christi Bay** near the Gulf of Mexico. West says:

> *[Shrimpers] always listen to the weather report. If waters are too rough, then you just don't go out. Otherwise we throw our nets in the water all day. If the winds get too high, we pick our nets up and go back to the dock.*

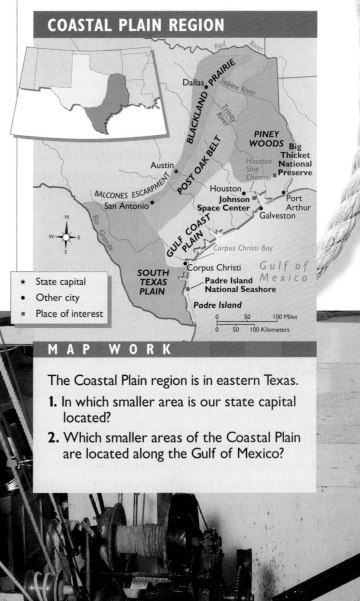

COASTAL PLAIN REGION

- ★ State capital
- • Other city
- ■ Place of interest

MAP WORK

The Coastal Plain region is in eastern Texas.

1. In which smaller area is our state capital located?
2. Which smaller areas of the Coastal Plain are located along the Gulf of Mexico?

LIVING AND WORKING

You have learned that Native Americans were the first people to live in Texas, and that immigrants came later to find a better life. Almost all these people chose to make their homes on the Coastal Plain. They found that this region is good for farming and fishing. The Coastal Plain also has important natural resources. Forests provide wood. A plentiful supply of oil lies beneath the Gulf of Mexico. It is gathered by offshore wells. The many rivers flowing across the Coastal Plain provide water for crops. Early Texans also found that the flat land of this region was good for building on.

Today, two out of three Texans live on the Coastal Plain. Are you one of them? Many people of the Coastal Plain live in **metropolitan areas**. A metropolitan area is a large city or group of cities together with their nearby suburbs. Houston, **Dallas**, **Austin**, and San Antonio are four of our state's biggest metropolitan areas. They are all located on the Coastal Plain.

Service Industries

Many major **industries** in the Coastal Plain are **service industries**. An industry is all of the businesses that make one kind of product or provide one kind of service. The service industry is made up of people whose job is to help other people.

Doctors, nurses, salespeople, and teachers work in the service industry. So do government workers such as police officers, postal workers, and firefighters.

The service industry is important in all parts of our state. In metropolitan areas, where there are many people, there is a greater need for service workers. Austin is the capital, where our state government is based. State workers provide services such as building roads and caring for the environment.

San Antonio's River Walk attracts visitors from all over the world. The hotel managers, restaurant chefs, and visitor information workers who take care of them are part of the service industry.

Dallas is an important business center. Here, many service workers are bankers. They help take care of people's money.

Service workers at Johnson Space Center use computers to control space shuttles.

A service worker at Space Center Houston might help you learn about the nearby Lyndon B. Johnson Space Center. This is where astronauts train to go into space. At Space Center Houston you can touch a rock that astronauts brought back from the moon!

The next time you visit a big city, try to count the service workers you meet. Don't be surprised if you have to count very high!

Transportation Centers

The cities of the Coastal Plain are important centers of local and world transportation. The Dallas-Fort Worth International Airport is the second busiest in the nation, with more than 2,000 flights daily.

Houston is the third largest port city in the nation. A port is where ships load and unload their goods. You would expect such a major port to be right on the coast. But Houston is not directly on the Gulf of Mexico. To reach the city, ships must travel the 50-mile Houston Ship Channel. Each day these ships bring products to Houston from around the world. Others leave Houston carrying Texan goods such as oil and cotton.

WHY IT MATTERS

Because it is located beside the Gulf of Mexico, the Coastal Plain region has a mild climate and enough rainfall to grow a variety of crops. Its many resources include forests, oil, and fish. This is one reason why so many Texans live in this region. In the next lesson, you will learn about the North Central Plains.

Reviewing Facts and Ideas

SUM IT UP

- The Coastal Plain of Texas has barrier islands, beaches, lowlands, and prairies.
- Many people of the Coastal Plain live in metropolitan areas.
- Many people of the Coastal Plain work in service industries.

THINK ABOUT IT

1. What is a barrier island?
2. Name two service jobs people might do in Austin.
3. **FOCUS** What are some special features of the Coastal Plain region?
4. **THINKING SKILL** What _effect_ do location and climate have on the way of life in a region?
5. **WRITE** Suppose you went shrimp fishing with Ruth West in Corpus Christi Bay. Write a poem about your experience.

Welcome to Dallas/Fort Worth International Airport

THE NORTH CENTRAL PLAINS OF TEXAS

Focus Activity

READ TO LEARN

Why is the North Central Plains region of Texas good for raising cattle?

VOCABULARY

mesa
butte
mesquite
rodeo
ranch
hailstorm

PLACES

Cross Timbers
Fort Worth
Wichita Falls
Abilene
Metroplex

READ ALOUD

"Fort Worth is where the West begins." This well-known Texan saying refers to the three regions of our state left for us to study. They share a lonely beauty. This is cowboy country.

THE BIG PICTURE

The land of the North Central Plains has a higher elevation than the Coastal Plain. It is a region of rolling hills, and it rises as you go west. Geographers divide the North Central Plains into three smaller areas. These are called the Grand Prairie, the Cross Timbers, and the Rolling Plains. You'll find these areas on the map on the next page.

The North Central Plains region of Texas is also called the Interior Lowlands region. This region is part of the area of the United States called the Interior Plains. You read about this landform in Lesson 1.

Farmers grow cotton, wheat, corn, and other crops in the North Central Plains. There are also large, grassy prairies which make this region good for raising animals that eat grass, such as horses and cows. You can see thousands of them here, wandering beneath the open sky.

THE LAND

Mesas are a special kind of landform found in the North Central Plains. The word *mesa* means "table" in Spanish. This landform got its name because it is a wide, flat-topped hill with steep sides, like a table. **Buttes** (BYOOTS) are another type of landform here. A butte is a narrow hill with a flat top that stands alone in the landscape.

Mesquite (mes KEET) trees are another common sight in the North Central Plains. These small, thorny trees have long roots that grow deep to find water. Mesquites can be found in places that are too hot and dry for other trees.

Rural Areas

The North Central Plains are more rural than the Coastal Plain. Here you will find towns like Stamford and Vernon.

Every year in Stamford, people from around the Southwest compete in the Texas Cowboy Reunion. This is a **rodeo** or contest of cowhand skills. Events include roping cattle and riding broncos. A bronco is an untamed horse.

The town of Vernon is the headquarters of the huge W. T. Waggoner **Ranch**. A ranch is a large area of land used to raise cattle, sheep, or horses. The Waggoner Ranch is the largest ranch in Texas. It has more than 14,000 cattle. That's more cattle than there are people living in the town of Vernon!

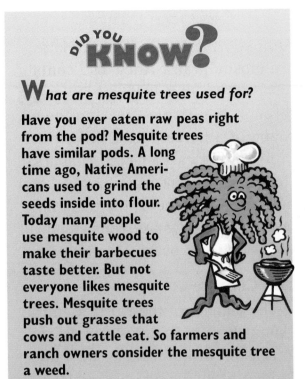

DID YOU KNOW?

What are mesquite trees used for?

Have you ever eaten raw peas right from the pod? Mesquite trees have similar pods. A long time ago, Native Americans used to grind the seeds inside into flour. Today many people use mesquite wood to make their barbecues taste better. But not everyone likes mesquite trees. Mesquite trees push out grasses that cows and cattle eat. So farmers and ranch owners consider the mesquite tree a weed.

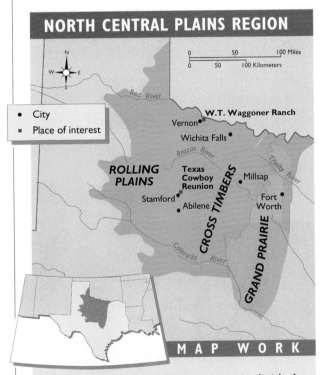

NORTH CENTRAL PLAINS REGION

- City
- Place of interest

MAP WORK

The North Central Plains region is divided into three smaller areas.

1. Which two cities lie between the Brazos River and the Colorado River?
2. Which area do you think might have had large forests at one time?

CROSS TIMBERS

Although the North Central Plains are mostly prairie, they also contain woods. Two thin strips of forest cut through the prairies, making the shape of a horseshoe. These strips of forest are called Cross Timbers. Here you will find oak, hickory, and pecan trees. Some of the trees have been cleared to make room for fruit, vegetable, and peanut farms.

The Climate

The climate of the North Central Plains changes greatly from season to season. In the winter, snow and sudden blasts of cold air called northers are common. In the summer, temperatures can reach 100°F or higher. In spring and fall, storms occur when cold air from the north meets warm air from the south. These conditions often cause **hailstorms**. Hailstorms, which usually happen along with thunderstorms, are showers of small, rounded chunks of ice. Hailstorms can ruin crops by crushing them.

Royce and Kim Wright are peanut farmers in Millsap. The weather is very important to them. Royce Wright says:

> You have to have just the right amount of rain, but not too much. We need spring rains, then rain when we plant. But at harvest time the conditions should be dry so that the water content of the peanuts is not too high. My dad, who was also a farmer, once said to me, "I spent my whole life wishing it would rain or wishing it wouldn't."

Living and Working

You have learned that much of the North Central Plains is rural. But the region is home to other businesses besides ranching and farming. Companies here make computers, soft drinks, and aircraft. Many people who do these jobs live in the cities of Fort Worth, Wichita Falls, and Abilene.

The Wright family looks over their peanut farm in Millsap and smiles at the good harvest.

Major Cities

Fort Worth began in the 1840s as a fort for a few dozen soldiers. Today Fort Worth is home to about half a million people. Its neighbor—on the Coastal Plain—is Dallas. Together these cities form a huge metropolitan area called the Metroplex. Fort Worth has long been known as a cattle town. Now, in addition to meat-packing plants, it has companies that build aircraft such as F-16 fighter planes.

Abilene was founded in 1881, when the railroad was built through this part of our state. Ranchers came to Abilene to sell their cattle and send them to other parts of the United States. Today, Abilene is also an important oil center in our state. There is so much oil here that in 1981 when an oil drilling rig was demonstrated at the West Texas State Fair, it struck oil!

WHY IT MATTERS

Grassy prairies make the North Central Plains region an ideal place to raise cattle and crops. The major cities of the area, Fort Worth and Abilene, are key business centers for the cattle industry.

Reviewing Facts and Ideas

SUM IT UP

- The North Central Plains are a region of rolling hills and prairies.
- Cattle owners in this region graze their animals on large ranches.
- Some people in the North Central Plains work in the oil, aircraft, or meat-packing industries.

THINK ABOUT IT

1. What is a butte?

2. How did mesas get their name?

3. **FOCUS** Why are the North Central Plains good for raising cattle?

4. **THINKING SKILL** _Compare_ and _contrast_ the North Central Plains with the Coastal Plain.

5. **GEOGRAPHY** Look at the map on page 57. Find the part of the North Central Plains region with the most cities. Why do you think they are there?

GEOGRAPHYSKILLS

Using Latitude and Longitude

VOCABULARY

latitude
parallel
degree
longitude
prime meridian
meridian
global grid

WHY THE SKILL MATTERS

In the last lesson you read about the North Central Plains. Suppose you are exploring this region to find a lost treasure buried deep in the ground there. The only clue you have is an old map. The writing on the map is faded, but you can just make out some lines that cross each other a little like a tic-tac-toe grid. Each line has a number on it.

You discover that these are imaginary lines invented long ago by mapmakers. The lines describe the location of a particular place. They provide an "address" for every place on Earth.

Airline pilots use this same system of lines to keep track of where they are. Up among the clouds a pilot must be sure of a plane's location at all times. Pilots also need an exact way to explain where they are going.

The faded lines on the map will help you to find the treasure in the North

Central Plains. You will use other imaginary lines on maps in this book and in many other books.

USING LATITUDE

Let's study these imaginary lines. Look at the map on this page and place your finger on the equator. This is the starting point for measuring **latitude**. Latitude is a measure of how far north or south a place is from the equator.

Geographers also call lines of latitude **parallels** because they are parallel lines. Parallel lines always remain the same distance apart.

Each line of latitude has a number. You can see that the equator is labeled 0°, meaning zero **degrees**. Degrees are used to measure the distance on

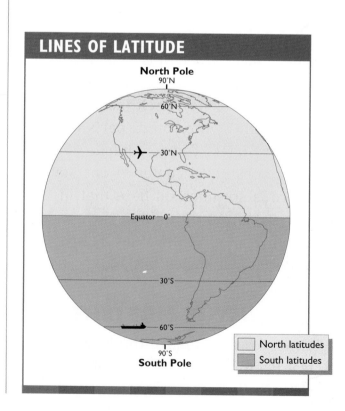

LINES OF LATITUDE

North Pole
90°N
60°N
30°N
Equator — 0°
30°S
60°S
90°S
South Pole

North latitudes
South latitudes

Earth's surface. The symbol ° stands for degrees. Look again at the map. What is the latitude of the equator?

Now look at the lines of latitude north of the equator. Notice that these parallels are labeled N for "north." The North Pole has a latitude, too, which is 90°N. The parallels south of the equator are labeled S for "south." The latitude of the South Pole is 90°S.

Find the ship on the map. The ship is sailing west. It is located at 60°S. Now find the small airplane on the map. Along which parallel is it flying?

USING LONGITUDE

Now look at the map on this page. It shows lines of longitude. Like parallels, these are imaginary lines on a map or globe. But instead of measuring distance north or south, they measure distance east or west of the prime meridian. Prime means "first." Lines of longitude are also called meridians. The prime meridian is the first line, or starting place, for measuring lines of longitude. That's why the prime meridian is marked 0° on the map. Put your finger on the prime meridian. It runs through the western parts of Europe and Africa.

Look at the meridians to the west of the prime meridian. These lines are labeled W for "west." The lines to the east of the prime meridian are labeled E for "east." Longitude is measured up to 180° east of the prime meridian and up to 180° west of the prime meridian. Since 180°E and 180°W fall on the same

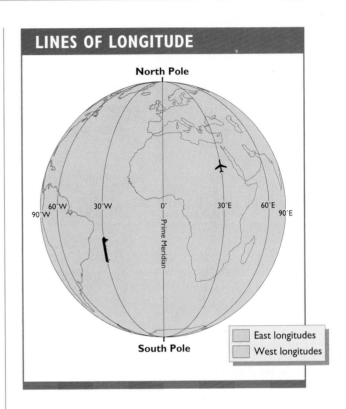

LINES OF LONGITUDE

North Pole

90°W · 60°W · 30°W · 0° · 30°E · 60°E · 90°E

Prime Meridian

South Pole

East longitudes
West longitudes

line, this line is marked neither E nor W. The line labeled 180° runs through the Pacific Ocean.

Unlike lines of latitude, meridians are not parallel to one another. Earth is round. Meridians divide Earth into pieces like the sections of an orange. Look at the map on this page again. As you can see, the meridians are far apart at the equator. They meet, however, at the North Pole and the South Pole.

Lines of longitude measure degrees east and west. Look at the ship on the map. It is sailing along the meridian known as 30°W. Now look at the airplane on the same map. It is flying over the continent of Africa. What meridian is it flying over? In which direction is the airplane traveling?

GEOGRAPHYSKILLS

GLOBAL GRID

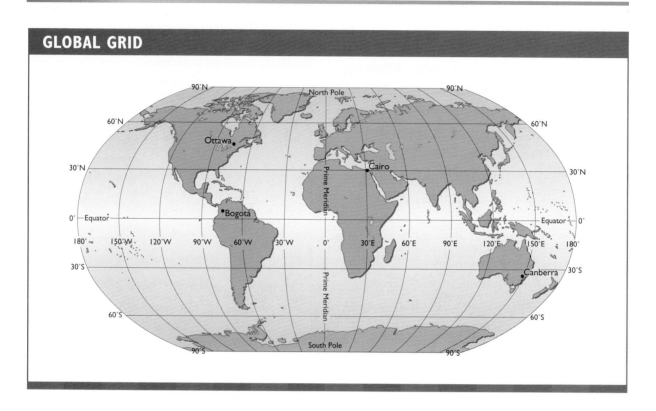

FINDING PLACES ON A MAP

In order to use latitude lines and longitude lines to find places, you must combine them on the same map. Look at the map of the world on this page. You can see that the lines of latitude and the lines of longitude cross to form a grid on the map. A grid is a set of crisscrossing lines.

The grid on this map is called a **global grid** because it covers Earth entirely. By using the global grid, you can locate the "address" of any place in the world.

Look at the map again. Find Canberra, Australia, and Bogotá, Colombia. Which of these two cities is closer to the equator? How can you tell?

Now find Ottawa, Canada. Is this city east or west of the prime meridian? Find Cairo, Egypt. Is Cairo east or west of the prime meridian? Is Cairo north or south of the equator?

Look at the latitude and longitude map of the 48 states on the opposite page. Find the city of Beaumont, Texas. As you can see, it is located near 30°N latitude. It is also located near 95°W longitude. So we say that the location, or "address," of the city of Beaumont is about 30°N, 95°W.

Remember that when you locate a place on a map, you must always give the latitude first and the longitude second. You also must remember to give north or south for the latitude, and east or west for the longitude. To describe a place that is not exactly at the point where two lines cross, you must use the closest lines.

TRYING THE SKILL

Try to find a city in the United States by its "address." This city is located at about 30°N, 105°W. What is the name of the city? Now describe the location of New Orleans, Louisiana, using latitude and longitude.

On your buried-treasure map are the following numbers: 35°N, 100°W. Do you understand what those numbers mean now? In what city is the treasure located? Start digging!

REVIEWING THE SKILL

Many maps include a grid of latitude and longitude. Use the 48 states map below to answer these questions.

1. What are lines of latitude and longitude? How can they be helpful?

2. Give the location of San Antonio, Texas, using latitude and longitude.

3. Name two cities on the map that share the same line of latitude. Then name two cities that share the same line of longitude.

4. How did you find the answers to the last questions?

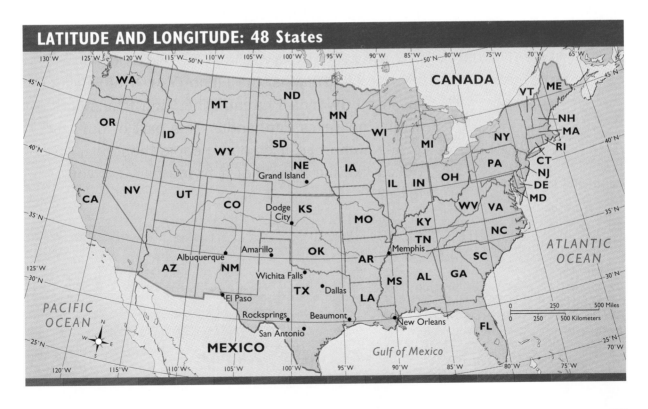

LATITUDE AND LONGITUDE: 48 States

63

THE GREAT PLAINS OF TEXAS

READ ALOUD

Margaret Woodward raises nearly 10,000 sheep on her ranch in West Texas. "The best part of raising sheep is lambing season in March. That's when the newborn lambs follow the mama sheep around."

THE BIG PICTURE

You have read that the Great Plains are a region of the United States. Part of the Great Plains lies in our state. This region is a high plateau. There is little rainfall here so farmers use irrigation to grow crops. Irrigation is the practice of using pipes or ditches to bring water to croplands.

Geographers divide the Great Plains of Texas into the High Plains, the Llano (YAHN oh) Basin, and the Edwards Plateau. The High Plains lie within the Texas Panhandle. This part of our state got its name because some people thought it looked like the handle of a frying pan. Do you agree?

Focus Activity

READ TO LEARN

Why is irrigation important in the Great Plains region of Texas?

VOCABULARY
irrigation
mohair
helium

PLACES
Edwards Plateau
Permian Basin
Midland
Odessa
Cap Rock Escarpment
Amarillo
Lubbock

64

THE LAND

Just west of the Balcones Escarpment, the Edwards Plateau is marked with hills and deep valleys. This area is Texas Hill Country, where President Lyndon Baines Johnson was born. Visitors can still see the one-room schoolhouse where he went to school.

Much of the wool produced in the United States comes from sheep that graze on the Edwards Plateau. Find the Edwards Plateau on the map below. In addition, nearly half the world's mohair comes from this area. Mohair is the hair of the angora goat. People use mohair to make soft, warm sweaters and other clothing. More than 100 years ago, ranchers brought this animal here from Turkey in Asia. Turkey's climate is similar to that of our state's Great Plains.

The Permian Basin

The Permian (PUR mee un) Basin is one of the largest oil-producing areas in the world. The cities of Midland and Odessa are located in the Permian Basin. Huge metal oil pumps dot the landscape here. These oil pumps are bringing petroleum, or "black gold," up from beneath Earth's surface.

Climate

Summers are hot and dry in the Great Plains. Winters can be very cold and snowstorms are common in the Panhandle.

The Great Plains can also be windy. People have built windmills to make use of the wind's power. These machines pump water from aquifers to homes and farms.

GREED PLAINS REGION

GREAT PLAINS REGION

N
W—E
S

Canadian River
Amarillo
CAP ROCK ESCARPMENT
HIGH PLAINS
Lubbock
Tahoka
OGALLALA AQUIFER
Brazos River
Odessa
Midland
Colorado River
PERMIAN BASIN
Pecos River
San Angelo
EDWARDS PLATEAU
LLANO BASIN
L.B. Johnson National Historical Park
Rio Grande

- City
- Place of interest

0   50   100 Miles
0   50   100 Kilometers

MAP WORK

The Great Plains region stretches through the Texas Panhandle.

1. What aquifer is located in this region?
2. Where is the Permian Basin located?

LIVING AND WORKING

A well-known Texas landform, the **Cap Rock Escarpment**, divides the Great Plains from the North Central Plains. West of the Cap Rock Escarpment, cotton is a major crop. Wayne Huffaker's family has been growing cotton here since 1918. The Huffaker family farm is located in the town of Tahoka in the southern part of the Panhandle.

Wayne Huffaker irrigates his cotton crop with water from the Ogallala Aquifer. In November early periods of cold weather called freezes make the leaves fall off the cotton plants. Then the plants are harvested by machine.

The cotton is packed into bales. A bale of cotton is the size of a large refrigerator. Each bale weighs about 500 pounds. Wayne Huffaker can harvest one bale of cotton from each acre of his 4,000 acres.

Major Cities

The two largest cities in the Great Plains region are **Amarillo** and **Lubbock**. The word *amarillo* means "yellow" in Spanish.

Amarillo is a center for the cattle industry. People come from all over the region, the rest of Texas, and neighboring states for the weekly cattle auction. An auction is a public sale where things are sold to the person who offers the most money. Over 200,000 cattle are sold here each year.

Amarillo is also the place where most of the world's supply of **helium** (HEE lee um) is found. Helium is a very light gas, found underground, that has no color or smell. Helium is lighter than air. The next time you're at a birthday party or a parade, think of Amarillo when you see the helium balloons!

Lubbock is a center for industry, oil, and farming. It processes more cottonseed than any other place in

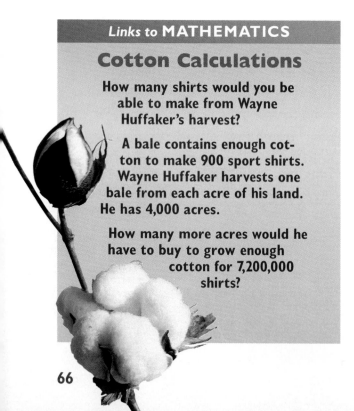

Links to MATHEMATICS

Cotton Calculations

How many shirts would you be able to make from Wayne Huffaker's harvest?

A bale contains enough cotton to make 900 sport shirts. Wayne Huffaker harvests one bale from each acre of his land. He has 4,000 acres.

How many more acres would he have to buy to grow enough cotton for 7,200,000 shirts?

Cattle at the Western Stockyards (left) are sold at auction in Amarillo. Sunflowers grow near Lubbock (below).

the world. Cotton seeds are used to make cooking oil, soap, candle wicks, rope, paper, fertilizer, fuel, and plastics. The cotton grown on the Huffaker family farm might be brought to factories in Lubbock. Some factories here use the cotton fibers to make the cloth that some of our clothes are made from.

WHY IT MATTERS

The Great Plains have a higher elevation than the Coastal Plain or North Central Plains regions. In parts of the Panhandle, the land rises more than 4,000 feet above sea level. The region is good for raising sheep and goats.

For many years, people thought the Great Plains region of our state was too dry for growing crops. But irrigation makes it possible to grow cotton, corn, and wheat. People must use water wisely here to make sure that the Ogallala Aquifer doesn't run dry. In the next lesson, you will read about the last of our state's four regions.

✓// Reviewing Facts and Ideas

SUM IT UP

- The Great Plains region of our state includes the High Plains, the Edwards Plateau, and the Llano Basin.
- Almost half the mohair in the world comes from the Edwards Plateau.
- Amarillo and Lubbock are two major cities on the Great Plains.

THINKING ABOUT FACTS

1. What is irrigation?
2. What is the landform that divides the Great Plains from the North Central Plains?
3. **FOCUS** Why is irrigation important to farmers living in the Great Plains region of Texas?
4. **THINKING SKILL** How are the resources of the Coastal Plain the _same_ as the Great Plains? How are they _different_?
5. **WRITE** From what you have read write a list of all the natural resources in the Great Plains region of our state. Then, next to each one, write down two products made with that resource.

THE MOUNTAINS AND BASINS OF TEXAS

Focus Activity

READ TO LEARN
How is the Mountains and Basins region of Texas different from all other Texas regions?

VOCABULARY
border
reservoir
time zone
tourist

PLACES
Chisos Mountains
Davis Mountains
El Capitan
Chihuahuan Desert
El Paso
Ciudad Juarez
Big Bend National Park
Guadalupe Mountains
   National Park

READ ALOUD

Dennis Vasquez is a nature expert in western Texas. He has some advice for visitors:

1. *It is very dry, so always bring water.*

2. *The sun is very hot, so wear a hat.*

3. *There are about 30 kinds of snakes, so never put your hands or feet where you can't see them. Have a good hike!*

THE BIG PICTURE

The Mountains and Basins region, in the western corner of Texas, is a place of unusual beauty. Our state's highest mountains are here. In between are low areas of bone-dry desert.

The mountains of western Texas are part of the Rocky Mountain chain. As you have read, the Rockies stretch from Canada to Mexico. In Texas, they include three smaller ranges of mountains. These ranges are the Chisos Mountains, the Davis Mountains, and the Guadalupe Mountains.

The Mountains and Basins region of our state borders the country of Mexico. A border is a line people agree on to separate two places. People from the United States and Mexico walk and drive back and forth across the border every day. Mexican culture has played a major role in the way of life here. Many people in this area speak Spanish.

THE LAND

You read in Chapter 1 that Guadalupe Peak in the Guadalupe Mountains has the highest elevation in Texas. El Capitan is another high mountain in this range.

In the Davis Mountains, you can visit the McDonald Observatory and look through its huge telescope. A clear sky at night makes viewing the stars easy.

In the bowl-shaped basins between the mountains, you'll find the Chihuahuan (chi WAH wun) Desert. Find this desert on the map. This is a flat, dry area that stretches into northern Mexico. At first glance you might think the desert is lifeless. But if you look closely, you'll find many interesting plants.

Climate

The Mountains and Basins region is the driest part of our state. It is dry because it is farthest away from the Gulf of Mexico's moist winds. The mountains of this region are cooler than the desert areas. Their temperature is lower because they have a higher elevation.

Summer temperatures in the desert can be the hottest in all Texas. At night, though, the desert can get quite cold. Why does the temperature drop at night? Air over the desert contains very little water in it. As a result, there are few clouds. Clouds hold heat over the land. Without clouds, the temperature drops after sunset. The dryness makes the heat more bearable for the people who live here.

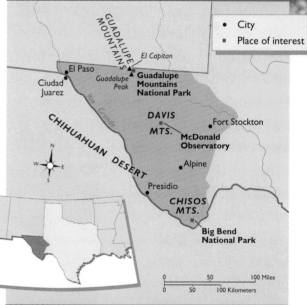

The kangaroo rat gets water from the seeds of plants in the Chihuahuan Desert (below).

MOUNTAINS AND BASINS REGION

- • City
- ■ Place of interest

GUADALUPE MOUNTAINS

El Capitan

El Paso

Ciudad Juarez

Guadalupe Peak

Guadalupe Mountains National Park

Rio Grande

DAVIS MTS.

McDonald Observatory

Fort Stockton

CHIHUAHUAN DESERT

Alpine

Presidio

CHISOS MTS.

Big Bend National Park

| 0 | 50 | 100 Miles |
| 0 | 50 | 100 Kilometers |

MAP WORK

The Mountains and Basins region is in western Texas.

1. Which mountains are close to Big Bend National Park?
2. What separates El Paso from Ciudad Juarez?

LIVING AND WORKING

Spaniards in the early 1600s called this region of Texas the *despoblado* (des poh BLAH doh)—"a place without many people." Today little has changed in some places. You can drive for a hundred miles here without seeing a town. Because there is so little rain, farming and ranching are difficult. Water is stored in **reservoirs** because there are few lakes here. A reservoir is a storage area for water. It collects water from rainfall. The reservoirs here also supports the region's metropolitan area.

El Paso

Over half a million people live in the city of **El Paso**. It is one of the largest cities in Texas. It is also far away from the other cities you have read about in this chapter. In fact, El Paso is so far west that it is located in a different **time zone** from most of our state. A time zone is a region in which all the clocks are set to the same time. When it is seven o'clock in El Paso, it is eight o'clock in most of Texas!

El Paso is located where the borders of Texas, New Mexico, and Mexico meet. Cross a bridge over the Rio Grande and you are in the Mexi-

can city of **Ciudad Juarez** (see oo DAHD HWAHR ez). In Spanish, *ciudad* means "city." Together El Paso and Ciudad Juarez are a major metropolitan area with over a million people. Because El Paso is so close to Mexico, there is a strong Hispanic culture here. Hispanics are people of Spanish heritage.

El Paso has many factories that make cowboy hats and other clothing. One factory is so large that supervisors work on roller skates! Factories in El Paso and Ciudad Juarez often work together. People at a factory in El Paso might cut up fabric for blue

Clothes and boots (right) are made in El Paso and Ciudad Juarez (below).

jeans. The pieces are then sewn together in another factory in Ciudad Juarez. When they are finished, the blue jeans are sent back to the United States to be sold. This kind of cooperation shows one way the two cities are interdependent.

Tourism

Texas has two national parks, and both of them are in the Mountains and Basins region. Many **tourists** come here to hike and enjoy the views. Tourists are people who travel for the fun of seeing new sights.

Dennis Vasquez is the chief naturalist at **Big Bend National Park**. The area is called Big Bend because it is located within a bend, or turn, in the Rio Grande. You have already read Vasquez's advice to visitors on page 68. He also might tell people that Big Bend has beautiful canyons, mountain lions, rattlesnakes, and more than 450 kinds of birds!

The walls of the mountains in **Guadalupe Mountains National Park** hold fossils. Fossils are the remains of living things from long ago. Today visitors to the park can see fossils of sea creatures in the rock as they walk along the mountain paths.

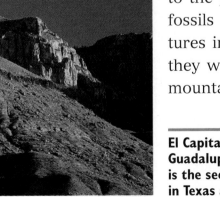

El Capitan is part of the Guadalupe Mountains. It is the second highest peak in Texas at 8,085 feet.

WHY IT MATTERS

The Mountains and Basins region has a very dry climate. Farming is difficult. Animals and plants that live here have special abilities that allow them to live without much water. Most of the people in this region live in El Paso.

The Mountains and Basins region has the highest mountains and some of the most breathtaking landscapes in our state. It attracts many tourists from all over the world.

✓// Reviewing Facts and Ideas

SUM IT UP

- The Mountains and Basins region contains part of the Rocky Mountain chain.
- The Chihuahuan Desert stretches from Texas south to Mexico.
- Many factories in El Paso are linked to factories in the Mexican city of Ciudad Juarez. This is an example of interdependence.

THINK ABOUT IT

1. Why are nights cool in the desert?
2. Why is Mexican culture a major part of life in this region?
3. **FOCUS** Why do tourists come to the Mountains and Basins region?
4. **THINKING SKILL** _Compare_ and _contrast_ the Mountains and Basins region and the Coastal Plain. Why do more people live on the Coastal Plain?
5. **WRITE** Write an advertisement to encourage tourists to visit the Mountains and Basins region.

THINKINGSKILLS

Decision Making

VOCABULARY

decision

WHY THE SKILL MATTERS

Decision making is a skill that people use every day. Making a decision is the same as making a choice. You have to make up your mind what to do. Decisions may be simple, like deciding what clothes to wear, or more difficult, like deciding where to live. To make a good decision, you have to know what your goal is.

When immigrants came to this country they made many decisions. First they made the important decision to leave their homeland. Their goal was to find a better life. When they arrived in this country they had to decide where they wanted to live.

Most early immigrants to Texas decided to live on the Coastal Plain. As you know, this region has a mild climate and plenty of rainfall. Newcomers used the wood from forests to build their homes. They cleared the land to plant crops. They fished in the waters off the coast. They used the natural resources in the Coastal Plain to build a new life.

USING THE SKILL

Today newcomers in Texas have more choices. They can decide to live in any one of our state's four regions. Of course, most people live where they can find work. Let's read about one recent newcomer who is deciding where to live.

Larry Bukaty has arrived in Texas from Europe. He is staying with relatives in Houston while he makes his plans. His relatives want him to remain in Houston to be near them. But Larry has never lived in a flat area before. He misses the mountains of his homeland. He is thinking about moving to the western part of the state. But that would mean he would be hundreds of miles away from his relatives.

Here are some possible results of each choice.

- Larry may find it difficult to adjust in a new location where he has no family.
- Larry may learn to like living on the Coastal Plain.
- Larry may continue to miss the landscape that he prefers.

If your goal were to find a good place to live, what decision would you make?

TRYING THE SKILL

Suppose your family is planning to take a summer vacation. Your family must choose a place to go camping. Your two choices are in different regions of our state.

The first is Padre Island National Seashore, on the Gulf of Mexico. Here your parents can relax and lie in the sun. Padre Island would be a good place to watch sea turtles. You and your older brother might also enjoy looking for shells on the beach. Other things to do at Padre Island are swimming and fishing.

The other choice is Big Thicket National Preserve. The preserve is a part of the Piney Woods located on the Coastal Plain. It is a forest, but there's a lot more to see than just trees. Hawks circle overhead. Alligators live in the bayous. A bayou is a stream that flows slowly through low, wet land. Big Thicket is a good place for hiking and canoeing.

Each member of your family has one vote. You will have to decide which location to choose. Use the Helping Yourself box for hints. What is your goal for the vacation? What do you think the results of either choice might be?

REVIEWING THE SKILL

1. What is a decision?
2. Look at the section called Trying The Skill. If your goal were to learn how to canoe, how would you have voted?
3. How will predicting possible results help you to make a good decision?
4. Why is it important to know how to make a good decision?

GEOGRAPHY OF THE WESTERN HEMISPHERE

Focus Activity

READ TO LEARN
What natural features does Texas share with other parts of the Western Hemisphere?

VOCABULARY
tundra
canal
province

PLACES
Canada
Great Lakes
Amazon River
Andes Mountains
Panama Canal
Amazon Rain Forest
St. Lawrence Seaway
Prince Edward Island

READ ALOUD

The Canadian poet Robert Service wrote these lines about northern Canada:

> *It's the great, big, broad land 'way up yonder,*
> *It's the forests where silence has lease [lives];*
> *It's the beauty that thrills me with wonder,*
> *It's the stillness that fills me with peace.*

THE BIG PICTURE

In this chapter, you have learned about some geographic features of Texas and the rest of the United States. Other countries in the Western Hemisphere share some of these natural features. For example, the Rocky Mountains stretch from Canada to Mexico. And the Great Lakes lie in both the United States and Canada.

Some parts of the Western Hemisphere have natural features that we do not have in the United States. For example, the Amazon River winds through Peru and Brazil in South America. South America also has the Andes Mountains, which are larger than the Rockies. In this lesson and in the Infographic on page 78 you will learn more about the special places found in the Western Hemisphere.

AMERICA, NORTH AND SOUTH

The Western Hemisphere stretches from the North Pole to the South Pole. Both the polar areas are very cold and covered with ice. Just south of the North Pole, in Alaska and northern Canada, you find the tundra. The tundra is a huge plain that is frozen for most of the year. South of the tundra is the Great Plains. You have learned in Lesson 1 that wheat grows there as far as the eye can see.

Traveling to South America

Continuing south, you pass through Texas and then Mexico. You cross the Panama Canal, which links the Atlantic and Pacific oceans. A canal is a waterway dug across land. You're now in South America.

If you travel south into Brazil, you enter the world's largest tropical rain forest. Here in the Amazon Rain Forest it is hot and humid almost all year long. At least 50,000 kinds of plants fill this forest along the Amazon River. On the west coast of South America are the towering Andes Mountains. They include Mt. Aconcagua (ak un KAUG wuh)—the tallest mountain in the Western Hemisphere.

Continuing south, you cross the pampas (PAHM pahs) of Argentina, a grassy region similar to the Great Plains of North America. When you reach the southern tip of South America, you find icy waters and bone-chilling winds—much like what you left behind in Alaska!

Climate in the Western Hemisphere

Did you know that when it is summer in Texas and other parts of North America, it's winter in much of South America? The seasons are opposite in the northern and southern halves of the Western Hemisphere. So if you like to ski in July, South America is the place to go!

The Panama Canal (left) and the tundra of Canada (below) are both in the Northern Hemisphere, but their climates are different.

OUR COUNTRY'S NORTHERN NEIGHBOR

Canada is our northern neighbor. It shares the northern border of the United States. Canada is a very large country. It occupies nearly four million square miles. That's the size of the United States plus two more states the size of California!

You know that the United States is made up of 50 states. Canada is also made up of smaller parts. It is divided up into ten provinces and two territories.

The northern part of Canada is far from the equator. Summers there are short and winters can be cold and hard. Not many people live in these cold northern parts of the country. Towns are far apart. In fact, the writer Andrew Malcolm has compared Canada's scattered towns to "a few specks of pepper on a huge freezer-room floor."

There are about 28 million people in Canada—less than twice the number of people in Texas.

The Seaway

In 1959 the United States and Canada together completed the St. Lawrence Seaway. This huge waterway allows ships to make round trips easily along the St. Lawrence River between the Atlantic Ocean and the Great Lakes.

Canals were built along the route. Now ships can carry wheat, corn,

The St. Lawrence Seaway (right) begins near Montreal (below). Montreal is the largest French-speaking city in the world after Paris.

and other goods from the heartland of North America to ports on the Atlantic Ocean. Like the Houston Ship Channel in our state, the St. Lawrence Seaway is an important shipping route.

An Island Climate

Near where the St. Lawrence River pours into the Atlantic Ocean you will find Prince Edward Island.

Prince Edward Island has a milder climate than much of Canada. It also has rich fertile soil. This combination makes it possible for many kinds of plants and trees to grow there. How does the writer Lucy Maud Montgomery describe a part of Prince Edward Island in her book *Anne of Green Gables*? Can you think of any ways in which this place is similar to Texas?

MANY VOICES LITERATURE

Excerpt from *Anne of Green Gables* by Lucy Maud Montgomery, written in 1908.

*On both sides of the house was a big orchard, one of apple trees and one of cherry trees, also showered over with blossoms; and their grass was all sprinkled with dandelions. In the garden below were lilac trees purple with flowers, and their dizzily sweet **fragrance** drifted up to the window on the morning wind.*

*Below the garden a green field lush with clover sloped down to the **hollow** where the brook ran and where **scores** of white birches grew.*

fragrance: smell
scores: a lot
hollow: valley

Infographic

Geography of the Western Hemisphere

In this lesson you have read about some of the geographic features found in North America and South America. What other landforms are in the Western Hemisphere?

North America

Brooks Range
Alaska Range
Greenland
Canadian Rockies
ROCKY MOUNTAINS
St. Lawrence River
Great Lakes
Missouri
Great Plains
Great Salt Lake
Sierra Nevada
Coast Ranges
Mississippi River
APPALACHIAN MTS
Coastal Plains
ATLANTIC OCEAN
Gulf of Mexico
West Indies
Caribbean Sea
Central America
PACIFIC OCEAN
ANDES MOUNTAINS
Amazon River
Amazon Rain Forest
SOUTH AMERICA
Atacama Desert
Pampas
Patagonia

CANADIAN ROCKIES

These rugged mountains form part of the huge chain that stretches through the western United States and into Mexico.

ATACAMA DESERT, CHILE

Rain almost never falls in some parts of this desert. Minerals such as copper, gold, and sulfur are found here.

LAS PAMPAS

Many cattle and sheep ranches are found on this huge grass-covered plain.

AMAZON RAIN FOREST

Half the variety of the world's plants and animals can be found in the more than two million square miles of this forest.

AMAZON RIVER

This is the second longest river in the world. It flows for 3,900 miles. Nearly 2,000 different kinds of fish live here.

WHY IT MATTERS

Texas and the rest of the United States share some landforms and bodies of water with other countries in the Western Hemisphere. Other important natural features are found only in specific countries. In the next chapter you will learn about the first people who came to Texas and the rest of the Western Hemisphere.

✓ Reviewing Facts and Ideas

SUM IT UP

- The Amazon River and the Andes Mountains are two natural features of South America.

- The northern and southern halves of the Western Hemisphere have opposite seasons.

- The St. Lawrence Seaway allows ships to travel between the Great Lakes and the Atlantic Ocean.

THINK ABOUT IT

1. What is a canal?

2. How is Canada divided?

3. **FOCUS** Which Texas landform is also found in two other countries of the Western Hemisphere?

4. **THINKING SKILL** Suppose you could travel to any country in the Western Hemisphere to learn more about a landform mentioned in this lesson. Which one would you visit? How did you _make_ your _decision_?

5. **WRITE** Write a letter to a Canadian pen pal. What questions will you ask about life in Canada?

CHAPTER 2 REVIEW

THINKING ABOUT VOCABULARY

Number a sheet of paper from 1 to 10. Beside each number write the word from the list that matches the description.

barrier island   reservoir
irrigation   service industry
mesquite   source
prairie   tributary
rain shadow   vegetation

1. The starting point of a river
2. A small river that feeds into a larger one
3. The dry side of a mountain range
4. Plant life
5. A narrow island between the mainland and the ocean
6. Jobs in which people help others by providing a service
7. Flat or rolling land covered with tall grass
8. The practice of using pipes or ditches to bring water to dry fields
9. A storage area for water
10. A small, thorny tree with long roots

THINKING ABOUT FACTS

1. Which landforms are found in the Southeastern region of the United States?
2. Where does the Mississippi River begin?
3. How are the Central Plains and the Great Plains of the Middle West different?
4. In which state are the tallest trees in the world found?
5. How are the regions of the United States interdependent?
6. Why is autumn the favorite season of many Northeasterners?
7. Which states make up the Southwestern region of the United States?
8. Which famous landform is located in the Southwestern region?
9. How do ships travel from Houston to the Gulf of Mexico?
10. Which two national parks are located in the Mountains and Basins region?

THINK AND WRITE

WRITING A SUMMARY

Write a summary of Lesson 3. Describe the land, the climate, the crops, and the major cities in the North Central Plains.

WRITING AN EXPLANATION

Write a paragraph explaining why the temperature of the desert drops at night. Be sure to explain the importance of the desert's dryness.

WRITING A LETTER

Suppose you are taking a vacation in Canada. Write a letter describing Canada to a friend back home. Be sure to describe how Canada and Texas are alike and how they are different.

APPLYING GEOGRAPHY SKILLS

LATITUDE AND LONGITUDE

Answer the following questions about the map on page 63 to practice your skill at using latitude and longitude.

1. What do latitude and longitude lines on a map help you to do?
2. What city is located at 30°N, 95°W?
3. The capital of our state is located on the same line of longitude as what other United States cities? How can you tell?
4. Give the approximate location of your own hometown, using latitude and longitude.
5. Why is it important to know how to use latitude and longitude?

APPLYING THINKING SKILLS

DECISION MAKING

Suppose that you and your friends are riding bikes in your neighborhood. You notice a dog wandering around your street. It has a broken chain attached to its collar. What do you do about the dog? Answer the following questions to practice your skill at making decisions.

1. What goal do you set for yourself?
2. What are the choices you have to reach your goal?
3. What might the results of each choice be?
4. Which choice will you make?
5. Do you think you made a good decision? Why?

Summing Up the Chapter

Use the table below to organize information from the chapter. Complete the table by writing down geography words that apply to each main topic. Use the table to write a paragraph that answers this question: "How does the geography of our state compare to the rest of the United States and Canada?"

UNITED STATES	CANADA	COASTAL PLAIN	NORTH CENTRAL PLAINS	GREAT PLAINS	MOUNTAINS AND BASINS

UNIT 1 REVIEW

THINKING ABOUT VOCABULARY

Number a sheet of paper from 1 to 10. Beside each number write **C** if the underlined word is used correctly. If it is not, write the word that would correctly complete the sentence.

1. A <u>basin</u> is a high, flat area that rises above the surrounding land.

2. An <u>environment</u> is an area where very little rain falls.

3. Something in the environment that people can use is a <u>natural resource</u>.

4. Minerals are examples of <u>renewable resources</u>.

5. <u>Prairies</u> are flat or rolling land covered with tall grasses.

6. The way of life that people share is called their <u>culture</u>.

7. A person who comes from another land to live in a new country is an <u>ancestor</u>.

8. A <u>hurricane</u> is a swirling funnel of wind that moves very quickly.

9. A <u>spring</u> is a layer of rock under the soil that absorbs water like a sponge.

10. A <u>time zone</u> is a region in which all the clocks are set to the same time.

THINK AND WRITE

WRITING A LETTER

Suppose you have a pen pal in another state. Your pen pal knows very little about Texas. Write a description of your state. Be sure to include information about the environment, the people, and the heritage of Texas.

WRITING A BROCHURE

Choose a region of our state and write your own travel brochure describing to others why it would be a fun and interesting place to visit.

WRITING A LIST

Write a list of five vocabulary words from Unit 1. Then write a paragraph with five sentences, using each of the vocabulary words in a sentence.

BUILDING SKILLS

1. **Elevation maps** Suppose you are planning a hiking trip to Big Bend National Park. Explain why it would be important to have an elevation map with you on your trip.

2. **Elevation maps** Using the elevation map on page 27, find the approximate elevation of the area where you live. Then find the approximate elevation of the Balcones Escarpment. Finally, find the approximate elevation of our state's capital.

3. **Latitude and longitude** Using the map on page 63, find the town that is located near 30°N latitude and 95°W longitude. Find the nearest latitude and longitude of Rocksprings.

4. **Decision making** What is a good first step to take when making a decision? Describe one decision you have made today. What steps did you take to make it?

5. **Decision making** Why do you think it is important for you to learn how to make decisions?

YESTERDAY, TODAY &
TOMORROW

When the first immigrants came to Texas, they may have thought that our resources would never run out. Now we know that many of these resources can be used up or polluted. Do you think that conservation efforts will be able to preserve our state's resources? Why or why not?

READING ON YOUR OWN
Here are some books you might find at the library to help you learn more.

THE ARMADILLO FROM AMARILLO
by Lynne Cherry
An armadillo learns about the geography, history, and environment of Texas.

THE FIRST TEXANS
by Carolyn M. Burnett
Read factual information about the way early Native American Texans lived.

THE LEGEND OF THE BLUEBONNET
by Tomie De Paola
A young Comanche girl gives up something she loves to save her people.

UNIT PROJECT

Make a State Model

1. In Unit 1 you learned about the geography of Texas. Write the names of five main cities in Texas, two state rivers, three mountain ranges, two escarpments, and the gulf located on the eastern end of Texas.
2. On a map of Texas, locate each of the places you named.
3. Next trace an outline of Texas onto a piece of oaktag.
4. Using your outline map as the base, create a model of Texas out of clay. With small pieces of clay, mold the mountain ranges and escarpments.
5. Finally cut out one paper rectangle for each place on your list. Write the name of the place on the rectangle and then glue it to a toothpick. Insert each flag in its proper place on the model.
6. Share your model with the class.

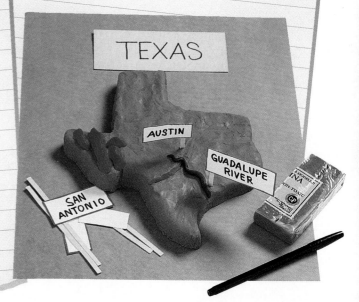

Institute of Texan Cultures

EARLY FRENCH SPEAR; NATIVE
AMERICANS OF THE PLAINS;
SPANISH MISSION OF 1720

Settling the Western Hemisphere

"... the most watchful ... of people ..."

from the book of Alvar Núñez Cabeza de Vaca
See page 124.

WHY DOES IT MATTER?

Who were the first people to live in our state? Why did they come? How did they get here? How did people live in Texas in the distant past? Who else came to Texas over the years that followed?

Read on. You will find out how the first people may have arrived in the Western Hemisphere. You will learn about the great civilization that rose up, much later, in Mexico. You will see how people from other parts of the world made the Western Hemisphere their home. You will discover the first settlers of Texas and the legacy they have left for us today.

CHRISTOPHER COLUMBUS

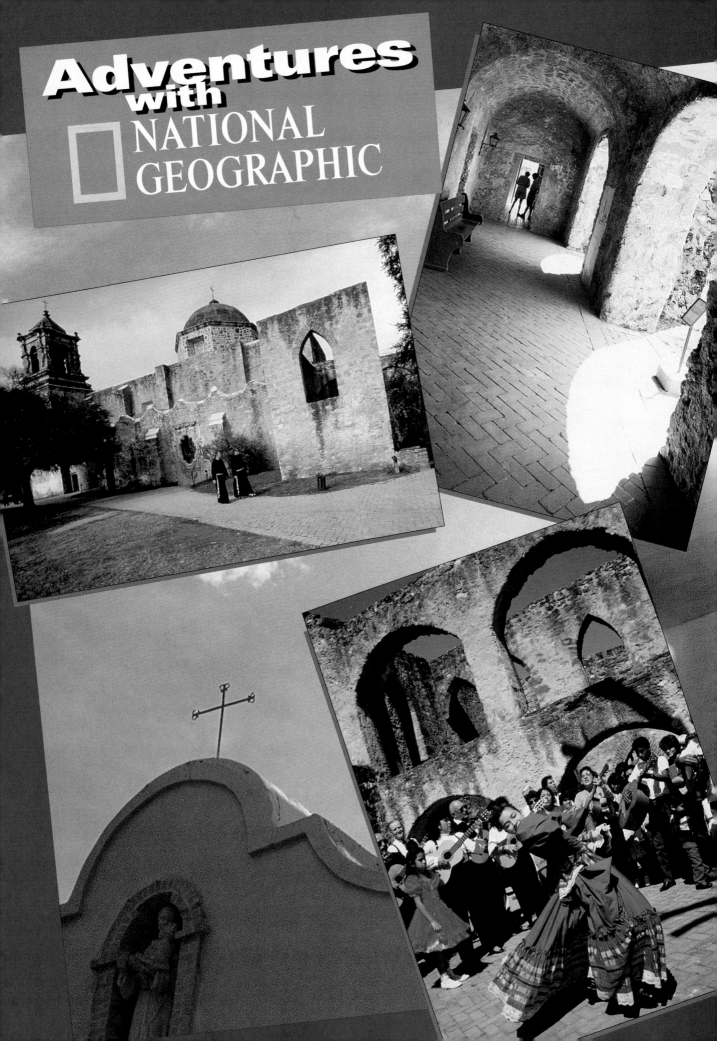

Adventures with NATIONAL GEOGRAPHIC

MEET ME AT THE MISSION

The Spanish priests who established missions in Texas hundreds of years ago might not be surprised to find that their missions are still thriving. After all, they built the places to last! Today, tourists from Texas, from across the United States, and from other countries visit missions to learn about Texas past. Festivals and celebrations take place at some missions; the courtyards echo with the sounds of music and dancing feet. And for some Texans, missions are still centers of religious life, just as they were long ago.

GEO JOURNAL

Describe buildings in your area that look something like the missions pictured here.

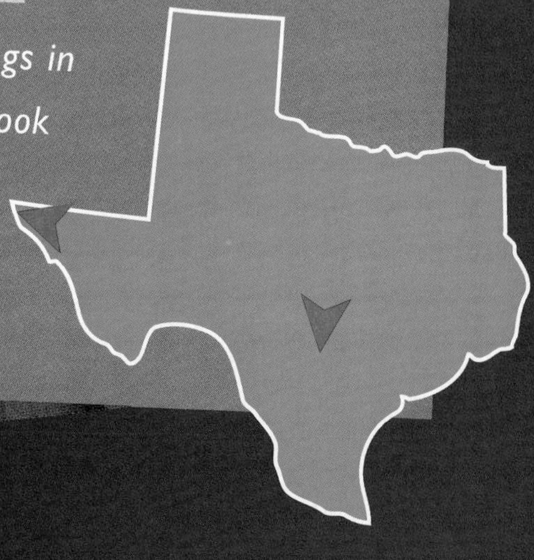

CHAPTER 3

People Come to the Western Hemisphere

THINKING ABOUT GEOGRAPHY AND HISTORY

How did people first arrive in Texas? According to many historians, the first people in the Western Hemisphere may have walked over land from Asia 40,000 years ago. As people spread out through North America and South America, they began to live in different ways. Read on to find out what Texas was like long, long ago.

PACIFIC OCEAN

9,500 years ago	1325	1500s
NEAR LUBBOCK	**LAKE TEXCOCO, MEXICO**	**GULF COAST**
Early people hunt giant bison and other animals	The Aztec begin building the city of Tenochtitlán	The Karankawa use canoes to move their campsites frequently

UNITED STATES

Lubbock

TEXAS

Piney Woods

Gulf Coast

Gulf of Mexico

MEXICO

Lake Texcoco

CENTRAL AMERICA

1500s

PINEY WOODS

Caddo communities pitch in to build permanent houses

THE FIRST AMERICANS

Focus Activity

READ TO LEARN
When and how did people first come to Texas?

VOCABULARY
Ice Age
glacier
history
prehistory
archaeology
artifact
atlatl
marsh

PLACES
Beringia
Bering Strait

READ ALOUD

"See that blood-spitting panther flanked [bordered] by what looks like a baseball bat and three balls? I think it depicts [shows] a hunt. The bat and the balls could represent weapons. . . ." This is how tour guide John Freeman describes one of the thousand-year-old drawings, like the panther below, in Seminole Canyon. Why might drawings like these be important to Texans today?

THE BIG PICTURE

Each year over 70,000 visitors come to Seminole Canyon State Historical Park near Langtry. They come to see some of the oldest art in the world. The Seminole Canyon drawings were made by people who lived in our state thousands of years ago. By studying their drawings we can learn a lot about how these first Americans lived. The drawings are among the many clues scientists use to tell us about life here thousands of years ago.

LIFE IN THE ICE AGE

Icy winds howled as the people walked across the frozen ground. They wore animal skins to keep warm. For food, they hunted wild animals and gathered plants. They were following the animals they hunted as they traveled east across lands where people had never lived.

Life may have been much like this description many thousands of years ago during the Ice Age. This was a time when glaciers (GLAY shurz), or huge sheets of ice, covered much of Earth's surface.

Traveling Across a Land Bridge

Before the glaciers formed, large bodies of water had separated Asia from North America. But during the Ice Age the level of the oceans dropped because so much water became frozen into glaciers. During this period a land bridge called Beringia (buh RIHN jee uh) connected Asia with North America. Today the land bridge is gone. The Bering Strait, a body of water 56 miles across, separates North America from Asia.

The First Americans

No one really knows when or how people came from Asia to North America. Some scientists believe that people crossed Beringia about 40,000 years ago. Slowly, many different groups of hunters and gatherers spread out through North and South America. Each group had its own culture. Look at the map on this page to see the routes that they might have taken.

These first Americans were ancestors of the people now known as Native Americans. The word *native* means "one of the first people to live in a land." Many Native Americans, however, do not believe their ancestors crossed Beringia. They believe they have always lived in North and South America.

Some scientists believe that people first reached Texas about 12,000 years ago. They lived in small groups and moved to follow their sources of food.

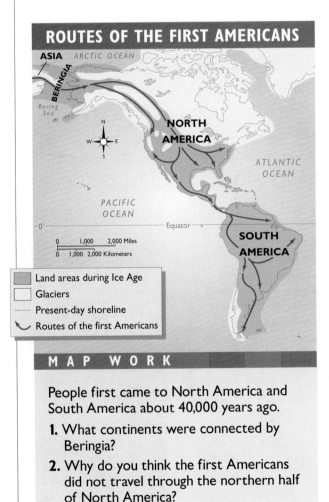

ROUTES OF THE FIRST AMERICANS

ASIA   ARCTIC OCEAN
BERINGIA
Bering Sea
NORTH AMERICA
ATLANTIC OCEAN
PACIFIC OCEAN
Equator
SOUTH AMERICA

0   1,000   2,000 Miles
0   1,000   2,000 Kilometers

Land areas during Ice Age
Glaciers
Present-day shoreline
Routes of the first Americans

M A P   W O R K

People first came to North America and South America about 40,000 years ago.

1. What continents were connected by Beringia?
2. Why do you think the first Americans did not travel through the northern half of North America?

STUDYING THE PAST

These early peoples left no written records. How do we know about them? We use the word history to describe past events that are preserved in written records. The time before written records is known as prehistory. You will be able to understand the difference between these two words by remembering that pre means "before."

The study of prehistoric people is archaeology (ahr kee OL uh jee). Archaeologists dig up the remains of ancient cities, villages, burial sites, and even garbage dumps. They study drawings like the ones found in Seminole Canyon. They find tools made by prehistoric people. They may find bits of bones, pottery, clothing, and ashes from a campfire. Objects made by people in the past are called artifacts.

Archaeologists study artifacts to learn about the past. Changes in pottery or tools may show that other groups of people moved into an area. Bones of ancient people and animals give clues about what they might have looked like. Archaeologists use special equipment to find out how old artifacts are. With this information and other clues they can solve part of the mystery of how people lived long ago.

Learning About Artifacts

In the Read Aloud, you read about the drawings in Seminole Canyon. This canyon is just one place where important archaeological discoveries have been made in our state.

More than 100 years ago, a traveler named Amos Andrew Parker noticed a series of mounds rising from the ground as he passed through eastern Texas. In his journal he wrote, "I have seen no satisfactory explanation given of the origin and use of these mounds."

Archaeologists digging in the Caddoan Mounds (right) hope to find artifacts like these arrowheads (below).

Archaeologists in Texas look for clues to the past as they study mammoth bones.

After studying the mounds, archaeologists learned that they were built by the Caddo (KAD oh) people. Today visitors who come to Caddoan Mounds State Historical Park near Alto can see these mounds.

Archaeologists think that some of the many mounds were probably used for Caddo burial and religious ceremonies. The mounds are full of artifacts. Some of the artifacts date back at least 10,000 years. Others, such as pottery and tools, are more recent. Archaeologist Dr. Dee Ann Story says that at Caddoan Mounds:

> We have . . . information that reveals a good deal about [Caddo] belief systems, their [community], and . . . their sources of food.

The Oldest Clues to Life in Texas

In the 1960s archaeologists digging at a site in Val Verde County discovered signs of early Texans. They found the points of wooden tools called **atlatls** (AHT laht ulz). Atlatls were throwing sticks that early peoples attached to the end of their spears in order to make them go faster and farther. Archaeologists in Val Verde County also found a large number of bison bones.

An atlatl could make a spear fly about 50–75 yards and pierce the tough hide of a woolly mammoth. A mammoth was like a huge elephant that grew to be fourteen feet tall. That's as tall as two seven-foot-tall basketball players—one standing on the shoulders of the other!

This atlatl (below) was found in West Texas in 1933. It was probably used for early spear hunting (right).

CHANGING WAYS OF LIFE

Drawings were not the only clues that archaeologists found in Seminole Canyon. They also discovered artifacts, such as stone tools, spear points, sandals, and baskets. Archaeologist Joe Labadie says:

> [T]he people who lived here were hunters and gatherers. They knew all the animal trails. They knew that every month—even during the winter—at least one plant blooms and comes in season out here. One of the leafy desert plants these people probably ate was the sotol (SOH tohl).

But about 2,100 years ago, some groups of people in Texas stopped moving from place to place to hunt. Instead they stayed in one place for longer periods of time.

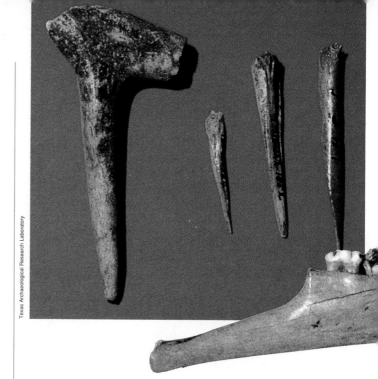
Texas Archaeological Research Laboratory

The First Farmers

Groups of people who began to farm the land and grow crops became the first Texan farmers. Archaeologists know that at this time, people in the central part of Mexico had already developed more advanced farming methods.

How do you think farming changed the lives of early Texans? As they farmed the land, people began to settle in villages and larger towns. They no longer had to move from place to place in search of food, hunting animals. Farming allowed these people to have a regular food supply and even to grow more than they needed. As a result, some people could spend more time making clothing, tools, and pottery. People also had more time to spend on community activities and religious practices.

DID YOU KNOW?

How many different ways did early Americans use the sotol plant?

A sotol plant is a small leafy desert plant with spines, or thorns. The sotol became important because early Americans found many uses for its different parts. First they used a sharp stone to strip the spines off the leaves of the plant. Then they wove the leaves into mats, baskets, and sandals. They dug up the sotol's underground bulbs and baked them in pits in the ground. The baked bulbs were used for winter food.

The earliest farmers used tools such as these (left and right), which were made from animal bone.

Many Cultures

Over time, early Texans developed different cultures. Each culture had its own language, ways of working and playing, and beliefs. They also had their own types of clothing and shelter. A group's culture developed as the group adapted to and then changed the environment in which it lived. For example, people who lived in the forest area of the Coastal Plain region were farmers. They made clearings in the forest in order to plant crops.

Other groups who lived along the Gulf of Mexico were hunters as well as fishers. They probably didn't need to farm because they lived on a kind of wetland called a **marsh**. A marsh is an area of low wetland that is covered mostly with tall grasses. Near the Gulf of Mexico the marshes are filled with salty seawater. Saltwater marshes are home to many birds, fish, and shellfish. The people who lived here probably had plenty to eat.

WHY IT MATTERS

To learn how early Texans lived and worked thousands of years ago, archaeologists dig up the remains of ancient villages, burial sites, and mounds. They search for clues such as art, artifacts, and bones.

At the same time that people came to Texas, other groups were living in different parts of the Western Hemisphere. You will learn more about these groups and their cultures in the next lesson.

✓ Reviewing Facts and Ideas

SUM IT UP

- Archaeologists use artifacts to learn about people who lived thousands of years ago.
- Some scientists think that people crossed Beringia from Asia to America about 40,000 years ago.
- About 2,100 years ago people in Texas began to farm the land.

THINK ABOUT IT

1. What is the difference between history and prehistory?

2. How do archaeologists learn about the past?

3. **FOCUS** When and how did the first people come to Texas?

4. **THINKING SKILL** What *decisions* might have led early Texans to become farmers?

5. **WRITE** Write a description of an artifact pictured in this lesson. Explain what that artifact suggests about the people who made it.

THINKINGSKILLS

Making Conclusions

VOCABULARY
conclusion

WHY THE SKILL MATTERS

In Lesson 1 you read about when and how people first came to Texas. You also read about how archaeologists study artifacts and drawings to make conclusions about how some of these groups lived.

When you make a conclusion, you pull together several pieces of information and decide what they mean. A conclusion does not repeat specific facts. Instead, it adds up these facts and tells how they are connected.

USING THE SKILL

In the last lesson you read about several artifacts found in Midland. These artifacts were similar to the ones you see in the photographs on this page. Now read these statements:

- Archaeologists found a spear point stuck in the rib of a giant bison.
- Archaeologists know that spear points were used during the Ice Age.
- Atlatls, which were throwing sticks that early people attached to their spears, were discovered in the same place as the spear point and the bison.

First ask yourself what all these statements have in common. All of these statements give information about artifacts found in the same place. Now put together these different pieces of information. A conclusion you might make is, "People who lived during the Ice Age used spears with atlatls to hunt bison." This conclusion connects all three statements. It finds a common idea behind the statements and describes it in a sentence. Like all good conclusions, this one is based on facts.

Mammoth bones

Flint point

Atlatl found in West Texas

Texas Archaeological Research Laboratory

Institute of Texan Cultures

96

TRYING THE SKILL

You have practiced making a conclusion about early Texans based on the finding of artifacts. Now you are ready to make a conclusion on your own. Read the following statements about the artifacts found at Seminole Canyon. You can see examples of similar artifacts in the photographs below. Then make a conclusion from the statements. Use the Helping Yourself box for hints.

- Artifacts from Seminole Canyon include sandals and woven baskets.
- The spiny sotol plant grew in Seminole Canyon.
- The bulbs of the sotol plant can be cooked and eaten. Other parts of the sotol can be used for weaving.
- People who lived in Seminole Canyon ate plants that grew there.

HELPING Yourself

- Making **conclusions** is a way of "adding up" several facts or statements to see how they are connected.
- Skim through the information for a common idea.
- State this meaning in your own words.

What common theme or meaning did you find in all four statements? How do they "add up" to a conclusion? What conclusion can you make about the people who used the artifacts?

REVIEWING THE SKILL

1. How did you reach your conclusion? Is your conclusion based on facts?

2. What did the four statements suggest about early people who lived in Seminole Canyon? How do you know?

3. How might making conclusions help you learn about prehistory?

4. Name some occasions in school when you might find it useful to make conclusions.

This woven basket probably carried food. The tied grass may have been used as a paintbrush.

Texas Archaeological Research Laboratory

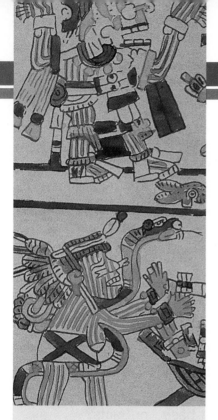

THE RISE OF CIVILIZATIONS

READ ALOUD

With our darts,
with our shields,
the city lives.

These words were written by an unknown Aztec poet. The Aztec were a group of people who lived hundreds of years ago in what is today Mexico. The "darts" and "shields" in the poem are weapons of war. As you will see, war was a part of Aztec life.

THE BIG PICTURE

At the same time small groups of Native Americans were living in what is today Texas, civilizations were developing in many other parts of the Western Hemisphere. A civilization is an organized culture. There were three major civilizations in the Americas during this time.

Two of those civilizations were the Maya of Central America and the Inca of South America. In this lesson you will read about the other great civilization—the Aztec. They lived in an area of present day Mexico that had many natural resources. They used these resources to build an empire. An empire is a large area containing different groups of people who are all ruled by a country or a single leader. Today the remains of some Aztec buildings can be seen in Mexico.

Focus Activity

READ TO LEARN
What was life like for the Aztec in the Valley of Mexico?

VOCABULARY
civilization
empire
tribute
religion

PLACES
Valley of Mexico
Tenochtitlán

THE VALLEY OF MEXICO

The Mexica, or Aztec, were a group of people who lived in what is today northern Mexico. According to Aztec sources, sometime during the 1100s they left their homeland because the land had become too dry. Over many years they traveled south. As they moved they met other groups of Native Americans. From these groups the Aztec learned how to farm. All the while, though, they kept looking for a sign from their sun god Huitzilopochtli (weet sih loh POCH tlee) to show them where to settle for good.

The Aztec eventually reached the Valley of Mexico. Lake Texcoco (tay SKOH koh) is located in the valley. About 1325, on a small island in the lake, the Aztec found the sign they were looking for. An eagle stood on a cactus, holding a snake in its mouth. The Aztec took this sign to mean they had found a home.

The environment around Lake Texcoco was ideal. The lake had water to drink and fish and birds to eat. In the lake, builders found tall grasses with which they could construct houses. At the lake's edge, farmers built gardens that appeared to float. They put thick poles into the water and filled the spaces between the poles with mud. Here they grew squash, corn, and beans.

A City Called Tenochtitlán

The Aztec built a city on the island. They named their city Tenochtitlán (te noch tee TLAHN), or "place of the prickly pear cactus." This cactus grew well on the island. Find Tenochtitlán on the map. It became the Aztec capital.

The Aztec were highly skilled builders. They built temples, homes, outdoor markets, and schools. They created three bridges to connect the island with the mainland, where they had also settled.

By the middle 1400s, Tenochtitlán was one of the largest cities in the world. Over 200,000 people lived there. More people lived there than in the city of Corpus Christi today.

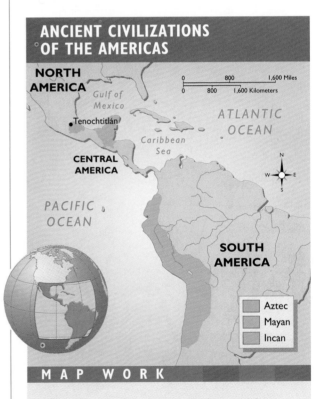

ANCIENT CIVILIZATIONS OF THE AMERICAS

NORTH AMERICA

Gulf of Mexico

• Tenochtitlán

ATLANTIC OCEAN

Caribbean Sea

CENTRAL AMERICA

PACIFIC OCEAN

SOUTH AMERICA

Aztec
Mayan
Incan

MAP WORK

This map shows where the Aztec, Maya, and Inca civilizations lived.

1. Which civilization lived on the largest area of land?

2. Did these three cultures make their homes inland or near water? Why do you think they all made this choice?

AZTEC LIFE

Most of the Aztec in Tenochtitlán were farmers or fishers. People also worked as potters, builders, and weavers. Find the weaver in the diagram on this page.

War and Worship

The Aztec often started wars with neighboring groups of people. One of their goals was to have other people pay them tribute. A tribute was payment in the form of valuable goods and services. Tribute could include food, clothing, and valuable stones. This payment was one of the ways in which the Aztec empire became rich.

In addition to valuable goods, Aztec soldiers often brought prisoners back to the city of Tenochtitlán. Men, women, and children were forced into slavery. Some had to work to build large buildings. Other people were killed and offered to the god of the Aztec, Huitzilopochtli.

What activities took place in Tenochtitlán?

temple

floating garden

bridge

central plaza

bridge

pottery

weaving

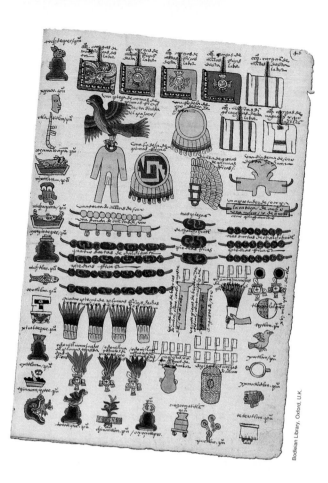

Bodleian Library, Oxford, U.K.

This Aztec drawing is actually a list—the symbols represent the different objects that the Aztec empire collected as tribute.

Religion was very important to the Aztec. Religion is the way people worship God or the gods they believe in. The Aztec worshiped their sun god through prayers and offerings. They believed that soldiers who died in battle and people who were killed as offerings would join the sun as it moved across the sky. The Aztec hoped that by pleasing Huitzilopochtli they would have good harvests and victory in battle.

WHY IT MATTERS

The Aztec were just one of many groups living in the Western Hemisphere at this time. Tenochtitlán was the center of Aztec civilization. In the next chapter, you will learn how the Aztec empire ended.

Though the empire no longer exists, parts of Aztec culture remain today. Some Mexicans still speak the Nahuatl (NAH wah tul) language of the Aztec. In fact, some words we use such as *Mexico* and *chocolate* come from the Aztec. In the next lesson you will read about Native Americans in Texas.

Reviewing Facts and Ideas

SUM IT UP

- The Aztec, Maya, and Inca created great civilizations in the Western Hemisphere.

- In about 1325 the Aztec began to build the city of Tenochtitlán in the Valley of Mexico.

- The Aztec empire grew wealthy as it took control over other groups of people and forced them to pay tribute.

THINK ABOUT IT

1. What is an empire?

2. Why did the Aztec build their city in the Valley of Mexico? What natural resources did they use?

3. **FOCUS** What was life like for the Aztec in the Valley of Mexico?

4. **THINKING SKILL** What _conclusions_ can you make about how the place in which the Aztec lived influenced their food and ways of life?

5. **GEOGRAPHY** Look back at the map on page 99. Which of the three civilizations was farthest south?

Focus Activity

READ TO LEARN

How did some of the early Native Americans of Texas live?

VOCABULARY

teepee
band

NATIVE AMERICANS OF THE GULF COAST AND THE PLAINS

READ ALOUD

In 1530 a Spaniard lived with a group of Native Americans in Texas. Many years later he wrote about their dances. What made one dance different from another, he wrote, was "the instruments which they play for them. For the festive ones they play a tambourine that is made of a tortoise shell . . . and a whistle [made] of reeds. . . . For the sad ones they play . . . [an] instrument they call the caymán."

THE BIG PICTURE

As you have read in Lesson 1, many different groups of Native Americans lived in North America in the 1500s. These groups are divided into four different cultures, or ways of life. They are the Native Americans of the Gulf Coast, the Plains, the desert, and the forest.

Archaeologists have learned about some of these groups of Native Americans from the writings and drawings of European sailors. However, we have to be careful when we read these records. Most Europeans did not speak Native American languages. They probably did not understand some of what they saw.

PEOPLE OF THE GULF COAST

The coastline along the Gulf of Mexico was home to the Karankawa (kah ran KAH wah) and also to the Coahuiltecan (kwah weel TE kan). They lived in the marshes of the Coastal Plain. Find these groups on the map. In this lesson you will read about the Karankawa.

The Karankawa

Much of our information about the Karankawa comes from the writings of some of the first Spaniards in Texas. In the next chapter you will read about how these people met the Karankawa.

Fishing was at the center of Karankawa life. Besides fish, they ate clams, turtles, and underwater plants. They also hunted deer, bear, and alligators. Women gathered nuts, berries, and seeds for food.

The Karankawa moved their campsite from place to place every few weeks, traveling to wherever the fishing was best. They traveled in large canoes made from hollowed-out tree trunks. Because they moved often, they needed houses that could be taken down easily. These houses were made of willow poles

Courtesy of the Witte Museum

The Karankawa used arrowheads like this one for hunting. It was made of glass left by the Spanish explorers.

covered with animal skins and woven mats.

The Spaniard from the Read Aloud also wrote about how the Karankawa treated their children. He said they "love their offspring the most of any in the world, and treat them with the greatest mildness."

Few Karankawa remained when Texas became part of the United States in 1845. Many had died from diseases brought unknowingly by early Europeans. Others had moved to Mexico or were killed in wars with other Native Americans or new settlers from the United States.

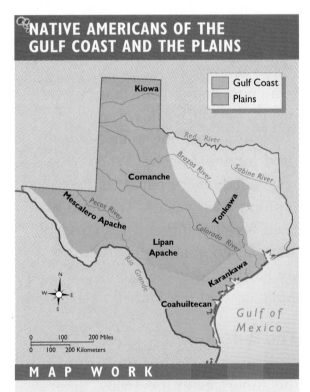

NATIVE AMERICANS OF THE GULF COAST AND THE PLAINS

Gulf Coast
Plains

Kiowa
Red River
Brazos River
Sabine River
Comanche
Mescalero Apache
Pecos River
Tonkawa
Colorado River
Lipan Apache
Rio Grande
Karankawa
Coahuiltecan
Gulf of Mexico

0   100   200 Miles
0   100   200 Kilometers

MAP WORK

Many Native American groups once lived on the Gulf Coast and the Plains.

1. Which Native American group lived in the northern Panhandle?

2. How do you think the location of the Karankawa influenced their way of life?

PEOPLE OF THE PLAINS

By the 1800s five groups of Native Americans lived on the plains of western Texas. They are sometimes called the Plains Indians. These groups were the Lipan Apache, Kiowa, Mescalero Apache, Tonkawa, and Comanche. In this lesson you will read about the Lipan Apache.

The Lipan Apache

Unlike the Karankawa, the Lipan Apache lived as hunters of buffalo. But like the Karankawa they moved their villages from place to place according to the seasons. You can see what an Apache village looked like in the Infographic on page 106. The Apache carried their homes, called teepees, with them. A teepee is a cone-shaped tent that can be put up and taken down quickly.

Buffalo were the main source of food for the Apache. When a buffalo was killed, every part was used and nothing was wasted. The hide was used for clothing and for covering teepees. Look at the chart to see some other ways in which the Apache used the buffalo.

The Buffalo Hunt

Spanish sailors brought horses to the Americas in the 1500s. Before that time the Apache and other Native Americans hunted on foot. Horses allowed them to move about faster and farther. What might it have been like to hunt buffalo with the Apache?

Suppose you are a ten-year-old Apache boy joining a buffalo hunt for the first time. Apache hunting leaders have located a herd. They begin to surround it on horseback.

As the huge, shaggy animals run by you the ground shakes. You

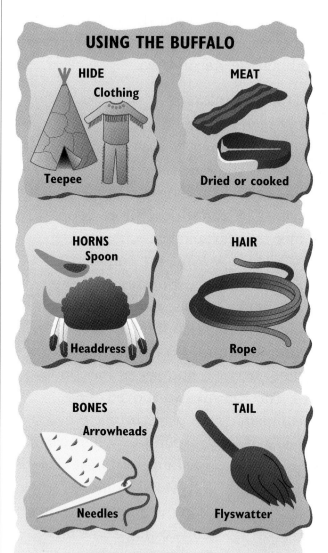

USING THE BUFFALO

HIDE — Clothing — Teepee

MEAT — Dried or cooked

HORNS — Spoon — Headdress

HAIR — Rope

BONES — Arrowheads — Needles

TAIL — Flyswatter

CHART WORK

The Lipan Apache did not waste any part of the buffalo.

1. How did the Apache make use of the hair of the buffalo?
2. Why do you think the Apache needed to make needles from the bones?
3. Why do you think the buffalo were important to the Apache?

know that the herd could trample you to death. Each buffalo is taller than an adult and weighs as much as ten people.

As the hunters close in on the herd you follow along. You ride up close to a buffalo. You aim and shoot your arrow straight into its side. You've killed your first buffalo!

The Apache Band

Each Apache was part of a small family group called a **band**. A band had a peace chief and a war chief. The bravest Apache were chosen to be chiefs.

The Apache were known as skilled riders and warriors. Boys and girls alike were good riders by an early age. Before they could become warriors, boys had to prove they could survive many hardships. For example, they had to stay outdoors for long periods of time in extreme heat and cold with little clothing.

Apache Children

Days after an Apache baby was born, it was laced into a wooden frame covered with deerskin. Apache women spent their days making clothing, raising maize and beans, and doing other chores. They had little time to look after their babies. These wooden frames, or cradleboards, kept children safe.

Apache children were educated mostly by their grandparents. Grandparents taught children

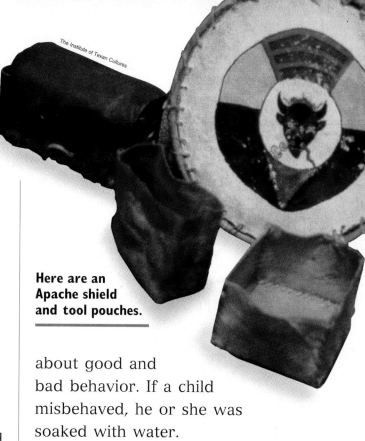

The Institute of Texan Cultures

Here are an Apache shield and tool pouches.

about good and bad behavior. If a child misbehaved, he or she was soaked with water.

Apache Life Today

Today the descendants of Apache groups live throughout the United States. Most live in Arizona, New Mexico and Oklahoma. There are, however, at least 2,500 Apache who make their homes in Texas.

***Lead Singer* is a modern Apache sculpture.**

1995, The Heard Museum

Infographic

Life in a Lipan Apache Village

The Lipan Apache lived on the plains in much of the western half of what is today Texas. They gathered wild plants, grew crops, and hunted buffalo. Let's take a closer look at what life was like in a Lipan Apache village nearly 200 years ago.

MOBILE HOMES The Lipan Apache lived in teepees made of buffalo skins and wooden poles. Teepees could be folded up to be moved.

A VALUABLE RESOURCE The Lipan Apache used the buffalo to meet many of their needs. They dried buffalo meat on racks to preserve it. They sewed buffalo hides to make clothing and teepee covers.

FOOD STORAGE The Lipan Apache used baskets to store food. Pitch from pine trees helped waterproof them. Animal skins were also used.

WHY IT MATTERS

The Karankawa and the Lipan Apache are two of the many Native American groups who lived on the Gulf Coast and the plains of Texas. Archaeologists have studied their artifacts and the writings of Spaniards to learn more about these groups of people.

In the next lesson you will read about other groups of Native Americans who lived in our state. Later on you will read why many Native Americans had to leave Texas.

✔️ Reviewing Facts and Ideas

SUM IT UP

- By the 1500s many Native American groups lived in Texas.
- The Karankawa were fishers who lived along the Gulf of Mexico.
- The Apache were hunters who lived on the plains of Texas.

THINK ABOUT IT

1. What natural resources did the Karankawa rely on?

2. Why were teepees good homes for the Apache?

3. **FOCUS** What were the ways of life of the Karankawa and the Apache?

4. **THINKING SKILL** List two ways your life is the _same_ as and _different_ from the Karankawa way of life.

5. **WRITE** What if a Karankawa artifact were found near your school? Write a paragraph telling how you could learn more about it.

A VISUAL HISTORY Paintings on buffalo hides showed the group's history. The pictures and symbols referred to important past events.

NATIVE AMERICANS OF THE DESERT AND THE FOREST

Focus Activity

READ TO LEARN
What were the ways of life of the Native Americans of the desert and forest?

VOCABULARY
pueblo
adobe
trotline
crop rotation

READ ALOUD

A European traveler described a Caddo village on the Red River in 1687.

"We saw several cottages. . . . In some of them are 15 or 20 families, each of which has its nook or corner, bed, and other utensils. . . . The cottages are round at the top, after the manner of a beehive."

THE BIG PICTURE

The Native Americans of the desert and of the forest had very different ways of life. However, they did have something in common. Both groups were farmers who lived in permanent villages. As you will read, both groups used the natural resources in their environment to meet their needs and wants. Look at the map on the opposite page. Find the groups of the desert and forest.

PEOPLE OF THE DESERT

Different groups of Pueblo peoples lived in the Southwest of what is today the United States. In Spanish *pueblo* means "village." The Pueblo who lived in Texas were the Tigua (TEE gwah), the Concho, and the Jumano (hoo MAH noh). Find these groups on the map. You will read more about the Tigua in Making a Difference on page 113.

The Jumano

Not much is known about Jumano culture. One group of Jumano were hunters and traders. They lived in the Mountains and Basins region of Texas. Many other Jumano were farmers who lived along the Rio Grande from El Paso to the Big Bend.

The Jumano lived in the desert. Farming was not easy because the land was always dry. The Jumano adapted to their dry environment by using the water from creeks or streams to irrigate their land. Some of the crops that the Jumano grew were corn, squash, and beans. To add to their food supply, the Jumano also hunted and fished.

The Jumano had a way of cooking called "stone boiling." A Spaniard described it like this:

> *They fill the half of a large calabash [gourd] with water, and throw on the fire many stones. . . . When hot, they are taken up with tongs of sticks and dropped into the calabash until the water boils. . . . Then whatever is to be cooked is put in, and until it is done, they continue taking out [cold] stones and throwing in hot ones.*

The Jumano built their houses out of adobe. Adobe is brick made from clay and straw that has been dried in the sun. Adobe walls helped to keep the inside of the houses cool in summer and warm in winter.

The Jumano villages along the Rio Grande disappeared hundreds of years ago. Historians are not sure why. Some people believe that the Jumano moved to Mexico.

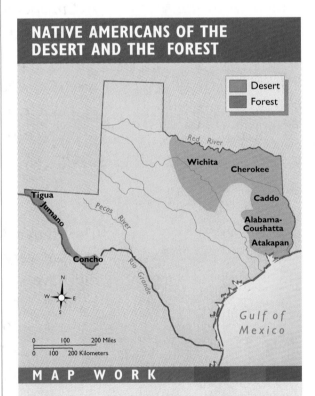

NATIVE AMERICANS OF THE DESERT AND THE FOREST

Desert
Forest

Red River
Wichita
Cherokee
Tigua
Jumano
Pecos River
Caddo
Alabama-Coushatta
Atakapan
Concho
Rio Grande
Gulf of Mexico

N W E S

0   100   200 Miles
0   100   200 Kilometers

MAP WORK

Native Americans of the desert and the forest farmed as their way of life.

1. Did the Caddo live in the eastern or western part of what is now Texas?

2. Why do you think the Jumano lived differently from the Karankawa, whom you read about in Lesson 3?

109

PEOPLE OF THE FOREST

The Native Americans of the forest culture lived in the Piney Woods. The Caddo were the first to live there. The Atakapan, the Wichita, the Cherokee, and the Alabama Coushatta (koo SHA tuh) moved there later. The Alabama Coushatta still live in eastern Texas today. In this lesson you will read about the Caddo.

Meeting the Caddo

In Chapter 1 you read that the name of our state comes from the Caddo word for "friends." Suppose you were entering a Caddo village for the first time in the year 1687.

The people would ride out to greet you with gift baskets filled with corn meal. How would such a greeting make you feel?

How the Caddo Lived

The Piney Woods provided many natural resources making it a good place to live. There was plenty of rain to grow the crops they needed. The forests were full of animals and plants for food, and the waters were full of fish.

To fish, the Caddo ran a trotline across a stream. A trotline is a long,

What activities can you find in this mural showing life in a Caddo village?

The Institute of Texan Cultures

heavy fishing line that has several baited hooks on it. It also has weights to keep it under water. A trotline could catch more fish than a single line could.

The Caddo cut down trees in order to farm. In the fertile soil, they grew corn, beans, pumpkins, squash, and melons. The community worked together to plant these crops so that they would provide enough food for hundreds of people.

As you read earlier, soil is a natural resource that needs to be enriched after years of farming. The Caddo knew this fact about soil. Therefore, they planted a different crop each year in the same soil. They did this so the soil would not wear out. This method of farming is called **crop rotation**. Crop rotation is still practiced today by farmers around the world.

A House-Raising

As described in the Read Aloud, the Caddo lived in large round houses that looked like domes or beehives. These houses were 25 to 45 feet wide. The largest could provide shelter for 20 to 30 people from several families.

Whenever a house was needed, the whole community pitched in to build one. The women gathered grass to cover the house. Groups of men placed long poles in the ground. Then they tied the tops of the poles together. Others covered the frame with wood. Then the grass covering was put on. The families who were going to live in the new house prepared a meal of corn and meat for the workers to eat. With so many people working, the job took less than a morning to do.

In 1690 a Spanish priest named Damian Massanet described the house of a chief. How is the chief's house different from your home? How is it similar?

Excerpt from a letter by Father Damian Massanet in 1690.

In the middle of the house is the fire which is never [put out]. . . . Arranged around one half of the house inside, are ten beds, which consist of a rug made of reeds, laid on four forked sticks. Over the rug they spread buffalo skins, on which they sleep. . . . In the other half of the house where there are no beds, there are some shelves . . . and on them are arranged large round baskets made of reeds in which they keep their corn, nuts, acorns, beans.

THE CADDO THEN AND NOW

Each Caddo group had a chief called a *caddi*. This position of honor was usually passed down from fathers to their sons. But Caddo women sometimes became caddi. The caddi gave orders, made decisions, and supervised projects.

Harvest Celebration

The most important Caddo ceremony was a harvest celebration. At this ceremony religious leaders went for days without food, drink, or sleep. They wanted to show how thankful they were to their god for the good harvest. The leaders also prayed for a good future for their people.

The Caddo Today

The Caddo remained in Texas until 1859. War and disease had reduced their number to only a few hundred. Newcomers to Texas wanted to build on Caddo land and the Caddo were forced to move to what is today Oklahoma. Their descendants still live there.

The Caddo today sometimes wear traditional dress for special celebrations.

WHY IT MATTERS

The Jumano and the Caddo were farmers. Historians know little about the life of the Jumano and why they disappeared from Texas. Though the Caddo do not live in Texas today, their descendants continue to celebrate their heritage in other parts of the United States.

✓ Reviewing Facts and Ideas

SUM IT UP

- The Native Americans of the desert and the forest cultures lived in permanent villages.
- The Jumano used the natural resources of the desert to meet their needs and wants.
- The Caddo used the natural resources of the Piney Woods to meet their needs and wants.

THINK ABOUT IT

1. What is adobe? Why did the Jumano build adobe houses?

2. Which activity did Caddo men and women share?

3. **FOCUS** How were the ways of life of the Native Americans of the desert and forest cultures alike?

4. **THINKING SKILL** List three *questions* that you might have asked a Caddo to learn more about his or her way of life.

5. **GEOGRAPHY** If the Caddo had lived in the Mountains and Basins, how might their lives have been different?

Keeping Tigua Culture Alive

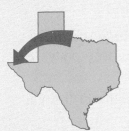

EL PASO, TEXAS—The Tigua of western Texas are the oldest living group of Native Americans in our state. They have lived here since 1681. Many Tigua live in El Paso at Ysleta del Sur Pueblo (ees LAY tuh del soor POOEH bloh). *Ysleta del Sur Pueblo* is Spanish for "little island of the south pueblo".

The culture of the Tigua today mixes Indian traditions with Spanish and Mexican customs. The Tigua have many ways of keeping these traditions alive. On weekends in the summer, the Tigua Indian Dance Group shares music, song, and dance with visitors to the pueblo at its cultural center. Young dancers, ages 10 to 21, perform Tigua dances like the eagle dance and the butterfly dance. They twirl around the floor in costumes of traditional colors: yellow for the sun, green for plants, red for earth, and white for clouds. Drums and chanting provide the music.

Nancy Hisa (HEE sah) is a Tigua dancer. She explains that she learned the dances "so that I would know more about where I came from and I could explain our traditions to others."

Nancy and her sister Susie helped teach the younger children the dances when the group first formed. Nancy says: "My favorite dance is the fancy shawl dance because it starts off slow, but then goes really fast. We have to keep up with the beat. We are really tired afterwards, but it's fun. I also like the butterfly dance. The butterfly fluttering over the growing crops was a sign of a good harvest to come. When we're dancing, we hold black and white feathers. It looks like a butterfly moving."

In the final dance of each performance, the dancers invite the audience to join them. Nancy says that "this dance is special because it's a circle of friendship, life, and peace. When other people dance with us they are sharing in a Tigua tradition."

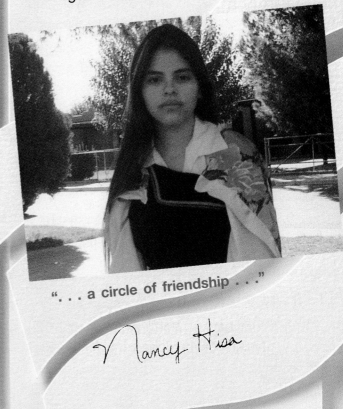

". . . a circle of friendship . . ."

Nancy Hisa

113

CHAPTER 3 REVIEW

THINKING ABOUT VOCABULARY

Number a sheet of paper from 1 to 10. Next to each number write the word from the list that best completes the sentence.

archaeology   marsh
artifact   prehistory
band   pueblo
empire   religion
glacier   trotline

1. A huge sheet of ice on the surface of Earth is a _____.

2. _____ is the time before written records.

3. An object that was made by people in the past is an _____ .

4. _____ is the study of prehistoric people.

5. A _____ is an area of low, wet land covered mostly with tall grasses.

6. A large area with different groups ruled by one leader is called an _____.

7. The way people worship the God or the gods they believe in is known as _____.

8. A _____ is a small family group of Native Americans.

9. _____ means "village" in Spanish.

10. A _____ is a long, heavy fishing line strung across a stream.

THINKING ABOUT FACTS

1. What part of North America did the glaciers cover during the Ice Age?

2. What body of water exists today where there was once a land bridge?

3. Who built the mounds found in eastern Texas?

4. What did archaeologists find in Seminole Canyon? What did these finds tell the scientists?

5. What happened about 2,100 years ago that changed the way early Texans lived?

6. Why did the Aztec settle in the Valley of Mexico?

7. What were the four cultural groups of Native Americans living in Texas in the 1500s?

8. Why did the Jumano use adobe to build their houses?

9. What custom did the Caddo practice when greeting people for the first time?

10. Which group of Native Americans practiced crop rotation?

THINK AND WRITE

WRITING A REPORT

Suppose you were on an archaeological dig and you were the first scientist to uncover an atlatl. Write a report about your discovery.

WRITING A DESCRIPTION

Write a description of the Aztec empire in the middle 1400s.

WRITING A DIARY

Suppose you are a young Karankawa child. Write an entry in your diary describing your day.

APPLYING THINKING SKILLS

MAKING CONCLUSIONS

1. What is meant by making a conclusion?

2. What steps should you follow when making a conclusion?

3. Read the section under "Changing Ways of Life" on page 94. What conclusion did Joe Labadie make about the people who lived in Seminole Canyon? Do you agree with his conclusion?

4. Read the first paragraph under "Why It Matters" on page 95. What conclusion could you make about people who decide to become archaeologists?

5. Why is it important to make conclusions about what you read?

Archaeologists hope to find artifacts that help them make conclusions about the past

Summing up the Chapter

Use the following word maps to organize information from the chapter. Copy the word maps on a sheet of paper. Then write at least one piece of information in each blank circle. When you have filled in the maps, use them to write a paragraph that answers the question "How did environment and natural resources affect the way Native Americans lived in Texas?"

People of the Gulf Coast

People of the Plains

People of the Desert

People of the Forest

CHAPTER 4

Newcomers to the Americas

THINKING ABOUT
GEOGRAPHY AND HISTORY

For thousands of years only Native Americans lived in Texas. In the 1500s something happened that would change the lives of these people and of others around the world. Europeans came in ships to the Western Hemisphere. Read Chapter 4 to find out how this contact changed life in Texas forever.

PACIFIC OCEAN

1520–1521
TENOCHTITLÁN, MEXICO

Cortés defeats Moctezuma and founds New Spain

1541
CÍBOLA, NEW MEXICO

Coronado meets the Pueblo while seeking gold

1681
EL PASO

Spanish missionaries build the first mission in Texas

UNITED STATES

Cíbola

El Paso   TEXAS

Gulf of
Mexico

MEXICO

Tenochtitlán

CENTRAL
AMERICA

ARRIVAL OF EUROPEANS

Focus Activity

READ TO LEARN
How did the arrival of Europeans in the Western Hemisphere affect the Native Americans?

VOCABULARY
explore
colony
conquistador

PEOPLE
Christopher Columbus
Hernando Cortés
Moctezuma II
Doña Marina

PLACES
Spain
New Spain

READ ALOUD

For thousands of years, the way of life of the many groups of Native Americans throughout the Americas changed very slowly. Then in 1492, something happened that changed Indian cultures—and cultures everywhere—forever.

THE BIG PICTURE

In August 1492 Christopher Columbus, an Italian sea captain, sailed from Spain. He commanded three ships—the *Niña*, the *Pinta*, and the *Santa María*. He was trying to find a route from Europe to the Indies in Asia by sailing west across the Atlantic Ocean. But instead, he reached the Bahama Islands in the Atlantic Ocean. Find the Bahama Islands on the Atlas map on page R14. Later, many Europeans said that Columbus had discovered a "New World." To the Native Americans already living here, North America and South America were not "new" at all. What happened when Columbus arrived? Who were the first people to meet him?

CHRISTOPHER COLUMBUS

On October 12, 1492, a sailor on one of Columbus's ships shouted *Tierra! Tierra!* ("Land! Land!"). Columbus was sure that he had reached the Indies. He called the people who lived there "Indians."

Columbus and the Taino

The people Columbus met called themselves the Taino (TĪ noh). They were one of many Native American groups living on islands in the Caribbean Sea. To travel from island to island, they used boats that were made of hollowed-out logs.

Today, a word used in English, *canoe*, comes from the Taino word for "boat." You know other Taino words. Have you ever relaxed in a *hammock*? The Taino wove hammocks from cotton. The sailors from Europe found that hammocks were comfortable. Soon, many sailors were using hammocks as beds.

Changes Brought by Europeans

After reaching the Western Hemisphere, Columbus set out to explore the Caribbean islands. To explore is to travel in unfamiliar places in order to find out and learn about them. Columbus and the Europeans who followed him were explorers. One of their goals was to set up colonies in this New World. A colony is a place that is ruled by another country.

Columbus took gold, parrots, and various plants back to Spain. Crops from the Western Hemisphere such as corn, potatoes, and peanuts were in time brought to countries in Europe, Africa, and Asia.

Europeans brought crops to the Americas that were unknown there, such as wheat and sugar cane. They also brought, unknowingly, diseases such as measles. These diseases killed many Native Americans, who had never come in contact with them before.

This ancient astrolabe (above) is an instrument Columbus might have used to help guide his way. The replicas of his three ships (left) can be seen in Corpus Christi.

CORTÉS AND THE AZTEC EMPIRE

One of the early explorers to follow Christopher Columbus was Hernando Cortés (cor TEZ). Cortés was a conquistador (kon KEES tah dawr) from Spain. In Spanish *conquistador* means "conqueror," one who takes ownership by force. Cortés went to Mexico with more than 500 soldiers. He was determined to conquer lands, find gold, and spread the Roman Catholic religion.

The Spaniards Arrive

In Chapter 3 you read about the rich Aztec empire in Mexico. In 1502 Moctezuma (mahk tuh ZOO muh) II became its ruler. Moctezuma was a powerful leader. In 1519 he heard that newcomers had landed along the coast of Mexico. Moctezuma did not know why the newcomers had come or what they wanted.

Gifts of Gold and Silver

Moctezuma sent gifts of gold and silver to Cortés. He hoped that the conquistadors would take the gifts and go home. Cortés wanted more gold. Nothing could stop him from trying to conquer Tenochtitlán, the capital of the Aztec empire.

Marching toward Tenochtitlán, Cortés came to several Indian cities. In one city, he met an Indian woman the Spanish called Doña Marina (DOH nyah muh REE nuh). She helped Cortés communicate with Indian groups. With her help

The Granger Collection

The Granger Collection

When Cortés (left) defeated Moctezuma II (right) the Americas were changed forever.

Cortés learned about the sufferings of Indians under Moctezuma's rule. Many Indians joined Cortés. They wanted to attack Moctezuma and his city of Tenochtitlán.

Cortés Meets Moctezuma

In 1519 Moctezuma welcomed Cortés to his grand city. The Spaniards were amazed at what they saw. One of them wrote:

> *Who could count the multitude [number] of men, women and children which had come out on the roofs, in their boats on the canals, or in the streets, to see us?*

The Aztecs were just as surprised. One Aztec described the Spaniards as ". . . clothed in iron." After arriving, Cortés, the Spaniards, and their Indian followers took Moctezuma prisoner and ruled the city.

The End of an Empire

The Aztecs and the Spaniards were soon locked in battle. Moctezuma was killed during the fighting. But the

Spaniards were forced to leave the city of Tenochtitlán.

In 1521 Cortés returned to Tenochtitlán with more soldiers. Again, many Indians joined him in battle. The Spaniards conquered and burned Tenochtitlán. Cortés renamed the empire New Spain after his homeland. New Spain included Mexico and the land of what is today Texas. This event marked the joining of two cultures, Mexican Indian and Spanish. Today you can visit the remains of Tenochtitlán in Mexico City.

Look at the drawing below. What are some differences between Spanish weapons and Mexican Indian weapons?

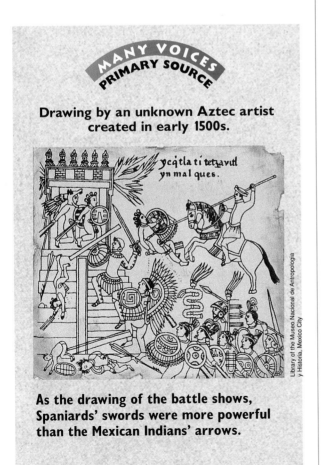

MANY VOICES
PRIMARY SOURCE

Drawing by an unknown Aztec artist created in early 1500s.

Library of the Museo Nacional de Antropología y Historia, Mexico City

As the drawing of the battle shows, Spaniards' swords were more powerful than the Mexican Indians' arrows.

WHY IT MATTERS

Columbus and Cortés were among the first of millions of Europeans who came to explore, conquer, and settle the Americas. Soon Africans would be brought to the Americas. The linking of the Eastern and Western hemispheres would change the way of life for people all over the world. You will read more about European exploration in the next lesson.

Reviewing Facts and Ideas

SUM IT UP

- In 1492 Christopher Columbus reached North America.
- The Taino were the first Native Americans that Columbus met.
- In 1521 Cortés established the colony of New Spain.

THINK ABOUT IT

1. Why did Europeans call the Western Hemisphere the "New World"?

2. What is a conquistador?

3. **FOCUS** What happened to many Native Americans when the Europeans arrived?

4. **THINKING SKILL** What _questions_ might you want to ask Columbus, Cortés, or the Indians they met?

5. **GEOGRAPHY** Look at the Atlas map on page R14. What bodies of water separate the Eastern and Western hemispheres? How did this affect the lives of people before and after Columbus and Cortés sailed?

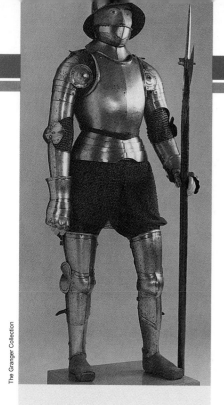

The Granger Collection

EXPLORING THE SOUTHWEST

Focus Activity

READ TO LEARN
Who were the first Europeans to explore the land now called Texas?

VOCABULARY
expedition

PEOPLE
Alonso Alvarez de Piñeda
Pánfilo de Narváez
Alvar Núñez Cabeza de Vaca
Estevanico
Fray Marcos de Niza
Francisco Vásquez de Coronado
Hernando de Soto
Luis de Moscoso de Alvarado
René Robert Cavelier, Sieur de la Salle

PLACES
Portugal
England
France

READ ALOUD
"We Spaniards suffer from a disease of the heart which can only be cured by gold." So wrote Hernando Cortés, conqueror of the Aztec empire.

THE BIG PICTURE

After Cortés defeated the Aztec in 1521, stories of great wealth in the Western Hemisphere spread throughout Europe. Countries, such as Portugal, sent their best explorers to South America to search for gold and silver. The coins below were made from silver found in the Americas. With their strong weapons, explorers conquered Native Americans, seized their land, and set up colonies. Meanwhile, other European nations, such as England and France, began to send explorers to North America to establish colonies. In a race for land, Spain moved quickly by planning a series of new journeys to North America. Spanish sailors were eager to find more gold and silver and declare ownership of more land.

[Texas]

Gulf of Mexico

92°

122

THE FIRST EUROPEANS IN TEXAS

In 1519, a Spanish explorer named Alonso Alvarez de Piñeda (ahl LAHN soh AHL vah rayz day pihn YAY dah) sailed along the coast of what is today Florida. He was the leader of an expedition, or a journey of exploration. His journey took him along the Gulf of Mexico from the west coast of Florida to Mexico. Crew members drew maps of the coastline. You can see their map below. You can trace their route on the map in the Infographic on page 126. Some historians believe Piñeda and his crew were the first Europeans to see the land of Texas.

Some historians once thought Piñeda sailed up the Rio Grande or the *Rio de las Palmas,* the "River of the Palms." But today some believe the Pánuco (PAHN uh koh) in Mexico was the river. Piñeda wrote back to Spain encouraging settlers to come.

Shipwrecked!

Using Piñeda's maps, an expedition of 400 Spaniards led by Pánfilo de Narváez (PAHN fee loh day nahr VAH ays) reached the west coast of Florida in 1528. Narváez and about 300 members of his crew walked overland to find a place to build a colony. But several were killed by Native Americans defending their villages. Others died from hunger. Because of the slowness of the journey overland, the expedition gave up. But they were far from their ships so they decided to build boats and try to sail to Mexico.

In September 1528, about 240 men left the Florida coast on these boats, but few survived. Near the Texas coast, a storm wrecked the boats and many drowned. A few survivors reached land—probably Galveston Island. On the island they were met by the Karankawa.

The Granger Collection

This statue (below) represents Piñeda, who many believe is responsible for the first map of Texas (left).

SPANISH EXPLORERS IN TEXAS

One of the men who survived the shipwreck was **Alvar Núñez Cabeza de Vaca** (NOON yayz kah BAY zah day VAH kah). Two other Spaniards, Alonso del Castillo Maldonado and Andrés Dorantes also survived the shipwreck. So did a man named **Estevanico** (es tay vah NEE koh), who had been enslaved by Dorantes earlier. Estevanico came from the country of Morocco, in North Africa. Some historians believe that Estevanico was the first African in Texas.

Journey to New Spain

The survivors were enslaved by the Karankawa. They dug roots for food and collected driftwood for fires. They did whatever they were told to do.

In 1534, after six difficult years, the four explorers escaped. They went west, looking for Mexico.

Along the way, they met many groups of Native Americans. The explorers journeyed about 3,000 miles before arriving in Mexico City.

Years later, Cabeza de Vaca wrote about his travels. How does he describe a group of Native Americans he met?

MANY VOICES PRIMARY SOURCE

Excerpt from the book of Alvar Núñez Cabeza de Vaca, 1542.

They are the most watchful in danger of any people I ever knew. . . . They often come out from their houses, bending to the ground in such manner that they cannot be seen, looking and watching on all sides to

From the title page of Cabeza de Vaca's book.

The Institute of Texan Cultures

catch every object. If they perceive anything about, they are at once in the bushes with their bows and arrows, and there remain until day.

---

perceive: notice

Cities of Gold

Cabeza de Vaca heard many stories from Native Americans about cities of gold. The Spaniards called them the Seven Cities of Cíbola (SEE buh luh). Spanish officials in Mexico asked Cabeza de Vaca to find those cities. Cabeza de Vaca, however, was exhausted from exploring. He returned to Spain.

In 1539 Spanish officials sent **Fray Marcos de Niza** (fray MAHR kos day NEE sah) to find the Cities of Gold. With Estevanico and hundreds of Mexican Indians he journeyed hundreds of miles north from Mexico. Estevanico was sent to scout ahead.

Estevanico reached the Zuni village of Cíbola along what is today the border of Arizona and New Mexico. He sent a message to Fray Marcos that he had found the golden cities! Today we know that he was mistaken. What he saw was the sun glowing on adobe pueblos.

Fray Marcos went on to Cíbola. There he learned that Estevanico had died. Some historians think Estevanico never made it to Cíbola. Others think he may have been killed by the Zuni who lived there.

A Mighty Expedition

Fray Marcos returned to Mexico with reports of gold. The Spanish officials put together a mighty expedition to go to Cíbola. A Spanish conquistador, **Francisco Vásquez de Coronado** (VAHS kays day kohr oh NAHD oh), was put in charge. In 1540 Coronado led 300 Spaniards and 1,000 Mexican Indians north through Mexico into Texas.

When the expedition crossed the Texas Panhandle they were surprised by their first sight of buffalo. Coronado wrote, "Their eyes bulge on the sides so that, when they run, they can see those who follow them."

When they arrived at Cíbola they saw buildings of adobe, not gold. Disappointed they continued. In 1542, after exploring 7,000 miles, Coronado and his expedition returned to Mexico without gold.

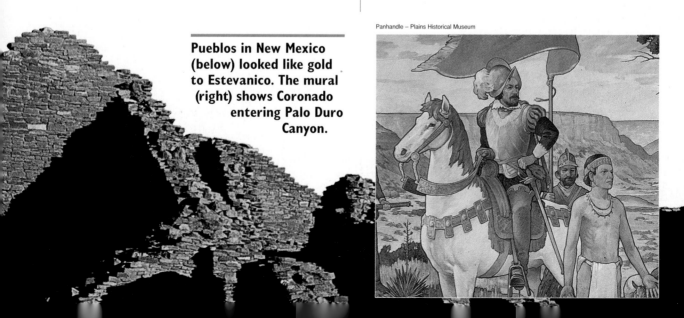

Pueblos in New Mexico (below) looked like gold to Estevanico. The mural (right) shows Coronado entering Palo Duro Canyon.

Panhandle – Plains Historical Museum

Infographic

Routes of the European Explorers

After Columbus's voyage to North America in 1492, other European explorers and conquistadors followed. The search for riches took some of them to Texas and the rest of the Southwest. Study the Infographic to learn about the routes of the explorers and the expeditions of the conquistadors in North America.

Alonzo Álvarez de Piñeda
1520

Along with his crew, he is believed to have been the first European to see the land of what is today Texas.

de Soto-Moscoso
1539–1542

After de Soto's death, Moscoso sailed down the Mississippi River to the Gulf of Mexico to reach Mexico.

Hernando Cortés
1519–1521

After defeating the Aztec, Cortés claimed the land of their empire for Spain and named it New Spain.

Francisco Vásquez de Coronado
1540–1542

He led a search for the Seven Cities of Gold. But the expedition returned to Mexico without finding gold.

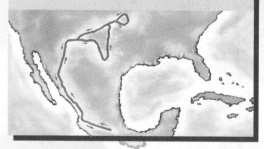

Álvar Núñez Cabeza de Vaca
1528–1536

After being shipwrecked on the coast of Texas, he reached Mexico with stories about gold.

René Robert Cavelier, Sieur de la Salle
1682–1689

After sailing past the mouth of the Mississippi, he landed in what is today Texas and built Fort St. Louis.

MORE EXPLORERS IN TEXAS

In 1539, before Coronado began exploring the Southwest, the Spanish explorer Hernando de Soto (er NAHN doh day SOH toh) had begun an expedition in the Southeast. He died in 1542. It was then that Luis de Moscoso de Alvarado (loo EES day mohs KOHS oh day ahl vah RAH doh) became the leader. Moscoso tried to lead his men to Mexico by traveling across what is now Texas. But the land was difficult to cross, and the Native Americans were unfriendly. So the group left Texas and went to the Mississippi River. The group built boats in which they sailed to the Gulf of Mexico and then on to Mexico.

In 1682, French explorer René Robert Cavelier, Sieur de la Salle (re NAY roh BAIR cah vuhl YAY sihr de lah SAL) sailed down the Mississippi River to the Gulf of Mexico. He claimed all the surrounding land for France. He named it Louisiana in honor of his king, Louis XIV. Then he returned to France.

In July 1684 La Salle tried to return to Louisiana with more than 300 colonists. But instead he landed along the Texas coast, east of what is now Corpus Christi. There the French colonists built Fort St. Louis in 1685. But many became sick and died. In 1689 Fort St. Louis was destroyed by the Karankawa.

WHY IT MATTERS

Spain lost interest in exploring the Southwest because Spanish explorers did not find gold. By the early 1700s several French settlements were built in Louisiana. Spanish officials became alarmed that France might claim Texas and build many more settlements. In the next lesson you will read about Spain's renewed interest in Texas.

✔ Reviewing Facts and Ideas

SUM IT UP

- In 1520 Piñeda mapped many miles of the Texas coastline.
- Cabeza de Vaca, Estevanico, and Coronado all searched for gold in Texas but never found any.
- In 1685 La Salle built Fort St. Louis. But it was soon destroyed.

THINK ABOUT IT

1. What is an expedition?
2. How did Piñeda's maps help Spanish explorers who came later?
3. **FOCUS** Who were the first Europeans to arrive in Texas and what were they looking for?
4. **THINKING SKILL** Why do you think Coronado made the _decision_ to continue exploring after he did not find gold in Cíbola?
5. **WRITE** What might it have been like to travel with Coronado? Write a journal entry as if you were there.

STUDY SKILLS

Reading Time Lines

VOCABULARY

time line

WHY THE SKILL MATTERS

In Lesson 1 you read about Columbus's voyage to America in 1492. This was just one event in Columbus's life. In order to raise money for his voyage, Columbus presented a plan to King Ferdinand and Queen Isabella of Spain. This was another event in Columbus's life.

To understand history, you need to know when events happened. You also need to know in which order they happened. Columbus sailed to South America. He also sailed to Central America. And he sailed to Trinidad and Hispaniola.

In what time order did he do these things? To help answer these questions, you can use a time line. A time line is a diagram that shows when events took place. It also shows the amount of time that passed between events. The way a time line is drawn helps to give a sense of sequence, or order, to history. The time line below shows important events in Columbus's life.

USING THE SKILL

Look at the time line. As you can see, the name of each event appears above or below the date it happened. The earliest event—the birth of Columbus—is on the left side. The most recent event—the death of Columbus—is on the right.

Like most time lines, this one is divided into equal parts. Each part represents a certain number or years. Each part of

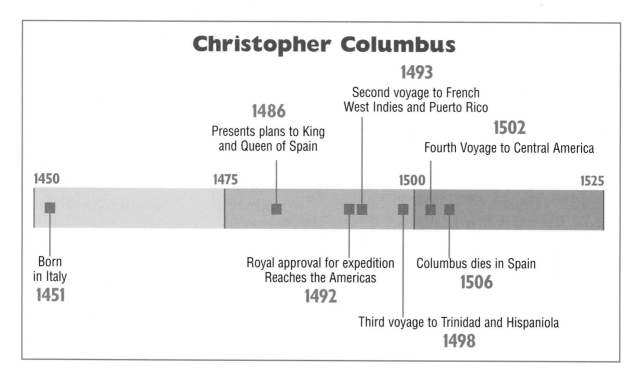

Christopher Columbus

1493
Second voyage to French
West Indies and Puerto Rico

1486
Presents plans to King
and Queen of Spain

1502
Fourth Voyage to Central America

1450   1475   1500   1525

Born
in Italy
1451

Royal approval for expedition
Reaches the Americas
1492

Columbus dies in Spain
1506

Third voyage to Trinidad and Hispaniola
1498

Columbus's time line represents 25 years.

Now read the time line from left to right. Which event took place between 1500 and 1506?

TRYING THE SKILL

Now read the time line of Texas Explorers and Settlers. Use the Helping Yourself box for hints.

What period of history does the time line cover? What event on the time line happened first? In what year did Cabeza de Vaca and Estevanico meet the Karankawa? Did Piñeda explore the Pánuco before or after Coronado searched for the Seven Cities of Gold? Which event happened in 1685?

REVIEWING THE SKILL

Use the information on the time line below to answer the following questions.

1. How does a time line help you to place events in the right order?
2. Which of these events took place in 1718?
3. How much time passed between Cabeza de Vaca's and Estevanico's meeting with the Karankawa and Coronado's search for gold?
4. Did Coronado's expedition happen before or after La Salle built Fort St. Louis?
5. In what other subjects would a time line be useful?

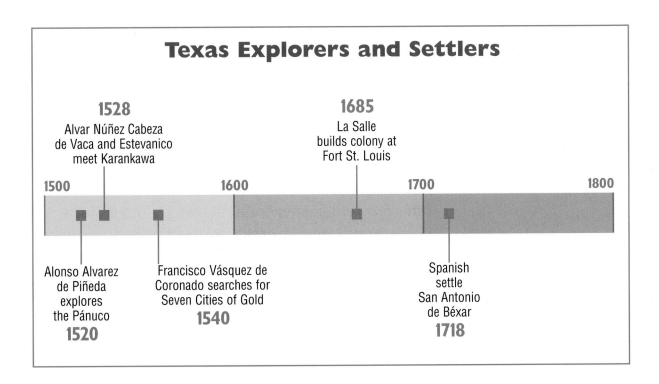

Texas Explorers and Settlers

1528 Alvar Núñez Cabeza de Vaca and Estevanico meet Karankawa

1685 La Salle builds colony at Fort St. Louis

1500   1600   1700   1800

Alonso Alvarez de Piñeda explores the Pánuco **1520**

Francisco Vásquez de Coronado searches for Seven Cities of Gold **1540**

Spanish settle San Antonio de Béxar **1718**

129

1400   1500   1600   1681   1731   1800

LIFE IN SPANISH TEXAS

Focus Activity

READ TO LEARN
What was life like in New Spain under Spanish rule?

VOCABULARY
mission
presidio
mestizo
missionary

PLACES
Mexico City
Ysleta Mission
San Antonio de Valero
San Antonio de Béxar

READ ALOUD

A Texan who grew up in San Antonio in the 1700s described life there like this:

"We were of the poor people . . . to be poor in that day meant to be very poor indeed . . . But we were not dissatisfied . . . There was time to eat and sleep and watch the plants growing. Of food, we did not have overmuch—beans and chili, chili and beans."

THE BIG PICTURE

By the 1700s Spain renewed its interest in Texas. By the middle 1700s many Spanish settlements were built along the Rio Grande valley southward from what is today Laredo. Some Spaniards were given large amounts of land on which to build ranches, called ranchos. Cattle and horses were raised on ranchos. Other newcomers built and lived in towns called villas. There were also settlements called **missions** where Europeans taught the Christian religion to Native Americans. To protect the different settlements from attacks by other Europeans and Native Americans, the Spanish also built **presidios** near the settlements. A presidio was a fort where soldiers lived. How did some of these settlements affect the lives of Native Americans who were already living in Texas?

130

CREATING AN EMPIRE

The largest Spanish settlement in New Spain was Mexico City, built on the ruins of Tenochtitlán. To remind them of home, the Spaniards constructed the city to look like a city in Spain. They built Roman Catholic churches, a university, a post office, and a central *plaza*, or town square.

The Blending of Cultures

As Spain's empire grew, Spanish and Mexican Indian cultures blended together to create a new culture. Spaniards saw foods such as *maize* (corn), potatoes, beans, and tomatoes for the first time. Mexican Indians were introduced to food brought from Europe—grapes, onions, and wheat. Large ranches were started for the Spaniards' cattle and horses.

Mexican Indians and Spaniards sometimes married. Their children were mestizos, people who were part Spanish and part Mexican Indian. Today their descendants live in Mexico and in many places in the United States.

The Spread of Missions

In the 1500s Spain sent priests to New Spain as missionaries. A missionary is a person who teaches his or her religion to others who have different beliefs. Spanish missionaries believed they had a duty to make sure that their religious ideas were taught to others. Look at the map to see where missionaries started settlements called missions in Texas. Often Spanish missions included homes for soldiers and Spanish settlers, rooms for Native American workers, kitchens, and workshops. The first mission in Texas was Ysleta (ee SLAY tah) Mission. It was built in 1681. You can see it in the photograph on the opposite page.

Spanish missions often were set up where Native Americans lived and worked. The Spaniards promised to provide the Native Americans with places to live at the missions.

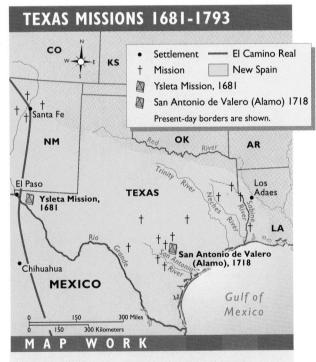

TEXAS MISSIONS 1681-1793

- • Settlement
- † Mission
- Ysleta Mission, 1681
- San Antonio de Valero (Alamo) 1718

El Camino Real
New Spain
Present-day borders are shown.

MAP WORK

The Spanish set up missions all over Texas.

1. How many missions were located on the Sabine and Neches rivers?
2. Through which three cities did El Camino Real run?
3. How do you think the San Antonio de Valero mission might have gotten the first part of its name?

MISSION LIFE

Look at the diagram. Suppose you lived at a mission in 1700. Your day would revolve around community living, with the Roman Catholic church as the center.

You would get up at sunrise and gather with others for prayer led by the missionaries. After breakfast you might help in the fields, growing beans, corn, or fruit. Or you might make baskets, pottery, or tools in one of the workshops.

At noon there would be more prayers and a midday meal. Afterwards it would be back to work until evening prayers. At sunset you and the others would go to bed.

Changes for Native Americans

Most Native Americans were made to work very hard on missions. They had very little choice about how things were done. They had to obey the missionaries. The Spaniards sometimes overworked Native Americans. Some died because they were treated cruelly. Many who survived were unhappy with the missionaries' attempt to change their religion and their way of life.

However, some Native Americans felt safe behind mission walls. They were protected from unfriendly groups who lived nearby.

Use the diagram to find the part of the mission where pottery (right) was made. Where else do mission workers do jobs?

Cornfields

Vegetable garden

Mission Church

Workshops

Native American village

The Settling of San Antonio

In 1718 a group of missionaries and Spanish settlers stopped at the source of the San Antonio River. The area was rich in natural resources such as wood, water, and building stone. The natural features of the land probably helped them to decide that this was a good place for the mission of San Antonio de Valero (day vah LAIR oh). The mission's church later became known as the Alamo. The presidio, called San Antonio de Béxar (day BAY hahr), was built to protect the mission. In 1731, a villa, San Fernando de Béxar was founded between the two. Four other missions were later built in the area. A villa grew up around these missions and later became the city of San Antonio.

Settlements Grow

In the early 1700s most people who lived in what is now Texas were Native Americans. But that soon changed. Mestizo settlers arrived from Mexico. Spaniards came from Spain and other parts of New Spain. A few Africans were brought from Africa to work as servants for Spanish families. Free Africans also came to Texas. Some people who were enslaved in the Carribbean Islands were allowed to make money in their spare time to buy their freedom. Others escaped from their owners and came to Texas.

WHY IT MATTERS

Between the late 1500s and early 1700s, Spain built a powerful empire in the Western Hemisphere. This empire expanded as new settlers arrived and settlements and missions were established. The Spanish brought a different language, different ways of life, and the Roman Catholic religion. Spanish influences can be seen throughout our state today. You will read about some of them in the Legacy on pages 134–135.

Reviewing Facts and Ideas

SUM IT UP

- Spanish settlements included ranchos, villas, missions, and presidios.
- The culture of New Spain was a blending of Spanish and Mexican Indian ways of life.
- Spanish missions helped to expand Spain's empire into Texas.
- Spanish settlements grew into towns such as San Antonio.

THINK ABOUT IT

1. What was a mission?
2. How did the lives of Native Americans change in New Spain?
3. **FOCUS** What was life like in New Spain under Spanish rule?
4. **THINKING SKILL** Make a conclusion about why New Spain established missions in Texas.
5. **GEOGRAPHY** Look at the map on page 131. Why do you think San Antonio de Béxar was located along the river?

Spanish Influence in TEXAS

These Mexican folk dancers are celebrating Diez y Seis. The festival brings people together to remember Mexican Independence.

You have read that Mexico and what is today Texas were once part of the Spanish colony of New Spain. Today Spanish and Mexican influences continue to be an important part of life in our state.

Spanish architecture is found in the missions, which were built long ago. Today many historic missions are still used as churches.

Food in Texas has been strongly influenced by Mexico. There's even a name—Tex-Mex—for our state's unique blend of Texan and Mexican foods.

The Spanish language is part of everyday Texas life. Many Texans are bilingual. *Bilingual* means "two languages." In this case, it means that many Texans speak both English and Spanish. Many Texan streets, towns, and cities have Spanish names. In these and other ways Spanish influence is a legacy that remains an important part of our state today.

Texans of all ethnic groups enjoy eating tortillas, which are thin, flat pancakes of corn or wheat.

These signs remind us of the lasting legacy of the Spanish language in Texas.

SAN MARCOS   13
SAN ANTONIO   63

Ysleta Mission in El Paso is a fine example of Spanish-style architecture. It is the oldest mission in our state, dating back to 1681.

COLONIES IN THE WESTERN HEMISPHERE

Focus Activity

READ TO LEARN
Why did European colonists settle in the Western Hemisphere?

VOCABULARY
pilgrim

PEOPLE
Pedro Alvares Cabral

PLACES
Jamestown
Plymouth
Brazil

READ ALOUD

In 1681 William Penn invited settlers to his colony in what is today Pennsylvania. He encouraged people to come but added, "They that go must wisely count the cost. . . . A winter goes before a summer." That was Penn's way of warning the colonists that before they could make better lives for themselves, they might face many hardships.

THE BIG PICTURE

Making a new life in the Western Hemisphere was hard work for colonists from Europe. But thousands of people were willing to try. Men, women, and children risked their lives crossing the dangerous waters of the Atlantic Ocean. Why would anyone make such an uncertain journey to live in a land unknown to them? They came in search of a better life for their families. Some dreamed of fortune. Many longed for religious freedom that they did not have in Europe.

These immigrants came from countries such as Spain, Portugal, England, and France. Find these places on the Atlas map on page R14. Some of these immigrants might have been your ancestors.

136

THE ENGLISH IN AMERICA

While Spain was building more and more missions in New Spain, people from England were also settling in North America. By 1733 they established 13 English colonies along the Atlantic Coast. These colonies were the beginning of the United States. Find them on the map on this page.

The Thirteen Colonies

In 1607 colonists from England arrived in what is now Virginia. They named their colony Jamestown after their king. It became the first permanent English settlement in America.

In 1620 the Pilgrims sailed from England to North America on the *Mayflower*. A pilgrim is a person who travels to a place for religious reasons. In England the Pilgrims did not have the right to practice their own religion. In America they settled in a place called Plymouth, in what is now Massachusetts. There they hoped to find the freedom to pray and live in their own way.

In an English Colony

Meet James Collins. James lives in a small town in the colony of Massachusetts with his family. The year is 1678 and James is 10 years old.

James is lucky—there is a school in this town. But he will attend long enough only to learn to read and write. Then James must work for many years to learn a trade. James might choose to become a black-smith like his father. James could also learn to make saddles, shoes, candles, or furniture.

He has little time to play. James and his sister Mary are expected to do chores at home. He fetches water every day and brings in wood for the fire. Mary is also learning to sew and cook. Like most girls, she does not attend school, but learns to read at home.

After supper, James and his family study the Bible. Their religion is very important to them. On Sunday they attend a church service that lasts all day.

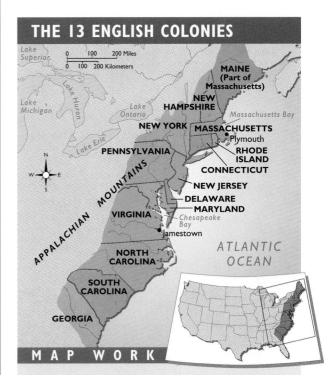

THE 13 ENGLISH COLONIES

MAP WORK

This map shows the 13 English colonies in North America.

1. In which colony was Jamestown located? In which colony was Plymouth located?

2. Why do you think so many of these colonies were on the coast?

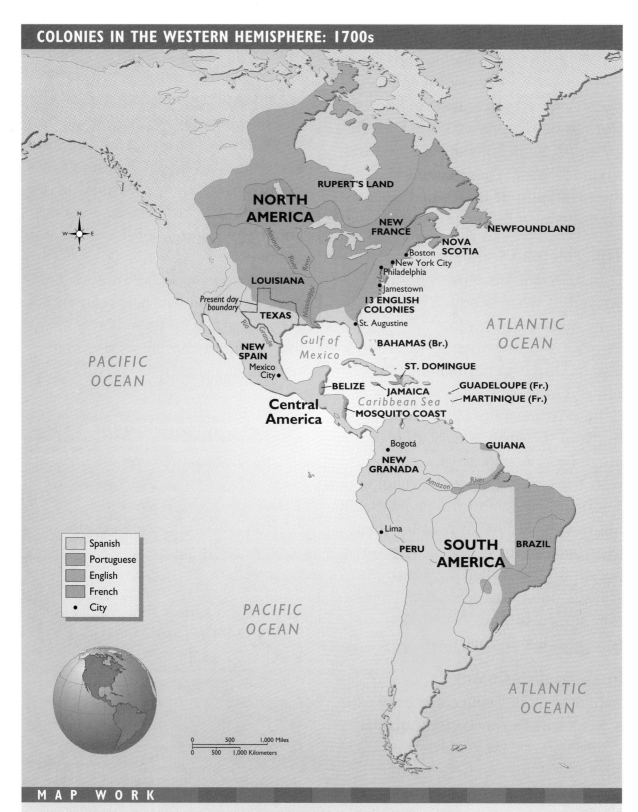

NORTH AMERICA

RUPERT'S LAND

NEW FRANCE

NOVA SCOTIA

NEWFOUNDLAND

Missouri River

River

LOUISIANA

• Boston
• New York City
Philadelphia

• Jamestown

13 ENGLISH COLONIES

Present day boundary

TEXAS

Mississippi

• St. Augustine

ATLANTIC OCEAN

Rio Grande

Gulf of Mexico

NEW SPAIN

Mexico City •

BAHAMAS (Br.)

ST. DOMINGUE

PACIFIC OCEAN

BELIZE

JAMAICA

GUADELOUPE (Fr.)

MARTINIQUE (Fr.)

Central America

Caribbean Sea

MOSQUITO COAST

Bogotá •

GUIANA

NEW GRANADA

Amazon River

Lima •

PERU

SOUTH AMERICA

BRAZIL

PACIFIC OCEAN

ATLANTIC OCEAN

Legend:
- Spanish
- Portuguese
- English
- French
- • City

0   500   1,000 Miles
0   500   1,000 Kilometers

MAP WORK

The Western Hemisphere was largely colonized by Europe in the 1700s.

1. To which country did the colony of Brazil belong?

2. Which country claimed most of Central America in the 1700s?

3. Name four cities that were located in English colonies.

OTHER COLONIES IN THE WESTERN HEMISPHERE

Different countries began colonies in the Western Hemisphere for different reasons.

In 1500 the Portuguese explorer Pedro Alvares Cabral (AHL vahr ez cah BRAHL) reached what is today Brazil when his ship was blown off course. Brazil is located along the northeast coast of South America. Portugal claimed Brazil as a colony and Cabral was the first Portuguese explorer to land there. The land of Brazil became a valuable natural resource for Portugal.

In 1608 French colonies were set up in Canada. The first French people in Canada were fur traders who came seeking beaver fur. Beaver fur hats were so popular in Europe that beaver fur was almost as valuable as gold to the French. Look at the map on the opposite page. Where else did France have colonies in the Western Hemisphere?

WHY IT MATTERS

In the 1600s and 1700s many colonists from Europe came to the Americas. Most hoped to find better lives, wealth, and the religious freedom they did not have in Europe.

This top hat was made of valuable beaver fur.

The arrival of European colonists affected the lives of Native Americans who lived and worked on the land where colonies were built. Some helped the colonists learn to survive in a land new to them. Many Native Americans, however, were killed trying to defend their villages.

In the next unit, you will read about why more and more people headed for present-day Texas.

Reviewing Facts and Ideas

SUM IT UP

- Immigrants came to the Western Hemisphere in search of a better way of life.
- By 1733 there were 13 English colonies along the Atlantic Coast of North America.
- Portugal and France started other colonies throughout the Western Hemisphere.

THINK ABOUT IT

1. Name England's first permanent colony in North America.

2. What is a pilgrim?

3. **FOCUS** Why did people come from Europe to the Western Hemisphere?

4. **THINKING SKILL** _Compare_ and _contrast_ the reasons Europeans came to Texas and the reasons Europeans came to Plymouth.

5. **WRITE** Suppose you live in an English colony as James and Mary Collins did. Write a letter to a friend back in England describing your life.

CHAPTER 4 REVIEW

Major Events

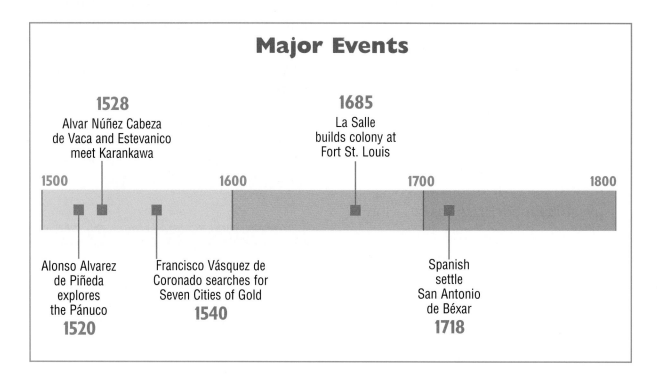

1528
Alvar Núñez Cabeza de Vaca and Estevanico meet Karankawa

1685
La Salle builds colony at Fort St. Louis

1500   1600   1700   1800

Alonso Alvarez de Piñeda explores the Pánuco
1520

Francisco Vásquez de Coronado searches for Seven Cities of Gold
1540

Spanish settle San Antonio de Béxar
1718

THINKING ABOUT VOCABULARY

Number a sheet of paper from 1 to 5. Next to each number write the letter of the definition that best matches the word.

1. colony

a. A place discovered by an explorer

b. A country that is ruled by a king

c. A place ruled by another country

2. expedition

a. A trip to find religious freedom

b. A mission of peace

c. A journey of exploration

3. mission

a. A fort where soldiers lived

b. A settlement where Europeans taught Native Americans the Christian religion

c. A farm where cattle and horses were raised

4. pilgrim

a. A person who travels to discover new lands

b. A person who travels to find gold

c. A person who travels to a place for religious reasons

5. presidio

a. A fort where soldiers lived

b. A settlement where people practiced religion

c. A farm where cattle and horses were raised

THINKING ABOUT FACTS

1. What happened in 1492?

2. What did Columbus take back to Spain? What did Columbus and the Europeans that followed him bring to the Americas?

3. Why did Cortés go to Mexico?

THINK AND WRITE

WRITING A LETTER
Suppose you are Alvar Núñez Cabeza de Vaca. You have survived the expedition that ended in a shipwreck. Write a letter describing your experiences.

WRITING A LIST
Suppose that you were able to interview Christopher Columbus. Write a list of three questions you would ask him. Then write the answers he might give.

WRITING A SUMMARY
Write a summary describing how the city of San Antonio was settled. Include details about the natural resources of the area.

APPLYING STUDY SKILLS

TIME LINES
Use the Major Events time line on the opposite page to answer the following questions.

1. How many years does the time line cover?
2. When did Coronado search for the Seven Cities of Gold?
3. How many years later did La Salle build a colony at Fort St. Louis?
4. Did the Spanish settle the mission of San Antonio de Béxar before or after La Salle built the colony at Fort St. Louis?
5. How are time lines useful for studying history?

Summing Up the Chapter

Use the following cause-and-effect chart to organize information from the chapter. Fill in the blank spaces and use the information to write a paragraph answering the question "How did the land that is now Texas change after the explorers from Europe arrived?"

CAUSE	EFFECT
Columbus landed in the Bahamas.	
Cortés conquered the Aztec civilization.	
	Many Native Americans died from diseases. Their ways of life changed in many ways.
	This brought more settlers to the areas. Some Native Americans lived and worked in the missions.

UNIT 2 REVIEW

THINKING ABOUT VOCABULARY

Number a sheet of paper from 1 to 10. Beside each number write the word or term from the list below that best matches the description.

adobe   Ice Age

atlatl   mestizo

colony   missionary

conquistador   teepee

history   tribute

1. A time when glaciers covered much of Earth's surface

2. A word to describe past events that are preserved in written records

3. A throwing stick that is attached to the end of a spear to make it go faster and farther

4. A payment in the form of valuable goods and services

5. A cone-shaped tent that can be put up and taken down quickly

6. Brick made from clay and straw that has been dried in the sun

7. One who takes ownership by force

8. A person who is part Spanish and part Mexican Indian

9. A person who teaches his or her religion to others who have different beliefs

10. A place that is ruled by another country, such as New Spain

THINK AND WRITE

WRITE A DESCRIPTION

In this unit you have read about shelters. Write a description of the different kinds of shelters made by Native Americans.

WRITE AN EXPLANATION

History tells us about past events that were preserved in written records. Write an explanation telling how we have learned about prehistory.

WRITE A NEWSPAPER ARTICLE

Suppose that you are a newspaper reporter for the Tenochtitlán Times. Cortés arrives in your city for the first time. Write an article for the newspaper describing his visit.

BUILDING SKILLS

1. **Making conclusions** What steps should you follow when making a conclusion?

2. **Making conclusions** In Chapter 4, you read about the Seven Cities of Gold. Historians made the conclusion that Cíbola was not a City of Gold. How do you think the historians arrived at that conclusion?

3. **Time lines** Draw a time line that begins with the year 1492 and ends with 1845. Place five events that you read about in Unit 2 on the time line.

4. **Time lines** Draw a time line that begins with your birth year and ends with this year. Place three events on the time line.

5. **Time lines** How do time lines help you understand history?

YESTERDAY, TODAY & TOMORROW

Native Americans depended on many natural resources to survive. How do we use resources differently from the early Native Americans? What can we learn from the way Native Americans used natural resources? How could this knowledge help us use natural resources more wisely in the future?

READING ON YOUR OWN

Here are some books you might find at the library to help you learn more.

EXPLORERS IN EARLY TEXAS
by Betsy Warren
Read about six Spanish explorers who traveled in Texas between 1519 and 1778.

SHIPWRECKED ON PADRE ISLAND
by Isabel R. Marvin
A young girl loses her bracelet in a 1554 shipwreck, linking her to a 1993 Padre Island visitor.

TALES OF OLD-TIME TEXAS
by J. Frank Dobie
In "The Texas Bluebonnet," a Native American girl helps save her people.

UNIT PROJECT

Guess Who?

1. Suppose you are one of the following people:
   - an early United States settler
   - a Karankawa
   - a Spanish explorer
2. Gather information from your textbook and your school library about the person you chose to be in step 1.
3. Write about a day in the life of the person. Be sure to mention where you live, how you get your food, who your family is, and what your job is.
4. Trade papers with a partner. Challenge your partner to guess which person from the list is being described.

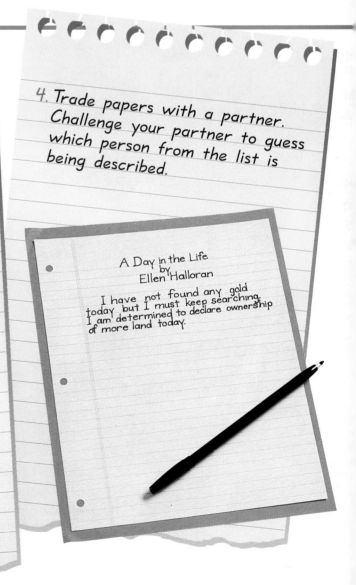

A Day in the Life
by
Ellen Halloran

I have not found any gold today but I must keep searching. I am determined to declare ownership of more land today.

SUZANNA DICKENSON;
THE ALAMO

Archives Division—Texas State Library

THE LONE STAR FLAG;
SAM HOUSTON

Independence and Statehood

"... our journey's end safe ..."

from an account by Mary Crownover Rabb
See page 155.

WHY DOES IT MATTER?

Long ago Texas was owned by Spain, a country in Europe. Nearly all the countries of North America were owned by European countries at one time.

What happened? How did our state change from being part of Spain to one of the 50 United States? What did Texans think about these changes? What are the "six flags" that have flown over Texas at different times?

Read on. As you do, you will discover more of the fascinating and exciting story that is the history of our state.

STEPHEN F. AUSTIN;
POSTER ADVERTISING LIFE
IN THE TEXAS COLONY

IN THE NEW CAPITAL OF TEXAS IN JANUARY 1.1840

Awesome Austin

Things are big in Texas—including the State Capitol building in Austin. It looks like the United States Capitol, in Washington, D. C., but it's seven feet taller! Austin became the capital of the Republic of Texas in 1839. Back then, legislators conducted business in a modest building with a shady porch—and the Lone Star flag flying proudly from the roof. Early Austin citizens enjoyed the beauty of the Colorado River and the surrounding hills. Today, Austin is a city of half a million people. But the great outdoors is still close. You can canoe just south of downtown!

GEO JOURNAL

You're a citizen of Austin in the early 1840s. Describe what it's like to live in the new capital.

CHAPTER 5

The Struggle for Independence

THINKING ABOUT
GEOGRAPHY AND HISTORY

You have read that the land that is now Texas was once the home only of Native Americans. You have learned how it became part of New Spain. Read on to discover the events that led to an independent Texas.

1821

SAN ANTONIO

Stephen F. Austin meets with Spanish governor Antonio Martínez

1823

LA GRANGE

Mary Crownover Rabb and other settlers begin moving to Texas

1832

SAN FELIPE DE AUSTIN

Texan settlers hold a convention on relations with Mexico

UNITED STATES

TEXAS

San Jacinto
River

San Felipe
de Austin

La Grange

San Antonio

MEXICO

Gulf of
Mexico

1836

SAN ANTONIO

**Mexican troops capture
The Alamo from American
and Tejano defenders**

1836

SAN JACINTO RIVER

**Texan soldiers capture
General Santa Anna at
the Battle of San Jacinto**

1810   1820 1825   1830   1840   1850

THE AUSTINS

READ ALOUD

In 1829, eight years after starting a colony in what is today our state of Texas, Stephen F. Austin wrote: "Texas . . . whether viewed with reference to . . . its soil, its climate, [or] the number of its rivers . . . may be [favorably] compared with any portion of North America."

THE BIG PICTURE

In 1803 President Thomas Jefferson bought a huge area of land from France for the United States for $15 million. This land, called the Louisiana Territory, stretched from the Mississippi west to the Rocky Mountains. The Louisiana Purchase doubled the size of the United States.

By 1820 land in the eastern United States had become too crowded and costly for many Americans. Land in the West was cheap and plentiful. Many people decided to move west as pioneers. A pioneer is a person who is among the first of a group of people to settle in a new region. People began packing up their belongings and heading west. One of these pioneers was Stephen F. Austin. He was continuing a plan begun by his father, Moses Austin, to bring pioneers from the United States to Texas. By 1825, nearly 300 families were living in Austin's Texas colony. These early colonists became known as The Old Three Hundred.

Focus Activity

READ TO LEARN
Why is Stephen F. Austin called "the Father of Texas"?

VOCABULARY
Louisiana Purchase
pioneer
The Old Three Hundred
frontier
empresario
Tejano
vaquero

PEOPLE
Thomas Jefferson
Stephen F. Austin
Moses Austin
Jane Long
Antonio Martínez
Don Martín de León
Patricia de la Garza
  de León

PLACES
Louisiana Territory
San Felipe de Austin
Victoria

150

COLONIZING TEXAS

Among The Old Three Hundred was a brave woman named Jane Long. Long had been to Texas before with her husband, who led an expedition to try to free Texas from Spain in 1820. Jane Long spent a cold, lonely winter that year near Galveston. There she had a daughter, the first child born in Texas to parents from the United States. Long is often called "the Mother of Texas."

Moses Austin also traveled to Texas in 1820. He was a businessman from Missouri who wanted to settle the Texas frontier. *Frontier* is the word that United States settlers used to describe land on the edge of their settlement. Moses Austin rode to San Antonio to ask the Spanish governor for permission to bring settlers from the United States to Texas.

Governor Antonio Martínez (mahr TEE nez) agreed. Soon after returning home in 1821, however, Moses Austin died. His wife, Maria, wrote to their son Stephen: "He called me to his bedside and . . . begged me to tell you to take his place."

Stephen F. Austin Takes Over

After receiving his mother's letter, Stephen F. Austin, only 27 years old, traveled to San Antonio. Governor Martínez agreed to let Austin take over his father's plan.

Then Austin rode across south central Texas looking for a good place to build his colony. Austin chose the coastal plain between the Colorado and Brazos rivers. He described this area as "land first rate, plenty of timber, fine water."

When Austin returned to the United States, nearly 100 letters from eager colonists awaited him. But these people had to prove to Stephen F. Austin that they were hardworking and honest. By the end of 1821, Austin's first colonists began arriving in Texas.

Many people left their homes to come to Texas after reading advertisements like this one in the newspaper.

TEXAS COLONY ASSOCIATION!
Rapid Development of a Glorious Country.
INCREASE OF POPULATION 400,000 IN TWO YEARS.
The Most Healthy and Agreeable Climate,
The Best Timber,
The Richest Minerals,
The Most Fertile Soil,
The Largest Stock Region,
AND THE GREATEST VARIETY OF PRODUCTS TO BE FOUND IN THE WORLD.
GO TO TEXAS!

THE TEXAS COLONY ASSOCIATION
LAWRENCE
KAUFMAN COUNTY.
THE PLAN OF THE COLONY

AUSTIN'S SUCCESS

In 1822 Stephen F. Austin again traveled to San Antonio. When he got there, he learned that Mexico had won its independence from Spain in 1821. Now Austin had to get new permission to settle his colony. While waiting for permission, he wrote a letter to settlers in his colony. You can read a part of Austin's letter below. What were some of his concerns?

MANY VOICES
PRIMARY SOURCE

Excerpt from a letter written by Stephen F. Austin from Mexico, 1822.

I fear some of the Settlers may have become a little discouraged at my long absence, and at the uncertainty in which they have remained, but I assure you that I have been [working] hard the whole time for your Good. . . . I think I shall be with you sometime in September, when I flatter myself with the pleasing hope of finding you all in peace and happiness.

Early Settlers

After a year of delays, the new Mexican government approved Austin's plan and he started back to his colony. When he arrived in 1823, Austin discovered that some settlers had returned to the United States. Also, some Karankawa and Tonkawa had attacked settlements. They were angry that the colonists were settling on their hunting grounds.

But the colony survived. In 1823 Austin chose a town on the Brazos River as his colony's capital. The Mexican governor of Texas named the town San Felipe de Austin.

More members of The Old Three Hundred arrived. At this time Mexican law allowed slavery. Some settlers brought enslaved people with them. They wanted these workers to help clear land and raise crops.

Stephen F. Austin granted land to settlers who often built log cabins like this one.

Empresarios

Empresarios (em pre SAH ree ohs) were people who were given a large piece of land by the government and allowed to sell the land to settlers. In 1824 the Mexican government set up an empresario system in Mexico and in Texas. Stephen F. Austin was an empresario, for example.

Another early empresario was Don Martín de León (dohn mahr TEEN day lee OHN). He and his wife, Patricia de la Garza de León, were two of many Tejanos, or Mexican people living in Texas. De León brought 200 families from Mexico to settle in Texas. In 1824 Patricia de la Garza de León used $10,000 of her own money to help her husband found the town of Victoria.

Many Tejanos became ranchers. To help them, they hired vaqueros (vah KAIR ohs). Vaqueros were ranch workers from Mexico who became the first cowboys.

WHY IT MATTERS

As the United States expanded, people became interested in moving west. After Mexico declared its independence from Spain in 1821, Texas was ruled by Mexico. Stephen F. Austin brought hundreds of families to Texas. Because of his important role in our state's history, Austin is often called "the Father of Texas."

✓✓ Reviewing Facts and Ideas

SUM IT UP

- Stephen F. Austin fulfilled his father's plan to bring United States settlers to Texas.

- After winning its independence from Spain in 1821, Mexico governed Texas.

- Empresarios like Austin and de León brought many new settlers to Mexican Texas.

THINK ABOUT IT

1. What is a pioneer?

2. Why did many people from the United States settle in Texas?

3. **FOCUS** Why is Stephen F. Austin called "the Father of Texas?"

4. **THINKING SKILL** Suppose you lived in the United States in 1825. Would you _decide_ to settle in Mexican Texas? Why or why not?

5. **WRITE** Write a letter to Stephen F. Austin. Tell him why he should let you settle in his colony.

This painting shows Don Martín de León overseeing the building of his town, Victoria.

The Institute of Texan Cultures

The Institute of Texan Cultures

LIFE IN MEXICAN TEXAS

Focus Activity

READ TO LEARN
How did colonists live in Mexican Texas?

VOCABULARY
dugout
subsistence farming
cash crop
barter

PEOPLE
Mary Crownover Rabb

READ ALOUD

"Those persons . . . who shrink from hardship and danger . . . [and who] know not how to . . . adapt themselves to all sorts of circumstances, had better stay where they are."

Mary Holley visited Texas in 1831. Although she thought Texas was a wonderful place, she also knew it would take hard work for settlers to make it a home.

THE BIG PICTURE

In the 1830s and 1840s, new settlers came to Texas from all over the United States and from other countries. Families from Missouri to Massachusetts moved to Texas. Others traveled north from Mexico. Later, immigrants came from Europe—Irish, Germans, Danes, French, Jews, Italians, Norwegians, and Swedes. They were joined by hundreds of free African Americans and thousands of enslaved African Americans. Each group brought its own language, customs, and beliefs.

You have already read that Mexico governed Texas at this time. Many leaders of Mexico hoped that these hardworking newcomers would create a strong Texas. They hoped the growing business and trade of Texas would help the entire nation of Mexico. Before long, Texas had grown more than anyone had expected.

"GONE TO TEXAS"

Getting to Texas in the 1820s was not as easy as it is today. Many settlers came to Texas across the prairie on horseback or in covered wagons. Others came down the Mississippi River on flatboats and steamships. From New Orleans they continued on small sailboats to Matagorda and other ports on the Texas coast. Even one of the main roads in Texas, El Camino Real, was little more than a dirt trail.

A Hard Journey

Overland travelers faced problems from washed-out roads to broken wagon wheels to wild animals. Those who traveled by ship faced spoiled drinking water, rotten food, and poor weather conditions.

One early settler, Mary Crownover Rabb, traveled to Stephen F. Austin's colony from her home in Arkansas. A member of The Old Three Hundred, Rabb wrote about her experiences in a book that was published after she died. How do you think Rabb felt when she finally arrived in Texas?

Modern-day reenactments like this one help us understand what life was like for early settlers traveling by covered wagon.

MANY VOICES PRIMARY SOURCE

Excerpt from _Travels and Adventures in Texas in the 1820s_ by Mary Crownover Rabb, published in 1962.

We started October 1, 1823. . . . Your Pa [and me] had about 16 or 18 head of small cattle. . . . We also had six head of horses.

We traveled on about one hundred miles, and our cattle got sick . . . and we had to stop driving them. . . . After . . . a few days, we met up with James Gilliland and his family . . . and then we drove on. . . .

Barker Texas History Center

We [came] to . . . where La Grange now is, but there was no house there then nor nothing but a wilderness. . . . We went up . . . above La Grange. . . . We got there about the 15 of December, 1823. There we . . . got to our journey's end safe.

LIFE IN THE COLONIES

Once the journey to Texas was over, there was no time to rest. After checking their land claim with the empresario, settlers went to work building their homes.

Getting Settled

Homes on the prairie were sometimes simply dug out of the side of a hill. These homes were called **dugouts**. Dugouts provided shelter from the wind and dust. But they were dark and damp.

Most settlers built their homes from logs. Mary Crownover Rabb described her first home in Texas:

> The house was made of logs. They made a chimney [for] it. The door shutter was made of thick slabs split out of thick pieces of timber. . . . We had an earthen floor in our house.

Farming in the Colonies

The first United States settlers who came to Texas practiced **subsistence farming**. This means they used all of the crops they grew for their own survival.

On subsistence farms men, boys, and women did the plowing and planting and also took care of livestock. Women and girls also sewed clothes, made candles, cooked, and tended vegetable gardens. Sometimes when a dozen or more families settled in an area, they all helped to build a school. Then they hired a teacher.

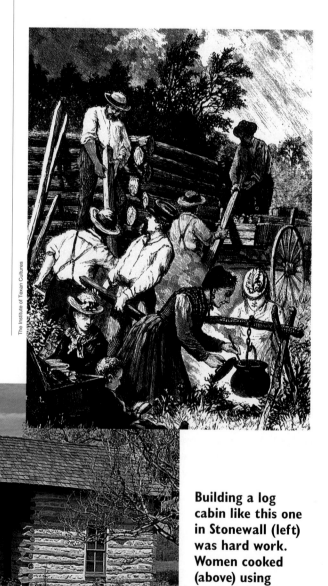

The Institute of Texan Cultures

Building a log cabin like this one in Stonewall (left) was hard work. Women cooked (above) using utensils like these (right).

Later many farmers began to grow **cash crops**. Cash crops are crops that farmers sell. Sometimes farmers would **barter** their crops. To barter is to trade things for other things without using money.

By the 1830s Texas farmers were growing large amounts of cotton, corn, and sugarcane. Ranches raised cattle for beef and hides. Towns grew up as places for farmers and ranchers to sell their products. In towns, people could also buy goods they couldn't make or grow.

A Community of Texans

Women gathered together and made quilts. Men competed in hunting and log-rolling contests. Sallie Reynolds Matthews fondly remembered quiet evenings as a girl in her home in West Texas:

> *On winter evenings . . . the family gathered around the fire. Often the boys would be molding bullets, Mother and Sister sewing, knitting or mending. Many pecans, which had been gathered . . . were cracked and sometimes roasted over the fire.*

Music was a great source of enjoyment too. European, Mexican, and African American music could be heard on farms and ranches.

WHY IT MATTERS

By 1833 46,500 settlers were living in Texas. Most of them were from the United States. Although the United States settlers had promised to be loyal to the country of Mexico, many saw themselves as Texans first. Mexican government leaders began to wonder whether these new Texans would remain loyal to Mexico.

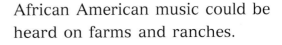

Reviewing Facts and Ideas

SUM IT UP

- Settlers came from many places to make new homes in Texas.
- The journey to Texas was often long and difficult.
- At first settlers practiced subsistence farming. Later many grew cash crops.

THINK ABOUT IT

1. Which two routes did most United States settlers take to Texas?

2. What is subsistence farming?

3. **FOCUS** As a young person in Mexican Texas, what might your day have been like?

4. **THINKING SKILL** What three *questions* could you *ask* a settler to learn more about his or her life?

5. **GEOGRAPHY** Look at the Atlas map on page R8. What do you think were the best routes from St. Louis, Missouri, to the coast of Texas? Why?

STUDYSKILLS

Reading Circle and Line Graphs

VOCABULARY
graph
circle graph
population
line graph

WHY THE SKILL MATTERS

In the last two lessons, you read about the people who came to Texas in the early 1800s. You learned about the way of life of settlers who arrived during that time.

Did the numbers of settlers increase each year? Decrease? Who were the different groups that came to Texas? What group was the largest?

It may be hard to make a conclusion from a lot of different numbers. A graph can help you make conclusions. Graphs are special diagrams that show information in a clear way. By presenting facts in a picture, they tell you a lot with only a few words.

USING CIRCLE GRAPHS

Look at the graph on this page. It is a circle graph. This kind of graph can show you how the parts of something make up or fit into the whole. Because each part may look like a slice of pie, a circle graph is sometimes called a pie graph.

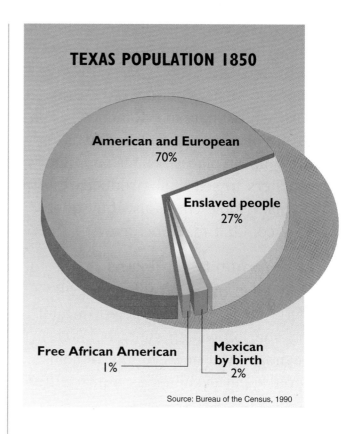

TEXAS POPULATION 1850

American and European 70%

Enslaved people 27%

Free African American 1%

Mexican by birth 2%

Source: Bureau of the Census, 1990

Read the title of the graph. This circle graph shows the population, or number of people, living in Texas in 1850.

The "slices" show the different groups of people who made up the population in 1850. Study the key. You can tell that the largest population group was "American and European" because this is the largest "slice" of the graph.

USING LINE GRAPHS

Unlike a circle graph, a line graph shows you how a piece of information changes with time. A line graph often shows an increase or decrease in number.

Look at the line graph on page 159. Start by reading the title. The title tells you that this is a graph of population in Texas from 1821 to 1850.

Read the label at the left side of the graph. This gives the number of people. The dates at the bottom of the graph tell you the years the population was measured.

Trace the line with your finger. Each dot on the line stands for the number of people in Texas during a particular year. As you can see, the population increased sharply between 1833 and 1847.

TRYING THE SKILL

Now study the circle graph of the population of Texas in 1850. Were there more enslaved people or more free African Americans? Were there more Americans and Europeans or Mexicans?

Now look at the line graph of population in Texas from 1821 to 1850. How many people lived in Texas in the year 1821? How many lived in our state in the year 1850?

REVIEWING THE SKILL

1. Between which years did the population of Texas rise the least? What did you do to find the answer?

2. What can you conclude from the line graph about the population of Texas between 1821 and 1850?

3. How do line and circle graphs differ? How do graphs make it easier for you to understand information?

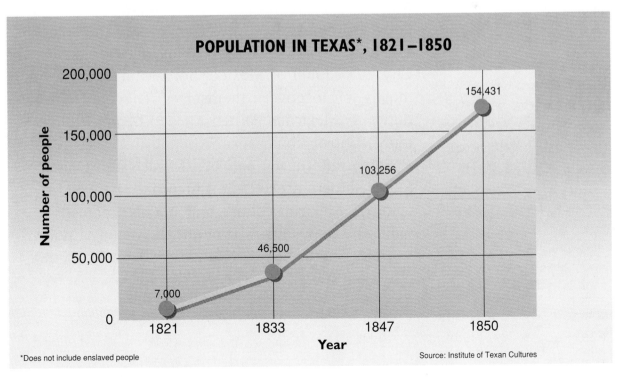

POPULATION IN TEXAS*, 1821–1850

Number of people / Year

7,000 (1821), 46,500 (1833), 103,256 (1847), 154,431 (1850)

*Does not include enslaved people

Source: Institute of Texan Cultures

GROWING UNREST

READ ALOUD

In 1827 a Mexican traveler, José Sánchez, noted that some Texans in San Felipe de Austin were unhappy about Mexico's government. He warned:

". . . the spark that will start the [fire] that will deprive us of Texas will start from this colony. All because the government does not take [strong] measures to prevent it. Perhaps it does not realize the value of what it is about to lose."

THE BIG PICTURE

Empresarios such as Stephen F. Austin and Don Martín de León worked to keep relations friendly between the Mexican government and the colonists. But East Texas was hundreds of miles from Mexico City, the capital of Mexico. Settlers in Texas were mostly left to govern themselves. They had no real duties as Mexicans. When Mexico began to take more control, some Texans began to resist.

Some differences between Mexico and United States settlers arose from differences between their cultures. Mexican culture was mainly Spanish, while the new settlers brought the mainly English-speaking culture of the United States with them.

Focus Activity

READ TO LEARN
Why did many Texans want independence from Mexico?

VOCABULARY
bilingual
convention
delegate
dictator
tax
Texas Revolution

PEOPLE
Sam Houston
Antonio López de
 Santa Anna
William B. Travis
Martín Perfecto de Cós
George Collinsworth
Ben Milam
Frank Johnson

PLACES
Gonzales
Goliad

160

GROWING TENSION

By the late 1820s, the warning you read in the Read Aloud was coming true. Mexico was in danger of losing its rule over Texas.

Different Ways of Life

One important difference between Mexico and United States settlers was language. In Texas all government papers were written in Spanish, the language of Mexico. Most new settlers from the United States, on the other hand, spoke English. Some people, like Stephen F. Austin, were bilingual. This word describes people who are able to speak two languages. Stephen F. Austin and some other bilingual people in Texas spoke Spanish and English.

Religion was another area of conflict. Mexican law required that all colonists accept the beliefs of the Roman Catholic Church. Many new settlers, however, were not Catholic. They believed that people should be free to choose their religion.

The issue of slavery also divided Mexico and United States settlers. Mexican law increasingly restricted slavery. However, many settlers from the United States brought their slaves with them. The enslaved people helped to build the successful farms and ranches of the growing Texas colonies.

Mexico Takes Action

The Mexican government began to worry that settlers in Texas would try to break away from Mexico. On April 6, 1830, Mexico passed a law stopping all immigration to Texas from the United States.

The Decree of April 6, as this law came to be called, went even further. It put limits on trade between Texas and the United States. This law angered the colonists. Towns and farms were growing, and business was booming. The new law would put a stop to this growth. The law also separated many families from their relatives in the United States.

Archives Division—Texas State Library

Many settlers brought to Texas by Stephen F. Austin did not want to be part of Mexico.

TEXANS TAKE ACTION

Colonists throughout Texas were unhappy with the Mexican immigration law of 1830. They decided to gather together and discuss what could be done.

Texans Meet

In October 1832, Texans gathered for a convention in San Felipe de Austin. A convention is a formal meeting held for a special purpose. The purpose of this convention was to discuss ways to improve relations between Texas and Mexico.

Sixteen different areas of Texas sent delegates to the convention. A delegate is a person who is chosen to speak for a group. The delegates were led by Stephen F. Austin. They had two main concerns. First they wanted immigration from the United States to continue. Second they wanted Texas to become its own state within Mexico. If Texas was a state, Texans would have more power to make decisions for themselves.

Another convention was held in April 1833. One delegate was Sam Houston. He had been governor of Tennessee and a soldier in the United States Army. At this convention Stephen F. Austin agreed to take the colonists' demands to the Mexican government.

Austin Goes To Mexico

Austin traveled to Mexico City. When he got there on July 18, 1833, the president of Mexico, Antonio López de Santa Anna, was away. Austin met with other government officials, but no one could act on the requests from the Texas convention.

Austin waited to meet with Santa Anna for five months. Discouraged, he wrote a letter to Tejano leaders in San Antonio. He said the Mexican leaders were not paying attention to his requests. He asked the Tejanos to work with settlers from the United States to set up a state government for Texas.

Santa Anna (left) wrote the story of his life (right). He ruled from Mexico City (below).

Austin and Santa Anna

When Santa Anna returned to Mexico City, he met with Austin. Santa Anna would not let Texas become a Mexican state. But he did agree to allow immigration from the United States to continue. Hopeful for the future, Stephen F. Austin started his journey back to Texas on December 10, 1833.

What Austin did not know was that the Mexicans had gotten hold of his letter to Tejano leaders in San Antonio. When Austin reached northern Mexico, he was arrested and accused of disloyalty. For three months, he sat alone in a tiny jail cell with no windows. Austin wrote to his brother-in-law: "I am in good health and have borne it with . . . patience." Austin was put in prison twice, and did not return home until 1835.

Hints of Conflict

By 1835 many Texans believed that Santa Anna was becoming a dictator. A dictator is a leader with complete control over the government. To strengthen his power over Texans, Santa Anna sent troops to Texas. He also sent officials to collect taxes. A tax is money people must pay to a government.

These actions angered Texans. Many, such as William B. Travis, wanted to break away from Mexico. Early in 1835, Travis led a group of about 20 men to confront Mexican soldiers at the town of Anáhuac (an NAH wok). Caught unprepared, the Mexicans surrendered. Some colonists disapproved of Travis's actions. They were afraid that Santa Anna would order more Mexican soldiers to Texas.

Benson Latin American Collection

William B. Travis (left) was born in South Carolina. He fought for Texas after moving here in 1831.

163

THE TEXAS REVOLUTION BEGINS

In September 1835, Santa Anna sent over 350 soldiers to San Antonio. They were led by General Martín Perfecto de Cós (pair FEK toh day COHS). Texans planned a convention for October 15 to decide what to do next. But before they met, fighting began. This was the start of the Texas Revolution. A revolution is a sudden change of government, usually by force. The Texas Revolution was the fight for Texas's independence from Mexico.

Early Battles

The first battle of the Texas Revolution took place at Gonzales on October 2, 1835. The map on the next page shows some Texas Revolution battle sites. Mexican soldiers were sent there to bring back a cannon that had been loaned to the Texans. Armed Texans refused to give up the cannon. They created a sign which read "Come and take it." A battle followed. After one Mexican soldier was killed, the Mexican Army retreated to San Antonio.

A week later about 50 Texans, led by George Collinsworth and Ben Milam, fought a battle in the town of Goliad. The Texans won again.

On to San Antonio

Word of the battles spread. More volunteers joined the Texas Army. These soldiers had no uniforms and many carried their own weapons. The Texans at San Antonio chose Stephen F. Austin as their commander-in-chief. They fought several minor battles while they surrounded San Antonio and waited.

On December 5, 1835, the Texan soldiers, led by Ben Milam and Frank Johnson, attacked San Antonio. They were outnumbered three to one, and Milam was killed in the fighting. However, the Texans were victorious. After four days, Cós gave up and led

Institute of Texan Cultures

Mexican General Martín Perfecto de Cós's (above) attempt to capture this cannon (left) in Gonzales was the first battle of the Texas Revolution.

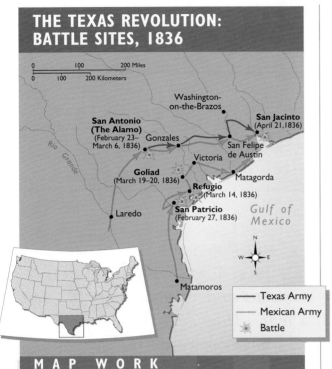

THE TEXAS REVOLUTION: BATTLE SITES, 1836

Washington-on-the-Brazos

San Antonio (The Alamo)
(February 23–March 6, 1836)

Gonzales

San Jacinto
(April 21, 1836)

Victoria

San Felipe de Austin

Goliad
(March 19–20, 1836)

Matagorda

Refugio
(March 14, 1836)

Laredo

San Patricio
(February 27, 1836)

Gulf of Mexico

Rio Grande

Matamoros

Texas Army
Mexican Army
Battle

0   100   200 Miles
0   100   200 Kilometers

MAP WORK

Groups of Texan soldiers were often sent off from the main part of the Texas Army to fight battles in other cities.

1. Where did the Texas Army travel from San Antonio?

2. What battle was fought on February 27? What other battle was taking place at that time?

the Mexican Army out of Texas. When Santa Anna heard the news he was furious. He planned to lead another attack himself.

A New Texas Government

On November 3, 1835, before the victory in San Antonio, delegates met in San Felipe de Austin. They wanted to set up a temporary government. They asked Stephen F. Austin to go to the United States to ask for money, supplies, and volunteers. They also chose Sam Houston to lead the Texas Army and decided to meet again in March 1836.

WHY IT MATTERS

As more settlers came to Texas from the United States, their unhappiness with the Mexican government grew. When Santa Anna came to power in Mexico, the situation got worse. Texans won several early battles of the Texas Revolution. However, Santa Anna was not ready to give up control of Texas.

Reviewing Facts and Ideas

SUM IT UP

- Differences in language and religion created tensions between United States settlers and Mexico.

- Tensions increased when Santa Anna gained power and became a dictator in Mexico.

- The Texas Revolution began with small battles between Texan settlers and Mexican troops. The first battle was at Gonzales.

THINK ABOUT IT

1. What is a delegate?

2. Why did Mexico worry about the growing numbers of United States settlers in Texas?

3. **FOCUS** Why were the settlers from the United States unhappy with Mexican rule?

4. **THINKING SKILL** Why do you think Stephen F. Austin _made a decision_ to encourage Texas's independence?

5. **WRITE** Suppose you were a settler in Texas in 1834. Write a letter to Santa Anna telling him why he should free Stephen F. Austin from prison.

THE BATTLE OF THE ALAMO

Focus Activity

READ TO LEARN
Why does The Alamo hold such an important place in the history of Texas?

VOCABULARY
Battle of The Alamo
Texas Declaration of
   Independence
constitution
Goliad Massacre

PEOPLE
David Crockett
James Bonham
Jim Bowie
Juan Seguín
Gregorio Esparza
José Antonio Navarro
Francisco Ruíz
Suzanna Dickenson
David G. Burnet
Lorenzo de Zavala
James W. Fannin

PLACES
The Alamo
Washington-on-the-
   Brazos

READ ALOUD

"I am besieged [attacked], by a thousand or more of the Mexicans under Santa Anna . . . and have not lost a man—The enemy has demanded a surrender. . . . I have answered the demand with a cannon shot, and our flag still waves proudly from the walls—I shall never surrender or retreat. Then, I call on you in the name of Liberty . . . to come to our aid." These stirring words were written by William B. Travis, as he defended The Alamo with a small group of Texans in 1836.

THE BIG PICTURE

The San Antonio de Valero mission, started by the Spanish in San Antonio in 1718, is also called The Alamo. This name comes from the Spanish word for "cottonwood tree."

The Alamo had been a quiet place for almost 120 years. All that changed in 1836. When the Texas Revolution began, San Antonio became a battle zone. Now The Alamo would become the most famous battle place in our state's history.

PREPARING FOR BATTLE

After the Texas victory at San Antonio in December 1835, most of the Texan soldiers had scattered. Farmers had to return to their crops and new immigrants wanted to claim land. Only about 100 Texan soldiers remained in San Antonio.

The Texas Army

In January 1836 word spread that Santa Anna's troops were marching northward from Mexico. Small groups of Texan soldiers began to move into San Antonio to prepare in the event of a battle.

Led by David Crockett, about 12 volunteers arrived from Tennessee. James Bonham arrived, as did a group of men from Gonzales. Jim Bowie brought about 25 men. William B. Travis came with 25 men from San Felipe de Austin. Juan Seguín (HWAHN say GEEN) and his company of Tejano men were among this group. One of Seguin's men, Gregorio Esparza brought his family into The Alamo.

Historians are not sure how many soldiers were present. The soldiers set up their defenses inside The Alamo. The Texans did not think Santa Anna would reach San Antonio until spring. They thought there was time to prepare for battle.

The Mexican Army Advances

Santa Anna's soldiers, about 5,000 strong, marched north in colorful uniforms. They were followed by 1,800 mules loaded with food and 200 ox-carts carrying supplies. They reached the Rio Grande in February.

Santa Anna's army reached San Antonio on February 23. The Mexican general ordered a red flag to be flown from the church bell tower. It was a signal to the Texans to give up or be killed upon defeat. From The Alamo, William B. Travis and Jim Bowie answered by firing a cannon. They would not give in. Santa Anna then attacked. The Battle of The Alamo had begun.

San Antonio was a small town (left) when Jim Bowie (above, far left) and David Crockett (above, left) became heroes at The Alamo.

The Granger Collection

The Institute of Texan Cultures

DEFENDING THE ALAMO

The Texans sent messages for aid. But no help came. They also sent Seguín for help. When he returned he could not get back inside The Alamo. The Texans were still outnumbered, but they fought on.

On the morning of March 6, Santa Anna ordered his army to set up ladders against The Alamo and climb over the walls. Look at the diagram to see the mission courtyard where the soldiers on both sides fought. When the battle was over, Travis, Bowie, and Crockett were all dead. Not one of the Texan soldiers survived.

Three days before The Alamo fell, Travis had written a letter to a friend asking him to take care of his son. How did Travis want his son to remember him?

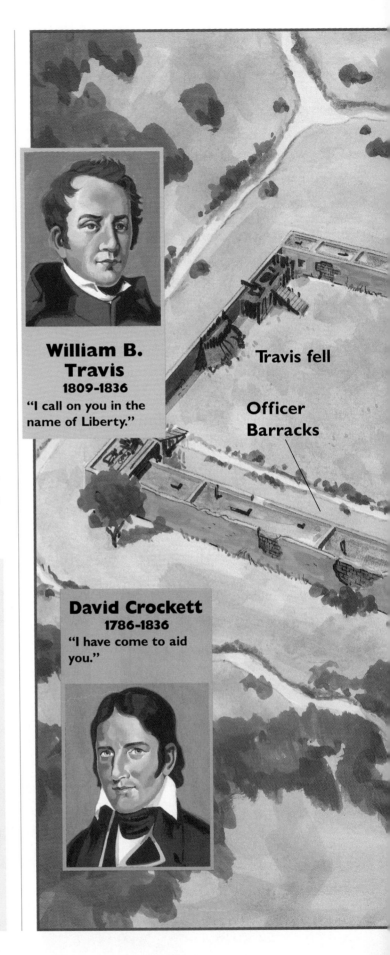

William B. Travis
1809-1836
"I call on you in the name of Liberty."

Travis fell

Officer Barracks

David Crockett
1786-1836
"I have come to aid you."

PRIMARY SOURCE

Excerpt from a letter written by William B. Travis to David Ayers March 3, 1836

*Take care of my little boy. If the country should be saved, I may make for him a splendid fortune; but if the country be lost and I should **perish**, he will have nothing but the proud **recollection** that he is the son of a man who died for his country.*

perish: die
recollection: memory

THE ALAMO

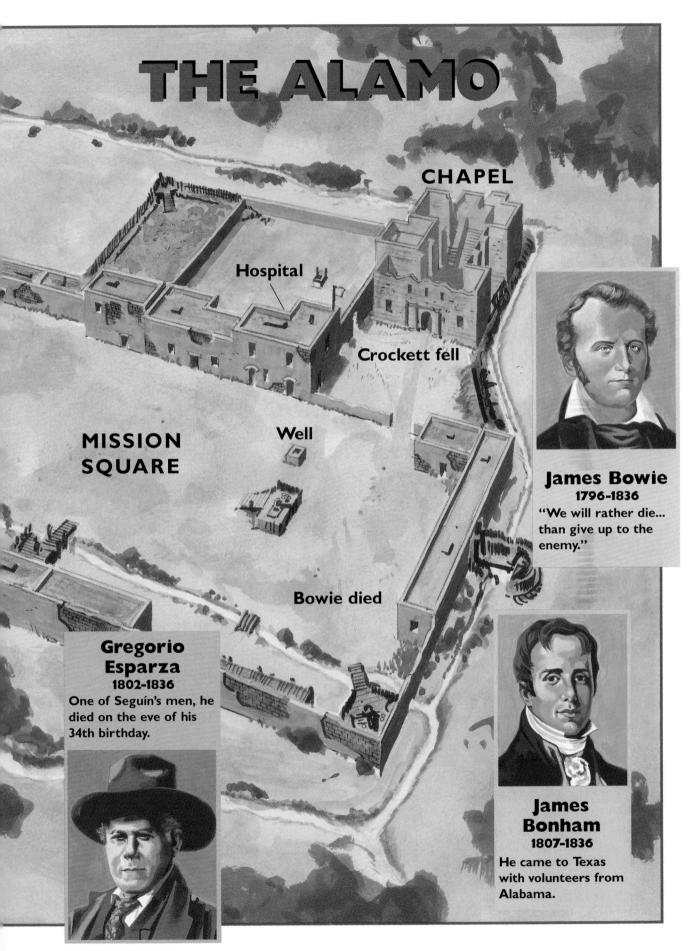

CHAPEL

Hospital

Crockett fell

MISSION
SQUARE

Well

Bowie died

James Bowie
1796-1836
"We will rather die...
than give up to the
enemy."

**Gregorio
Esparza**
1802-1836
One of Seguín's men, he
died on the eve of his
34th birthday.

**James
Bonham**
1807-1836
He came to Texas
with volunteers from
Alabama.

SURVIVORS OF THE ALAMO

No one knows for sure how many people died at The Alamo. Historians think that at least 189 Texans and possibly 250 died at The Alamo along with 800 Mexicans. Suzanna Dickenson and her daughter, Angelina, were two of the survivors. They helped spread the word of the disaster through Texas.

The Battle of The Alamo was being fought while Texas delegates met at a convention in the town of Washington-on-the-Brazos. On March 2, 1836, the delegates signed the Texas Declaration of Independence, declaring their separation from Mexico.

Suzanna Dickenson cooked for and nursed the sick during the Battle of The Alamo.

Links to CURRENT EVENTS

Learning About The Alamo

How do historians know what actually happened inside The Alamo? Since there were so few survivors, historians are uncertain about many details of the Battle of The Alamo. Letters, journals, and eyewitness reports have provided much information. In 1995 archaeologists tried to uncover the well that provided drinking water for The Alamo. They did not find the well, but they did find a small piece of copper and a ceramic cup, probably from the early 1900s. Read your local newspaper to learn if archaeologists uncover more artifacts in the future.

Declaring Independence

Among the signers of the Texas Declaration of Independence were José Antonio Navarro and Fransisco Ruíz. They were Mexicans who had been born in Texas.

At the convention, a constitution for an independent Texas was prepared. A constitution is a plan of government. David G. Burnet and Lorenzo de Zavala (day zah VAH lah) were chosen to serve as President and Vice President until Texans could vote for their own candidates.

Lorenzo de Zavala was Vice President after the Texas Declaration of Independence.

The Struggle Continues

Encouraged by victory at The Alamo, Santa Anna sent troops to the town of Goliad. About 300 Texans, led by James W. Fannin, waited. After hearing of the fall of The Alamo, however, General Houston ordered Fannin to retreat.

About 20 miles out of Goliad, the Texans were surrounded by Mexican troops. After a brief battle, Fannin surrendered. He and his troops were imprisoned at Presidio La Bahia. Then Santa Anna ordered that the Texans be shot. This event is known as the Goliad Massacre.

A massacre is the brutal killing of many people.

WHY IT MATTERS

Texans were defeated at The Alamo and Goliad, but the struggle for independence continued. The brave people who fought are remembered as heroes of the Texas Revolution. Although the settlers of Texas had declared their independence from Mexico, Santa Anna was not ready to give them their freedom.

✓ Reviewing Facts and Ideas

SUM IT UP

- The Alamo is the site of the most famous battle in our state.
- Texans fought to defend The Alamo, but they fell to the much larger Mexican forces.
- Texans wrote a Declaration of Independence and a constitution in 1836 to form a new country.

THINK ABOUT IT

1. What do you think was the purpose of the Texas Declaration of Independence?

2. What advantage did Santa Anna's army have over the Texan Army at The Alamo?

3. **FOCUS** Why is The Alamo important to Texans?

4. **THINKING SKILL** What _conclusions_ can you make about the volunteers who came to help the Texans?

5. **WRITE** Suppose you are a delegate at Washington-on-the-Brazos. Why do you think this is the time to write a constitution for Texas?

THINKING SKILLS

Identifying Cause and Effect

VOCABULARY

cause
effect

WHY THE SKILL MATTERS

You have read that the Texans' desire for independence led to the Battle of The Alamo. This desire for freedom was a cause. A cause is something that makes something else happen. The battle was an effect of this desire for independence. An effect is what happens as a result of something else.

Understanding cause and effect allows you to put facts together in a meaningful way. It helps to explain *why* things happen. It shows connections between one event and another. Use the Helping Yourself box for some word clues that may help you find causes and effects.

USING THE SKILL

As you read the passage below, look for a cause and an effect. Try to find some clue words that can help you identify the effect.

David Crockett was one of the soldiers at the Battle of The Alamo. Crockett was born in Tennessee in 1786. In 1827 he was elected to represent Tennessee in Washington D.C., the capital of the United

States. When Crockett ran for reelection in 1835, he was defeated. As a result of his loss, Crockett began to think about leaving his home in Tennessee.

Crockett had heard that many Texans were talking about breaking away from Mexico's rule. He knew that if Texas became independent from Mexico, it would likely become part of the United States. Crockett began to think that he might be elected to represent Texas in Washington, D.C. Therefore, Crockett moved to Texas shortly after losing his election in Tennessee.

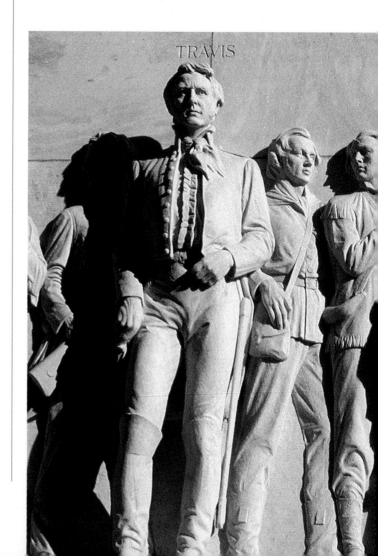

Crockett's loss was the cause of his move to Texas. Leaving Tennessee for Texas was the effect of his loss for reelection. Some clue words that helped you tell the effect were *as a result of* and *therefore*.

TRYING THE SKILL

Now read this passage. Look for any causes and effects. Remember to watch for word clues.

On February 11, 1836, William B. Travis took

command of the Texan soldiers at The Alamo. However, most of the men there were volunteers, not members of the regular army. They were loyal to Jim Bowie, who had earned their respect with his leadership at San Antonio.

The volunteers demanded the right to choose their own leader. As a result of their admiration for Bowie, they chose him. Bowie then became leader of the volunteers. Their numbers were far greater than the 25 Texan Army soldiers that Travis continued to command.

What was the cause of Bowie's victory over Travis in the election at The Alamo? Is Travis's loss a cause or an effect? How do you know?

REVIEWING THE SKILL

1. What is a cause? What is an effect?

2. How could David Crockett's loss in the Tennessee election also be seen as an effect?

3. On February 24, 1836, Jim Bowie became ill with a fever. He handed command of his men to William B. Travis. Was Bowie's illness a cause or effect in this case? Explain.

4. How might identifying cause and effect help you understand history?

CROCKETT

WINNING INDEPENDENCE

READ ALOUD

After the defeats at The Alamo and Goliad, the Texans had no choice but to retreat. Falling back, however, did not mean surrender. "By falling back," Sam Houston said, "Texas can [come together] and defeat any force that can come against her."

THE BIG PICTURE

The mood of Texans turned from hopeful to gloomy. The Mexican Army was on the move from San Antonio. Antonio López de Santa Anna had given orders to his troops to destroy every town and farm that they came across. He hoped to wipe out the colonies of the Texas settlers forever.

Once word of Santa Anna's advance spread through Texas, many people panicked. Thousands of settlers packed up what they could and fled their homes. The roads leading east out of the colonies were soon clogged with wagons, livestock, and people. Later, Texans would call this flight the Runaway Scrape.

The Texas Army, led by Sam Houston, also retreated. His small army seemed no match for Santa Anna's well-armed troops. As a result, the Mexican general believed he would have no problem defeating the Texas Revolution. Houston, however, was confident that Texans would win the war.

Focus Activity

READ TO LEARN
How did Sam Houston lead the Texans to victory?

VOCABULARY
Runaway Scrape
Battle of San Jacinto
treaty
Treaty of Velasco
republic

PEOPLE
Antonio López de
    Santa Anna
Sam Houston
Erastus Deaf Smith
Hendrick Arnold
Henry Karnes

PLACES
San Jacinto River

BEFORE THE BATTLE

Five days after the fall of The Alamo, General Houston reached Gonzales. There he met Suzanna Dickenson and heard the story of The Alamo. He also learned from his scout, Erastus Deaf Smith, that Santa Anna was marching toward Gonzales with thousands of soldiers. Houston ordered that everyone leave Gonzales, and that the city be burned.

Houston in Charge

As Texans everywhere scattered for safety, Houston marched 800 soldiers to a farm along the Brazos River. President Burnet wrote to Houston: "The enemy are laughing. . . . You must fight them." Houston waited for two weeks, training his army and collecting supplies. During that time, Hendrick Arnold, an African American scout, pretended to be a runaway slave. This way he could get into the Mexican Army camps and send information to General Houston.

As the Mexican Army came eastward, Houston headed south to the San Jacinto River to meet them. Find this river on the map. Houston set up camp where the San Jacinto River meets the Buffalo Bayou.

Santa Anna's Mistake

Fully expecting another victory, Santa Anna and about 700 soldiers set up camp only about a mile away from the Texans. Look at the map below to see just how close the two armies were. No Mexican soldiers were even assigned to watch out for Texan soldiers. One day Santa Anna's forces were caught off guard by a surprise attack from Houston's army.

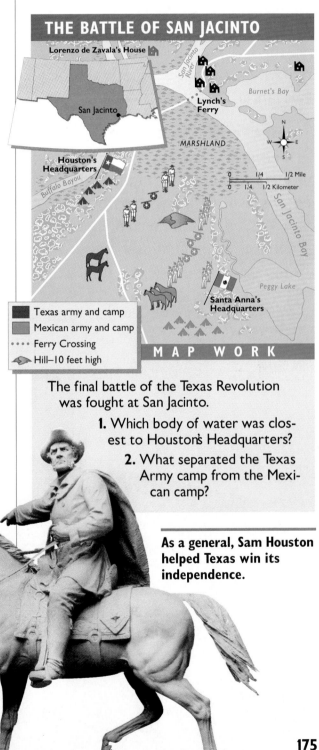

THE BATTLE OF SAN JACINTO

Lorenzo de Zavala's House

San Jacinto River

Burnet's Bay

San Jacinto

Lynch's Ferry

MARSHLAND

Houston's Headquarters

Buffalo Bayou

San Jacinto Bay

Peggy Lake

Santa Anna's Headquarters

0   1/4   1/2 Mile
0   1/4   1/2 Kilometer

- Texas army and camp
- Mexican army and camp
- Ferry Crossing
- Hill–10 feet high

MAP WORK

The final battle of the Texas Revolution was fought at San Jacinto.

1. Which body of water was closest to Houston's Headquarters?

2. What separated the Texas Army camp from the Mexican camp?

As a general, Sam Houston helped Texas win its independence.

175

REMEMBER THE ALAMO

As April 21 dawned, Santa Anna's forces were joined by General Cós and about 540 more soldiers. Houston put a plan into action to trap the Mexicans. To block them from retreating, Houston sent scouts Erastus Deaf Smith and Henry Karnes to destroy a bridge over nearby Simms Bayou. This bridge was the only way in or out of the area where both the Texan and Mexican armies were camped.

The Battle of San Jacinto

General Cós's troops had marched through the night and settled down to rest. By afternoon many of Santa Anna's soldiers were napping after their midday meal.

Meanwhile, the Texans were preparing for battle.

General Houston drew his sword and the Texas Army rose up out of the woods to attack. When they got close to the enemy, the Texan soldiers shouted "Remember The Alamo!" and "Remember Goliad!" as they opened fire with rifles and cannons. The Mexican Army was completely taken by surprise.

The Texans rushed into the Mexican camp and quickly attacked the Mexican troops. General Houston was wounded in the ankle. Two horses were shot from under him. But he continued leading the army.

Although the Battle of San Jacinto was won in 18 minutes, the killing continued for several hours. The Texans chased Mexican troops

The Battle of San Jacinto (below) put an end to Mexico's rule over Texas. The battle was a great defeat for Santa Anna, whose glove is shown (left).

into the bayou, where many drowned. When the day was done, more than 600 Mexicans had died. Fewer than 10 Texans had fallen.

The Capture of Santa Anna

When he saw that the battle was lost, Santa Anna escaped from the battlefield. That night he hid in tall grass, wearing the uniform of a common soldier. The next day Texan soldiers found him. They brought him back to camp, not knowing who he was. As they approached, a group of Mexican prisoners called out, "El Presidente!" Only then did the Texans realize that the man they had captured was Santa Anna.

Santa Anna was brought before Sam Houston, who was lying injured under an oak tree. The Texan soldiers expected Santa Anna to be killed. But Houston refused. He knew this was his chance to trade Santa Anna's freedom for the freedom of Texas.

Treaty of Velasco

While Houston was being treated in the hospital, President Burnet met with Santa Anna at the town of Velasco. They signed a treaty that ended the war. A treaty is a formal agreement between countries.

In the Treaty of Velasco, Santa Anna promised never again to fight against Texas. He agreed to send all Mexican forces out of Texas and to exchange prisoners of war. He and Burnet agreed that the southern border of the newly independent Texas was at the Rio Grande.

In another treaty, which was kept secret, Santa Anna promised the Mexican government would recognize Texas as independent. In the fall, Santa Anna returned home to Mexico.

WHY IT MATTERS

Texans won independence from Mexico at the Battle of San Jacinto. Texas was now a republic. A republic is a form of government in which people choose leaders to represent them. As you will read, Mexicans and Texans would continue to disagree in the years to come.

Reviewing Facts and Ideas

SUM IT UP

- As Santa Anna's army advanced through Texas, many settlers fled.
- General Sam Houston led the Texas Army to victory over Santa Anna at the Battle of San Jacinto.
- After the victory at San Jacinto Texas became a republic.

THINK ABOUT IT

1. What was the Runaway Scrape?
2. Why did Texans shout "Remember The Alamo?"
3. **FOCUS** How was Sam Houston a good leader for the Texans?
4. **THINKING SKILL** Name one *cause* and one *effect* of the Battle of San Jacinto explain your answer.
5. **GEOGRAPHY** Look at the map on page 175. Which of the two armies made its camp closer to San Jacinto Bay?

Landmarks OF
★ TEXAS HISTORY ★

You have already seen the most famous landmark in our state—The Alamo. Landmarks have been set aside to preserve the memory of important Texans and events in history. Some landmarks are monuments or statues. Others are buildings or parks.

Our state has a rich history that began hundreds of years ago. People with courage took part in that history. Today we remember these people because of their important roles in the story of Texas. We also remember important events and the places where they occurred.

Historic sites help to keep these memories alive. These landmarks are a legacy that will continue to remind Texans of the people and events that contributed to our state's history. Perhaps you will visit one of them some day.

This statue of Stephen F. Austin sits proudly in the state park named in his honor in San Felipe.

Lyndon B. Johnson (right) served as the 36th President of the United States from 1963 to 1969. Today LBJ's childhood home (above) is a museum in Johnson City.

Nuestra Señora de Loreta Presidio at La Bahía is the site where Colonel James Fannin's men were killed in the Texas Revolution.

CHAPTER 5 REVIEW

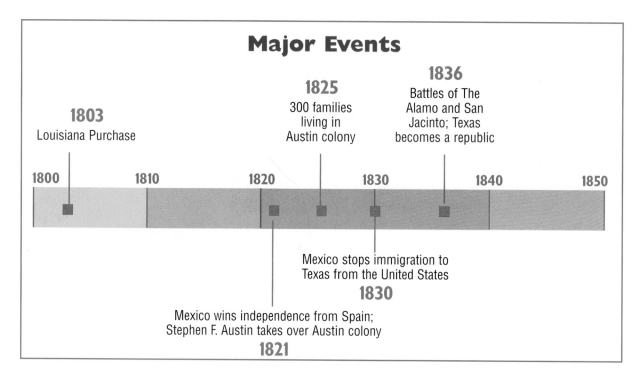

Major Events

1803
Louisiana Purchase

1825
300 families living in Austin colony

1836
Battles of The Alamo and San Jacinto; Texas becomes a republic

1800   1810   1820   1830   1840   1850

Mexico stops immigration to Texas from the United States
1830

Mexico wins independence from Spain; Stephen F. Austin takes over Austin colony
1821

THINKING ABOUT VOCABULARY

Number a sheet of paper from 1 to 10. Next to each number write the word or term from the list below that best matches the statement.

delegate   treaty
empresario   vaquero
frontier

1. A person who was given a large piece of land by the government and allowed to sell the land to settlers

2. A person who is chosen to speak for a group

3. A worker from Mexico who became one of the first cowboys

4. The edge of settlement

5. A formal agreement between countries

THINKING ABOUT FACTS

1. Who were the "Old Three Hundred"?

2. Describe differences between Mexican and American settlers in Texas.

3. Why is April 16, 1830 important?

4. What importance did The Alamo play in the fight for Texan independence?

5. What was the Treaty of Velasco?

THINK AND WRITE

WRITING A LIST
List five vocabulary words from Chapter 5. Write a paragraph using all the words.

WRITING A COMPARISON
Write a paragraph comparing the battles of The Alamo and of San Jacinto.

WRITING A NEWSPAPER ARTICLE
Suppose you were a reporter at the signing of the Treaty of Velasco. Write a newspaper article describing the event.

APPLYING STUDY SKILLS

READING CIRCLE AND LINE GRAPHS

1. Describe how a circle graph and a line graph are different.
2. Look at the circle graph on page 158. Which group made up the largest portion of the population?
3. Look at the line graph on page 159. About how many people lived in Texas in 1821?
4. Which kind of graph, circle or line, would you use to show how the temperature in Houston changes from August to December?
5. How do graphs make some information easier to understand?

APPLYING THINKING SKILLS

IDENTIFYING CAUSE AND EFFECT

1. What is a cause? What is an effect?
2. Name one cause for the Runaway Scrape.
3. What was a cause of the conventions in San Felipe de Austin in 1832 and 1833? What was an effect of the conventions?
4. Sam Houston led the Texas army to victory at San Jacinto. Identify one effect of the victory.
5. Why is understanding cause and effect useful when you are studying history.

Summing Up the Chapter

Use the following word maps to organize information from the chapter. Copy the word maps on a sheet of paper. Then write at least one piece of information in each blank circle. When you have filled in the maps, use them to write a paragraph that answers the questions, "What are the important events that led to the independence of Texas? Who were the important people?"

TEXAN LEADERS

MEXICAN LEADERS

BATTLES

CHAPTER 6

The Road to Statehood

THINKING ABOUT
GEOGRAPHY AND HISTORY

You have read how the Texas Revolution was won and Texas became an independent republic. Yet, as you know, Texas is now one of the United States of America. In this chapter you will learn about the Republic of Texas and Texas's early years as a state.

PACIFIC OCEAN

1839
AUSTIN

Austin becomes the capital of the Republic of Texas

1845
AUSTIN

Citizens of Texas debate whether to join the United States

1848
GUADALUPE HIDALGO, MEXICO

A treaty signed here ends the Mexican War

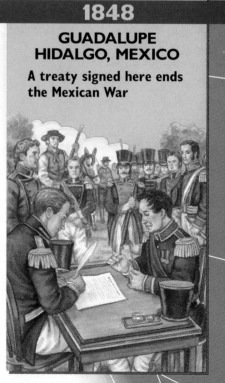

UNITED STATES

TEXAS

Austin

Panna Maria

MEXICO

Gulf of
Mexico

Guadalupe
Hidalgo

CENTRAL
AMERICA

1854

PANNA MARIA

**Polish settlers build a
new community in Texas**

The Granger Collection

Focus Activity

READ TO LEARN
Who were the leaders of the Republic of Texas?

VOCABULARY
congress
Texas Rangers
debt

PEOPLE
Sam Houston
Philip Bowles
Mirabeau B. Lamar

PLACES
Columbia
Austin

THE REPUBLIC OF TEXAS

READ ALOUD

"[Although] . . . few in numbers . . . we dared to proclaim [announce] our independence. . . . As yet our course is onward. We are only in the outset of the campaign of liberty."

In 1836 Sam Houston gave his first speech as President of the Republic of Texas. He reminded Texans that independence was just the beginning of their struggle to make Texas strong.

THE BIG PICTURE

On March 2, 1836, after years of Spanish and then Mexican rule, Texas became a republic. Texas was now an independent country with its own government. It had the right to declare war, make laws, and raise money through taxes. Now Texans voted for their own President and members of their own congress. Congress is the branch of government that makes laws.

Independence did not solve all of the problems in Texas, however. The new nation had little money. Some Texans still feared more attacks from Mexico. Some were fighting with Native Americans for control of land. Many Texans thought Texas would be better off if it joined the United States. Others believed Texas could grow strong and powerful on its own.

The Granger Collection

A NEW REPUBLIC

The new republic needed a capital city. In 1836 the leaders of the republic chose the town of Columbia on the Brazos River. Later that year however, the capital was moved to the larger city of Houston. Some Texans thought Houston was too far from the western part of Texas. So in 1839 the leaders of the republic decided to move the capital again. They chose a village named Waterloo and renamed it Austin. Can you tell why?

The first leaders of the Republic of Texas also chose a flag. Several designs were tried before one flag was adopted in 1839. A lone star was chosen to represent the new republic. This Lone Star flag is still the flag of Texas today.

Although Texans had won their freedom from Mexico, the fighting was not over. Mexico continued to send soldiers to try to recapture the land it had lost. Texas did not have money to pay for a large army. So the leaders of the republic turned to the Texas Rangers.

Who made the first flag of Texas?

Joanna Troutman probably used a silk skirt to make the first Lone Star flag in 1836. It had a blue star instead of the white star we see on our state flag today. Another woman, Sarah Dodson, also made a Lone Star flag during the first year of the Texas Republic. Her flag flew over the building where the Texas Declaration of Independence was signed.

Archive Division
Texas State Library

Texas Rangers

The Texas Rangers were formed in 1835. They were white farmers, ranchers, and townspeople who volunteered to defend the republic. Today the Texas Rangers are part of our state police force.

President Sam Houston

In 1836 Sam Houston became President of Texas. One of President Houston's major problems was the republic's large debt, or amount of money owed to others. During the revolution Texas had borrowed money to pay for military supplies. The new government did not even have enough money to buy paper for writing official letters!

Culver Pictures Inc.

The capital was Columbia (right) and then, in 1840, Austin (left).

185

HOUSTON AND NATIVE AMERICANS

Many Texans felt fear and anger toward Native Americans because of the fighting that had occurred between them. President Houston, however, admired Native Americans. He had lived for three years with the Cherokee in Tennessee. Houston thought it was wrong for the new settlers to force Native Americans off their land.

During the revolution Houston had signed a treaty with Cherokee Chief **Philip Bowles**. Under the treaty the Cherokee agreed not to attack settlers on the frontier. In exchange, Texas would give the Cherokee the right to live on land in East Texas. As President, Houston tried to turn this treaty into a law. The Texas congress refused.

Sam Houston (left) and Chief Philip Bowles (below) worked for peace between Texans and the Cherokee.

President Mirabeau B. Lamar

President Houston thought the republic's problems would be solved more easily if Texas were a state of the United States. **Mirabeau B. Lamar** (MIHR uh boh luh MAHR), who became President of the republic in 1838, had other plans for Texas. Lamar did not want Texas to join the United States. He thought Texans could build a strong nation on their own. He valued education as the foundation for a strong Texas. Therefore, he set aside land on which to build schools and colleges. Today Lamar is still remembered as the "father of Texas education."

Ships and Swords

President Lamar printed extra paper money to try to solve Texas's debt. But with so much paper money in print, it soon became almost worthless. Lamar also bought ships for the Texas Navy. As a result, the republic's debt continued to grow.

Lamar's ideas about how to get along with Native Americans were very different from Houston's. Lamar wanted to take all the land in Texas away from Native Americans. "If peace can be obtained only by the sword, let the sword do its work," he said. At the Battle of the Neches in 1839, Chief Bowles and many other Cherokee were killed. Cherokee villages were burned. The Texas

The Republic of Texas "redback" $50 note (top and center) was printed by Mirabeau B. Lamar (above). Can you see how it got its name?

Army drove the survivors across the Red River into the Indian Territory in what is today Oklahoma. A year later the Comanche suffered a major defeat in battle and were driven farther west in Texas.

WHY IT MATTERS

The Texas Republic lasted only nine years. During this time, a capital was named for Stephen F. Austin. A flag was chosen, and land was set aside for schools. Sam Houston became President again in 1841. He continued to work to make Texas part of the United States.

✓ Reviewing Facts and Ideas

SUM IT UP

- The Texas Republic was an independent nation.
- President Sam Houston tried to keep peace with Native Americans. He wanted Texas to become part of the United States.
- President Mirabeau B. Lamar helped establish schools in Texas. He wanted to keep Texas an independent nation.

THINK ABOUT IT

1. What were two problems faced by leaders of the new Republic of Texas?

2. Why did Texas have a debt?

3. **FOCUS** Who were the first two Presidents of the Republic of Texas? What was one way their beliefs were different?

4. **THINKING SKILL** *Make a conclusion* about the way the Texas government treated Native Americans.

5. **WRITE** Write a speech for either President Houston or President Lamar explaining why the Republic of Texas should or should not join the United States.

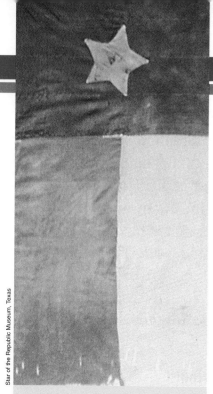
Star of the Republic Museum, Texas

THE LONE STAR STATE

READ ALOUD

During his last speech as President of Texas, Sam Houston described his dream for its future. "If the United States shall . . . ask [Texas] to come into her great family of states, you will then have other [leaders], better than myself, to lead you into the beloved land from which we have sprung—the land of the broad stripes and bright stars."

THE BIG PICTURE

Texans wanted other countries to recognize their new republic. France, Great Britain, and the United States had recognized Texas as an independent country by 1840. Mexico, on the other hand, refused to accept this new country.

Many Texans did not want to continue as an independent nation, however. In 1836 they had voted to become part of the United States. And yet, Texans did like being independent in some ways. They wanted to keep control of their public land. This land would help Texas bring in money and new settlers.

By 1840 a new idea, called Manifest Destiny, was sweeping the United States. This idea was that the United States should grow as far west as the Pacific Ocean and as far south as the Rio Grande. The belief in Manifest Destiny meant Texas would soon become part of the United States.

Focus Activity

READ TO LEARN
How did Texas become part of the United States?

VOCABULARY
Manifest Destiny
annexation
territory
resolution

PEOPLE
Anson Jones
James K. Polk
James Pinckney
  Henderson

ANNEXATION OR INDEPENDENCE

You have read that President Houston wanted Texas to join the United States. He supported annexation (an ek SAY shun). Annexation means bringing a territory into a country. A territory is land owned by a country that does not have the full rights of a state.

Texans who favored annexation pointed out that the United States had a strong army and a strong money system. Texas had neither. Also, many Texans had family in the United States. These Texans wanted to be a part of the same country.

Other Texans, such as former President Lamar, wanted Texas to remain an independent nation. They thought that soon Texas would use its own resources to become rich. But if it joined the United States, they feared Texas would have to give up its land and its independence. In Viewpoints on page 194 you will read more about what Texans thought about becoming a state.

Debate in the United States

As you just read, many people in the United States believed in the idea of Manifest Destiny. Annexing Texas seemed a natural step toward expanding the borders of the United States. Look at the map below to see how the United States was growing.

On the other hand, people in the United States knew Mexico was angry about losing Texas. Many feared war with Mexico. The question of the annexation of Texas also became part of the debate about slavery in the United States. At that time the United States Congress was evenly divided between states that allowed slavery and states that did not. Texas allowed slavery. Adding Texas might upset the balance in the United States Congress between free states and "slave states."

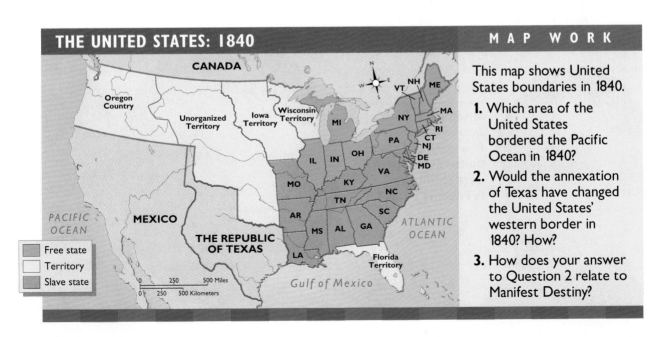

THE UNITED STATES: 1840

Free state
Territory
Slave state

MAP WORK

This map shows United States boundaries in 1840.

1. Which area of the United States bordered the Pacific Ocean in 1840?

2. Would the annexation of Texas have changed the United States' western border in 1840? How?

3. How does your answer to Question 2 relate to Manifest Destiny?

THE LAST DAYS OF THE REPUBLIC

Early in 1844 representatives from Texas and the United States agreed that Texas would become a territory of the United States. The agreement said that Texas would give all its public lands to the United States. In return, the United States would pay all of the debts owed by Texas. Although this agreement was not everything Texans had wanted, many still wanted to join the United States as a state. Therefore, many Texans were willing to accept the agreement.

But when it was time for the United States Congress to accept this agreement, it refused. Concerns about slavery and war with Mexico were the main reasons.

When Sam Houston's second term as Texas President ended in 1844, two men wanted the job. Anson Jones supported annexation, and Edward Burleson was against it. Anson Jones was chosen President of the Republic.

Support for Texas in the United States

In 1844 the people of the United States were choosing their own President. Texas became the focus of this race.

James K. Polk was chosen President. Polk was a friend of Sam Houston and supported the annexation of Texas.

In February 1845, just before Polk took office, the United States Congress passed a joint resolution [rez uh LOO shun], or decision. The resolution said that Texas could become a state. Texas would have to give up its forts and other military buildings. Texas would be able to keep its vast public lands. To pay its debt, Texas would raise money by selling some of this land. The resolution also said that Texas could be divided into as many as five new states. This resolution gave Texans almost everything they wanted.

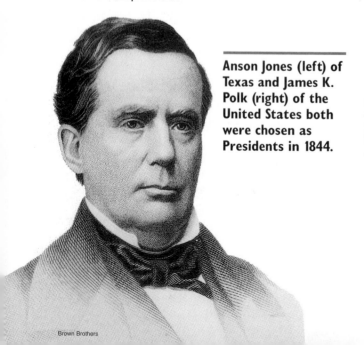

Anson Jones (left) of Texas and James K. Polk (right) of the United States both were chosen as Presidents in 1844.

The 28th State

Now it was time for Texas to decide what to do about the United States resolution. President Jones and the Texas congress held a convention in Austin on July 4, 1845.

Mexico did not want the United States to grow larger and stronger. Before the Austin convention voted, Mexico tried to make a deal with Texas. Mexico agreed to recognize the Republic of Texas and stop sending soldiers there. In exchange for peace, Mexico wanted Texas to remain independent. Texans turned down the deal. All but one person at the convention voted for statehood.

Later that year, the people of Texas showed their support for this decision. More than 4,000 people voted to become a state. Only 267 voted against it. Texans also voted to approve a state constitution.

On December 29, 1845, President Polk signed the law that made Texas the 28th state of the United States. On February 19, 1846, Anson Jones stepped down as the last President of the Republic of Texas. From now on Texas would be led by a governor. Our state's first governor was James Pinckney Henderson. At a ceremony, the Lone Star flag was lowered and replaced with the United States flag. Jones said, "The final act in this great drama is now performed: the Republic of Texas is no more." In the Infographic on page 192 you can see the six flags that have flown over our state.

The Institute of Texan Cultures, San Antonio, Texas

How can you tell that this United States flag (left) was made after Texas became the 28th state? James Pinckney Henderson (above) became our state's first governor.

191

Infographic

Six Flags Over Texas

Have you ever heard the phrase "Six Flags over Texas"? It refers to the flags of the six different nations that have ruled our land. How do these flags remind us of our state's history and its special heritage?

 Spain

Gallery of the Republic

1519-1685; 1690-1821

Early Spanish explorers claimed the land of Texas for Spain. Spanish expeditions searched for gold. But they didn't find any, and the Spanish left Texas in 1685. The Spanish returned a few years later.

3 Mexico

Gallery of the Republic

1821-1836

After Mexico won its independence from Spain, the Mexican flag became the third to fly over Texas land.

2 France

Gallery of the Republic

1685-1690

French explorer La Salle claimed the land of Texas for France. He established Fort St. Louis, but it did not survive long. Spain soon reclaimed the land.

4 The Republic of Texas

Star of the Republic Museum

1836-1845

After the Texas Revolution, Texas became an independent republic. The Lone Star Flag is still used today as our state flag.

5 The Confederate States of America

Gallery of the Republic

1861-1865

As you will learn in Chapter 7, Texas joined with the Confederate States of America during the Civil War. The Confederate flag flew over our state for four years.

6 The United States of America

1845-1861; 1865-present

After Texas became the 28th state, the American flag with 28 stars flew throughout the country. Today our 50-star flag flies proudly throughout Texas and the rest of our country.

WHY IT MATTERS

Texas is the only state in our nation that was once a republic. Both Texas and the United States had to weigh many issues before deciding to unite. Among them were slavery and growth. Mexico did not allow slavery and was unhappy about the annexation. The United States would soon find itself at war with its new southern neighbor.

✓ Reviewing Facts and Ideas

SUM IT UP

- The United States, Great Britain, and France recognized the Republic of Texas but Mexico refused.
- People in Texas and the United States had different ideas about annexation.
- Texas became the 28th state of the United States in 1845.

THINK ABOUT IT

1. What is Manifest Destiny?

2. What signal did the United States send to Texas by choosing James K. Polk as President?

3. **FOCUS** How did Texas become part of the United States?

4. **THINKING SKILL** What *effect* did the idea of Manifest Destiny have on the debate in the United States about Texas annexation?

5. **GEOGRAPHY** Look at the map on page 189. Name three territories that belonged to the United States. How did their locations reflect Manifest Destiny?

CITIZENSHIP
VIEWPOINTS

1800s: WHAT DID TEXANS THINK ABOUT JOINING THE UNITED STATES?

This 1936 drawing by Norman Price shows Anson Jones lowering the flag of the Republic of Texas on February 19, 1846.

In 1836 the majority of voters in the Republic of Texas were in favor of joining the United States. Most Texans, including President Sam Houston, felt that they would be safer and grow richer as a part of the United States. However, the United States Congress delayed acting on the Texas request to become a state. By the early 1840s, therefore, many Texas leaders were uncertain about whether or not annexation would ever occur.

Not all Texans favored annexation. Some, such as President Mirabeau B. Lamar, were strongly against it. They argued that, as United States citizens, they would be governed by people who did not understand their needs. Juan Seguín, who had left Texas to make his permanent home in Mexico, also argued against annexation. He knew that Mexico had offered to recognize Texas's independence.

Read the three different viewpoints about annexation. Then answer the questions that follow.

Three DIFFERENT Viewpoints

1 SAM HOUSTON
President of the Republic of Texas
Excerpt from Letter to United States President Andrew Jackson, written in 1836

My great desire is that our country Texas shall be annexed to the United States . . . . It is [popular] to hold out the idea . . . that we are able to [support and protect] ourselves against any power . . . yet I am free to say to *you* that we cannot do it. . . . I look to you as [a] friend and . . . the [helper] of mankind to [get involved] in our behalf and save us.

"I look to you as [a] friend . . ."

2 MIRABEAU B. LAMAR
President of the Republic of Texas
Excerpt from Inaugural Address, 1838

When I reflect upon the invaluable rights which Texas will have to [give] up with the surrender of her independence—the right of making either war or peace; the right of controlling the Indian tribes within her borders . . . I cannot regard the annexation of Texas to the American Union in any other light than as the grave of all her hopes of happiness and greatness.

". . . the grave of all her . . . hopes . . ."

3 JUAN SEGUÍN
Soldier for Texas in the Texas Revolution
Excerpt from Letter to Texas President Anson Jones, 1845

I know that the true happiness of Texas . . . consists in preserving its independence from any other power other than Mexico . . . Mexico is . . . resolved to recognize the independence of Texas by way of treaties.

". . . true happiness of Texas . . ."

BUILDING CITIZENSHIP

1. What was the viewpoint of each person? How did each one support his views?
2. In what ways are some of the viewpoints alike? In what ways are the viewpoints different?
3. What other viewpoints might people have had on this issue?

SHARING VIEWPOINTS

Suppose you and your classmates were living at the time of the debate about annexation. Discuss what you agree with about these viewpoints. Then as a class, write two statements that all of you could have agreed with about annexation.

The Granger Collection

THE MEXICAN WAR

Focus Activity

READ TO LEARN
Why did the United States go to war with Mexico?

VOCABULARY
Mexican War
Treaty of Guadalupe Hidalgo

PEOPLE
Zachary Taylor
Sarah Borginnis
Winfield Scott

PLACES
Nueces River
Rio Grande
Chapultepec

READ ALOUD

On May 11, 1846, President James K. Polk asked the United States Congress to declare war on the country of Mexico.

"Mexico has . . . invaded our territory and shed American blood upon the American soil. . . . We are called upon . . . to [uphold] with decision the honor, the rights, and the interests of our country."

THE BIG PICTURE

As you read in Lesson 2, the idea of Manifest Destiny swept the United States in the 1840s. Once Texas joined the United States, many Americans wanted our country to keep expanding westward. American businesses wanted to increase trade with countries in Asia. Ports along the coast of the Pacific Ocean would make more trade possible. But first the United States had to own the land as far west as the Pacific Ocean.

Much of the land that is now the southwestern and western United States belonged to Mexico at the time. After the annexation of Texas, the Mexican government ordered its representative in Washington, D.C., to come home. This act was a signal that Mexico was angry about losing Texas to the United States. Tension was growing between the two countries.

TROUBLES BETWEEN THE UNITED STATES AND MEXICO

The United States and Mexico disagreed about the borders of Texas. Mexico said Texas was still a part of Mexico eastward to the Nueces River. The United States said Texas as its state extended all the way to the Rio Grande. Look at the map on this page to see where the countries placed their national boundaries.

In 1845 President James K. Polk sent a special representative to Mexico City, Mexico. Polk wanted to buy from Mexico the land of what is today California and several Southwest states. He also wanted to talk about the southern border of Texas. Polk said he was trying to keep peace between the two countries. At the same time, however, he was preparing for war.

The Mexican government refused to speak with Polk's representative. Although many Americans opposed war with Mexico, Polk sent about 3,500 United States soldiers to the Rio Grande in February, 1846. Their leader was General Zachary Taylor. Taylor was popular with his soldiers because he was always willing to risk his own safety.

Taylor and his men had been camped at the Nueces River. Moving them south to the Rio Grande was a major step. Polk was giving Mexico a signal that the United States would defend this area of Texas as its own.

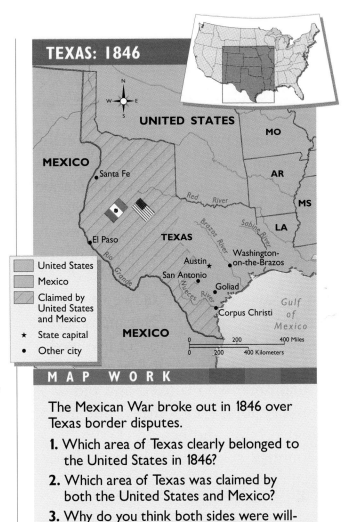

TEXAS: 1846

- United States
- Mexico
- Claimed by United States and Mexico
- ★ State capital
- • Other city

MAP WORK

The Mexican War broke out in 1846 over Texas border disputes.

1. Which area of Texas clearly belonged to the United States in 1846?
2. Which area of Texas was claimed by both the United States and Mexico?
3. Why do you think both sides were willing to fight over the borders?

War Breaks Out

Mexico, in turn, also sent its soldiers to the Rio Grande. The two armies camped on opposite sides of the river. The United States Army played our country's national anthem, "The Star-Spangled Banner," on musical instruments such as fifes and drums. The Mexican soldiers responded by playing their own country's songs. Finally, Mexican soldiers attacked and killed a group of United States soldiers. The United States declared war on Mexico on May 13, 1846.

THE ROLE OF TEXANS IN THE WAR

Men from across the United States responded to the declaration of war with Mexico. Of course, Texans had a special interest in the **Mexican War**. More than 8,000 Texans signed up, including six groups of Texas Rangers. Governor Henderson even took time out from his official duties to be in the army.

Women were not allowed to fight in the Mexican War. But many women found ways to get involved. One such person was **Sarah Borginnis**, who cooked and did laundry for Taylor's army. She also loaded guns and helped carry wounded soldiers off the battlefield.

Fighting Reaches Mexico City

Soon after the war began, General Taylor's army crossed the Rio Grande into Mexico. The soldiers defeated Santa Anna, who was again President of Mexico, at the Battle of Buena Vista (BWAY nuh VEE stuh) early in 1847. Later that year the United States Army led by General **Winfield Scott** landed at Veracruz, Mexico. After heavy fighting the army reached Mexico City.

General Scott decided to attack **Chapultepec** (chuh PUL tuh pek). This huge fort was on a hill overlooking Mexico City. On September 12, Scott's army attacked the fort. After a fierce battle, Scott captured the fort. The United States flag was raised over Chapultepec and Santa Anna's army soon retreated. The next day a white flag was raised over Mexico City. The United States had won the Mexican War.

The End of the War

On February 2, 1848, the United States and Mexico signed the **Treaty of Guadalupe Hidalgo** (gwahd ul OOP ay hih DAHL goh). Under this treaty Mexico had to recognize the Rio Grande as its border with the United States. It also had to give up land that now makes up part or all of the states of California, Arizona, Nevada, Utah, New Mexico,

United States soldiers followed General Zachary Taylor into Mexico soon after the Mexican War began.

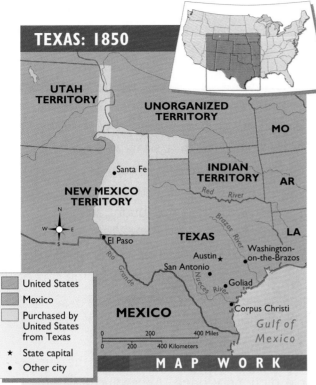

TEXAS: 1850

United States
Mexico
Purchased by United States from Texas
★ State capital
• Other city

UTAH TERRITORY
UNORGANIZED TERRITORY
MO
Santa Fe
NEW MEXICO TERRITORY
INDIAN TERRITORY
AR
Red River
El Paso
Brazos River
TEXAS
LA
Austin ★
Washington-on-the-Brazos
San Antonio
Nueces River
Goliad
Rio Grande
MEXICO
Corpus Christi
Gulf of Mexico

200   400 Miles
200   400 Kilometers

MAP WORK

By 1850 the borders of present-day Texas were established.

1. What area was purchased by the United States from Texas?

2. What river formed the southwestern border of Texas in 1850?

3. How did this purchase of land help the United States to continue growing?

Wyoming, and Colorado. In exchange for this land, the United States paid Mexico $15 million.

Texas still had one more border problem to settle. Texans claimed all the land west to the Rio Grande. That land included half of what is now New Mexico. In 1850 the United States paid Texas $10 million to give up that land. Look at the map to see the borders of Texas today.

WHY IT MATTERS

The annexation of Texas and the United States' desire to extend its land to the Pacific Ocean led to the Mexican War. The war began in 1846 and ended in 1847 after General Winfield Scott captured Mexico City.

Under the Treaty of Guadalupe Hidalgo in 1848, Mexico had to give up huge areas of land to the United States. Now Texas and the new area of the United States were ready to receive thousands of new settlers.

✓ Reviewing Facts and Ideas

SUM IT UP

- The United States and Mexico disagreed about the southern border of Texas.

- The United States declared war against Mexico on May 13, 1846.

- Mexico's defeat resulted in losing much of its land and recognizing the Rio Grande as the southern border of Texas.

THINK ABOUT IT

1. According to the United States, which river formed its border with Mexico?

2. Where did the Mexican War begin? Where did it end?

3. **FOCUS** What were the main reasons that led the United States and Mexico to fight in the Mexican War?

4. **THINKING SKILL** *Compare* and *contrast* the Mexican War with the Texas Revolution.

5. **GEOGRAPHY** Find the Nueces River and the Rio Grande on the map on page 197. Why do you think Mexico wanted the Nueces River to serve as its border with the United States?

STUDYSKILLS

Using Reference Sources

VOCABULARY
reference source
dictionary
guide word
encyclopedia
CD-ROM

WHY THE SKILL MATTERS

In the last lesson you read about General Zachary Taylor, General Winfield Scott, the Mexican War, and the Treaty of Guadalupe Hidalgo. You might like to find out more about any of these topics—let's say, the Treaty of Guadalupe Hidalgo.

You could find the information you want in reference sources. These are books and other sources that contain facts about many different subjects. They can be found in a special part of the library called the reference section.

USING A DICTIONARY

To begin, you might want to know the exact meaning of the word *treaty*. To find out, you would look in a dictionary. A dictionary gives the meanings of words. It shows how to pronounce and spell each word. Sometimes a dictionary explains where a word comes from, or uses it in a sentence. Some dictionaries also provide synonyms, or words with similar meanings.

The words in a dictionary are arranged in alphabetical order. To make your work faster, you can refer to the guide words. These appear at the top of each page of the dictionary. They tell you the first and last words that are defined on that page.

Look at the guide words on the sample dictionary page. According to them, what is the last word to be defined on the page? Would the word *treasure* appear on this page? Now find the word *treaty*. What does this word mean?

treadmill/trial

treadmill A device turned by animals or persons walking on moving steps or on a belt formed into a loop. Treadmills produce motion to run machines, raise water from wells, and perform other tasks.
tread-mill (tred'mil') *noun, plural* **treadmills.**

treason The betraying of one's country by helping an enemy. Giving the army's battle plans to the enemy was an act of *treason.*
trea-son (trē'zən) *noun.*

treasure Money, jewels, or other things that are valuable. A chest of gold coins was part of the pirates' *treasure. Noun.*
—To think of as being of great value or importance; cherish. We *treasure* the memory of our grandparents. *Verb.*
treas-ure (trezh'ər) *noun, plural* **treasures;** *verb,* **treasured, treasuring.**

treasurer A person responsible for taking care of the money of a club or business.
treas-ur-er (trezh'ər ər) *noun, plural* **treasurers.**

treasury 1. The money or other funds of a business, government, or other group. The club paid for a party out of its *treasury.* 2. **Treasury.** A department of the government in charge of the country's finances.
treas-ur-y (trezh'ə rē) *noun, plural* **treasuries.**

treat 1. To behave toward or deal with in a certain way. The principal *treated* the student fairly. 2. To talk or write about; consider or discuss. The Sunday paper *treats* the week's sports events in detail. 3. To give medical care to. The doctor *treated* my burned hand with an ointment. 4. To subject to a process. You can *treat* cloth with a chemical to make it waterproof. 5. To pay for the entertainment of another person. I will *treat* you to the movie. *Verb.*
—Something that is a special pleasure. Going to the circus was a *treat. Noun.*
treat (trēt) *verb,* **treated, treating;** *noun, plural* **treats.**

treatment 1. The way something or someone is treated. That scratched record has had rough *treatment.* 2. The care or medicine used to help cure a sick or injured person. Rest was the recommended *treatment.*
treat-ment (trēt'mənt) *noun, plural* **treatments.**

treaty A formal agreement between countries. A *treaty* was signed to end the war.
trea-ty (trē'tē) *noun, plural* **treaties.**

tree A plant with a single main stem or trunk that is made up of solid, woody tissue. Trees have branches and leaves at a distance above the ground. *Noun.*

—To chase up a tree. The dog *treed* the squirrel. *Verb.*
tree (trē) *noun, plural* **trees;** *verb,* **treed, treeing.**

trellis A frame of crossed strips of wood or metal for a plant to grow on.
trel-lis (trel'is) *noun, plural* **trellises.**

tremble 1. To shake with cold, fear, weakness, or anger. The wet kitten *trembled.* We *trembled* at the sound of thunder. 2. To move or vibrate. The building *trembled* from the explosion.
trem-ble (trem'bəl) *verb,* **trembled, trembling.**

tremendous Very large or great; enormous. A *tremendous* clap of thunder shook the house.
tre-men-dous (tri men'dəs) *adjective.*

tremor A shaking or trembling. Earthquakes cause *tremors* in the earth.
trem-or (trem'ər) *noun, plural* **tremors.**

trench A long, narrow ditch. The soldiers fought from *trenches* in the battlefield.
trench (trench) *noun, plural* **trenches.**

trend A direction or course that seems to be followed; tendency. There is a *trend* toward higher prices in this country.
trend (trend) *noun, plural* **trends.**

trespass To go on another person's property without permission. The swimmers *trespassed* on the private beach. *Verb.*
—A sin. *Noun.*
tres-pass (tres'pəs *or* tres'pas') *verb,* **trespassed, trespassing;** *noun, plural* **trespasses.**

trestle A framework used to hold up a railroad bridge or other raised structure.
tres-tle (tres'əl) *noun, plural* **trestles.**

tri- A prefix that means having or involving three. A *triangle* is a figure with three sides.

trial 1. The examination of a person accused of a crime in a court of law. 2. A trying or testing of something. 3. A test of someone's strength, patience, or faith; hardship. The cold winter was a *trial* for the Pilgrims.
tri-al (trī'əl) *noun, plural* **trials.**

trellis

764

USING AN ENCYCLOPEDIA OR A CD-ROM

Another useful reference book is the encyclopedia. This book or set of books gives information about people, places, things, and events. Like a dictionary, the topics in an encyclopedia are arranged in alphabetical order. Most encyclopedias also use guide words.

Let's say you want to learn more about the Mexican War. You would look in the volume, or book of the set, with M on the spine. Which volume would you look in to learn more about Zachary Taylor?

A newer kind of reference source is the CD-ROM. This is a compact disc that you "read" with the aid of a computer. Like an encyclopedia, a CD-ROM contains facts about many subjects. It also may include sounds, music, and even short movies! Your teacher or librarian will help you use this type of reference source.

TRYING THE SKILL

You have practiced using reference sources. Now suppose that you want to write a report on General Winfield Scott. Which reference sources would you use? How would you find the information you need? Use the Helping Yourself box before you begin your report.

REVIEWING THE SKILL

1. What is a reference source?

2. Which reference source or sources would you use to find the meaning of the word *republic*?

3. Some encyclopedias have guide words on their spine instead of letters. Suppose you had a volume covering everything from *library* to *medicine*. Would this volume contain an article about Mexico City?

4. When are reference sources useful?

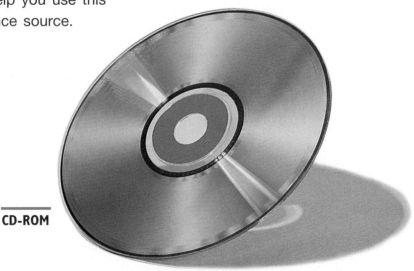

CD-ROM

201

NEW SETTLERS

READ ALOUD

". . . here one can get a house very easily [because] everybody builds his house for himself."

This is how an immigrant described Texas in a letter to his family in Poland. Like other people who came from far away, Polish settlers found that Texas offered many chances and challenges.

THE BIG PICTURE

If you had lived in Mississippi or another state near Texas during the middle 1800s, you might have seen empty houses with signs that read "GTT." These letters stood for "Gone to Texas." Many people moved to Texas after it won its independence from Mexico. They kept coming when Texas became part of the United States. These new settlers came for land. Texans had so much land that they gave it away for free!

People came to Texas from other states in the United States and from more than 26 countries. These new settlers became part of the long history of pioneers who had come to Texas. Not all people came to Texas of their own free will, however. Thousands of enslaved people were brought to Texas by their owners.

Focus Activity

READ TO LEARN
What was life like for the new pioneers in Texas?

PEOPLE
Henri Castro
Patricia de la Garza
   de León

PLACES
Castroville
Panna Maria
New Braunfels
Fredericksburg

MANY ROADS TO TEXAS

White men and their families were given free land when they arrived in Texas. Advertisements and letters written home by these pioneers helped spread the news. In 1836, when Texas won its independence, more than 35,000 people lived here. By 1860, the number of Texans had grown to more than 600,000.

From Around the World

Most pioneers came from other parts of the United States. They came from Louisiana, Mississippi, Arkansas, Tennessee, Georgia, Illinois, New York, and other states.

Other pioneers came from Europe. They left their homelands because they wanted to find better job opportunities or because they faced political or religious problems.

Many French immigrants were drawn to Texas by a Frenchman named Henri Castro. He created the town of Castroville. People from what is now the Czech and Slovak republics settled in southeast Texas. Norwegians came to the northeast. Records show Irish and Swedish immigrants also settled here. Almost one-third of the new people that came to Texas were enslaved African Americans.

On Christmas Eve in 1854, a small group of people from Poland arrived in an unsettled part of Texas. They celebrated the holiday under an oak tree, and named the place Panna Maria. Panna Maria, which means Virgin Mary, was the first Polish settlement in the United States. The oak tree still stands beside the church they built.

Often new people found their way to Texas with help from others. For example, the Society for the Protection of German Immigrants in Texas brought thousands of people to central Texas. They built the towns of New Braunfels and Fredericksburg.

Eleven-year-old Caroline von Hinueber (fun HIHN ee ber) came with her family to Texas from Germany in 1831. How did she describe their first house?

MANY VOICES PRIMARY SOURCE

Excerpt from
Life of German Pioneers in Early Texas
by Caroline von Hinueber, published in 1899.

[It] was covered with straw and [had] six sides, which were made out of moss. The roof was by no means waterproof, and we often held an umbrella over our bed when it rained at night. . . . Of course we suffered a great deal in the winter . . . we were afraid to light a fire because of [our straw roof]. So we had to shiver.

From which country did pioneers bring plates like this one to Texas?

Star of the Republic
Museum, Texas

PIONEER LIFE

Pioneer life in Texas was never easy. Building new homes and farms took hard work and courage. Pioneers found that life was filled with many challenges, from dangerous rattlesnakes to terrible drought.

Some people faced additional difficulties. Tejano settlers, such as Patricia de la Garza de León, about whom you read in Chapter 5, often were treated badly by new settlers. De León had sided with Texas during the revolution. However, she and her family were driven off the land by Texans who were angry with Mexico.

Most pioneers were farmers. They had come to Texas with few belongings. So they had to make almost everything they needed for life on their farms.

You can visit pioneer cabins that have been recreated like this one in Fredericksburg.

Life on the Farm

Farmers made clothing, furniture, and tools. One pioneer wrote that within five years he had made a "wheel, a coffin, a cradle, a bucket, an ox yoke, and a pair of shoes." The settlers found a use for everything. Corn husks were used to stuff mattresses, and corn cobs were burned for heat. In rural areas, parents also served as schoolteachers.

Most farmers planted corn, cotton, and potatoes. They often raised cattle and pigs. Rocky soil made it hard to plant crops, and food was often scarce. Many families lived on corn bread, sweet potatoes, and pork preserved in salt.

Pioneers built their homes out of the natural resources they found nearby. Where there were trees, people built log cabins. In other areas, people built homes from stone, adobe, or sod.

Shopping in Towns

Farmers sometimes came to towns to buy what they could not make or grow themselves. Unlike farms, towns were more crowded and had many businesses. The shops belonged to saddlemakers, tailors, brickmakers, and wheelmakers. Milliners made hats for women. Tanners turned animal skins into leather for clothing, shoes, and bags.

Transportation

Texas was soon bustling with people and goods being transported from place to place. River steamboats brought goods from Galveston and other ports to towns far from the Gulf of Mexico. Farmers sent food to town on wagons pulled by oxen. Stagecoaches were horse-drawn carriages that followed a fixed route. Cross-country fares were as much as $150. But if a passenger could hold on to the stagecoach from the outside, the fare was 10 cents a mile.

OVERLAND TO THE PACIFIC.

The San Antonio and San Diego Mail-Line.

Ads (above) offered stagecoach travel across Texas to the West. Wagon wheels (left) often met rough roads.

By 1860, Harrisburg, Houston, and Galveston were linked by train. The railroad company said that "a journey of *days* is now performed in the same number of hours."

WHY IT MATTERS

Many new settlers came to Texas between 1836 and 1860. Pioneers had to start from almost nothing. They built houses, grew their own food, and made their own clothes. These settlers helped change the land and life of our state.

Reviewing Facts and Ideas

SUM IT UP

- Settlers came to Texas from other states and countries such as France, Germany, and Poland.
- Pioneers used whatever resources they had in order to survive.
- Wagons, trains, and steamboats were used for transportation.

THINK ABOUT IT

1. Why did many new settlers come to Texas?

2. Where did many of the new settlers to Texas come from?

3. **FOCUS** What were some of the challenges faced by new settlers?

4. **THINKING SKILL** How did new forms of transportation help *cause* the state of Texas to grow?

5. **WRITE** Suppose you are a Texas pioneer in 1860. Write a letter to your old home in Europe or the United States. Describe your new life.

INDEPENDENCE IN THE WESTERN HEMISPHERE

Focus Activity

READ TO LEARN

How did European colonies in the Western Hemisphere gain their independence?

VOCABULARY

American Revolution
Plan of Iguala

PEOPLE

George Washington
Miguel Hidalgo
José María Morelos
Agustín de Iturbide
Simón Bolívar

PLACES

Dolores
Venezuela

READ ALOUD

"Friends and countrymen, you are the sons of this land, yet have been for three centuries in bondage [slavery]. The Europeans have everything. . . . Come march with us for country and religion. . . . Death to the bad government!"

Miguel Hidalgo (mee GHEL hih DAHL goh), a Mexican priest, spoke these words on September 16, 1810, in Dolores, Mexico. The "Cry of Dolores," as this speech became known, was the first step in winning Mexico's freedom from Spain.

THE BIG PICTURE

In Chapter 5 you read about how Texas won its independence from Mexico in 1836. Mexico had won its independence from Spain in 1821.

Even earlier, in 1776, the 13 English colonies had declared their independence from England. George Washington led the colonies' army in the American Revolution. After winning the American Revolution the colonies became the United States of America. The desire to be free spread throughout the Western Hemisphere. You will read about some of these struggles in this lesson.

MEXICO'S ROAD TO INDEPENDENCE

As you read in Chapter 4, Mexico had been under Spanish rule since 1521. For 300 years Mexico, as part of New Spain, was ruled by Spaniards. Most Indians and mestizos were poor and had no power.

The Cry of Dolores

Miguel Hidalgo was a priest who, in 1803, went to the church of Dolores in central Mexico. He tried to help Indian and mestizo farmers by showing them how to grow olives and grapes. Soon, however, Spanish government workers cut down the olive trees and grapevines. It was against the law to grow these crops in Mexico. Mexicans had to buy them from Spain.

Hidalgo saw that, as long as Spain ruled Mexico, life for the poor would not improve. On September 16, 1810, Hidalgo gave the famous "Cry of Dolores" speech at his church. Thousands joined Hidalgo to march to Mexico City. That day was the beginning of Mexico's war for independence.

Hidalgo was killed in 1811 and his army of men, women, and children was defeated. But José María Morelos (hoh SAY muh REE uh moh RAY lohs), a mestizo priest, continued the struggle. Morelos was killed in 1815.

Independence at Last

Independence finally was won by a military officer, Agustín de Iturbide (a goos TEEN day ee TOOR bee day). He was a mestizo. Iturbide had been chosen by the government to lead the Spanish forces. But he switched sides, hoping to win power for himself.

In 1821, Iturbide wrote the Plan of Iguala (ee HWA lah), his plan for Mexican independence. Under this plan, Mexico would be ruled by a king, and the Roman Catholic Church would remain Mexico's official church. The plan also promised equal rights for all Mexicans. On September 27, 1821, Iturbide and his army entered Mexico City and Mexico became an independent country. On July 25, 1822, however, Iturbide seized power and made himself the emperor.

Agustín de Iturbide (above left) is remembered during the annual Mexican Independence Day celebration in Mexico (above).

Independence in the Western Hemisphere

COUNTRY	COLONIAL RULER	YEAR OF INDEPENDENCE
Argentina	Spain	1816
Belize	Great Britain	1981
Bolivia	Spain	1825
Brazil	Portugal	1822
Canada	Great Britain	1931
Chile	Spain	1810–1818
Colombia	Spain	1810–1819
Costa Rica	Spain	1821
Cuba	Spain	1898
Dominica	Great Britain	1978
Dominican Republic	France and Spain	1821
Ecuador	Spain	1809–1822
El Salvador	Spain	1821
Grenada	Great Britain	1974
Guatemala	Spain	1821
Guyana	Great Britain	1966
Haiti	France	1804
Honduras	Spain	1821
Jamaica	Great Britain	1962
Mexico	Spain	1821
Nicaragua	Spain	1821
Panama	Spain	1821
Paraguay	Spain	1811
Peru	Spain	1821–1824
St. Kitts and Nevis	Great Britain	1983
St. Lucia	Great Britain	1979
St. Vincent and the Grenadines	Great Britain	1979
Suriname	Netherlands	1975
Trinidad and Tobago	Great Britain	1962
United States	Great Britain	1776
Uruguay	Portugal and Spain	1828
Venezuela	Spain	1821

CHART WORK

Much of the Western Hemisphere gained independence in the 1800s.

1. When did the United States become independent?

2. Which country was the last to gain independence? When did it happen?

3. Why do you think so many countries became independent in 1821?

INDEPENDENCE IN THE WESTERN HEMISPHERE

Mexico had not been Spain's only colony in the Western Hemisphere. During the early 1800s, other Spanish colonies also began to fight against Spanish rule. Look at the chart on the opposite page to see when the countries of the Western Hemisphere became independent.

The Story of Simón Bolívar

Simón Bolívar (see MOHN boh LEE vahr) was born in 1783 into a wealthy family in Caracas, Venezuela. Bolívar believed that conditions in Venezuela would improve only if Venezuela were free from Spanish control.

In 1813 he took command of a rebel army, leading it successfully against the Spanish. Venezuelans began to call Bolívar "The Liberator." But the Spanish soon sent many more troops and by 1815 Bolívar was forced to escape to Jamaica.

Bolívar returned to lead the fight in Venezuela in 1816 and Venezuela finally gained its independence in 1821. Bolívar spent the rest of his life helping other South American countries fight for independence.

WHY IT MATTERS

The desire for freedom from foreign rule spread through the Western Hemisphere. The American Revolution had made the 13 English colonies an independent country.

Mexico freed itself from Spain in 1821. Other colonies also decided it was time to be free of foreign rule. Struggles that lasted for many years finally ended in independence.

✓// Reviewing Facts and Ideas

SUM IT UP

- In the early 1800s many colonies in the Western Hemisphere gained independence.
- Miguel Hidalgo, José Morelos, and Agustín de Iturbide led the fight to end Spanish rule in Mexico.
- Simón Bolívar was a leader of the struggle for independence in South America.

THINK ABOUT IT

1. What were some of the problems faced by Mexican farmers under Spanish rule?

2. What important role did Miguel Hidalgo play in Mexico's war for independence?

3. **FOCUS** Look at the chart on page 208. Which was the first Spanish colony in the Western Hemisphere to begin to fight for independence? How long did it take?

4. **THINKING SKILL** Do you think Mexico's war for independence had an *effect* on Venezuela's fight for independence? Explain your answer.

5. **WRITE** Suppose that you lived in a colony in the Western Hemisphere. Write a speech in which you explain the need for independence.

CHAPTER 6 REVIEW

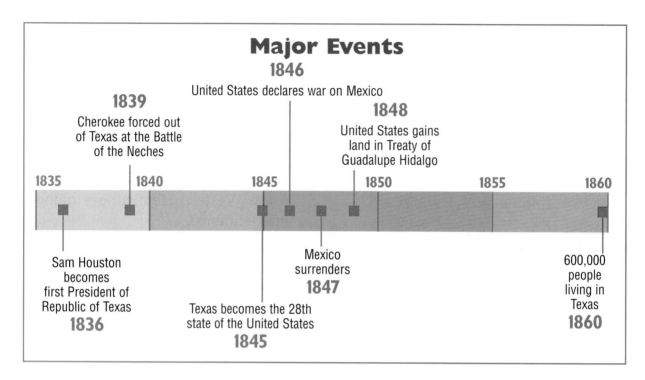

Major Events

1846
United States declares war on Mexico

1839
Cherokee forced out of Texas at the Battle of the Neches

1848
United States gains land in Treaty of Guadalupe Hidalgo

1835　　1840　　1845　　1850　　1855　　1860

Sam Houston becomes first President of Republic of Texas
1836

Texas becomes the 28th state of the United States
1845

Mexico surrenders
1847

600,000 people living in Texas
1860

THINKING ABOUT VOCABULARY

Number a sheet of paper from 1 to 10. Next to each number write the word or phrase from the list that best fits the definition.

annexation　　　Plan of Iguala
congress　　　　resolution
Creole　　　　　territory
debt　　　　　　Texas Rangers
Manifest Destiny　Treaty of Guadalupe Hidalgo

1. The branch of government that makes laws

2. A group of men who volunteered to defend the Republic of Texas

3. The idea that the United States would grow as far west as the Pacific and as far south as the Rio Grande

4. Incorporating a territory into a country

5. The agreement that ended the Mexican War

6. Land owned by a country that does not have the full rights of a state

7. A plan for Mexican independence

8. A person of Spanish and French descent

9. A decision

10. An amount of money owed to others

THINKING ABOUT FACTS

1. Why did Mexico oppose statehood for Texas?

2. Why was a star chosen to represent Texas on its new flag?

3. Describe two causes of the war between Texas and Mexico.

4. Why did the United States pay $15 million to Mexico under the Treaty of Guadalupe Hidalgo?

5. Name two promises included in the Plan of Iguala.

THINK AND WRITE

WRITING AN ESSAY

Write a short essay in which you explain how the idea of Manifest Destiny affected both the annexation of Texas and the Mexican War.

WRITING A PARAGRAPH OF COMPARISON

Write a paragraph comparing the opinions of Sam Houston and Mirabeau B. Lamar on whether or not Texas should become a state. Do you agree with Sam Houston or Mirabeau B. Lamar? Why?

WRITING A SUMMARY

Write a summary of Simón Bolívar's struggle for Venezuela's independence. How did Bolívar spend the rest of his life?

APPLYING STUDY SKILLS

USING REFERENCE SOURCES

1. What are reference sources? Name three different kinds.

2. Which reference sources would you use to learn more about Sam Houston?

3. Suppose the guide words on a dictionary page are *floor* and *flounder*. Would the word *flute* be found on the same page?

4. Suppose you wanted to listen to and watch speeches by Lyndon B. Johnson. Which kind of reference source would you use?

5. How might reference sources be helpful when you are studying history?

Summing Up the Chapter

Use the following time line to organize information from the chapter. Copy the time line on a piece of paper. Then fill in a major event from our state's history for each date on the time line. When you have filled in the time line, use the information to write an answer to the question "What are some of the events that took place in Texas during the years before and after statehood?"

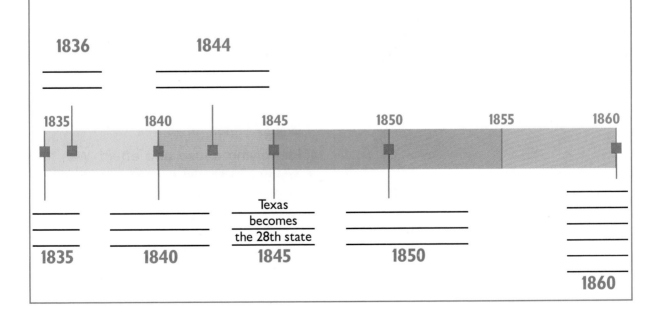

UNIT 3 REVIEW

THINKING ABOUT VOCABULARY

Number a sheet of paper from 1 to 10. Next to each number write the word or phrase from the list that best completes each sentence.

barter
bilingual
constitution
debt
delegate

empresario
pioneer
republic
Runaway Scrape
Tejano

1. A person who packed up his or her belongings and traveled west was called a _____.

2. A Mexican who lived in Texas was known as a _____.

3. Sometimes Texas farmers would _____ their crops instead of paying money for things they bought.

4. In 1832 each _____ to the convention had been chosen to speak for a group of Texans.

5. A document that contains the basic rules used to govern a state or a country is called a _____.

6. After the Battle of San Jacinto, Texas became a _____.

7. The early Republic of Texas had a large _____ because it had borrowed money during its revolution.

8. A person who is able to speak two languages is _____.

9. An _____ was given land by the government for bringing in settlers.

10. Thousands of settlers in Texas fled their homes during the _____.

THINK AND WRITE

WRITING A LETTER
Suppose you lived in Texas from 1835 to 1845. Write a letter to a friend in the East describing the changes that took place during that time.

WRITING A NEWSPAPER ARTICLE
Reread "Learning About The Alamo" on page 170. Write an article for your school newspaper on the discovery of artifacts at The Alamo.

WRITING A POSTER
Suppose you lived in Texas in 1840. Write and design a poster that supports one of the following: annexation to the United States or independence.

BUILDING SKILLS

1. **Reading circle and line graphs** Which kind of graph would you use to show the portion of Texans who work in service industries?

2. **Reading circle and line graphs** Look at the circle graph on page 158. In 1850 how many people in Texas were Mexican by birth?

3. **Identifying cause and effect** Identify the cause and the effect in the following sentence: *After the Treaty of Guadalupe Hidalgo, the size of the United States grew.*

4. **Identifying cause and effect** Was the Treaty of Velasco a cause or an effect of the Texas Revolution?

5. **Using reference sources** Which reference sources would you use to find the name of the state bird of Texas?

YESTERDAY, TODAY & *TOMORROW*

Some Texans do not know that their state was once an independent republic. Do you think it is important for people in Texas to know about events from the past? Do you think it will be important for people living in Texas 50 years from now to learn about our state's history? Why or why not?

READING ON YOUR OWN

Here are some books you might find at the library to help you learn more.

A PARADISE CALLED TEXAS
by Janice Shefelman
A story about a German family's journey into Texas during the middle 1800s includes hardship, tragedy, and adventure.

OUR TEJANO HEROES
by Sammye Munson
Outstanding Hispanic leaders of early and modern-day Texas come to life in this book.

SUSANNA OF THE ALAMO
by John Jakes
This exciting, true story is about a girl who survived the Battle of The Alamo.

UNIT PROJECT

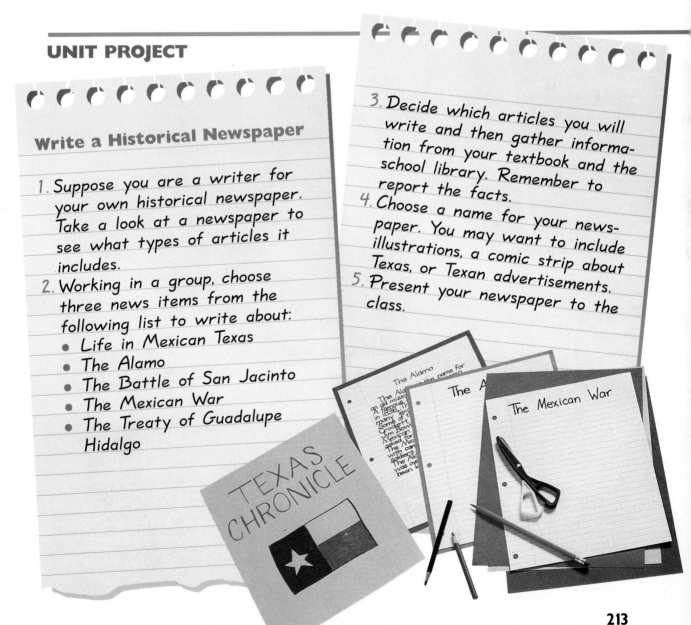

Write a Historical Newspaper

1. Suppose you are a writer for your own historical newspaper. Take a look at a newspaper to see what types of articles it includes.
2. Working in a group, choose three news items from the following list to write about:
   - Life in Mexican Texas
   - The Alamo
   - The Battle of San Jacinto
   - The Mexican War
   - The Treaty of Guadalupe Hidalgo

3. Decide which articles you will write and then gather information from your textbook and the school library. Remember to report the facts.
4. Choose a name for your newspaper. You may want to include illustrations, a comic strip about Texas, or Texan advertisements.
5. Present your newspaper to the class.

AN EARLY GRANGE
POSTER;
KIOWA CHIEF SATANTA

THE INTERIOR OF FORT SUMTER DURING THE BOMBARDMENT.—[SEE PAGE 257.]

BATTLE OF FORT SUMTER,
SOUTH CAROLINA; A DRUM
OF THE CONFEDERATE ARMY

214

Challenge and Growth

"... forever free ..."

from the Emancipation Proclamation, announced by President
Lincoln in September 1862
See page 233

The Granger Collection

WHY DOES IT MATTER?

Texas joined the United States in 1845, a difficult time in our country's history. Not even twenty years later, the Civil War would split our country apart. When the war was over, our state would face new challenges. There would also be new opportunities for Texans in our growing state.

Institute of Texan Cultures

What role did Texas play in the Civil War? How did life change for different groups of people living in our state? When the war was over, how did our state continue to grow?

Read on. You will learn about many major events that changed the state and people of Texas.

**LIZZIE JOHNSON WILLIAMS;
YOUNG TEXAN SOLDIER;
BUTTONS FROM
CONFEDERATE UNIFORMS**

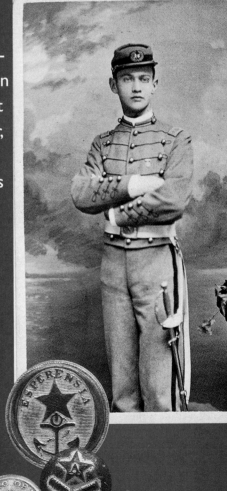

215

Adventures
with
NATIONAL
GEOGRAPHIC

Comin' Through Cowtown

How did Fort Worth come to be known as "Cowtown"? It all started in the 1860s, when long cattle drives passed through the town on their way to markets in Kansas. Then, in 1876, the Texas Pacific Railroad reached Fort Worth, allowing cattle to be shipped by rail directly from there. Before long, the Fort Worth stockyards were the largest in the world, and the city had become a major meat-packing center. Today, the stockyards area is a historic district, and the "cattle drives" there are just for show. But cattle remain Texas's biggest source of agricultural income.

GEO JOURNAL

Write lyrics for a song that cowboys might have sung around a campfire during a cattle drive.

The Civil War and Reconstruction

THINKING ABOUT GEOGRAPHY AND HISTORY

You learned that Texas joined the United States in 1845. But did you know that Texas seceded from, or left, the United States in the 1860s? The Civil War was fought between states that remained in the Union, and states, like Texas, that seceded. Read on to find out about the reasons behind the Civil War, how it ended, and how Texas rejoined the United States.

PACIFIC OCEAN

1861
AUSTIN

Texas secedes from the Union and joins the Confederacy

1863
SABINE PASS

The Davis Guards stop Union forces from invading Texas

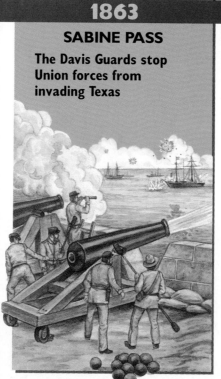

1865
PALMITO RANCH

The last land battle of the Civil War is fought

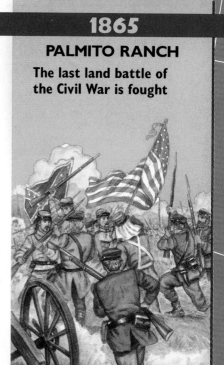

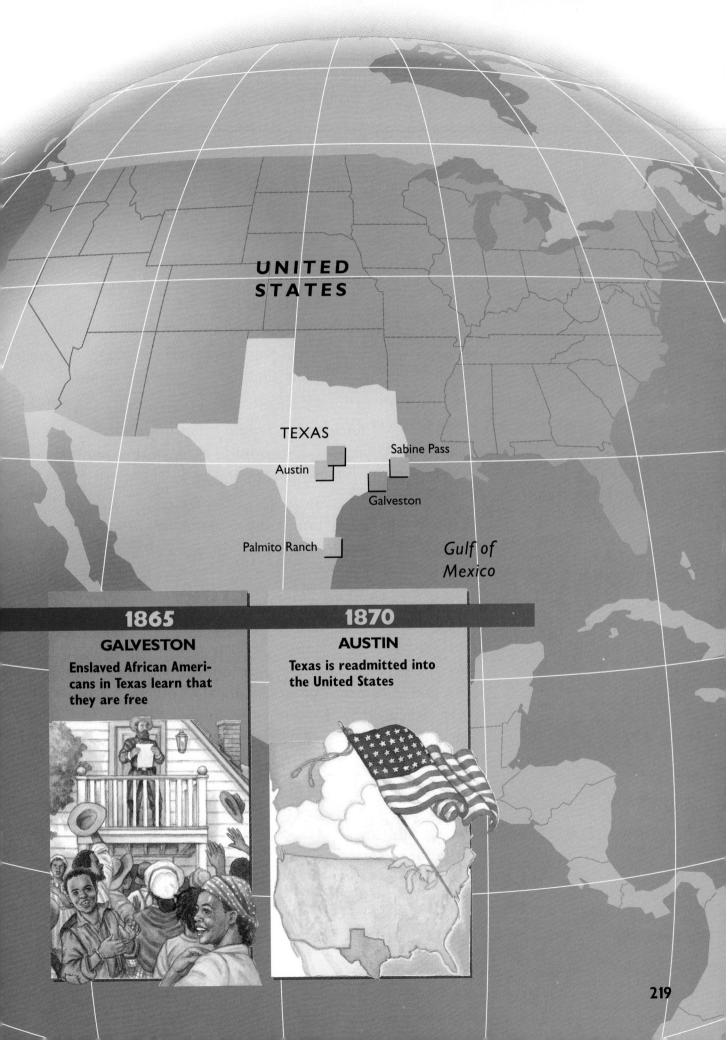

UNITED
STATES

TEXAS

Austin

Sabine Pass

Galveston

Palmito Ranch

Gulf of
Mexico

1865

GALVESTON

Enslaved African Americans in Texas learn that they are free

1870

AUSTIN

Texas is readmitted into the United States

SLAVERY IN TEXAS

READ ALOUD

In 1858 John B. Webster kept a diary about the work enslaved African Americans did on his large farm in Harrison County. What were some of the jobs?

Feb. 18 Charles and Emaline hauling cotton
Feb. 19 Patsey . . . dropping [planting] corn
Mar. 10 Emaline nursing the sick
June 7 Alsey spinning at the house
June 8 Patsey and Jane working in . . . garden
Aug. 6 Emaline and Malinda sewing

THE BIG PICTURE

Many African Americans, like those who were enslaved on John Webster's farm, did not come to our state freely. They were brought to work for no pay and with no hope of freedom. Although fewer than one in three Texas farmers owned slaves, large landowners in Texas came to depend on slavery. They believed that growing crops such as cotton required a huge number of unpaid workers if the landowners were going to make money. Without the work of enslaved people, many landowners thought that they could not have kept up their plantations. A plantation is a large farm on which crops such as cotton are grown.

Focus Activity

READ TO LEARN
What was life like for most African Americans in the 1850s?

VOCABULARY
plantation

PEOPLE
William Goyens

PLACES
Nacogdoches

KING COTTON

A popular saying in the southern United States in the 1850s was "Cotton Is King." Not only in Texas, but throughout the Southern states, cotton was the most important cash crop. As you have read, a cash crop is sold for money. Slavery was the key to making cotton "King." Look at the graph. How many more enslaved workers were there in 1855 than in 1845?

Life under Slavery

A plantation was like a small town. Its enslaved workers included blacksmiths, carpenters, and weavers. Most slaves, however, labored in the hot, dusty cotton fields from dawn to dusk. They filled sack after sack with bolls of cotton. Enslaved men and women were made to pick as much as 300 pounds of cotton a day. Smaller cotton sacks were made for children. Adeline Marshall, who worked in the fields as a child, recalled that "you went out to the field almost as soon as you could walk." Only Sundays, July 4, and Christmas week were sometimes free from work.

Enslaved women did all the household work for their owners, including the laundry. They hauled tubs to a well or river and filled them with water. Then they built fires to heat the water and they washed the clothes. When the clothes were dry the women ironed them. An iron often had a bell in it.

If the bell stopped ringing, the plantation owner knew that the worker had slowed down.

Not all slave owners were cruel, but some treated their "property" badly. They could beat or even kill slaves. The few laws that protected slaves were rarely enforced. Enslaved families could be broken up and the parents and children sold to different owners.

Slaves attempted to rebel many times. Some slaves stole crops or destroyed property. Others escaped to Northern states, Mexico, or Canada. A runaway who was caught could be severely punished.

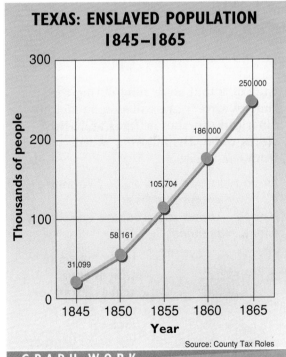

TEXAS: ENSLAVED POPULATION 1845–1865

Source: County Tax Roles

GRAPH WORK

Slavery in Texas increased in these years.

1. What was the enslaved population of Texas in 1845? What was it in 1865?
2. What do you think a chart of cotton production in Texas for the same time period would look like? Why?

A LASTING CULTURE

In spite of the hard work and lack of freedom they experienced, enslaved African Americans in Texas and other states kept alive a rich culture. Music, storytelling, and religion were all important parts of this culture.

Enslaved African Americans often sang together as they worked in the hot fields. They passed the day with songs that described their hardships, hopes, and beliefs. Some songs were ways of communicating with each other. Other songs called spirituals were more religious. These songs were based on rhythms from traditional African folk songs.

Links to MUSIC

Spirituals

Spirituals that were sung during the time of slavery are still sung in African American churches in Texas and other states today. The following words are from one spiritual.

Nobody knows the trouble I've seen
Nobody knows but Jesus.
Nobody knows the trouble I've seen
Glory, Hallelujah!

In the music section of your school library or public library, look up the words to another spiritual. What does the song talk about?

Dallas Museum of Art

This painting of an African American musician, titled *Old Slave*, was painted by William Henry Huddle in about 1889.

Stories of the Past

Oral traditions were an important part of the lives of African Americans. Stories were passed down from parents and grandparents to children. Some enslaved Texans were allowed to learn to read and write. Stories and songs, however, were a more common source for remembering the past. Read the words of Annie Mae Hunt who told a story about her grandmother. Why do you think she wanted to tell this story?

**Excerpt from *I Am Annie Mae*
by Ruthe Winegarten, in 1977.**

My grandmother was known as a house girl. That means you worked in the house with Old Mistress. . . . My grandmother always said she remembered very well the day they sold her mother. . . . And grandmother cried and cried. . . . That's all Grandma knew. She had sisters and a brother, and she never heard from them (again).

Free African Americans

By 1860 there were about 355 free African Americans in Texas. Some, like William Goyens, had settled in Texas before it became a republic. He served Sam Houston in the Texas Revolution, and then bought land which was later called "Goyen's Hill."

William Goyens and his wife

Mary lived in Nacogdoches (na kuh DOH chez) in East Texas. Goyens ran a blacksmith shop, an inn, and a mill. He started a freight-train line and bought and sold land.

Goyens could speak English, Spanish, and the Cherokee language. Sam Houston and Chief Bowles relied upon Goyens as an interpreter.

Although African Americans like Goyens had their freedom, life was difficult. Some white Texans treated them badly. In 1840 all free African Americans were ordered to leave Texas. In order to stay, individuals needed special permission from the Texas government. However, the law was not strictly enforced and many free African Americans remained in Texas—their home.

William Goyens was a wealthy businessman who owned a blacksmith shop, an inn, and a sawmill.

WHY IT MATTERS

As cotton became "King" in Texas, slavery became more common. Enslaved African Americans grew and harvested the cotton, built the buildings, did the laundry, and cooked the food on the plantations. They also created a rich African American culture that continues to be an important part of life in Texas today. In the next lesson you will read about how people in the United States became divided over the issue of slavery.

✔️ Reviewing Facts and Ideas

SUM IT UP

- Landowners believed they needed enslaved African Americans to do the work on their plantations.

- Enslaved African Americans led a hard life working on plantations.

- African Americans succeeded in creating a rich culture in spite of slavery.

THINK ABOUT IT

1. What is a plantation?

2. What were two important parts of African American culture in Texas?

3. **FOCUS** What was life like for enslaved people on a plantation?

4. **THINKING SKILL** What *effect* did the growth of cotton as a cash crop have on the growth of slavery?

5. **WRITE** With a partner or a group, write an essay, a story, a poem, or a song telling why it is important for all people to be free.

STUDY SKILLS

Writing Notes and Outlines

VOCABULARY
outline

WHY THE SKILL MATTERS

You have just read about African American life on plantations in Texas during the middle 1800s. What if you were asked to write a report about it? How would you collect information and organize it?

A plan for organizing written information about a subject is called an outline. First take notes in your own words as you read. Write down the main ideas of what you are reading. You should also jot down important facts that support the main ideas.

For your outline, place a roman numeral beside each main idea. Under each of your main ideas, group the facts that support it. Write a capital letter beside each fact.

USING THE SKILL

The following article describes the difficult life of slaves in the South. Try taking notes. Then study the outline below it to see how it organizes the information.

Slaves were up by daylight and worked until sunset. Many enslaved people planted the seed and harvested the crop. Other jobs included mending fences, and digging ditches.

Some slaves worked in the owner's house. Enslaved women cooked, did laundry, and took care of the owner's children. Some owners and their children taught enslaved people to read and write.

After a long day of work, enslaved workers returned to their cabin. At night enslaved women still had to do the cooking and laundry for their own families.

Enslaved families were sometimes broken up and sold to different owners. Family members might live nearby or be moved to another state.

According to the outline, what is the first main idea of this article? What facts support this idea?

I. The difficult life of enslaved people
   A. worked from sunrise to sunset
   B. enslaved women did their own cooking and laundry at night
   C. families were sometimes broken up

II. Field workers
   A. planted seed, harvested crops
   B. mended fences and dug ditches

III. House workers
   A. cooked, washed clothes, and took care of children
   B. sometimes learned to read

TRYING THE SKILL

Now read the article about why slavery was important to the South. Take notes as you read, then write an outline. Use the Helping Yourself box for hints. What are the main ideas? Be sure to use facts to support them. Do main ideas or supporting facts get roman numerals in your outline?

Slavery became a central part of life in the South. In all of the Southern states, the hard labor of enslaved workers kept the cotton plantations booming. Southern plantations also grew crops like tobacco, indigo, sugar, and rice. On these plantations, as well, enslaved workers were responsible for the success of the harvest. By 1860, one-quarter of all families in the South had enslaved African American workers.

Most slaveowners thought of their slaves as property. Enslaved workers were bought and sold at auctions. In addition, enslaved African Americans were often not allowed to learn to read or write. Slaveowners provided slaves with food and shelter. However, enslaved workers had to work until old age, and could never choose to leave.

Signs like this one advertised slave auctions.

REVIEWING THE SKILL

1. How does writing outlines help you to organize information?

2. How did you decide which statements were main ideas and which were supporting facts?

3. In your outline on slavery in the South, what are the supporting facts? How can you tell?

4. How can taking notes and writing an outline help you learn about history?

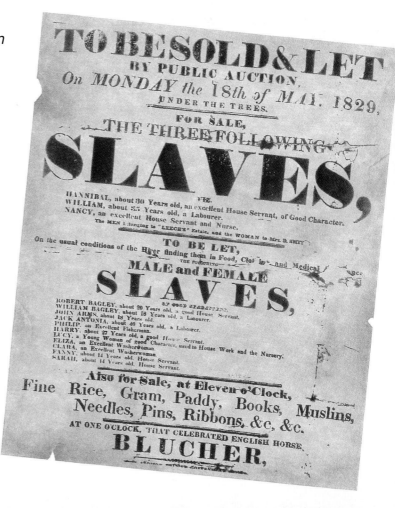

A DIVIDED NATION

READ ALOUD

"A house divided against itself cannot stand. I believe this government cannot endure [last] permanently half slave and half free. It will become all one thing or all the other." These words were spoken by Abraham Lincoln in 1858. Lincoln believed that our country could not last if it remained divided into two opposite ways of life.

THE BIG PICTURE

Life in the South was very different from life in the North. For example, most people in the South worked as farmers. Plantations grew larger and more farm workers were enslaved African Americans. By 1860 about one out of every four Texans was enslaved. In the North, however, people were moving from farms to cities to work in factories. Cotton grown in the South was shipped to the factories of the North, where it was made into cloth.

Slavery was against the law in most Northern states. Many Northerners believed that slavery should be ended everywhere in the United States. Many Southerners, however, believed that the voters of each state should be able to decide about slavery and other issues. This view was called states' rights. States' rights meant that states should be able to make their own laws about everything that had not been granted to Congress in the United States Constitution.

Focus Activity

READ TO LEARN
What led the people of the United States to fight against each other?

VOCABULARY
states' rights
abolition
Union
secede
Confederacy
Civil War

PEOPLE
Melinda Rankin
Sam Houston
Abraham Lincoln
Jefferson Davis
Edward Clark

PLACES
Fort Sumter

VOICES AGAINST SLAVERY

Many people believed slavery was wrong. Some wanted abolition, or an end to slavery. Abolitionists, both whites and free blacks, worked to end slavery.

Texans Against Slavery

Most white Texans thought that slavery was necessary in order to keep the cotton industry booming. Slave owners argued that they took good care of their slaves by providing food, clothing, and shelter. However, some other Texans disagreed.

Melinda Rankin was a Christian missionary who settled in the town of Brownsville in 1852. She became the director of a girls' school there. Rankin spoke out against slavery. Many people disagreed with her point of view. As a result, she was fired from her job.

When Jewish slave owners Joseph and Helena Landa from New Braunfels decided to free their slaves, their decision angered some Texans. Joseph was forced to flee to Mexico.

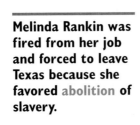

Melinda Rankin was fired from her job and forced to leave Texas because she favored abolition of slavery.

Division in Texas

Many white people in Texas and in other states where slavery was allowed disagreed with one another about the issues of states' rights and slavery. Some of these people even began to talk about leaving the Union. The word *Union* describes the group of states that make up the United States. Other Texans believed that our state should not leave the Union. They wanted to remain a part of the United States.

In 1859 Sam Houston became governor of our state. Read the passage below from a letter written by Governor Houston. What did Houston think about Texas leaving the Union?

MANY VOICES PRIMARY SOURCE

Excerpt from a letter written by Sam Houston in 1860.

If the Union be dissolved now, will we . . . have our rights better secured? After enduring civil war for years, will there be any promise of a better state of things than we now enjoy? Texas, especially, has these things to consider . . . I cannot believe that we can find at present more safety out of the Union than in it . . . Here, I take my stand! . . . I am for the Union as it is.

secured: protected
enduring: suffering through

A DIVIDED COUNTRY

The South and the North became divided over the issue of slavery. In 1861, Abraham Lincoln became President of the United States. Lincoln did not support abolition. However he was strongly against the spread of slavery. White Southerners worried that Lincoln might try to end slavery everywhere.

North and South

You have read that when Texas became a state in 1845, the country argued over slavery. Some people did not want Texas to join the Union as a slave state. Now the issue of slavery was threatening to split the Union in two.

The disagreements between Northern states and Southern states became angrier and angrier. The North and the South argued about states' rights and about slavery. As you have read, many white Southerners thought states should have the right to make laws about slavery and other matters. Many Northerners believed the national government should outlaw slavery.

Texas Leaves the Union

On January 28, 1861, leaders of the government of Texas met to decide whether or not to secede (se SEED) from, or leave, the Union. After four days of discussion, they voted to leave the Union. Texas and

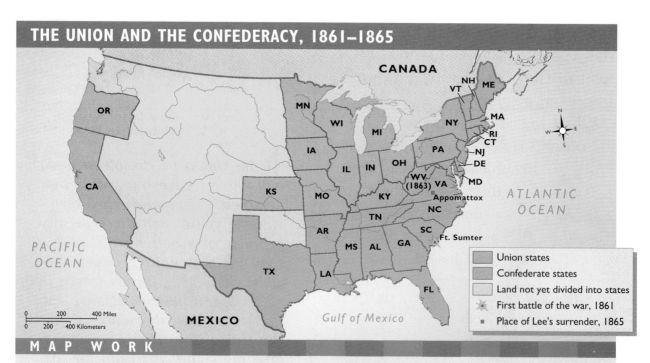

THE UNION AND THE CONFEDERACY, 1861–1865

Legend:
- Union states
- Confederate states
- Land not yet divided into states
- First battle of the war, 1861
- Place of Lee's surrender, 1865

MAP WORK

During the Civil War, the United States split into two separate countries.

1. In what state did the first battle of the Civil War take place?
2. Why did much of the western land belong to neither the Union nor the Confederacy?
3. How were the Union and the Confederacy divided geographically?
4. Looking at the map, why do you think Texas joined the Confederacy?

The Granger Collection

Confederate cannons (top) fired at Fort Sumter. Jefferson Davis (right) was President of the Confederacy.

ten other Southern states joined to form the new Confederate States of America, or the Confederacy. Jefferson Davis of Mississippi was elected President of this new country. Look at the map on page 228 to find the states of the Confederacy.

You have read that Governor Sam Houston did not want Texas to secede. He refused to take an oath of loyalty to the Confederacy and was removed from office. He was replaced as governor by Edward Clark. Clark took the oath willingly.

The Civil War Begins

In April 1861 Confederate soldiers fired at Fort Sumter, a Union fort in South Carolina. This started the bloodiest conflict in American

history. It was called the Civil War, or the "War Between the States." It would last over four years.

WHY IT MATTERS

In 1861, when Abraham Lincoln became President, arguments about states' rights and slavery became more heated. Texas and ten other states seceded from the Union and formed their own country called the Confederacy. This act led to the outbreak of the Civil War.

Reviewing Facts and Ideas

SUM IT UP

- The issues of states' rights and slavery divided the nation.
- Melinda Rankin and other Texas abolitionists spoke out against slavery.
- Texas and ten other Southern states seceded from the Union in 1861 and formed the Confederacy.
- The firing on Fort Sumter marked the beginning of the Civil War.

THINK ABOUT IT

1. What is an abolitionist?
2. Why did Texas decide to leave the Union and join the Confederacy?
3. **FOCUS** What were some of the events that led to the Civil War?
4. **THINKING SKILL** What were some of the reasons why Texas and other Southern states _decided_ to form the Confederacy?
5. **GEOGRAPHY** Look at the map on page 228. Name the states that made up the Union.

229

1800   1825   1861 1865   1900

TEXAS GOES TO WAR

The Granger Collection

Focus Activity

READ TO LEARN
What role did Texas play in the Civil War?

VOCABULARY
cavalry
Terry's Texas Rangers
Hood's Texas Brigade
Davis Guards
blockade
Emancipation
    Proclamation

PEOPLE
Rosanna Osterman
Robert E. Lee
Ulysses S. Grant

PLACES
Sabine Pass
Palmito Ranch

READ ALOUD

"Brother Joe made us his last visit in 1863. I saw him mount his horse, Grey Eagle, and ride away never to return. Oh, war, cruel, cruel war."

These words by Eudora Moore of Texas describe what war was like for many people in both the South and the North. Families were torn apart as fathers, sons, and brothers went off to war. Many never returned.

THE BIG PICTURE

When word of the Fort Sumter attack reached Texas in 1861, white men and boys across the state started joining the Confederate Army. Men as young as 17 joined up. Historians are not sure how many Texans fought in the Confederate Army— anywhere between 60,000 and 90,000. These soldiers fought in every major battle of the war. Not all Texans fought for the Confederacy, however. Between 2,000 and 3,000 men, including some former slaves, fought on the side of the Union Army.

230

TEXANS IN THE CONFEDERATE ARMY

Most of the fighting in the Civil War took place in eastern states such as Virginia and Maryland. To get to these states, Texas soldiers traveled far from their homes. Because of their experience with horses, many Texans fought in the cavalry. A cavalry is a group of soldiers who fight on horseback.

The Fighting Forces of Texas

Terry's Texas Rangers were cavalry soldiers led by Colonel Benjamin Franklin Terry. They loved to show off their skill with horses, and were known for their bravery. Terry's Texas Rangers fought in battles in half a dozen states east of the Mississippi River.

Hood's Texas Brigade was led by General John Bell Hood. Members of this brigade, or group, constantly put themselves in danger while fighting against Union soldiers.

Of the brigade's 4,480 members, only 557 were still alive at war's end.

The Battle of Sabine Pass

In 1863 Union forces tried to invade Texas. They planned to sail into Texas through the Sabine Pass and then capture Beaumont and Houston. The Sabine Pass is the place where Sabine Lake opens into the Gulf of Mexico. It was protected by Fort Griffin. Fewer than 50 soldiers were stationed at the fort. They were called the Davis Guards.

The Union Army arrived at the Sabine Pass with 5,000 soldiers and more than 20 ships. The Davis Guards were far outnumbered. But they damaged two Union gunboats and took about 350 prisoners. The Union Army was forced to turn back. This victory by Confederate soldiers came at an important time. The Battle of Sabine Pass restored people's confidence in the strength of the Confederacy.

Terry's Texas Rangers **wore hats like this one (below). Members of** Hood's Texas Brigade **(right) posed for this photo after the Civil War was over.**

LIFE AT HOME

While husbands, fathers, and sons were away at war, women, children, and enslaved workers struggled to keep farms and businesses going.

Wartime Changes

In addition to providing troops, Texas also supported the Confederate cause in other ways. Farmers turned their cotton fields into corn fields to help feed the soldiers. Texans built factories in Austin and Tyler to make weapons. Other factories were built here to make wagons, blankets, shoes, and saddles to be used by Confederate soldiers.

In Austin a group of women met at the Capitol Building to sew clothes for the soldiers. Other women served as nurses for soldiers.

Rosanna Osterman turned her mansion in Galveston into an army hospital. She used her sheets to make bandages and her carpets to make slippers for the soldiers.

Enslaved women worked even harder during the war. They had to take on more of the men's work and also helped make clothing for the soldiers. Some had to stay up until midnight spinning cotton. They then had to rise at dawn the next day.

Union leaders worried about all the products that Texas was sending to Confederate soldiers in the Southern states. They also worried about the cotton that Texas sent to Europe in exchange for goods needed for the Confederacy. In an effort to stop this flow, the Union Navy set up a blockade of Galveston and other ports.

These nurses (left) were among many women who served during the Civil War. The shoes (below) belonged to a Confederate soldier. The jacket and buttons (far left) were worn by soldiers from Texas.

During a blockade, troops shut off an area to prevent trade.

Thousands of slaveholders from other Southern states brought their slaves to Texas to escape the Union Army. By the end of the war, the number of enslaved people in Texas had grown from 186,000 to 250,000.

The End of Slavery and the Civil War

In September 1862 President Lincoln announced the Emancipation Proclamation (e man sih PAY shun prahk luh MAY shun). This official announcement said that on January 1, 1863, all slaves in the Confederate states would be "forever free." However, the enslaved people of Texas did not learn that they had been freed for another two years.

In April 1865 Confederate General Robert E. Lee surrendered to Union General Ulysses S. Grant at Appomattox, Virginia. But news of the war's end traveled slowly to Texans 1,000 miles away.

On May 13, 1865, after Lee had surrendered, the last land battle of the Civil War took place at Palmito Ranch. Union forces on Brazos Island moved inland and tried to capture Brownsville. They were defeated at nearby Palmito Ranch by Confederate troops. Union soldiers who were taken prisoner told the Confederates of Lee's surrender. You can see the site of this battle on the Infographic on page 234.

Freedom

On June 19, 1865, enslaved African Americans in Texas finally learned that they were free. Major General Gordon Granger of the Union Army stood on a balcony in Galveston. In a loud voice he read an order: "The people of Texas are informed that . . . all slaves are free." African Americans from Texas have celebrated June 19th, or *Juneteenth* for short, ever since.

When word of their freedom reached the enslaved Texans, they rejoiced. One former slave named Felix Haywood recalled, "Everyone was singing. We [were] all walking on golden clouds." Still, most knew life would be difficult. As one said, "Freedom could make folks proud, but it didn't make them rich."

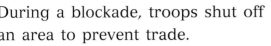

Where else in the United States is June 19th celebrated?

In 1979 June 19th became a state holiday in Texas. The holiday's official name is Emancipation Day. Many African Americans from Texas now live in other states, but they have kept the tradition of the June 19th celebration alive in their new homes. As a result, June 19th is now celebrated all over the United States, with barbecues, parties, and prayers.

Infographic

Major Battles of the Civil War

Although the major battles of the Civil War were fought in the Southeast, several important battles took place in Texas. In what part of Texas were they fought?

BATTLE OF SABINE PASS

September 8, 1863 Although greatly outnumbered, Lieutenant Dick Dowling and the Davis Guards turned back Union ships.

The Institute of Texan Cultures

The Institute of Texan Cultures

BATTLE OF GALVESTON

January 1, 1863 Soldiers led by General John B. Magruder returned Galveston to Confederate control.

BATTLE OF PALMITO RANCH

May 13, 1865 In a battle fought a month after the war had ended, Confederate Colonel John S. Ford's troops defeated Union soldiers near Brownsville.

Texas Southmost College

The Civil War was not fought only in Texas and South Carolina. The chart shows some of the major battles that took place in other states.

BATTLE	DATE & PLACE
Bull Run	1861, Manassas, VA
Monitor and Merrimac	1862, near Hampton Roads, VA
Bull Run	1862, Manassas, VA
Antietam	1862, Sharpsburg, MD
Fredericksburg	1862, Fredericksburg, VA
Vicksburg	1863, Vicksburg, MI
Gettysburg	1863, Gettysburg, PA

The Granger Collection

FORT SUMTER
April 12, 1861 The Confederate attack on Union soldiers at Fort Sumter was the first battle of the Civil War.

WHY IT MATTERS

After four long years the Civil War was over. The Confederacy was gone and the Union had survived. Soon after the war slavery was outlawed in the entire United States. But the cost of the Civil War was huge. More than 600,000 Americans had died, and the South and some of the North lay in ruins.

✓ Reviewing Facts and Ideas

SUM IT UP

- Between 60,000 and 90,000 Confederate soldiers came from Texas.
- Many women helped the war effort by sewing clothes or working as nurses.
- General Robert E. Lee surrendered to General Ulysses S. Grant in April 1865, ending the Civil War.

THINK ABOUT IT

1. Who were Terry's Texas Rangers?
2. Why is Emancipation Day celebrated on June 19th?
3. **FOCUS** What role did Texas play in the Civil War?
4. **THINKING SKILL** Put the following events in the *order* in which they occurred: the Emancipation Proclamation, the battle at Palmito Ranch, Juneteenth, the Battle of Sabine Pass, Lee surrenders to Grant at Appomattox.
5. **GEOGRAPHY** Look at the Infographic map on the opposite page. Why was it important for Texans to keep ports free of Union control?

Focus Activity

READ TO LEARN
What changes took place in Texas after the Civil War?

VOCABULARY
Reconstruction
Freedmen's Bureau
amendment
Black Codes
sharecropper

PEOPLE
Andrew Johnson
Edmund J. Davis
George T. Ruby

RECONSTRUCTION

READ ALOUD

"They love their school."

These were the words of a teacher who taught at a school for freed slaves in Texas after the Civil War. As you will read, many changes came to our state during this time.

THE BIG PICTURE

After the war, the people of Texas and other Southern states wondered how they would ever again be a part of the United States of America. President Lincoln believed that the South should not be punished. Instead, he promised to bring the Union back together "with malice toward none . . . and charity for all."

But before President Lincoln could carry out his plans, tragedy struck. On April 14, 1865, Lincoln was shot in a theater in Washington, D.C., and later died. Now his plans and goals were in the hands of a new President, Andrew Johnson. President Johnson faced the huge task of Reconstruction. Reconstruction is the time period in which the Southern states were brought back into the Union. The terrible wounds caused by four years of war between the North and the South had to be healed.

As part of Reconstruction, government and laws had to be redesigned. Many changes were made in Southern states. Slowly, people in Texas and throughout the South began to rebuild their lives and look to the future.

AFTER THE WAR

By the end of 1865, over 48,000 Union soldiers came to Texas. They were sent to make sure that enslaved people were freed and to make sure that Texans obeyed the laws of Reconstruction.

The Freedmen's Bureau

A month before President Lincoln died, the United States Congress established the Freedmen's Bureau. This organization helped former slaves, now known as freedmen, to build new lives. It started schools and hospitals throughout the South. Between 1865 and 1866 Texas had about 90 bureau schools, though most were Sunday schools and night schools. Church groups in the North helped support these schools. The Freedmen's Bureau also gave out food and clothing to poor people. It also helped African Americans to find jobs, and provided them with land to farm. In Making a Difference on page 241, you will read that helping others is still important to Texans today.

Classes were held in churches and even on some plantations throughout Texas. Also, new buildings were built to serve as schoolhouses. In some schools, former slaves worked as teachers. Most teachers, both black and white, were women. They taught reading, writing, arithmetic, and geography.

Although many African Americans were still unable to attend school, the Freedmen's Bureau was a big success in Texas. By 1870 about 20,000 black Texans had learned to read and write.

Archives Division, Texas State Library

Brazoria County Historical Museum

Isabella Dance and her husband Charlie Brown (above) were among many freed slaves who owned successful farms in Texas. Mariah Carr (right) spun thread to make a living.

RECONSTRUCTION LAWS

President Johnson tried to bring Southern states back into the Union "with malice toward none." Few Southerners were punished, and Johnson alowed Southern states to begin forming new governments. These new governments had to declare loyalty to the United States and agree to abolish slavery.

Amendments to the Constitution

Four months before the Civil War ended in April 1865, Congress passed the Thirteenth Amendment. An amendment is an addition to the United States Constitution. The Thirteenth Amendment, approved by the states after the war, ended slavery everywhere in the United States.

After the war, in order to make sure that African Americans would be treated fairly, Congress proposed another amendment to the United States Constitution. The Fourteenth Amendment gave former slaves all the rights of other citizens. Read these amendments on the chart.

The governments of the Southern states refused to accept the Fourteenth Amendment. They also passed laws called Black Codes that restricted the rights of freedmen. Under these laws, in some states African Americans were not allowed to own land. This angered many members of Congress. In 1867, as a result, Congress passed much tougher laws for Reconstruction. One of these new laws required Southern states to accept the Fourteenth Amendment before being allowed back into the United States.

Life Under Reconstruction

Texans faced many changes during Reconstruction. Farms suffered from the loss of enslaved workers. For African Americans the joy of freedom was replaced by a concern for survival.

Landowners had to do more work on their land without enslaved workers. They often had no money to pay the farm workers. For this reason, many owners divided their land and

AMENDMENTS TO THE UNITED STATES CONSTITUTION

THIRTEENTH AMENDMENT
Abolition of Slavery
Slavery is abolished, or made illegal, in the United States.

FOURTEENTH AMENDMENT
Rights of Citizens
Every citizen of the United States is also a citizen of the state in which he or she lives. No state may pass a law limiting the rights of citizens or take away a person's life, liberty, or property unfairly. Every person must be treated equally under the law.

CHART WORK

Congress can pass an amendment to make a change to the Constitution.
1. What did the Thirteenth Amendment change?
2. Why do you think the Fourteenth Amendment was needed?

rented it to sharecroppers. A sharecropper is a person who grows crops on someone else's land. The sharecropper then pays a *share*, or part, of that crop to the owner of the land. Some landowners gave sharecroppers a mule, seed, a plow, and other tools.

John Mosley and his family became sharecroppers. Mosley recalled that the landowner he worked for "hauled off all our crop, paid our debts and if there were any (money) left he gave us that, but most of the time . . . we would still be in debt."

Many freed African American families stayed and worked as sharecroppers on the plantations where they had been enslaved. Some former slaves went looking for family members from whom they had been separated. Still others traveled to cities and other states to find work.

A Change in Government

Many changes also took place in our state government during this time. A new state constitution protected the voting rights of African American men over the age of 21. But such changes angered many white Texans. Some joined secret groups such as the Ku Klux Klan. The Klan threatened, beat up, and sometimes killed African Americans and other people. Many whites believed that the new government was not treating them fairly. They thought that some new leaders, both white and black, were using their positions to become rich.

After the Civil War, many African Americans in Texas and throughout the South worked as sharecroppers.

TEXAS RE-ENTERS THE UNION

In 1870 Edmund J. Davis became governor of Texas. He followed the laws of Reconstruction and Texans accepted the Fourteenth Amendment. Texas was allowed back into the United States on March 30, 1870.

The Texas elections of 1869 marked an important change in Texas government. Thirteen African Americans were voted into state government for the first time. One of these new leaders was George T. Ruby. He had come to Texas in September 1866 to work for the Freedmen's Bureau. Later, he became president of the Loyal Union League of Texas, a group to which many African Americans belonged.

Archives Division, Texas State Library

George T. Ruby was elected to serve in the Texas state government in 1869.

WHY IT MATTERS

During Reconstruction people struggled to recover from the Civil War. African Americans gained freedom and many became involved in government. When Reconstruction ended in the United States in 1877, however, a number of these changes were reversed. In the next chapter you will read more about how our state changed.

✓ Reviewing Facts and Ideas

SUM IT UP

- Reconstruction began in 1865.
- The Freedmen's Bureau helped African Americans and other poor people during Reconstruction.
- Many freed African Americans became sharecroppers.
- Texas was accepted back into the United States in 1870.

THINK ABOUT IT

1. How did the Freedmen's Bureau help people in our state during Reconstruction?

2. What did the Fourteenth Amendment change about the Constitution of the United States?

3. **FOCUS** What changes took place in Texas after the Civil War?

4. **THINKING SKILL** *Compare* and *contrast* the life of African Americans in Texas before and after the Civil War.

5. **WRITE** Write a letter to a friend from a freed African American explaining why he or she decided to become a sharecropper.

CITIZENSHIP
MAKING A DIFFERENCE

ASTROS at Work

MESQUITE, TEXAS—The J.C. Austin ASTROS are not a team of space travelers. They are a team of talkers. Their name, ASTROS, stands for Austin Students Trying to Reach Other Students. These fourth-through-sixth graders at J.C. Austin Elementary School are peer mediators. This means they help settle arguments between students their own age. They call it "kids helping kids."

Mediators are elected by their classmates at the beginning of fourth grade. They receive training from school counselor Eunice Futrell, who started the program in 1989. "Most problems," says Mrs. Futrell, "start over rumor or gossip, ownership of personal property, name calling, or money." Sixth graders Antoine Hood and Amber Dugan have been mediators for three years.

Mediators are called in by teachers or the students involved in the argument. They go in pairs to the mediation table outside the library. First, students have to agree to certain rules. "They must agree," says Amber "to work to solve the problem, tell the truth, no name calling or put downs while the other person is talking, no interrupting, and no physical contact."

Antoine explains how the process works. "First we choose somebody to tell their side of the story. Then we restate what they said and how they felt about it. Then we ask the other person to tell their side of the story. Next we ask both people how they can solve the problem. If they can't think of a solution on their own, we give them some hints." Once a solution has been agreed upon, students sign a written agreement. "Mediation," says Antoine, "teaches people that arguing doesn't always solve the problem. It teaches them a better way to solve problems."

" . . . arguing doesn't . . . solve the problem."

Antoine Hood II

Amber Dugan

241

CHAPTER 7 REVIEW

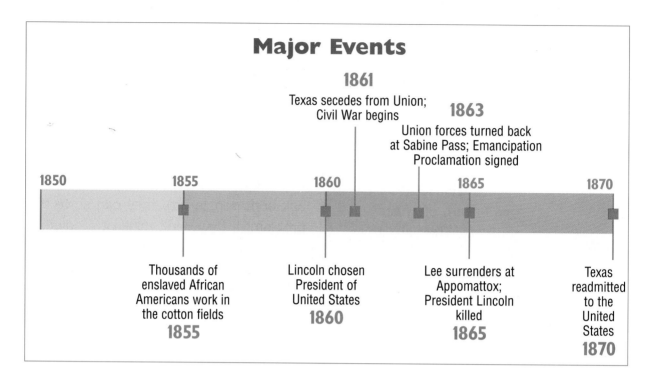

Major Events

1861
Texas secedes from Union;
Civil War begins

1863
Union forces turned back
at Sabine Pass; Emancipation
Proclamation signed

1850   1855   1860   1865   1870

Thousands of
enslaved African
Americans work in
the cotton fields
1855

Lincoln chosen
President of
United States
1860

Lee surrenders at
Appomattox;
President Lincoln
killed
1865

Texas
readmitted
to the
United
States
1870

THINKING ABOUT VOCABULARY

Number a sheet of paper from 1 to 10. Next to each number write the word or term from the list below that matches the statement.

abolition   plantation
amendment   Reconstruction
blockade   secede
cavalry   sharecropper
Confederacy   states' rights

1. A large farm on which great amounts of crops such as cotton are grown

2. Leave a group, such as the Union

3. The belief that each state should make its own laws

4. The term for an end to slavery

5. The name for the group of states that chose to leave the United States

6. A group of soldiers fighting on horseback

7. The shutting off of an area by troops and ships to prevent trade

8. An addition to the United States Constitution

9. The word used to describe the Confederate states being brought back into the Union

10. A person who grows crops on someone else's land

THINKING ABOUT FACTS

1. What was the most important cash crop in Texas in the 1800s?

2. Who was Melinda Rankin?

3. Name two of the issues that divided Southern and Northern states during the early 1800s.

4. Who was Jefferson Davis?

5. What was the purpose of the Freedmen's Bureau? Name three ways that the Freedman's Bureau helped former slaves.

THINK AND WRITE

WRITING A PARAGRAPH
Write a list of five new vocabulary words from Chapter 7. Then write a paragraph with five sentences using each of the words.

WRITING A SUMMARY
Reread Lesson 1 in Chapter 7. Then write a summary of the information you have read in the lesson.

WRITING A NEWSPAPER ARTICLE
Suppose that you were a newspaper reporter in Texas during the 1860s. Write a newspaper article describing the end of the Civil War. Be sure to include details such as the date, the location, and the names of the leaders from both sides.

APPLYING STUDY SKILLS

WRITING AN OUTLINE
1. What is an outline? How can writing outlines help you organize information?
2. What are the steps in writing an outline?
3. Read the section in Lesson 2 titled "Voices Against Slavery." Take notes as you read and then write an outline of the section.
4. Read the section in Lesson 3 titled "Life at Home." Then write an outline of the section.
5. How can taking notes and writing an outline help you to write a research report about the Civil War?

Summing Up the Chapter

Use the following cause-and-effect chart to organize information from the chapter. Copy the chart on a sheet of paper. Then fill in the blank spaces on the chart. When you have completed the chart, use it to write a paragraph that answers the question "How did the issues of states' rights and slavery change Texas history during the 1800s?"

CAUSE	EFFECT
Cotton is the most important cash crop in Texas.	
	All slaves in the Confederate States are "forever free".
Southern and Northern states disagree on states' rights and slavery.	
	Texas is readmitted to the United States in 1870.

CHAPTER
8

A Growing State

THINKING ABOUT
GEOGRAPHY AND HISTORY

In Texas the years after the Civil War were a time of new growth and new challenges. Railroads created new and exciting opportunities to connect distant parts of our state. Yet some people, such as cowboys and Native Americans, would find their ways of life changed forever. In Chapter 8 you will learn about the many ways Texas was growing and changing as the 1900s approached.

PACIFIC OCEAN

late 1800s	1869	1874
SAN ANTONIO	**HOUSTON**	**PALO DURO CANYON**
Cattle drives begin along the Chisholm Trail	Chinese immigrants arrive in Texas to work on the railroads	United States soldiers defeat remaining Native American villages

UNITED
STATES

Palo Duro
Canyon

TEXAS

Austin

Houston

San Antonio

Gulf of
Mexico

1876

AUSTIN

New state Constitution
is written

245

CATTLE TRAILS TO THE NORTH

Focus Activity

READ TO LEARN
What was the life of a cowboy like?

VOCABULARY
longhorn
brand
cattle drive
stampede
barbed wire

PEOPLE
Lizzie Johnson Williams
Joseph Glidden

PLACES
Chisholm Trail

READ ALOUD

"A cowboy . . . rose at dawn, shook down his clothing, pulled on his boots and hat, and dashed cold water on his gritty face. He seldom bothered to shave or brush his teeth. Then he tore into a breakfast of hot cakes swimming in syrup, bacon or salt pork, and sourdough biscuits with jam."

This is how writer Marian T. Place described the beginning of a cowboy's day in her book **American Cattle Trails East and West.**

THE BIG PICTURE

As you read in Chapter 4, Spanish explorers first came to Texas over 400 years ago. They brought along cattle for meat and horses to ride. Spanish and Mexican settlers soon became ranchers along the Rio Grande and the San Antonio and Nueces rivers. Their cattle were longhorns. The distance between the tips of their horns could be as much as six feet! Some of these longhorn cattle got away and ran wild.

Over the years many new settlers to Texas became ranchers. They raised the animals they brought with them and the wild cattle they caught. The number of cattle in Texas multiplied. By the end of the Civil War in 1865, Texas was known as the "cattle kingdom." Even today there are more livestock than people in our state.

ON THE PLAINS

The men who herded the cattle became known as cowboys. A cowboy's outfit was easy to spot. A broad-brimmed hat shaded his eyes. A bandanna kept the dust from the prairie out of his mouth. His deep-heeled boots rested easily in the saddle's stirrups.

Who were the cowboys? Many were Tejanos. Others came from different parts of the United States. At least one out of every seven cowboys were African Americans.

Working on the Range

What did the cowboys do? Millions of cattle roamed the open Texas plains at the time. There were no fences dividing the land. Ranchers hired cowboys to keep track of their herds. "Line riders" patrolled the boundaries of the ranch, protecting the cattle from thieves and wild animals.

The cowboys moved the longhorns from one grazing spot to another. They marked each animal with a brand or design. The brand identified the ranch to which the cattle belonged.

One rancher described the way cowboys talked about their horses. Why do you think this was a favorite topic for them?

MANY VOICES PRIMARY SOURCE

Excerpt from *The Story of the S.M.S. Ranch*, by Frank S. Hastings, 1919.

Every horse has a name and every man on the ranch knows every horse by name. . . . A man who does not love his mount [horse] does not last long in the cow business. . . . Cowboys' principal topic is their horses or of men who ride, and every night about the camp fire, they trade horses, run imaginary horse races, or romance [invent stories] about their pet ponies.

Texas longhorns like this one (below right) are tall and strong. Huge numbers were taken to market along the Chisholm Trail (below).

Henry Nelson, Wichita Art Museum

THE CATTLE DRIVE

By the middle 1860s there was a great demand for beef in the Northeast. There were not enough farms and ranches in the Northeast to feed the region's crowded cities. The number of cattle in the North had dropped because so many had been needed to feed the Union Army during the Civil War.

Cattle in Texas sold for $4 each. That same animal was worth $40 in the Northeast! Yet how could ranchers in Texas get their cattle to these faraway markets in the North? The answer was the cattle drive.

In a cattle drive, cowboys herded the cattle north from Texas. As you can see from the map on this page, the cattle trails led to railroad lines in Colorado, Nebraska, Kansas, and Missouri. From these places the animals were transported east by train. Between 1866 and 1890, about ten million cattle were driven from Texas to markets in Kansas and Missouri. The cattle industry became the biggest industry in the western part of the United States at that time.

Life on the Trail

Many ranchers drove their herds up the Chisholm (CHIHZ um) Trail. This route stretched about 800 miles from San Antonio, Texas, to Abilene, Kansas. Usually a herd could cover only about ten miles each day. As a result, the drive lasted three months or more.

During the 1880s Lizzie Johnson Williams was one of the few women to travel the Chisholm Trail. Williams used money she earned as a teacher

CATTLE TRAILS IN THE 1800s

Legend:
- • City
- — Cattle trail
- +++ Railroad
- Present-day borders are shown.

0 125 250 Miles
0 125 250 Kilometers

MAP WORK

Cattle trails were part of Texas from the 1860s to the 1880s.

1. Which trail ran from San Antonio to Ogallala?
2. Which trails stopped at the Kansas Pacific Railroad?

Lizzie Johnson Williams used the money she earned writing newspaper articles to begin her cattle business.

The Institute of Texan Cultures

and writer to buy longhorn cattle. Soon her ranch in Driftwood, near Austin, grew so large that she was called the "Cattle Queen of Texas." Unlike the cowboys who worked for her, Williams traveled in a horse-drawn buggy. All the same, she rose early each morning to count the cattle in her herd.

The members of a cattle drive included a trail boss, a group of cowboys on horseback, and a cook. The cook drove the chuckwagon. The chuckwagon was like a kitchen on wheels. It had a large box at the back end that contained food and cooking supplies to be used on the trail. The cook prepared beans, stews, beef dishes, biscuits, and coffee for everyone.

Danger on the Trail

A cattle drive was hard, dangerous work. A small number of cowboys guided thousands of longhorns across plains, deserts, and rivers. They faced droughts and violent thunderstorms. Sometimes the herd was attacked by outlaws.

Longhorns were a wild breed of cattle. If something frightened them, they were quick to take off and run. When a herd of cattle ran wild, cowboys shouted, "Stampede!" The worst stampedes usually happened at night. Storms with thunder and lightning probably caused more stampedes than anything else.

Cowboys slept with their boots on to be ready in case of a stampede.

To stop a stampede, they jumped on their horses and tried to make a circle around the cattle. Bringing the herd under control sometimes took several hours.

The life of the cowboy could be lonely. Cowboys spent many nights alone in the saddle guarding the herd. To pass the time, they sang songs. Some songs told tall tales about imaginary cowboys. In others, like the one on the next page, the singer longed for his distant home. The songs quieted the herd.

like the one on the next page

Links to HOME ECONOMICS

Trail Treats

With your family at home or your class at school, try baking biscuits like the ones cowboys ate. First make sourdough starter. In a glass jar, mix 1 package active dry yeast, 2 cups warm water at about 85°F, and 2 cups flour. Stir with a wooden (not metal) spoon. Let the mixture stand uncovered in a warm place for 4 to 7 days. Stir it once a day. When it bubbles and smells sour, it's ready! Store the sourdough starter in the refrigerator.

Then put 3/4 cup flour in a bowl. Make a hole in the center. Add 1 cup of sourdough starter. Stir in 1 teaspoon each of salt, sugar, and baking soda. Add 1 tablespoon of butter. Mix until crumbs form. Add more flour to make dough stiff. Pinch off dough for one biscuit. Form a ball and dip it in melted butter. Place the biscuit in an 8-inch cake pan. Continue with the remaining dough, filling the pan. Let the dough rise in a warm place for 30 minutes. Bake 15 to 20 minutes at 425°F.

249

THE TEXAS COWBOY

Traditional Cowboy Song
Arranged by Dan Fox

Oh, I'm a Tex-as cow-boy so far a-way from home. If I get back to Tex-as, I nev-er-more shall roam. Mon-tan-a is too cold for me, the win-ters are too long. Be-fore the round-ups do be-gin our mon-ey is all gone.

Fort Worth Star-Telegram

END OF THE CATTLE DRIVES

The period of great cattle drives lasted only a short time—about 25 years. Why did they end?

In 1873 an Iowa farmer named Joseph Glidden invented barbed wire. Barbed wire has sharp points. It was used for fences, which began to close in the vast open spaces. Cowboys needed open spaces for their cattle to move and graze on. As one angry trail driver put it in 1884: "Fences, sir, are the curse of the country." Luckily for ranchers, railroads were built through Texas and trains carried the cattle to market.

WHY IT MATTERS

In 1995 a group of cowboys held a cattle drive like those of the 1870s. They drove 250 longhorns from Fort Worth all the way north to Miles City, Montana. The trip was 1,600 miles, and it took six months. This cattle drive was different from ones of the past. Modern life created new challenges for these cowboys. For example, police cars were needed to get the cattle

On this modern cattle drive, cowboys used plastic bags for their garbage and the trail boss kept in touch with his Texas office through a fax machine.

across busy highways. However, it showed that the cowboy spirit still lives in our state and in the American West.

Reviewing Facts and Ideas

SUM IT UP

- Texas became the "cattle kingdom" after the Civil War.
- Cowboys moved cattle to and from grazing points and made sure they were safe.
- Cattle trails led to railroads that carried cattle to northern markets.

THINK ABOUT IT

1. When did the worst stampedes usually happen?

2. Who was Lizzie Johnson Williams?

3. **FOCUS** What was life like for cowboys on a cattle drive?

4. **THINKING SKILL** List three _questions_ you would ask if you could interview a cowboy.

5. **GEOGRAPHY** Look at the map on page 248. What bodies of water did cowboys come across along the trail?

STUDYSKILLS

Identifying Fact and Opinion

VOCABULARY

fact
opinion

WHY THE SKILL MATTERS

You have just read about cattle drives. Suppose someone told you that longhorn cattle grew more slowly than other cattle raised in our state today. This statement is a **fact**. You can check that it is true by looking up the information in a reference source, such as an encyclopedia. A fact is a statement that can be proven.

Suppose, however, that somebody told you that beef from a longhorn tastes better than any other kind of meat. This statement is an **opinion**. An opinion expresses one person's belief or feeling, not a fact that can be proven. Another person might believe that pork tastes better. Still another might prefer lamb.

Facts and opinions are very different kinds of statements. You must be able to tell them apart because the decisions you make should be based on facts. Use the Helping Yourself box to guide you in identifying these two kinds of statements.

USING THE SKILL

Read this passage about the beef cattle industry in Texas. Then identify the statements that are facts and those that are opinions.

> *Texas earns more than $5 billion a year from its beef cattle industry. The mild climate of Texas allows the cattle to graze outside all year. Some people think that large cattle ranches should be replaced by factories. They believe that more people would rather work in a factory than on a ranch.*

Which statements in the passage are facts? Which are opinions? The first two sentences are facts. They can be proven. You can check the information in a reference source.

The last two sentences are opinions. They contain word clues that often appear in opinions: *think*, *should*, and *believe*. Opinions do not always have word clues, however.

TRYING THE SKILL

You have practiced identifying facts and opinions in a passage about the cattle industry. Now read this passage about how one Texas cowboy became one of the greatest rodeo riders in history. As you read the passage, pay attention for some of the word clues that indicate when the writer is giving an opinion.

> Bill Pickett was a famous cowboy and rodeo rider. He performed with other famous cowboys such as Tom Mix and Will Rogers in the 101 Ranch Show. Some people think he invented the sport of bulldogging. Bulldogging is wrestling a bull to the ground with your bare hands and flipping the animal on its back. Zack Miller, owner of the 101 Ranch, believed Bill Pickett was "the greatest sweat-and-dirt cowboy that ever was."

Which statements do you think could be proven true? How? Which statements do you think are opinions? What did you do to identify the facts and the opinions?

REVIEWING THE SKILL

1. How is a fact different from an opinion?

2. Why does a word clue like *believe* often tell you that the speaker is expressing an opinion?

3. How would the reference section of the library be able to help you to decide whether certain statements were facts or opinions?

4. When is it useful to be able to tell a fact from an opinion?

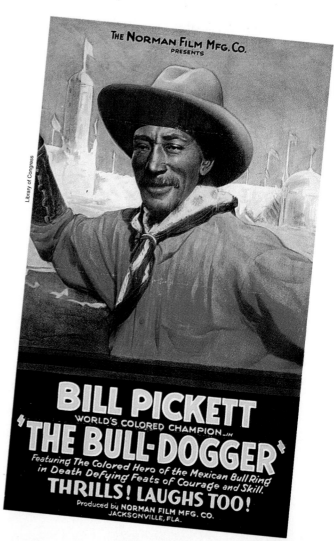

Library of Congress

THE NORMAN FILM MFG. CO.
PRESENTS

BILL PICKETT
WORLD'S COLORED CHAMPION *in*
"THE BULL-DOGGER"
Featuring The Colored Hero of the Mexican Bull Ring in Death Defying Feats of Courage and Skill.
THRILLS! LAUGHS TOO!
Produced by NORMAN FILM MFG. CO.
JACKSONVILLE, FLA.

Bill Pickett (right) was the first African American honored by the Cowboy Hall of Fame. Longhorns (left) graze on Texas ranches.

NEW CHALLENGES

Focus Activity

READ TO LEARN
What changes did railroads bring to Texas in the late 1800s?

VOCABULARY
Grange
reform
Texas Railroad Commission

PEOPLE
Norris Wright Cuney
Sarah Cockrell
Clara McDonald Williamson
James Hogg

READ ALOUD

In 1881 an El Paso newspaper reported that the railroad had arrived.

"Travel to this city is something almost unprecedented [unheard of]. Coaches [trains] . . . are running almost hourly to the end of the track, bringing in crowds of new residents and visitors."

THE BIG PICTURE

In the late 1800s railroads were built throughout Texas. Towns and cities sprang up wherever the railroads went. Traveling and transporting goods from place to place became easier and faster. Texas began to expand more quickly. Many people from East Texas and other parts of the United States moved to West Texas where land was cheaper.

Industries, both old and new, helped meet the needs of our state's growing population. At that time, cotton had become an old industry in Texas. Lumbering was new. Meat-packing was another growing industry. While our state became richer, it also developed new problems. Many farmers thought the railroads charged unfair prices to transport their goods to market and to bring farm supplies to Texas. Texans in state government disagreed about how Texas should be run.

CHANGES IN GOVERNMENT

In 1875 delegates held a convention to change the state constitution that had been written during Reconstruction. This new constitution, which went into effect in 1876, reduced the power of the governor and other officials. Under this new constitution, the government also cut expenses.

African Americans in Government

Between 1870 and 1900, 42 African Americans were elected to the Texas state legislature. Others were appointed to important jobs such as sheriff. African Americans also won elections in towns with large black populations.

During this time Norris Wright Cuney served in many positions in the state and federal governments. He worked to fight the separation between blacks and whites in Texas. He also became a successful businessman.

Despite gains in government and business, African Americans faced new challenges in Texas. After the Civil War, many Southern states, including Texas, passed laws called Black Codes. These laws restricted the rights of African Americans. The passage of the 14th Amendment in 1868 gave African Americans the rights of all citizens. Yet even after Reconstruction ended in 1877, Texas and other Southern states passed laws making it difficult for blacks to vote. These laws often required voters to pass a special test or pay money called a poll tax.

In the 1880s new laws forced the separation of blacks and whites in public places, such as trains. The facilities reserved for blacks were not as good as those for whites.

These delegates to the Texas Constitutional Convention of 1875 represented both whites and blacks.

J. L. GERMAN. W. B. WRIGHT. E. L. DOHONEY.

WM. REYNOLDS. B. B. DAVIS.

A. T. McKINNEY. J. S. MILLS. WM. E. BRADY.

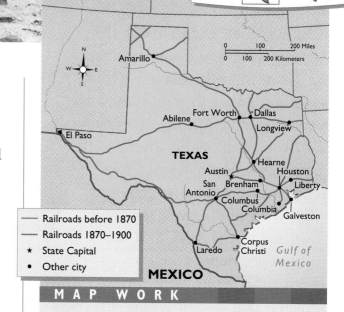

Tools like this spike and mallet (below left) were used by workers laying tracks across Texas (left). Many Chinese workers came to the West to build railroads.

RAILROADS IN TEXAS: 1900

Railroads before 1870
Railroads 1870–1900
★ State Capital
• Other city

Amarillo
El Paso
Abilene Fort Worth Dallas
Longview
TEXAS
Austin Hearne Houston
San Brenham Liberty
Antonio Columbus
Columbia Galveston
Laredo Corpus Gulf of
Christi Mexico
MEXICO

MAP WORK

Life in Texas changed greatly when railroads were built across our state.

1. Which part of Texas had the most railroads before 1870?

2. From El Paso, which two cities could you reach first by railroad?

RAILROADS ACROSS TEXAS

Before the Civil War about 500 miles of railroad lines had been built in Texas. Most people traveled on foot, by horse, or by horse-drawn carriage. After Reconstruction, our state government encouraged the building of railroads. The state offered land to railroad companies for each mile of track they laid. These companies sold the land to settlers to raise money to pay for the cost of building the track.

Look at the map on this page to see how the railroads grew between 1870 and 1900. About 10,000 miles of tracks had been laid in our state by 1900.

Building the Railroads

Much of the work of building the new railroads in Texas was done by Chinese immigrants. A small group of Chinese men and one woman, all in their 20s, arrived in Houston in 1869. They cleared the land and laid down rails for the Houston and Texas Central Railway. In the 1880s more Chinese people arrived to build rail lines all the way west to El Paso. The Chinese workers were often given the most difficult and dangerous work. After the railroads were finished, many Chinese people stayed in Texas. Many opened restaurants, grocery stores, and laundry shops to provide services in the growing Texas cities.

The Growth of Cities

The growth of cities in Texas was due largely to the railroads. Houston became an important railway and steamboat stop. Rails reached Austin, San Antonio, Dallas, and Fort Worth in the 1870s. They pushed on to Laredo in 1880 and El Paso in 1881. Trains brought new people and new businesses. El Paso's population and its wealth doubled in just two years.

Many people played important roles in starting new businesses in our growing cities. A business-woman named Sarah Cockrell helped Dallas grow during this period. She built a bridge across the Trinity River and charged people for crossing it. She also built a large hotel and owned part of a flour mill. Sarah Cockrell became the richest person in Dallas. When she died in 1892, she owned about one-quarter of the city's downtown.

Rails joined cities in Texas with one another and with cities in other states. When a railroad finally reached a town, it was cause for great celebration. In 1880, when the artist Clara McDonald Williamson was a little girl, she saw the first train pull into Iredell, near Waco. Many years later, Williamson recorded her memories of that day in a painting called *The Building of the Railroad*. Williamson put herself in the painting. She is wearing a blue dress. Can you find her?

MANY VOICES
PRIMARY SOURCE

The Building of the Railroad, painted by **Clara McDonald Williamson in 1949-50.**

In this painting, the artist shows how railroads were built in the 1880s. The train, loaded with ties, track, and supplies, ran to the end of the track. When new track was laid, the train moved forward.

A.H. Belo Corporation Foundation

257

RAILROADS AND INDUSTRY

Railroads were a great help to many industries. For example, the lumber industry now had a quick way to transport cut trees from the pine forests of East Texas. The cities of Orange and Beaumont became large sawmill centers. The wood they produced was used to build homes and furniture. It was sent by rail to other growing towns and cities.

Other industries produced and sold our state's mineral resources. They mined coal, salt, and iron ore. Today these industries still use the Texas railroads to transport their mineral products.

Farmers Band Together

Although industries and cities in Texas were booming, life was becoming harder for many farmers. Farmers were growing more crops than ever. However, because food and other farm products were in such large supply their prices dropped. From 1865 to 1895 cotton prices in our state dropped from 31 cents to 7 cents per pound.

While prices were dropping, farmers' costs were rising. Many farmers complained that railroad companies treated them unfairly. Farmers often were charged much more than large businesses to transport their goods.

Most banks would not lend money to farmers. Bankers worried that farmers would not be able to repay loans. Many farmers were caught in a trap. They had no way to get out of debt.

To help solve these problems, farmers throughout the United

Farmers hoped that the Grange could help force the railroads to lower the cost of transporting products like cotton.

States united in an organization called the Grange. The first local Grange in Texas was formed in 1873. By 1876, over 40,000 farmers throughout our state had become members.

The Grange worked for reforms. A reform is a change intended to make things better. Through the Grange, farmers were able to buy supplies at lower prices. Grange members shared information about raising crops and animals. Another reform group, the Farmers' Alliance, began in Texas in 1875. The goals of this group were similar to those of the Grange.

Governor Hogg and the Railroad Commission

Many people became concerned about railroads charging unfair prices. One of them was James Hogg who became governor of Texas in 1891. Governor Hogg had worked to create the Texas Railroad Commission in 1890. The commission stopped many of the railroads' unfair practices, such as charging more for short trips than for long ones. It even forced one railway line that had stopped sending trains to small towns to start up again. Hogg won the hearts of Grange members and other rural Texans.

WHY IT MATTERS

Texas underwent many changes after the Civil War. Railroads were

Governor Hogg helped farmers receive fair prices from the railroad companies.

built across our state. They carried people and goods. But these changes created problems for Native Americans in Texas. You will read about these problems in the next lesson.

Reviewing Facts and Ideas

SUM IT UP

- Many African Americans served in the government in Texas during the late 1800s.
- The building of thousands of miles of railroads helped Texas to grow quickly after the Civil War.
- Chinese immigrants helped build the railroads.
- The lumber and mineral industries grew because of the railroads.
- Governor Hogg made railroads treat farmers more fairly.

THINK ABOUT IT

1. What changes occurred for African Americans in the 1800s?

2. How did our state government encourage railroad construction?

3. **FOCUS** How did the new railroads change Texas in the late 1800s?

4. **THINKING SKILL** Identify one *fact* and one *opinion* about why so many farmers joined the Grange organization.

5. **WRITE** How did James Hogg help change the railroads in Texas?

Quilt-making

In the last lesson you read about artist Clara McDonald Williamson who painted important events during her life. Like Williamson, the quilter Gazzie Hill was also an artist.

Gazzie Hill was born in 1877 in LaGrange. One of her parents had been an enslaved African American. Gazzie Hill drew on her rich African heritage to sew beautiful quilts like this String Scrap Quilt. It is made of scraps of fabric from clothing and other material. All of the pieces were sewn together by hand.

Gazzie Hill lived to be 98 years of age. During her long life she made many wonderful quilts by piecing scraps of fabric together. She liked to rock in her chair and sing while she sewed her quilts.

Quilts have long been a way for people to remember the past. The stitches of each quilt tell a story—often a family story. Quilts are a legacy to future generations.

This quilt has a secret. Gazzie Hill sewed the alphabet into it. To find the letters, look at the quilt from all four directions. Don't expect the letters to appear in order. They're hidden, but they're there.

CONFLICT ON THE PLAINS

Focus Activity

READ TO LEARN
Why was there fighting between Native Americans and new settlers?

VOCABULARY
Treaty of Medicine Lodge Creek
reservation

PEOPLE
Satanta
Quanah Parker
Cynthia Ann Parker
William Tecumseh Sherman
Ranald S. MacKenzie
Henry O. Flipper

PLACES
Indian Territory
Palo Duro Canyon

READ ALOUD

In 1867 Kiowa Chief Satanta described how he felt about moving to a permanent settlement: "I don't want to settle. I love to roam over the prairies. There I feel free and happy, but when we settle down we grow pale and die. . . . A long time ago, this land belonged to our fathers; but when I go up to the river I see camps of soldiers. . . . These soldiers cut down my timber [forest], they kill my buffalo; when I see that, my heart feels like bursting."

THE BIG PICTURE

For thousands of years Native Americans lived freely on the land that is now Texas. As you read in Chapter 3, some Native American groups depended on the buffalo for their survival.

In Chapter 4 you read that the Spanish took some land away from Native Americans to begin towns, ranches, and missions. Later, when Texas became a republic and then a state, more newcomers wanted to settle on Native American lands.

After the Civil War the growth of railroads brought even more new settlers to our state. As the frontier pushed westward, Native Americans like Chief Satanta became angry. They did not want to give up their land. To protect their way of life some Native Americans decided to fight back.

WARRIORS AND SOLDIERS

In an effort to protect their land, Native Americans began a series of raids on settlers' ranches and farms. In 1866 the United States government sent soldiers to stop these raids.

The Search for Peace

In 1867 the United States sent representatives to Medicine Lodge Creek in Kansas. These representatives met with Comanche, Kiowa, Cheyenne, Apache, and Arapaho chiefs. The United States representatives and some of the chiefs signed the Treaty of Medicine Lodge Creek. This treaty said that the chiefs would move with their people to Indian Territory, in what is today Oklahoma. They agreed to live on reservations. A reservation is land set aside by the government for Native Americans.

In exchange, the United States offered to give the Native Americans food, clothing, tools, and money. However, Comanche Chief Quanah (KWAH nah) Parker refused to sign the treaty. He wanted the right to live freely on Comanche land.

Quanah Parker was the son of Chief Peta Nocona (PEE tuh nuh KOH nuh) and

Comanche Chief Quanah Parker (left), the son of a captured settler (below), refused at first to move to a **reservation**.

Cynthia Ann Parker. Cynthia Ann Parker was not a Comanche. Her parents were white settlers. In 1836, when she was nine, Parker was captured by a group of Comanche who adopted her. When she grew up, she married Nocona, who became a Comanche chief.

In 1860 Cynthia Ann Parker was captured by Texas Rangers. Though she wanted to return to the Comanche, she was sent to live with her uncle. Parker never saw her son, Quanah, again. She died four years later.

In 1869 a Native American gave these dolls to Sallie Reynolds Matthews. You read her words in Chapter 5.

FRONTIER WARS

The Treaty of Medicine Lodge Creek was soon broken by both sides. Raids on settlers' farms and ranches started up again. In 1871 the United States government sent **William Tecumseh Sherman** to Texas. Sherman had been a Union General during the Civil War. While he was in Texas, a group of settlers traveling in wagons were attacked by Native Americans. Seven settlers were killed. Satanta and two other chiefs were arrested and sentenced to death for the killings. Satanta was later set free in exchange for pledges of peace. Sherman, however, decided it was time for the United States to force the Native Americans of Texas onto reservations.

By 1900 only about 300 buffalo lived in the United States. Today buffalo are protected by law and their numbers have increased.

The End of the Buffalo

In the 1870s buffalo hunters came to Texas. They could become rich by selling buffalo hides for up to three dollars each. The hunters often killed hundreds of buffalo in a day. In 1878, about 100,000 buffalo were killed in Texas in two months.

As you have read, the Native Americans of the plains needed buffalo in order to survive. They ate buffalo meat, and they used other parts of the buffalo to make everything from clothing to rope. The buffalo hunters, on the other hand, took only the hides. They left the rest of the animals' bodies to go to waste. These hunters were killing so many buffalo that Native Americans worried about how they would survive without them.

The Red River Campaign

Quanah Parker and other chiefs led raids against buffalo hunters. Kicking Bird, a Kiowa chief, said: "Just as it makes a white man's heart feel to have his money carried away, so it makes us feel to see others killing and stealing our buffaloes."

The United States responded in 1874 by sending 3,000 soldiers to force Native Americans to stop the raids and move to reservations. The Texas Rangers helped the army. Left with few choices, most Native Americans agreed to move to reservations. But a few groups refused. They camped along the Red River and prepared for battle.

Ranald S. MacKenzie led United States soldiers at the Battle of Palo Duro Canyon.

The Battle of Palo Duro Canyon

On the morning of September 28, 1874, the most important battle of the Red River campaign began. Army scouts discovered a group of Comanche, Kiowa, and Cheyenne villages at the bottom of Palo Duro Canyon.

Colonel Ranald S. MacKenzie of the United States Army ordered 500 soldiers to climb down the canyon's steep walls for a surprise attack.

Many of the Native Americans in the villages escaped. But MacKenzie destroyed their food. He also had soldiers kill more than 1,000 of their horses. He wanted to make sure the Native Americans could not recapture their horses and use them in future battles. The soldiers also burned the villages.

The Native Americans who escaped could not survive long without horses, food, or shelter. By November most moved to reservations. Others held out until the spring. Quanah Parker finally led his people to a reservation in June 1875.

Native Americans had been forced from northern Texas. Some Kickapoo and Apache remained along the Mexican border. By 1880 they, too, had been forced to leave all lands in Texas.

Look at the Kiowa drawing of the Battle of Palo Duro Canyon below. How do the weapons of the Kiowa compare with the United States Army's weapons?

MANY VOICES
PRIMARY SOURCE

Kiowa Teepee Painting of the Battle of Palo Duro Canyon, late 1800s.

This painting on buffalo hide shows a Kiowa artist's viewpoint of the 1874 battle which ended the Red River campaign.

The Smithsonian Institute

THE BUFFALO SOLDIERS

Most soldiers in the United States Army during the late 1800s were white. However, two army units, the Ninth and Tenth Cavalries, were made up entirely of black soldiers.

The Ninth and Tenth Cavalries were sent to states such as Texas to fight Native Americans. They fought so well that they became known throughout the state. Native Americans developed great respect for the fighting ability of these soldiers. In fact, Native Americans came to call the black soldiers "buffalo soldiers" after the animal the Native Americans held sacred.

The buffalo soldiers built new roads and telegraph lines. They protected stagecoaches and wagon trains. Buffalo soldiers guarded the border between Mexico and Texas. They also fought against cattle thieves and other outlaws.

At that time, all army officers were white. In 1877 Henry O. Flipper became the first African American to graduate from West Point, a military school in New York. He became a lieutenant and then joined the Tenth Cavalry in Texas. Flipper served in the Panhandle, keeping peace between Native Americans and settlers.

Buffalo soldiers lived hard lives. Stationed in lonely places, they often could not visit their families for five years at a time.

WHY IT MATTERS

The Red River campaign caused great sadness and bitterness for Native Americans. Many Native Americans were killed in fighting or died from disease or hunger. Their days of hunting buffalo were over. They were no longer free to live on the open plains as they had for hundreds of years. Life was hard on reservations.

Today's Texans include members of over 300 Native American groups. They live and work in cities and towns throughout our state. In addition Texas has three reservations. The Tigua have a reservation in El Paso. The Alabama-Coushatta reservation is near Livingston. And the Kickapoo Traditional Tribe of Texas has a reservation near Eagle Pass.

DID YOU KNOW?

What was life like for the buffalo soldiers?

The buffalo soldiers were often treated badly by the army and by the white settlers they defended. The food they were given was of lower quality than the food white soldiers ate. Sometimes the buffalo soldiers were punished for crimes they did not commit. Henry O. Flipper was unfairly accused of stealing money. In 1882 he was forced to leave the army. Almost 100 years later, in 1976, the United States Army admitted that Flipper had been innocent.

Public Affairs Office / Department of Army

Reviewing Facts and Ideas

SUM IT UP

- The Treaty of Medicine Lodge Creek was a peace agreement between the United States and some Native American groups.
- Many Native Americans were forced to move from Texas to the Indian Territory.
- Buffalo hunters often killed hundreds of buffalo in a day, but they used only the hides.
- The Battle of Palo Duro Canyon forced the last Native Americans to leave northern Texas.
- The buffalo soldiers were African Americans sent to protect settlers in Texas.

THINK ABOUT IT

1. Who were the buffalo soldiers? What did they do in Texas?

2. Name two Native American leaders and describe their actions with the United States.

3. **FOCUS** Why was there fighting between Native Americans and new settlers?

4. **THINKING SKILL** *Make a conclusion* about why Quanah Parker did not want to agree to take his people to a reservation.

5. **GEOGRAPHY** How did the geography of Palo Duro Canyon help the United States Army win the battle there in 1874?

CHANGES IN THE WESTERN HEMISPHERE

Focus Activity

READ TO LEARN
How did life in other parts of the Western Hemisphere compare with life in Texas during the 1800s?

VOCABULARY
monarchy

PEOPLE
Dom João
Dom Pedro I
Dom Pedro II

PLACES
Brazil
Rio de Janeiro

READ ALOUD

"All Brazil is a fresh-blooming garden."

A Portuguese priest wrote this description of Brazil, Portugal's new colony, in the early 1500s. During the next 300 years, this "fresh-blooming garden" attracted many settlers from Portugal.

THE BIG PICTURE

You have read about the Civil War, cattle drives, railroads and the end of slavery. All of these brought great changes to our state. Around the same time, great changes were happening in other parts of the Western Hemisphere. From Canada in the north to Argentina in the south, people saw changes in government, business, and all parts of daily life.

In South America, for example, the country of Brazil was being transformed. Settlers in Brazil, like those in Texas, had huge plantations in the 1800s. The biggest crop in Brazil was sugarcane, although cotton was grown too. During the middle 1800s, thousands of immigrants came from Europe to settle in southern Brazil. Like the newcomers to Texas, they brought many of their own traditions with them. In this lesson you will read how Brazil had much in common with Texas. However, many things were very different too.

THE COLONY OF BRAZIL

In 1800 the Portuguese colony of Brazil had more than three million people. About two-thirds of them were enslaved workers. They or their ancestors had been brought by force to Brazil from Africa. Enslaved people worked on plantations, cattle ranches, or in gold and diamond mines. Slavery was harsher in Brazil than in Texas and other parts of the United States. Many enslaved people survived only about 10 years after arriving from Africa.

Brazilian life centered around the sugarcane and other plantations. Most plantations were huge. One was larger than all of Portugal. Brazil's few towns and cities served the plantations. Townspeople packed and shipped the sugar, cotton, and tobacco that the plantations produced.

In 1800 the largest city in Brazil was Rio de Janeiro (REE oh DAY jah NAIR oh). Rio had about 100,000 people—more people than in all of Texas at that time.

Moving Toward Independence

In 1821 the ruler of Portugal was Dom João (ZHWAU). In Portuguese, *Dom* means "sir", and *João* is "John". Dom João had put his son, Prince Pedro, in charge of Brazil. Dom João told his son: "If Brazil demands independence, grant it, but put the crown upon your own head."

In 1822, Prince Pedro declared Brazil's independence from Portugal. Pedro then became Dom Pedro I of Brazil. So Brazil, although finally independent, had become a monarchy, a country ruled by one person.

Africans were brought to Brazil on packed ships (right) and forced to work growing crops like coffee (below, above).

POPULATION IN THE WESTERN HEMISPHERE, 1825–1900

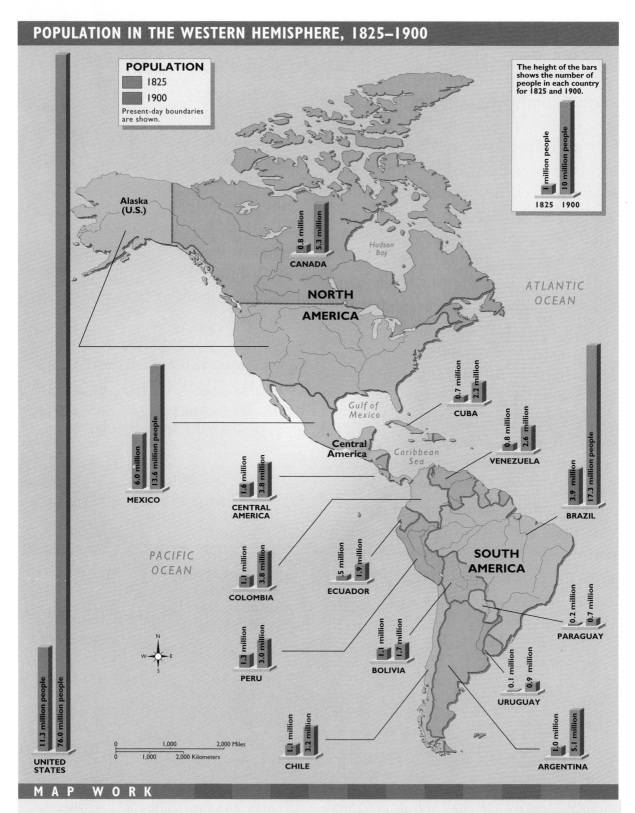

POPULATION
- 1825
- 1900

Present-day boundaries are shown.

The height of the bars shows the number of people in each country for 1825 and 1900.

1 million people
10 million people
1825 1900

Alaska (U.S.)

NORTH AMERICA

0.8 million / 5.3 million
CANADA

Hudson Bay

ATLANTIC OCEAN

Gulf of Mexico

0.7 million / 2.2 million
CUBA

0.8 million / 2.6 million
VENEZUELA

Caribbean Sea

6.0 million / 13.6 million
MEXICO

Central America

1.6 million / 3.8 million
CENTRAL AMERICA

3.9 million / 17.3 million
BRAZIL

SOUTH AMERICA

PACIFIC OCEAN

1.1 million / 3.8 million
COLOMBIA

.5 million / 1.9 million
ECUADOR

0.2 million / 0.7 million
PARAGUAY

1.3 million / 3.0 million
PERU

.1 million / 1.7 million
BOLIVIA

0.1 million / 0.9 million
URUGUAY

11.3 million people / 76.0 million people
UNITED STATES

0   1,000   2,000 Miles
0   1,000   2,000 Kilometers

1.1 million / 3.2 million
CHILE

1.0 million / 5.1 million
ARGENTINA

M A P   W O R K

The population of the Western Hemisphere grew from 1825 to 1900.

1. Which country had the largest population in 1900?

2. How many people lived in Brazil in 1825? How many in 1900?

3. What do you think a bar representing this year would show for most countries in our hemisphere?

THE END OF SLAVERY

Dom Pedro did not rule wisely. He gave the best government jobs to people from Portugal, and started a war with Argentina. By 1829 many Brazilians had turned against him. In 1831 fearing a rebellion, Dom Pedro turned the monarchy over to his son, Dom Pedro II, who had been born in Brazil.

Dom Pedro II proved to be a better ruler than his father. Under his leadership, Brazil began to modernize. Railroads were built.

Dom Pedro II was against slavery. The owners of the plantations, however, depended on it. To avoid trouble, Dom Pedro II planned to end slavery gradually, in steps. In 1871 he approved a law that freed children born to people in slavery. Then in 1885 he approved another law that freed all enslaved people over the age of 60. Finally, in 1888, the Brazilian government freed all remaining people in slavery.

The Republic of Brazil

The plantation owners were angry because they were not paid for the people who were freed from slavery. They blamed Dom Pedro II for the loss of enslaved workers. With the landowners' support, the army rebelled against Dom Pedro II. On a rainy night in 1889, Dom Pedro II boarded a ship and sailed to Europe. He no longer ruled Brazil. In that year Brazil became a republic with leaders chosen by the people.

WHY IT MATTERS

During the 1800s, millions of people came to the Western Hemisphere. Look at the map on the opposite page. As you have read, these people brought many changes to both Brazil and Texas.

You can make many more connections between Texas and Brazil in the 1800s. Plantations, slavery, and new independence are all things they had in common. Today trade and communications are two things that link Texas and Brazil across the Western Hemisphere.

Reviewing Facts and Ideas

SUM IT UP

- Brazil was a colony of Portugal.
- In 1822 Dom Pedro I became the first ruler of an independent Brazil. Brazil was then a monarchy.
- Dom Pedro II left Brazil in 1889, when Brazil became a republic.

THINK ABOUT IT

1. Why was Dom Pedro I unpopular?
2. Why did Dom Pedro II move to end slavery gradually?
3. **FOCUS** How was life in Texas and Brazil similar during the 1800s? How was life different?
4. **THINKING SKILL** _Compare_ and _contrast_ a monarchy with a republic.
5. **GEOGRAPHY** Look again at the map on page 270. Which parts of the Western Hemisphere had the most people? Why do you think this was so?

CHAPTER 8 REVIEW

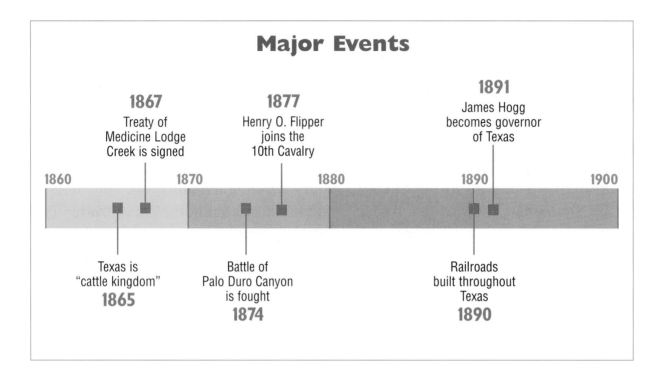

Major Events

1867
Treaty of
Medicine Lodge
Creek is signed

1877
Henry O. Flipper
joins the
10th Cavalry

1891
James Hogg
becomes governor
of Texas

1860   1870   1880   1890   1900

Texas is
"cattle kingdom"
1865

Battle of
Palo Duro Canyon
is fought
1874

Railroads
built throughout
Texas
1890

THINKING ABOUT VOCABULARY

Number a sheet of paper from 1 to 10. Next to each number write the word or term from the list below that best matches the statement.

brand
cattle drive
longhorn
stampede
monarchy
reform

Texas Railroad
 Commission
reservation
Treaty of Medicine Lodge
 Creek
barbed wire

1. A breed of cattle that has horns with tips very far apart

2. The way that cowboys moved cattle north from Texas

3. Wire with sharp points

4. Something a frightened herd of cattle might do

5. A group that stopped many of the railroad's unfair practices

6. A design burned into cattle's hide

7. A change for the better

8. An agreement between Native American chiefs and the United States government

9. Land set aside by the government for Native Americans

10. A country or a state that is ruled by a king or queen

THINKING ABOUT FACTS

1. Name two hardships faced by cowboys on a cattle drive.

2. Who were the "line riders"?

3. What was the purpose of branding cattle?

4. Why did the cattle drives of the late 1800s end?

5. What was the Grange? Why was it formed?

THINK AND WRITE

WRITING A LETTER

Suppose you are a cowboy on a cattle drive. Write a letter to your family describing your experiences.

WRITING A SUMMARY

Reread the section in Lesson 3 titled "Buffalo Soldiers." Then write a summary of what you have read.

WRITING AN EXPLANATION

Write a paragraph explaining why Native Americans were angry about the killing of the buffalo.

APPLYING THINKING SKILLS

1. What is the difference between a fact and an opinion?

2. What are some word clues that help you recognize opinions?

3. Identify the fact and the opinion in the following statement: *The first local Grange in Texas was formed in 1873. Farmers believed the Grange would improve their lives.*

4. Write a statement of your own including a fact <u>and</u> an opinion.

5. Why is it important to learn how to tell a fact from an opinion?

Summing Up the Chapter

Use the following time line to organize information from the chapter. Copy the time line on a piece of paper. Then add the events listed below in the correct places along the time line. When you have filled in the time line, use the information to write an answer to the question "How did cattle affect the history of Texas?"

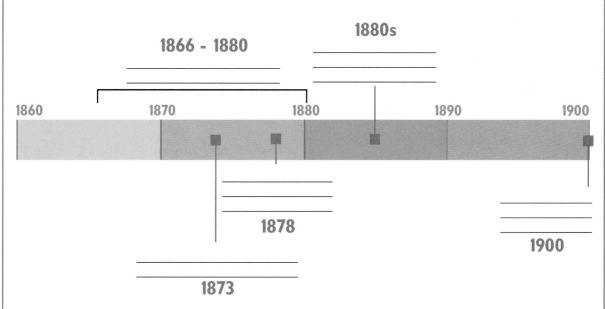

- 10,000 miles of railroad track in Texas
- Lizzie Johnson Williams travels Chisholm Trail
- 10 million Texas cattle transported to markets

- Joseph Glidden invents barbed wire
- 100,000 buffalo killed in two months

UNIT 4 REVIEW

THINKING ABOUT VOCABULARY

Number a paper from 1 to 5. Next to each number write the letter of the definition that best matches the word.

1. STATES' RIGHTS

a. The belief that national government should decide about states' issues

b. The belief that each state should build its own railroads

c. The belief that each state has the right to make its own laws

2. AMENDMENT

a. An addition to the United States Constitution

b. An addition to the Emancipation Proclamation

c. A law affecting African Americans

3. RECONSTRUCTION

a. The plan for helping freed slaves

b. The plan for fighting the Civil War

c. The period when the Southern states were brought back into the Union

4. RESERVATION

a. Land set aside for state buildings

b. Land set aside by the government for Civil War soldiers

c. Land set aside by the government for Native Americans

5. TREATY OF MEDICINE LODGE CREEK

a. An agreement that said Native Americans could keep their land

b. An agreement that said the United States Army would help Native Americans find food

c. An agreement that said Native Americans would move to reservations

THINK AND WRITE ◄▭▭▷

WRITING A PARAGRAPH OF COMPARISON

Choose one of the people you read about in Unit 4. Discuss your report with a classmate who wrote about a different person. Write a paragraph comparing these two people.

WRITING A SONG

You read about the spirituals sung by enslaved people. You also read about the songs sung by cowboys. Suppose that you were a Native American leaving home to live on a reservation. Write the words to a song of your own.

WRITING A NEWSPAPER ARTICLE

Suppose you were a reporter during the time of Reconstruction. Write an article describing the Freedmen's Bureau.

BUILDING SKILLS

1. **Notes and outlines** Read the section on pages 248–249 about cattle drives. Take notes as you read and then write an outline.

2. **Notes and outlines** How can writing outlines help you organize information?

3. **Fact and opinion** What are some clues to help you tell that a statement is a fact?

4. **Fact and opinion** What are some word clues that tell you the writer is expressing an opinion?

5. **Fact and opinion** Find one fact and one opinion in Unit 4. Explain how you made your choices.

YESTERDAY, TODAY &
TOMORROW

When railroads were built in our state during the 1800s, many changes followed. During the 1900s the invention of the automobile caused even greater changes. What kind of new technology do you think will cause changes in the future?

READING ON YOUR OWN

Here are some books you might find at the library to help you learn more.

CAMELS FOR UNCLE SAM
by Diane Yancey
A daring United States Army experiment during the late 1850s brings camels to Texas.

HANK, THE COWDOG
by John Erikson
This humorous story is about a ranch dog's adventures in solving mysteries.

THE MUSTANG PROFESSOR: THE STORY OF J. FRANK DOBIE
by Mark Mitchell
This story about J. Frank Dobie brings to life Texas's frontier heritage.

UNIT PROJECT

Weave a Tale

1. In Chapter 8 you read about Gazzie Hill's quilts and learned that quilts can tell a story. Work with a partner to make a quilt about your hometown.
2. Cut nine large squares out of colored construction paper. Use each square to tell a different part of your town's story.
3. Begin by researching information about your hometown. When was it founded? How has it grown? Write the answers before you make the quilt.
4. Think about how best to show each event. Will you draw or cut out pictures from a magazine? Will you use markers, crayons, or colored pencils?
5. Finally "weave" your quilt by placing the finished squares in three rows. Each row should have three squares. Make sure the squares are in the correct order and then glue the squares together to form a quilt.
6. Share the quilt with your class.

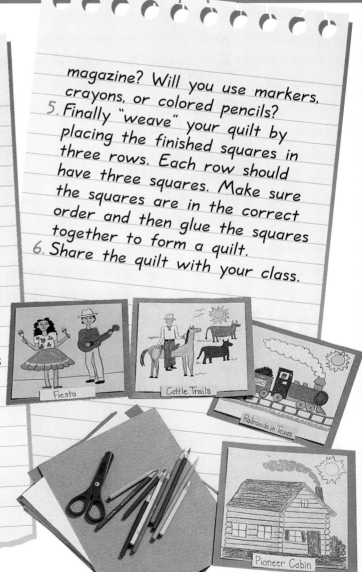

275

JOVITA IDAR;
"UNCLE SAM" ARMY POSTER

Institute of Texan Cultures

Library of Congress

FALLS THEATRE RIVER FALLS,

AN EPIC OF THE AIR

WINGS

WITH
CLARA BOW
CHARLES (Buddy) ROGERS
RICHARD ARLEN
and GARY COOPER

I WANT YOU
FOR U.S. ARMY
NEAREST RECRUITING STATION

POSTER FOR TEXAS MOVIE
"WINGS"; NASA ROCKET

276

A New Century

"... I took that opportunity ..."

from a statement by Astronaut Bernard A. Harris, Jr.
See page 310.

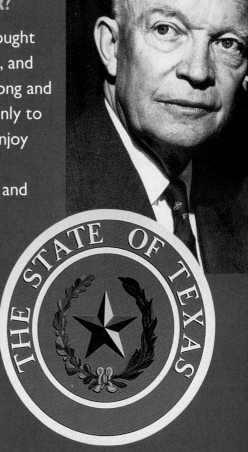

WHY DOES IT MATTER?

Although the twentieth century brought World War I, the Great Depression, and World War II, Texas remained a strong and growing state. Texans learned not only to get through difficult times, but to enjoy good times and build for the future.

How did Texans help each other and other Americans through the hard times? What job opportunities opened up for Texans? How did the economy and government of our state continue to be successful? Read on to see how Texas rose to meet the needs of a changing world.

DWIGHT DAVID EISENHOWER;
THE TEXAS STATE SEAL

Adventures
with
NATIONAL
GEOGRAPHIC

Birth of a Boom

I began on January 10, 1901. A well drilled into a hill called Spindletop, near the town of Beaumont, suddenly started gushing. Oil blew 100 feet into the air. A boom began! By 1903, derricks crowded Spindletop. After the "gusher," life in Texas—and the world—changed forever. People raced to the oil fields, seeking wealth. Oil came into use to fuel industry, power cars, and heat homes. Today, oil remains important to the economy of Texas. And Gladys City, the reconstructed "boom town" near the gusher that started it all, is a historic landmark.

GEO JOURNAL

List some things that would not be possible without oil.

CHAPTER 9

A Time of Change

THINKING ABOUT GEOGRAPHY AND HISTORY

The twentieth century brought good times and hard times to Texas. The discovery of oil brought new wealth and new jobs. New inventions such as the radio and the automobile made communication and transportation easier. As proud citizens of the United States, Texans fought alongside our countrymen in two world wars. In Chapter 9 you will read about all of these events in our state's history and more.

PACIFIC OCEAN

1901
SPINDLETOP
The first big "gusher" is struck

1917
SAN ANTONIO
The United States enters World War I

1920
DALLAS
Radio station WRR makes its first broadcast

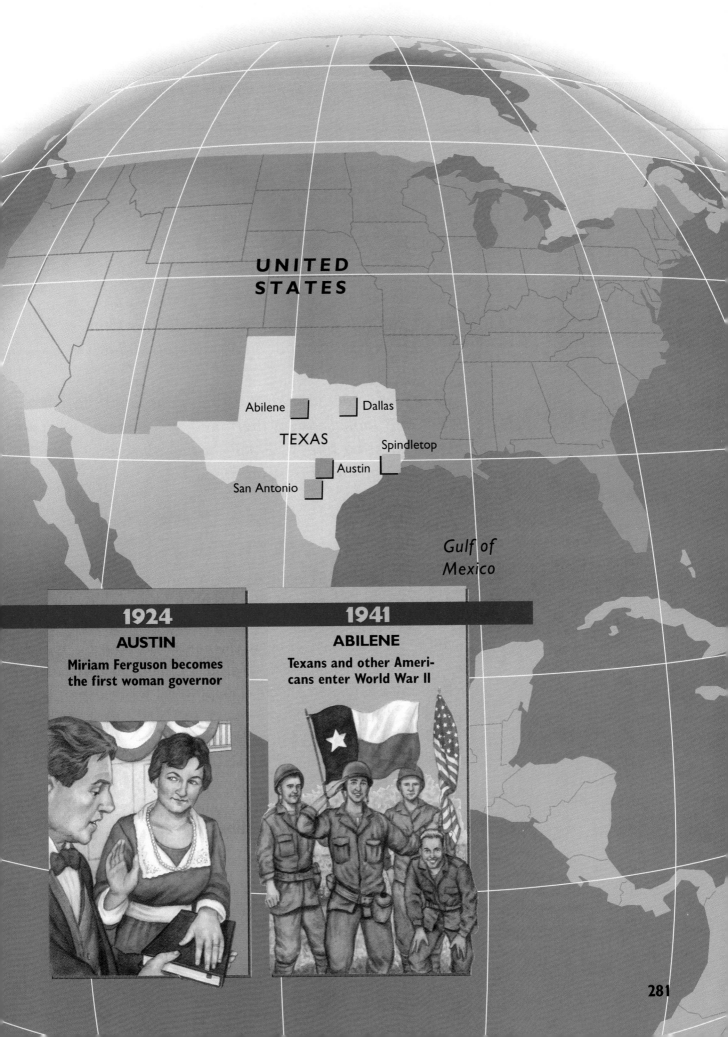

UNITED
STATES

Abilene Dallas

TEXAS

Spindletop

Austin

San Antonio

Gulf of
Mexico

1924

AUSTIN

Miriam Ferguson becomes
the first woman governor

1941

ABILENE

Texans and other Americans enter World War II

The Center for American History

GUSHER! BLACK GOLD

READ ALOUD

Oil worker Allen Hamill was an eyewitness the day oil was "discovered" in Spindletop Heights, in Beaumont, in 1901.

"I heard something kind of bubbling just a little bit and looked down there and this foaming oil was starting up. . . . Finally it just shot up clear through the top of the derrick."

THE BIG PICTURE

By 1900 people in Texas had been using petroleum for centuries. The Karankawa found it seeping up from the ground. They used it to make their bowls waterproof. The survivors of Hernando de Soto's expedition used petroleum to stop the leaks in their boats. Later, people collected seeping oil to grease tools and wagon wheels.

In the 1850s a new use was found for oil. When it was heated, petroleum produced kerosene. Kerosene could be burned as fuel in a lamp to provide light. This discovery made oil more valuable than ever. No wonder the sticky black substance came to be called "black gold"!

Focus Activity

READ TO LEARN
How did the discovery of oil change the way of life in our state?

VOCABULARY
kerosene
gusher
boom town
crude oil
refinery
petrochemical

PEOPLE
Pattillo Higgins

PLACES
Beaumont
Spindletop
Kilgore

RICHES FROM THE EARTH

As petroleum became more valuable, people began digging into the ground in hopes of finding more. They wanted to "strike oil" to sell it.

One of these people was Pattillo Higgins. This one-armed mechanic and real-estate developer lived in Beaumont in the late 1800s. One day he was walking over a nearby hill called Spindletop. He noticed gas bubbles escaping from a stream. Higgins wondered if there might be oil beneath the ground.

The Gusher at Spindletop

All through the 1890s Higgins tried drilling into Spindletop. He hit nothing but rock and mud. But on January 10, 1901, a crew was drilling near the bubbling stream. Suddenly mud exploded from the well. Then a cloud of gas hissed out.

For a moment the ground was quiet. Then a rumbling noise began to build. At last a fountain of oil, or a gusher, spouted 100 feet high.

As news of the gusher at Spindletop spread, people streamed into the town of Beaumont. Living in tents and shacks, they spent their days drilling for oil. Within months the population climbed from 10,000 to 50,000.

Boom Towns

Beaumont became a boom town—a community that grows rapidly. Boom towns appeared throughout Texas for many years.

In Kilgore, for example, drillers struck oil in 1930. Within days, thousands of people arrived. Crews began drilling everywhere—even through the floor of the local bank!

The oil boom also changed industries across the United States. Soon ships, trains, and factories were powered by this new fuel. And a new petroleum product—gasoline—made automobiles run.

The painting *Boomtown* (right) by Thomas Hart Benton, gives the artist's impression of such towns at the time Pattillo Higgins (above) found oil.

Memorial Art Gallery/Univ. of Rochester, N.Y.

THE BUSINESS OF OIL

How does petroleum get from deep underground to a gas pump? First, scientists study where oil may be located. Then workers use a steel bit to drill wells into the ground. Special pipes are lowered into the hole. These pipes lead oil to the surface.

The petroleum that lies near the surface is called crude oil. Crude oil must be transported to a factory called a refinery (ri FI nuh ree). There the crude oil is refined, or separated into parts to be used. The chart shows you how this is done.

From the parts, petrochemicals (pet roh CHEM i kulz) are produced. Among the chemicals made from petroleum are paint, plastics, fertilizers, pesticides, and even medicines.

Petroleum is often moved in huge pipes, or pipelines. Oil can also be carried in large ships called tankers. The largest of these tankers can hold over 3 million barrels of oil. A barrel is equal to 42 gallons.

What products listed in this chart might you find in your classroom?

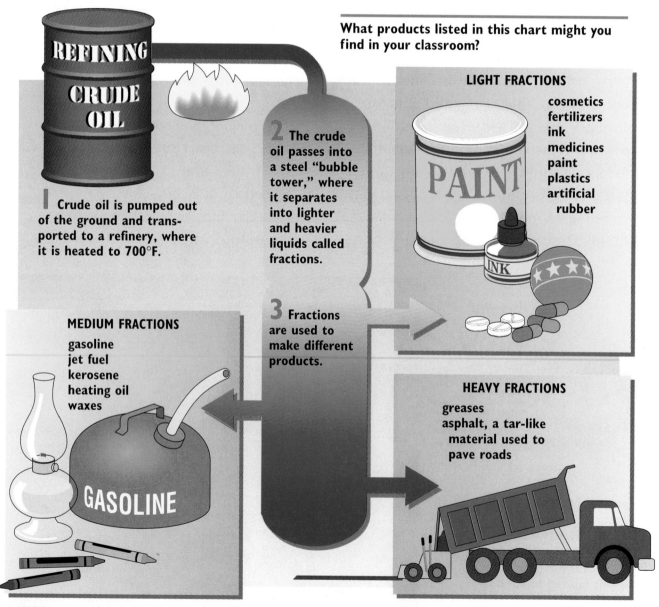

REFINING CRUDE OIL

1 Crude oil is pumped out of the ground and transported to a refinery, where it is heated to 700°F.

2 The crude oil passes into a steel "bubble tower," where it separates into lighter and heavier liquids called fractions.

3 Fractions are used to make different products.

LIGHT FRACTIONS
cosmetics
fertilizers
ink
medicines
paint
plastics
artificial rubber

PAINT

INK

MEDIUM FRACTIONS
gasoline
jet fuel
kerosene
heating oil
waxes

GASOLINE

HEAVY FRACTIONS
greases
asphalt, a tar-like material used to pave roads

Houston is the most important oil-refining center in the United States. Much of the Southwest and many other countries send their crude oil to refineries in Houston.

WHY IT MATTERS

The discovery of petroleum changed Texas forever. Boom towns appeared practically overnight. Oil has brought jobs, people, and wealth to our state. Today Texas produces about 1.4 million barrels of oil a day—about one-quarter of the total supply of the United States.

Plentiful fuel helped to make cars popular. Petrochemical products such as plastics, fertilizers, and medicines have changed the way we live today. In the next lesson you will read about how other businesses in our state have grown and changed.

DID YOU KNOW?

Where do plastics come from?

You know that wood comes from trees and that metals come from metal ores. Plastics are made from petrochemicals. Unlike wood or metal, plastics are made by people.

Plastics are all around us. They are even in toys you play with. One reason plastics are so useful is that they can be molded into many different shapes when they are heated. Thin layers of plastic are used to coat electrical wires. Thick layers of plastic may strengthen the floor of a building. Plastics are used to make sneakers, bicycle helmets, and parts of automobiles. They are even used to make paints and paintbrushes!

Reviewing Facts and Ideas

SUM IT UP

- Oil was used in many ways before 1900, but it was not a common or valuable resource in Texas.
- In 1901, drillers struck the first big Texas "gusher" near Beaumont.
- Crude oil must be refined before being sent to your local gas station or used in other ways.

THINK ABOUT IT

1. How did the development of kerosene affect the value of oil?
2. What is a boom town?

3. **FOCUS** What effect did the discovery of oil have on businesses throughout Texas and the rest of the United States?

4. **THINKING SKILL** *Make a conclusion* about why Houston has become the center of our nation's oil-refining industry.

5. **WRITE** Suppose you were a newspaper reporter present at Spindletop on January 10, 1901, the day of the first gusher. Write an article describing the events of the discovery.

THINKING SKILLS

Making Generalizations

WHY THE SKILL MATTERS

In Lesson 1 you read about the discovery of oil in Texas. Suppose you want to compare this with discoveries of resources in other states. After some research you notice some similarities. For example, other states also had gushers and boom towns. From these similarities you make a general statement about how the discovery of resources affects a state.

Your general statement would be a generalization. A generalization is a statement that ties together several different examples. It shows how the examples are connected by a single concept or idea.

Why is a generalization useful? Facts or events that seem very different may have some things in common. A generalization states how things that seem different may be related.

USING THE SKILL

Suppose you want to make a generalization about different kinds of transportation. You learned in the last lesson that oil led to the growing use of automobiles. You already know that some pioneers came to Texas in covered wagons. Still others came by boat.

Now compare the examples. You could ask yourself, "How were these forms of transportation used?" The car made it easier for families to get around. The covered wagon moved well on land that was mostly flat. Neither of them would be useful in the water, however. On water the ship would be the only kind of transportation.

Now you have the beginnings of a generalization. What do these examples have in common? The ways people travel are affected by the environment in which they live. You have made a generalization about transportation.

You might be able to make more than one generalization from the same information. Now try making a generalization.

Courtesy of Panhandle- Plains Historial Museum

Use the Helping Yourself box as a guide.

TRYING THE SKILL

Try making a generalization about inventions. Here are three examples: the automobile, the radio, the telephone. How are these inventions similar? What kinds of problems did these inventions solve? How did these inventions change people's lives? What generalizations can you make from these three examples? What steps did you take to make your generalizations?

REVIEWING THE SKILL

1. What is a generalization?

2. Think of forms of transportation other than those already mentioned. Do they support the generalization about transportation and the environment? Explain your answer.

3. Why is it important to have several examples in order to make a generalization?

4. How do generalizations help us to understand history?

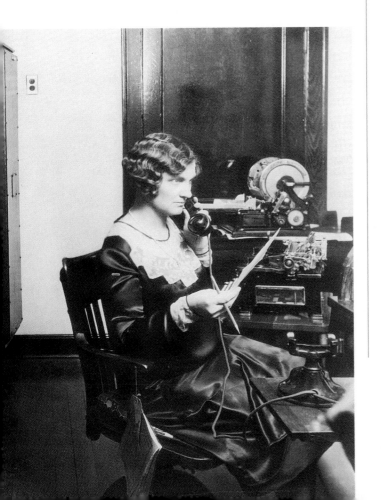

The telephone and the typewriter changed the way people worked (left). Automobiles (above) changed the way people traveled.

287

WAR AND GROWTH

READ ALOUD

In 1928 President Herbert Hoover exclaimed proudly: "We in America today are nearer to the final triumph over poverty than ever before in the history of any land." During much of the 1920s, many Americans would have agreed with what he said.

THE BIG PICTURE

Throughout the United States, the years between 1900 and 1914 were a time of steady growth. Electricity came to towns and cities. Plumbing moved indoors. An automobile might pass by. In Texas, of course, the discovery of oil was changing businesses and our way of life.

For most Americans the time was peaceful. The future seemed full of promise. Then a gunshot rang out in Europe, and the world changed. In June 1914 Archduke Francis Ferdinand, a noble in line to rule the empire of Austria-Hungary, was killed. This event triggered the start of what became known as World War I. For the first time in history, countries around the world would be at war with each other.

Focus Activity

READ TO LEARN
What changes did Texas experience during the "Roaring Twenties"?

VOCABULARY
World War I
Allied Powers
Central Powers
Roaring Twenties
invention
communication

PEOPLE
Marjorie Stinson
Katherine Stinson
Scott Joplin
Josephine Lucchese

PLACES
Austria-Hungary

I WANT YOU FOR U.S. ARMY
NEAREST RECRUITING STATION

WORLD WAR I

In 1917 the United States entered the war on the side of the **Allied Powers.** The Allied Powers included Great Britain, France, and Russia. The opposing countries were known as the **Central Powers**. The Central Powers included Germany, Austria-Hungary, and Italy.

At first most Americans wanted to stay out of World War I. But attacks by German submarines on ships carrying United States passengers began to make people angry. Finally the United States joined the war on the side of the Allied Powers on April 6, 1917.

Texas at War and at Home

About 200,000 Texan men served as soldiers, sailors, and marines during the war. Although women were not allowed to fight, hundreds served as nurses. Two other women, **Marjorie Stinson** and **Katherine Stinson** helped to train United States and Canadian military pilots at the Stinson School of Flying in San Antonio.

On the home front, Texans raised money for the war effort. They helped to build military equipment and to produce oil for ships and planes. They cut down on the foods they ate so that soldiers would have enough.

The war pulled Texans together. Yet it also led to conflicts. Some German Americans were treated as possible enemies. The German language was outlawed in many schools.

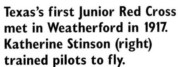

Texas's first Junior Red Cross met in Weatherford in 1917. Katherine Stinson (right) trained pilots to fly.

The Institute of Texan Cultures

THE ROARING TWENTIES

The Allied Powers defeated the Central Powers in 1918, ending World War I. The following 10 years were a time of exciting changes in our state and country. Texans, like all Americans, were happy the war was over. Businesses were growing. More people than ever had jobs. The 1920s became known as the Roaring Twenties.

New Inventions

What made the Roaring Twenties such an exciting time? Inventions of the time were changing the way Americans lived. An invention is a newly created product. Perhaps the invention that led to the biggest change in our way of life was the automobile.

Americans had been making and driving automobiles since the early 1900s. Now, however, their popularity grew quickly. In 1917 there were 200,000 cars in Texas. By 1926 more than a million cars were on the road in our state!

The wide use of the automobile made travel much easier than ever before. The automobile helped farmers bring their crops to market. And since cars are fueled by gasoline, they kept our oil industry booming.

Gasoline engines invented for automobiles also had other uses. Texans used them to power cotton gins and tractors. Motorized water pumps helped to irrigate many fields in our state.

Some inventions, like the vacuum cleaner, made household chores easier. So did new products like frozen foods and the refrigerator. Inventions such as the radio and telephone helped Texans to stay in touch with each other and the world. How would your life be different if these inventions did not exist today?

Sights and Sounds

Some inventions changed the ways that people had fun. In March 1920 the Dallas radio station WRR broadcast its first program. Now Texans could listen to the news,

The Library of Congress

AN EPIC OF THE AIR

WINGS

WITH CLARA BOW
CHARLES (Buddy) ROGERS
RICHARD ARLEN
and GARY COOPER

weather reports, and the first "soap operas." They could also hear music by fellow Texans like Scott Joplin or Josephine Lucchese.

At the same time, other forms of entertainment were becoming popular across the country. Millions of Americans went to the movies each week. Every city had its "picture palaces," where people cheered at silent movie westerns or laughed at comedians like Charlie Chaplin.

Both the radio and the movies marked the growth of the industry called communications. Businesses in communications are involved in the exchange of information between people.

The Institute of Texan Cultures

The 1920s movie "Wings" (left) was made in Texas. Texans Josephine Lucchese (above) and Scott Joplin (right) composed popular music.

WHY IT MATTERS

The first 30 years of the 1900s were a time both of pain and of excitement for Texans and all Americans. New weapons, such as machine guns, tanks, and airplanes made World War I especially deadly. New inventions changed the way Texans lived, worked, and played. In the next lesson you will learn that these "good times" would not last forever.

Reviewing Facts and Ideas

SUM IT UP

- The early years of the twentieth century were a time of change.
- The United States entered World War I in 1917. Many Texans fought overseas or helped at home.
- The Roaring Twenties brought excitement, wealth, and change to the lives of many Americans.

THINK ABOUT IT

1. Name the Allied Powers in World War I.
2. How did Texans help the war effort at home?
3. **FOCUS** What were some changes Texans experienced during the Roaring Twenties?
4. **THINKING SKILL** How do you think increased use of cars _affected_ the building of highways?
5. **WRITE** Suppose that you were living during the 1920s. Write a letter to a friend describing the effect of one new invention on your life.

LESSON 3

THE GREAT DEPRESSION AND WORLD WAR II

The Institute of Texan Cultures

Focus Activity

READ TO LEARN

How did the Great Depression and World War II affect Texans?

VOCABULARY

stock
Great Depression
New Deal
World War II
Axis Powers
Allies

PEOPLE

Franklin D. Roosevelt
Audie Murphy
Dwight D. Eisenhower
Oveta Culp Hobby

READ ALOUD

Carmen Perry, a teacher, had this to say about the difficult years of the 1930s. "They had cut my salary so badly. I don't know how a lot of people managed."

THE BIG PICTURE

The Roaring Twenties had been good years for the stock market. **Stocks** are shares, or parts, of ownership in a company. In the 1920s many people bought stocks. They hoped to earn money as businesses boomed and stock prices went up. In October 1929 many stockholders grew worried as prices began to fall.

On October 29, 1929, as people across the country rushed to sell their stocks, prices fell to rock bottom. The stock market "crashed."

The stock market crash marked the beginning of hard times for the people of our state and of the entire country. Many people had taken loans from banks but they did not have enough money to pay them back. As a result, many banks failed. People could not afford to buy things, so companies needed fewer workers. Many people lost their jobs and their savings. The **Great Depression** of the 1930s had begun.

The mural over Alamo Stadium was made by artists like Barney Villa in the WPA (above). The WPA was one of the New Deal programs created by Franklin D. Roosevelt (left).

THE DEPRESSION IN TEXAS

The Great Depression hit hard in our state. Between 1929 and 1933 more than 65,000 people lost their jobs. Many Texans lost their farms. Many moved to cities, but they could not find work there, either. How does Carmen Perry, whose words you read in the Read Aloud, describe how people helped each other during the Depression?

Excerpt by Carmen Perry from Women of the Depression by Julia Kirk Blackwelder, 1984.

We used the bus, we didn't have cars, and we made our own clothes. . . . We could buy T-bones [steaks] for 25 cents a pound, and hamburger for a dime. . . . We had to help each other. Sometimes at the end of the week we'd say, can you spare me a quarter until Monday? We'd share. We'd entertain ourselves by getting together and chatting. . . . Of course at school we put on plays. . . .

The Government Responds

In 1932 Americans chose a new President, Franklin D. Roosevelt. FDR, as he was called, promised to bring change. He started government programs to try to help struggling Americans get back on their feet. Roosevelt called his new programs the New Deal. Some New Deal programs aimed to help farmers, others to help banks, and still others to put people to work improving their communities.

Young men in the Civilian Conservation Corps, or the "CCC Boys," built parks, bridges, and schools. They built well-known landmarks such as the River Walk in San Antonio and the San Jacinto Monument at Buffalo Bayou near Houston.

Another New Deal program was the Works Progress Administration, or WPA. This program put artists, musicians, writers, and teachers to work throughout our state and throughout our country.

WORLD WAR II BEGINS

In 1939, while Americans were still struggling through the Great Depression, another world war broke out. World War II was started by the Axis Powers led by Germany, Italy, and Japan. They fought against the Allies led by Great Britain, France, and later the Soviet Union.

The United States at first tried to stay out of this conflict. But on December 7, 1941, Japanese planes bombed the United States naval base at Pearl Harbor, Hawaii in a surprise attack. The next day Congress declared war on Japan. Germany and Italy, in turn, declared war on the United States.

Texans in World War II

More than 750,000 men and women from our state served in the armed forces in World War II. Some became well-known. Lieutenant Audie Murphy from Hunt County was the most decorated hero during the war. General Dwight D. Eisenhower from Denison commanded Allied troops in Europe. Colonel Oveta Culp Hobby from Killeen helped organize and became the commander of the Women's Army Corps.

Thousands of African Americans from Texas served in the war. However, most were separated from white troops and were not allowed to fight in battles. Native Americans and Mexican Americans from Texas

Audie Murphy (above right) received the Congressional Medal of Honor in 1945. Dwight D. Eisenhower (right) led the Allies in Europe.

also served in World War II. Fourteen Texans received the Medal of Honor, including five Mexican Americans.

The War at Home

Texans at home worked hard to support the war effort. Communities collected scrap metal and old tires for military supplies. Texas provided much of the oil the military needed for fuel. Many Texans purchased war bonds to help pay the costs of the war. Because so many men were away fighting the war, women took over many of their jobs.

The war brought many changes to our state. The national government built many army training camps in Texas, including Fort Bliss near El Paso and Camp Barkeley near Abilene. The biggest change was that the war effort finally brought the Great Depression to an end. Industries built weapons and supplies and jobs became available throughout our state and country.

The government built 21 prisoner of war camps in Texas. These camps held 45,000 German, Italian, and Japanese soldiers by war's end. In Seagoville, Crystal City, and Kenedy the government also set up "relocation" camps. More than 5,000 Japanese Americans were confined to these camps until the war ended. Victims of fear and suspicion, most of these Japanese Americans were taken from their homes in California. They were forced to live in the camps until the war ended. In 1988 the United States issued an official apology for these actions.

This Texan woman is shown repairing tents for the United States soldiers in World War II.

Institute of Texan Cultures/San Antonio Light Collection

WHY IT MATTERS

In Texas, as in the rest of the United States, the Great Depression put an end to the Roaring Twenties. New Deal programs tried to help people through the Great Depression. Still, our state, like most states, did not fully recover until World War II.

In 1945 both Germany and Japan surrendered to the United States and the Allies. Texans, like other Americans, were anxious to get on with their lives.

✓// Reviewing Facts and Ideas

SUM IT UP

- In 1929 the stock market crashed and the Great Depression began.
- President Roosevelt's New Deal programs tried to help many Texans find jobs.
- The United States entered World War II in 1941. The war put an end to the Great Depression.
- World War II ended in 1945.

THINK ABOUT IT

1. What was the stock market crash?

2. How did the New Deal try to help the people of our state?

3. **FOCUS** How did the Depression and World War II affect Texans?

4. **THINKING SKILL** *Make a generalization* about how World War II helped Texas recover from the Great Depression.

5. **GEOGRAPHY** Look at the Atlas map on page R14. Why do you think the United States was able to stay out of World War II until 1941?

The Texas Collection of Baylor University

EQUAL RIGHTS FOR ALL

READ ALOUD

"Texas women are voters now; I helped . . . to make it possible."

Jane Y. McCallum of Austin used these words to describe how proud she felt about helping women in Texas gain the right to vote.

THE BIG PICTURE

Until 1920 women in our state and our country did not have the right to vote. The struggle for suffrage (SUF rihj), or the right to vote, lasted for many years. Lone Star women such as Eleanor Brackenridge started suffrage groups. They staged marches and held meetings to gain the right to vote.

Support for women's suffrage increased during World War I, when women took over many men's jobs in factories and offices. In 1920, two years after the war, the Nineteenth Amendment to the United States Constitution gave women the right to vote.

As you will read in this lesson, women are not the only group to struggle against discrimination. Discrimination is the unfair difference in the treatment of people. Other people, including African Americans, Mexican Americans, and Native Americans, have also worked hard for equal rights in the United States.

Focus Activity

READ TO LEARN
How have Texans fought for equality?

VOCABULARY
suffrage
discrimination
segregation
civil rights

PEOPLE
Eleanor Brackenridge
Miriam A. Ferguson
Ann Richards
Christia Adair
Martin Luther King, Jr.
Lyndon B. Johnson
Jovita Idar
Henry B. González
Mario Gallegos

296

EQUAL RIGHTS ON THE JOB

Gaining the right to vote was an important step in women's struggle for equality. Women then worked to elect government officials and to run for public office.

"Ma" Ferguson

In 1924 Miriam A. Ferguson was chosen the first woman governor of our state. She was called "Ma" Ferguson by many people. Some people believed that she was chosen to stand in for her husband, former Governor James Ferguson. He was removed from office in 1917 for breaking the law and was not allowed to run for governor again.

Ma Ferguson cut taxes and worked to help Texans during the Great Depression. She also fought against the Ku Klux Klan, a hate group that threatened and sometimes killed African Americans and others it opposed.

The Institute of Texan Cultures

DID YOU KNOW?

What are some organizations women have started to bring about change?

In 1882 the Women's Christian Temperance Union was started in Paris, Texas. This group of women believed that drinking whiskey and other kinds of alcohol should be against the law. This group brought many Texas women into the world of politics. Later some of these women would fight for the vote. In 1980 women concerned about deaths caused by drunk drivers started Mothers Against Drunk Driving (MADD).

Changes for Women

Since 1945 American women have continued to gain rights. In the 1960s and 1970s large numbers of women began to work outside the home. Many demanded to be paid the same as men for the same kinds of work.

The Institute of Texan Cultures

Today about one out of two women in our state work outside the home. Some Lone Star women have top jobs in state and local governments. Ann Richards was the second woman to be governor of our state.

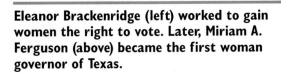

Eleanor Brackenridge (left) worked to gain women the right to vote. Later, Miriam A. Ferguson (above) became the first woman governor of Texas.

SEPARATE BUT NOT EQUAL

You read in Chapter 7 that blacks in Texas were freed from slavery in 1865. More than 100 years later, however, African Americans in Texas were still suffering from discrimination.

In big cities like Houston and small towns like Marshall, African Americans faced segregation (seg rih GAY shun). Segregation is the practice of keeping blacks and whites separate. Blacks were not allowed to join the same clubs, eat in the same restaurants, or go to the same schools as whites. Schools and other places that were used by African Americans were usually of poorer quality than those that were used by whites.

Christia Adair, an African American from Victoria, worked hard in the 1950s and 1960s to have signs for "whites only" taken down at the Houston airport. She also worked to have public places opened to African Americans.

The Civil Rights Act

Leaders such as Martin Luther King, Jr., of Georgia, led marches for civil rights. Civil rights are the rights of all people to be treated equally under the law. The largest civil rights march took place in Washington, D.C., in 1963. Finally, the United States Congress passed the Civil Rights Act in 1964 when Texan Lyndon B. Johnson was President.

Martin Luther King, Jr. looked on as President Johnson signed the Civil Rights Act in 1964.

LBJ Library Collection

Jovita Idar worked for equal rights for Mexican Americans in the early 1900s.

It was now against the law for businesses to treat people differently because of their race, sex, or religion. In 1965 the United States Congress passed the Voting Rights Act. This law made illegal the practices that were used to keep African Americans from voting.

Working for Change

Mexican Americans have also fought against discrimination. In the early 1900s Jovita Idar of Laredo formed the League of Mexican Women. She worked to provide free education for Mexican children. As a reporter for *La Cronica* and *El Progreso*, she spoke out against violence toward Mexican Americans.

Today Mexican Americans like former United States Representative Henry B. González of San Antonio and State Senator Mario Gallegos

of Houston continue to work for equal rights in jobs and education.

Native Americans also fought for equal rights. In the 1870s Native Americans were forced to move to reservations. In 1924 the Indian Citizenship Act gave Native Americans the rights of other citizens.

WHY IT MATTERS

Texans have joined people throughout the United States in an effort to win equal rights for all. But more still needs to be done. The fight to gain equal rights for all people continues.

✔️ Reviewing Facts and Ideas

SUM IT UP

- Miriam A. Ferguson became the first woman governor of our state in 1925.
- Congress passed the Civil Rights Act in 1964.
- Texans, like other Americans, continue to work for equal rights for all.

THINK ABOUT IT

1. What is discrimination?
2. What was the Civil Rights Act?
3. **FOCUS** In what ways have Texans fought for equality?
4. **THINKING SKILL** *Make a generalization* about different groups of people working for equal rights.
5. **WRITE** Suppose you lived before 1920. Write a letter to a newspaper explaining why you think women should be allowed to vote.

CHAPTER 9 REVIEW

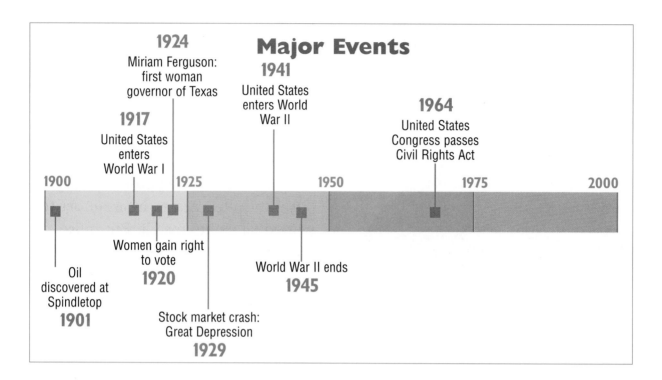

Major Events

1924
Miriam Ferguson: first woman governor of Texas

1941
United States enters World War II

1964
United States Congress passes Civil Rights Act

1917
United States enters World War I

1900   1925   1950   1975   2000

Women gain right to vote
1920

Oil discovered at Spindletop
1901

World War II ends
1945

Stock market crash: Great Depression
1929

THINKING ABOUT VOCABULARY

Number a piece of paper from 1 to 5. Next to each number write the word or term that matches the statement.

crude oil   suffrage
refinery   World War I
Roaring Twenties

1. A factory where crude oil is separated into parts to be used

2. The petroleum that lies near the ground's surface

3. The right to vote

4. A war that lasted from 1914 to 1918 and involved most of the nations of Europe

5. The decade of exciting changes that started shortly after the end of World War I

THINKING ABOUT FACTS

1. Name at least three products made from crude oil.

2. When did the United States enter World War I? Why?

3. List three inventions that helped to make the Roaring Twenties an exciting time.

4. When did women get the right to vote?

5. What was the Civil Rights Act? When was it passed?

6. What discovery turned oil into "black gold"?

7. When did the stock market crash?

8. How did the New Deal help Americans to recover from the Great Depression?

9. On which side did the United States enter World War II?

10. How were Japanese Americans affected by World War II?

THINK AND WRITE

WRITING A SPEECH

Suppose you were Eleanor Brackenridge, a suffrage leader from Texas. Write a speech explaining why women should have the right to vote.

WRITING AN EXPLANATION

Explain how crude oil is discovered and changed into products that you use every day.

WRITING A LIST

Suppose you are a newspaper reporter in Texas during World War I. Write a list of three questions you might ask Marjorie and Katherine Stinson.

APPLYING THINKING SKILLS

1. What is a generalization?

2. Reread Lesson 2 and Lesson 3. Make a generalization about the reasons the United States entered World War I and World War II.

3. Reread Lesson 4. Make a generalization about the reasons women, African Americans, Mexican Americans, and Native Americans have long fought for equal rights.

4. Look around your classroom. Make a generalization about your classmates that includes you.

5. How might making generalizations help you to understand history?

Summing Up the Chapter

Use the following spider map to organize information from the chapter. Copy the spider map on a sheet of paper. Then write at least one piece of information in each blank circle. When you have filled in the maps, use them to write a paragraph titled "What were some of the important changes that took place in Texas during the 20th Century?"

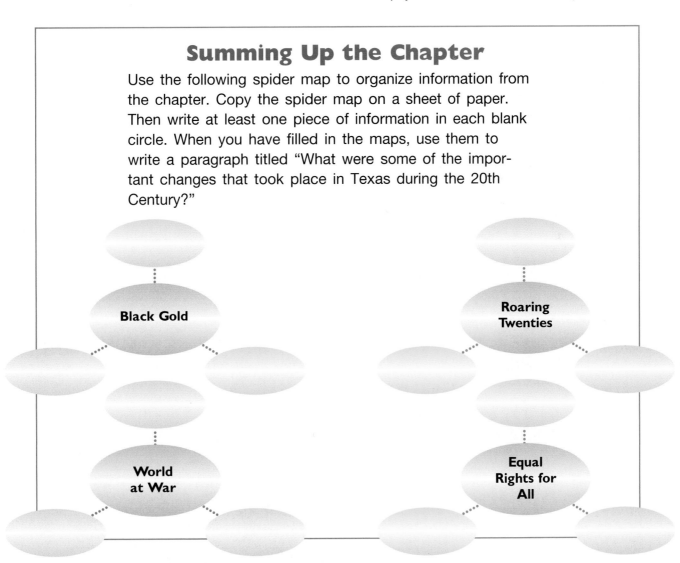

Black Gold

Roaring Twenties

World at War

Equal Rights for All

CHAPTER 10

Economic Growth

THINKING ABOUT GEOGRAPHY AND ECONOMICS

Texas provides many important goods and services to the economy of the United States. We are lucky enough to have rich farmlands, booming cities, and the headquarters for our country's space program! Read on to find out about the many kinds of economic growth in Texas.

UNITED STATES

Terry County

TEXAS

Terlingua

Houston

MEXICO

Gulf of Mexico

NASA

Oil Rigs
HOUSTON SHIP CHANNEL

These rigs in the Houston Ship Channel are just a part of the booming oil business in our state. "Black Gold" continues to be a very important industry in Texas.

Longhorn Ranch
NEAR TERLINGUA

You have read that western Texas is "cowboy country." But do you know how ranching affects our state's economy? Chapter 10 will explain.

NASA
NEAR HOUSTON

Texans are very proud that NASA, which runs our country's space program, is located right in Clear Lake, near Houston. NASA provides many service jobs for the people of our state.

Ogallala Aquifer
TERRY COUNTY

Both large and small farms in Texas play an important role in the growth of our state. In this chapter you will read about the ways farming is done in our state today.

303

A FREE-ENTERPRISE ECONOMY

Focus Activity

READ TO LEARN
How does the free-enterprise economy work in Texas?

VOCABULARY
economy
free-enterprise system
entrepreneur
profit
investor
consumer

PLACES
Tomball

READ ALOUD

Lorrie Hayes is the education manager for Junior Achievement in Houston. "Our purpose," explains Lorrie, "is to inspire young people to value free enterprise, understand business and economics, and to be ready for a job."

THE BIG PICTURE

One of the most important parts of life in Texas is its economy. The economy is the way a place uses its natural resources to meet people's needs and wants. Every time you spend or earn money, you are taking part in our economy.

One of the strengths of the economy in the United States is the free-enterprise system. Under this system people are free to own and run their own businesses. People in business decide what to make or buy. Shoppers can choose between many different products. The free-enterprise system allows Americans to make their own economic decisions.

Students at Tomball High created these dolls, called "Texas Guardian Angels."

304

A BUSINESS BLOOMS

People start thousands of businesses every year in our country. Here is how one business in Tomball, Texas, got its start.

Getting Started

In 1994 a group of 18 students at Tomball High School decided to learn about business by starting one themselves. They made 14 products that they thought the community would enjoy. One product was a T-shirt designed on a computer. Another product was a doll called the "Texas Guardian Angel" which you can see on the opposite page. The students also made cloth wreaths with the colors of the American flag and the Texas flag.

People who organize and run a business, such as these high school students, are called entrepreneurs (ahn truh pruh NURZ). Entrepreneurs take risks by creating products they think people will want to buy. When a business is successful, an entrepreneur makes a profit. Profit is the money a business earns after it pays for supplies, tools, salaries, and other costs. The profit is a return for hard work—and for taking a risk.

The First Steps

The group at Tomball chose one student, Christopher Mendel, as president and another, Jennifer Schultz, as executive vice president. The students decided to call their company "Taking Care of Business." The students also decided that if they got good advice, they would have a better chance of running a successful business. Debbie Redding, the manager of a local company and a successful businesswoman, agreed to help them out.

These student entrepreneurs started a business called "Taking Care of Business," or "TCB" for short.

After making products by hand (right), students created a display booth to sell their goods (left).

A CLOSER LOOK

Starting and running a business means a lot of work. Let's take a closer look at how the Tomball students made Taking Care of Business a success.

Investors and Consumers

Starting a business costs money. Most businesses need to borrow money to get started. Often businesses borrow money from investors. An investor is someone who puts money into a business. The investor usually expects to get some of the profit in return. The investors in Taking Care of Business were the 18 student entrepreneurs, other students at the school, and people in the community.

Taking Care of Business now had money to buy materials and tools. The students all helped to make the products. They designed labels to put on each one. When the products were finished, the students needed to let consumers know about their products. Consumers are the people who buy a product or use a service.

The Service Side

A student named Kelly Teichmiller was in charge of advertising. She and other students handed out flyers to shoppers at a local mall. They put notices up on bulletin boards in their school and throughout the town. They also wrote articles about their company. The articles were printed in the school and in the town newspapers.

The students decided to set up a booth at a local mall. Rachel Petrich was in charge of selling. "One of the most important things in selling," says Rachel, "is how you display your product." She and other students spent time decorating their booth. Kelly says, "When I talk to customers, I tell them why they need our product. I tell them how great it is and what it's good for."

Advertising and selling are two examples of service-industry jobs. Teachers, doctors, and police officers also provide services. Almost seven out of ten Texans work in the service industry.

A Successful Business

Taking Care of Business was a big success. All the investors made a profit of 60 cents for each dollar they put in. In just 16 weeks, the students sold $7,400 worth of goods. Their profit was over $600. They also won an international Junior Achievement award.

Taking Care of Business helped prepare 18 young people for a future in business. They gained first-hand business experience. Kelly says the experience helped her learn "how to get along with people—local businesspeople, consumers, and other students." Rachel summed up her experience this way: "I feel confident [sure] that when I go for a job. . . I can be a good employee."

WHY IT MATTERS

In a free enterprise system, people make their own economic decisions. Taking Care of Business made some good decisions to become a successful business. Our economy depends on people and businesses that are willing to take risks.

Different parts of our state have different resources and make different products. In the next lesson you will learn about other kinds of businesses in our state.

✔ Reviewing Facts and Ideas

SUM IT UP

- The economy is the way a place uses resources to meet people's needs and wants.
- In a free-enterprise system, people can start their own businesses.
- Services, such as advertising, are an important part of our economy.

THINK ABOUT IT

1. What is free about the free-enterprise system?
2. What are two ways in which you take part in your community's economy?
3. **FOCUS** How does Taking Care of Business show the free-enterprise system working in Texas?
4. **THINKING SKILL** *Sequence* the steps that the students took to make their business a success.
5. **WRITE** Suppose you worked for Taking Care of Business. Write an advertisement explaining why people should buy your products.

307

MODERN INDUSTRIES IN TEXAS

Focus Activity

READ TO LEARN
What kinds of jobs will there be in Texas when you finish school?

VOCABULARY
technology
food processing
manufacturing
high-tech industry

PLACES
Houston
Dallas
Johnson Space Center
Clear Lake
San Antonio

READ ALOUD

"Technology will create entirely new experiences in how people live, how we learn, how we work, and how we play."

Sherel D. Horsley works for a large technology company in Dallas. Like many Texans, he believes that technology will be more and more important to living and working in our state.

THE BIG PICTURE

During World War II Texas became a center for industry. As you read in Chapter 2, an industry is all of the businesses that make one kind of product or provide one kind of service. Between the years 1941 and 1945, thousands of Texans left farms and small towns for jobs in cities such as Houston, Dallas, and Fort Worth. Some worked in large factories making airplanes, tanks, trucks, and other equipment needed to fight World War II. Others helped to supply the gasoline needed to run all the new machinery.

The airplane, oil, and chemical industries in Texas continued to grow after World War II. Technology, or the use of skills and tools to meet human needs, also became more important. Thanks to our state's natural resources, warm climate, and our hard-working people, Texas has become a strong leader in the free-enterprise economy of the United States.

INDUSTRY TODAY

Texans work in all kinds of businesses, large and small. All these jobs keep our economy strong. In fact only ten countries in the world have larger economies than Texas!

Texas Oil

Today Texas is the largest producer of oil and natural gas in the United States. Thousands of Texans work in this business. Clet Landry, an engineer, is one of them. He goes out on ships to explore for oil in the Gulf of Mexico. Clet explains that there is:

> a room [on the ship] where people record sound echoes from deep inside Earth. . . . These recordings are [changed] into pictures in Houston by some of the world's largest computers so people can see where oil might be found.

A Leader In Many Industries

Texas is also a leader in food processing. Food processing is any of hundreds of ways of turning raw food into different kinds of products. For example, beef is packaged in Hereford, near Amarillo, and cottonseed oil is made in Lubbock.

Logging is another major industry in Texas. Logs are used in the manufacturing of wood products. Manufacturing is the making of goods by machinery. Some logs are cut into boards that are used to build houses and to make furniture. Other logs are chopped into wood chips. The chips are mixed with chemicals and then used to make paper.

High-Tech Texas

People from around the world buy electronic products made in Texas. Computers, as well as parts for VCRs and CD players, are all made in our state. These companies are part of the high-tech industry. The goods that this industry produces require a great knowledge of science and math. Technology is the "tech" in high tech.

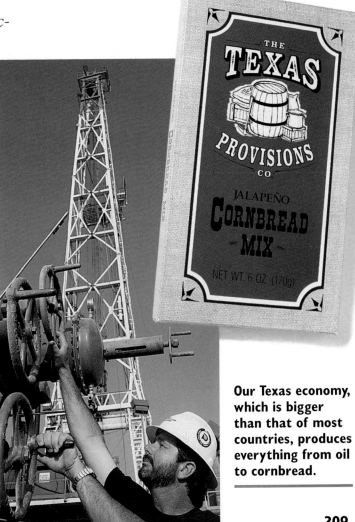

Our Texas economy, which is bigger than that of most countries, produces everything from oil to cornbread.

TECHNOLOGY TAKES US TO THE MOON

Millions of people from around the world watched their televisions to see Neil Armstrong become the first person to walk on the moon in July 1969. Texans were especially proud because it was Mission Control near Houston that controlled Armstrong's journey to the moon. Computers were used to control his space vehicle 240,000 miles away from Earth.

Johnson Space Center

Johnson Space Center is an important part of our state's economy. It is also an important part of the United States space program. Johnson Space Center is located in a suburb of Houston called Clear Lake. Today the space center provides jobs for about 3,500 scientists, engineers, and other service-industry workers. The space center also serves as a school where astronauts are trained to work in space.

Dr. Bernard A. Harris, Jr., trained to become an astronaut at Johnson Space Center in Clear Lake.

Dr. Bernard A. Harris, Jr., is an astronaut and also a Texan from Temple. Read about how Dr. Harris wanted to be an astronaut since he was a child. What opportunities did Dr. Harris take to reach his goal?

MANY VOICES
PRIMARY SOURCE

From
an interview with
Dr. Bernard A. Harris, Jr., in 1995.

As a child I had a dream and kept it alive. I knew I wanted to be a doctor as well as an astronaut. I used to watch space flights on television. Whenever there was an opportunity to read a book, watch a movie, or study space science, I took that opportunity.

Both of these dreams came true when I became a flight surgeon. A flight surgeon is a doctor who takes care of astronauts during a space mission. So far, I have been on two space flights and even walked in space. Traveling in space made me see that we are all one people.

BOOMING CITIES

Today, four out of five Texans live in urban areas. In fact, three of the ten largest cities in the United States are found in our state—Houston, Dallas, and San Antonio.

Big Cities, Big Economies

As you may know, Houston is the largest city in our state and the fourth largest city in the United States. Houston is located near rich oil fields. Of the 500 largest companies in the United States, 16 have their headquarters in Houston.

Today Dallas is the second largest city in Texas. Back in 1843, it was a town made up of just two log cabins! Today Dallas has about 4,000 factories. It is a center of high-tech industry, making products such as electronics, airplanes, and missiles.

San Antonio is the third of Texas's "big three" cities. In 1955 only about half a million people were living here. By 1995 the city's population had reached one million. The Alamo, River Walk, and other sights make tourism a major part of San Antonio's service industry. The chart shows how some jobs in Texas will grow in the future. The Info-graphic on page 312 will show you more about Texas's economy.

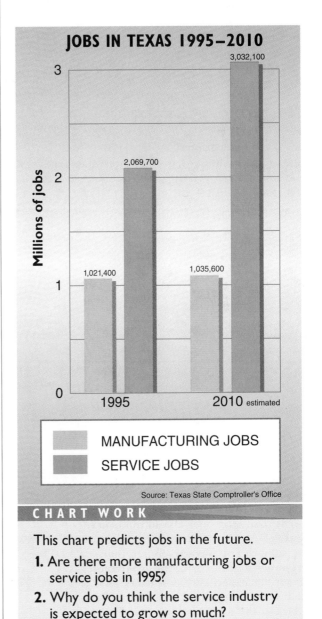

JOBS IN TEXAS 1995–2010

Millions of jobs

- 3,032,100
- 2,069,700
- 1,021,400
- 1,035,600

1995   2010 estimated

MANUFACTURING JOBS
SERVICE JOBS

Source: Texas State Comptroller's Office

CHART WORK

This chart predicts jobs in the future.

1. Are there more manufacturing jobs or service jobs in 1995?
2. Why do you think the service industry is expected to grow so much?

Infographic

The Economy of Texas

Oil is one of the most valuable resources in Texas, and refining is one of it's biggest industries. What other goods and services are important to our state's economy?

Hi Tech
Texas is second in the nation in making electronic products, such as computer parts and systems.

Stampede!
Texas is the leading state in raising cattle, sheep, and angora goats. Ranchers are in almost every part of our state.

The Great Outdoors
Beautiful scenery attracts many visitors every year to Texas's two national parks, Big Bend and Guadalupe Mountains. In 1994 more than half a million tourists enjoyed the great outdoors there.

Up, Up, and Away
The Dallas/Ft. Worth International Airport is the fourth busiest airport in the country, with 2,500 take-offs and landings each day. That's about 84 planes coming and going every hour!

Blast Off!
The Lyndon B. Johnson Space Center near Houston employs many scientists, engineers, technicians, and about 100 astronauts. Millions of tourists visit the Space Center every year.

Down on the Farm
There are more farms and farmland in Texas than anywhere else in the United States. Texas leads the country in producing spinach and watermelons. Other crops are wheat, corn, rice, vegetables, and fruits, especially citrus fruits. Milk is an important product in northeast Texas. Chicken and egg farms are found in eastern Texas. Hog farms are in the North Central Plains and the Panhandle.

It's a Deal!
Houston and Dallas are international business centers. More than 50 foreign governments have offices in Houston.

King Cotton
More cotton is grown in Texas than in any other state. Cotton grows near the gulf coast, on the central and northern prairies, and in the Rio Grande valley.

All Aboard
There are about 29 seaports along the Gulf Coast. The port of Houston is the second largest in the United States, with over 140 million tons of cargo passing through it each year.

WHY IT MATTERS

People in Texas have jobs in many fields—from high-tech industries to food processing. As our free-enterprise economy grows and changes, new jobs and businesses are created. As you grow older, you will play a more important part in our state's growing economy. In Viewpoints on page 314 you will read about our state's industries and the environment.

✓✓ Reviewing Facts and Ideas

SUM IT UP
- Major industries in our state include oil, logging, food processing, and high-tech industries.
- Johnson Space Center is an important part of our country's space program.
- Cities have grown in Texas because of business and industry.

THINK ABOUT IT
1. Why have many Texans moved from rural areas to cities?
2. What kinds of products do high-tech industries make?
3. **FOCUS** Which industries do you think will be important in Texas when you graduate high school?
4. **THINKING SKILL** *Predict* whether or not our state's cities will continue to grow. Explain the reason for your prediction.
5. **GEOGRAPHY** Look again at the Infographic. How do you think the geography and resources of Texas influence our economy?

CITIZENSHIP
VIEWPOINTS

Whooping cranes migrate 2,500 miles to their winter home on the Texas coast.

WHAT DO TEXANS THINK ABOUT PROTECTING THE WHOOPING CRANE?

At one time whooping cranes lived throughout North America. As cities, farms, and highways replaced plains and prairies, however, their natural homes disappeared. Today whooping cranes are an endangered species. They are dying out.

The largest group of wild whooping cranes spends its winters in or near the Aransas Wildlife Refuge on the Texas coast. To protect the cranes, no oil drilling can take place near the refuge during the winter months. Other rules prevent certain types of construction near the cranes' homes. Some Texans, such as David Hernandez, believe that the cranes should be protected. Others, like King Fisher, believe some rules protecting the birds are too costly. Some, like Deanna Appell, have mixed views. Read and consider three viewpoints on the issue. Then answer the questions that follow.

Three DIFFERENT Viewpoints

1 DEANNA APPELL
Tourboat Captain, Rockport
Excerpt from Interview, 1995

There are ways humans can work to benefit themselves while still helping wildlife. It takes a little more planning and effort. Wildlife is our first warning of anything going wrong in the environment. We should protect it. On the other hand, I have seen businesses go broke because of rules protecting some small animal.

". . . more planning and effort."

2 KING FISHER
Marine Construction Manager, Port Lavaca
Excerpt from Interview, 1995

The whooping cranes are overprotected. We need environmental protection, but we need a little common sense too. Oil and chemical spills on the waterway are less common than people think. There's a lot of taxpayer money spent on cranes that could be spent on better things.

". . . cranes are overprotected."

3 DAVID HERNANDEZ
Conservation Scientist, Austin
Excerpt from Interview, 1995

The loss of the whooping crane or any other species is an indicator that there is a big problem in the environment. Scientists estimate that one species goes extinct somewhere in the world every day. There is no separation between nature and humans. Protecting the crane protects many other species and our future as well.

". . . one species goes extinct . . . everyday."

BUILDING CITIZENSHIP

1. What is the viewpoint of each person? How does each person support his or her view?
2. In what ways do the viewpoints agree? How do they disagree?
3. What other viewpoints might people have? How could you find out more about this issue in your community?

SHARING VIEWPOINTS

Discuss what you agree with or disagree with about these and other viewpoints. As a class, make a chart showing the various ways the whooping crane might be protected without hurting businesses in our state.

GEOGRAPHYSKILLS

Using Map Scales

VOCABULARY

scale

WHY THE SKILL MATTERS

Suppose your new job requires you to travel to many cities in Texas. How can you find out how far apart these cities are? Scale on a map can tell you the answer. Scale is the relationship between the distance shown on a map and the real distance. A map has a scale because it is not the same size as the area it represents.

Look at the map of Texas on this page. It is marked Map A. Then look at the map of Texas on the facing page. It is marked Map B. The two maps are drawn to different scales.

Why are the two maps here drawn to different scales? Some maps need to include many details. To show many details, a map cannot include a very large area. A very detailed map that shows every street, tree, and building might cover an area of only a few blocks. If less detail is necessary, a map can show a much larger area.

USING THE SKILL

Look again at Map A on this page. Find the map scale. The top line shows how many miles on Earth are shown by one inch on the map. One inch stands

Map A: TEXAS

for 500 miles. The bottom line shows how many kilometers on Earth are shown by one and one-half centimeters.

Suppose you wanted to measure the distance from San Antonio to Brownsville. You might make a guess by looking at the map scale. However, you could make a more accurate measurement by using a scale strip.

Use the scale on the Texas map above to make a scale strip. Place a piece of paper below the scale and mark the distances. Your scale strip should look like this:

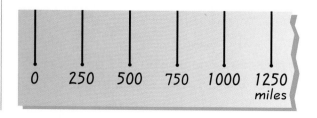

Place the edge of the scale strip between the symbols for the two Texas cities. Make sure the zero is directly below San Antonio. Then read the numbers beneath Brownsville. You can see that the distance between the cities is about 250 miles. How far is El Paso from San Antonio? What is this distance in inches on the map?

HELPING
Yourself

- **Different scales allow maps to show either more detail or a greater area.**
- **Study the scale on the map.**
- **You can make a scale strip to find out the real distance between points on a map.**

TRYING THE SKILL

Now look at Map B on this page. This map shows some of the same area of land as the first one. As you can see, however, the areas are different sizes. If you compare the two map scales, you will see that they are different. On which map does one inch stand for a greater distance? Which map shows more detail? Use the Helping Yourself box for hints.

Using your scale strip, measure the distance between San Antonio and Dallas. What is the distance in miles? On Map A, the two cities are half an inch apart. On Map B they are one inch apart. On which map does one inch stand for a smaller distance?

REVIEWING THE SKILL

1. What information does a map scale give us about a map?

2. How does using a scale strip help to make accurate measurements?

3. Which map would you use to find the distance between Odessa and Lubbock? What is the distance between the two cities in miles? What is the distance in miles between Amarillo and El Paso?

4. What information is shown on Map B that is not shown on Map A?

5. When might it be helpful to use maps drawn to different scales?

Map B: TEXAS

★ State capital
• Other city
— Major road
National park

NE   IA
KS
MO
OK
NM   Amarillo
AR
Red River
Lubbock   Wichita Falls
Guadalupe Mountains National Park
Midland   Fort Worth   Dallas
El Paso   Odessa   Colorado River
Pecos River   TEXAS   Brazos River   Trinity River
Presidio   Austin ★
Rio Grande   San Antonio   Houston
Big Bend National Park   Nueces River   Galveston
Corpus Christi
Laredo
MEXICO   Brownsville   Gulf of Mexico

N W E S

0   100   200   250 Miles
0   100   200   250 Kilometers

FARMING AND RANCHING

READ ALOUD

Clem Mikeska and his brothers grew up working in the meat business in Temple, Texas. Their father came from Czechoslovakia, which is now the Czech and Slovak republics. He was a farmer. Clem says, "The best thing in Texas to eat is beef. Texas beef!"

THE BIG PICTURE

Until the early 1900s over half the people in our state lived and worked on farms and ranches. As you read in the last lesson, many Texans moved from rural to urban areas to take jobs in industry during World War II. The move to the cities continued after the war. In 1940 there were 418,000 farms in Texas. In 1992 this number dropped to 183,000.

Another change that came to rural Texas was the growth of agribusiness. An agribusiness is a farm or ranch which is combined with other businesses, such as food processing. A family farm can be an agribusiness, too. These farms often grow several different crops and ship them across the country. Together they produce an astounding variety of food products that end up on kitchen tables across the United States and around the world. How do these farmers and ranchers do it?

Focus Activity

READ TO LEARN
How has modern technology changed farming and ranching in Texas?

VOCABULARY
agribusiness
agriculture

PLACES
Linn
King Ranch

MODERN FARMING

Today farming in Texas is big business. Modern equipment has made agriculture, or the business of growing crops and raising animals, a high-tech industry.

Farm Life Today

The Guerra (GAIR ruh) family farm is near the town of Linn, not far from our border with Mexico. The Guerra family has farmed this land for four generations. The Guerras grow peaches, jalapeño peppers, and watermelons on 1,500 acres. Much of the farm work is still done by hand, such as picking the peaches and cutting back trees.

When it comes to packing, however, modern technology takes over. The Guerras have special machines that sort and de-fuzz the peaches. They even have a special sensor that picks out overripe peaches.

The Guerra farm has modernized in other ways as well. For example, a new irrigation system has been installed below ground. As you have read, irrigation is a system that supplies water to dry land. A layer of plastic on top of the ground keeps water from evaporating in hot weather. Since water is in short supply, this new system helps preserve this precious resource. José Guerra says, "It's expensive, but you're growing produce with less water and making the most of the water you use. You also cut down on using chemicals to control weeds."

The Pick of the Crop

One of the most important crops in our state is cotton. More cotton is grown in Texas than in any other state. The soft fibers from this plant end up in everything from blue jeans to spacesuits.

The farmers of North Texas grow vast fields of wheat and a grain called sorghum. Near the Gulf Coast, rice is an important crop. Along the Colorado River, pecans and other nuts are grown. In the warm Rio Grande Valley, farmers raise vegetables and fruits, including oranges and grapefruits.

José Guerra says, "To see things grow and watch people enjoy the fruits of your labor—that sums up why I'm a farmer."

319

RANCHING TODAY

Ever since the Spanish first brought cattle to Texas 400 years ago, ranching has been part of life in Texas. Texans also raise poultry, hogs, and sheep. However, cattle remain the most important livestock. Today there are more cattle raised in Texas than anywhere else in the United States. Look at the map below to see the agricultural products that are grown in our state.

The King Ranch

Since much of the ranch land in Texas is very dry and has little vegetation, cattle need a lot of room to graze. One of the biggest ranches in the world is the King Ranch which is located in South Texas. This ranch spreads over 800,000 acres—larger than the whole state of Rhode Island.

Ranching today is different from when Richard King founded the ranch back in 1853. Now, two thousand miles of fences keep the 60,000 cattle inside the ranch. In addition to horses the ranchers use helicopters to travel around. The cattle are branded and electronic devices are attached to the ears of calves. This

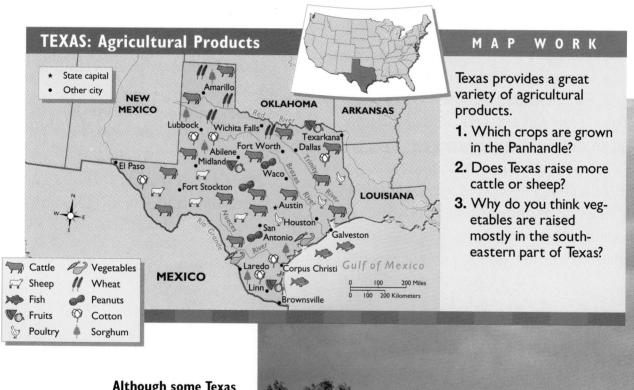

TEXAS: Agricultural Products

Legend:
★ State capital
• Other city

NEW MEXICO, OKLAHOMA, ARKANSAS, LOUISIANA, MEXICO

Cities: Amarillo, Lubbock, Wichita Falls, Texarkana, Fort Worth, Dallas, Abilene, Midland, El Paso, Waco, Fort Stockton, Austin, Houston, San Antonio, Galveston, Laredo, Corpus Christi, Linn, Brownsville

Rivers: Red River, Brazos River, Trinity River, Nueces River, Rio Grande

Gulf of Mexico

Map key:
- Cattle
- Sheep
- Fish
- Fruits
- Poultry
- Vegetables
- Wheat
- Peanuts
- Cotton
- Sorghum

Scale: 0 100 200 Miles / 0 100 200 Kilometers

MAP WORK

Texas provides a great variety of agricultural products.

1. Which crops are grown in the Panhandle?
2. Does Texas raise more cattle or sheep?
3. Why do you think vegetables are raised mostly in the southeastern part of Texas?

Although some Texas ranches are as small as 10 acres, some are so big that ranchers use helicopters to keep track of cattle.

helps keep track of their feeding schedules and health records.

There is a lot of activity on the King Ranch besides raising cattle. Scientists here study ways to find better feed to improve the health of the animals. They even created a special breed of cattle called Santa Gertrudis. This breed is very well suited to the hot and humid climate of South Texas.

WHY IT MATTERS

Agriculture is an important part of our state's economy. Modern technology has helped farmers and ranchers produce more food than in the past. Today, planes, trains, and ships help to transport Texas products all over the world.

Links to **ART**

Cattle Brands

Where did the tradition of branding cattle come from?

The Spanish brought the practice of branding cattle to Texas almost 300 years ago. They created pictographs, or picture–like symbols, to identify the owner of the branded cattle. In the United States a leaning letter was called "tumbling" and a letter resting on its side was called "lazy." The King Ranch brand is a "running" W, which means it has short, curved lines on top. It is still used at the ranch today.

Suppose that you own a ranch. Create a special brand for your cattle.

Reviewing Facts and Ideas

SUM IT UP

- Major Texas farm products include cotton, sorghum, wheat, rice, nuts, fruits, and vegetables.
- By using new technology, farmers and ranchers are finding better ways of raising crops and cattle.

THINK ABOUT IT

1. Name some major Texas crops.

2. Why are some ranches so big?

3. **FOCUS** How has technology changed farming and ranching in Texas?

4. **THINKING SKILL** *Compare* and *contrast* a modern Texas farm with one from 100 years ago.

5. **WRITE** Suppose you live on a farm or ranch. Write a journal entry telling about your day.

321

STATE FAIR

The farmers and ranchers in our state are among those who look forward to the State Fair of Texas in October. The fair is a time for them to see each other and have fun. The fair began over 100 years ago. Horse racing was the big attraction back then. Today the fair has many of the same events as it had 100 years ago.

Each year millions of people visit the fairgrounds in Dallas. There are livestock and horse shows. Boys and girls enter livestock they've raised themselves. They all hope to win a blue ribbon.

Texans from all over our state display their homemade jams, jellies, cookies, and cakes. Visitors enjoy music, dancing, parades, and amusement rides. There are lots of delicious foods to eat too.

The State Fair of Texas is an event that people look forward to each year. It is a legacy for all Texans to enjoy and share.

Big Tex, the 52-foot-tall cowboy, welcomes visitors to the State Fair of Texas. Fairgoers enjoy cooking and craft contests, concerts, rodeos, and fireworks displays. The fair has something for everybody.

The fairgrounds, called Fair Park, have been a National Historic Landmark since 1986. The Texas Star Ferris Wheel provides riders with a great view.

The livestock show is always a popular event. This nine-year-old girl has worked hard all year to raise her prize steer.

323

CHAPTER 10 REVIEW

THINKING ABOUT VOCABULARY

Number a sheet of paper from 1 to 10. Next to each number write the word or term from the list below that best matches the statement.

agribusiness

agriculture

consumer

economy

entrepreneur

food processing

free-enterprise system

investor

manufacturing

profit

1. The way a community uses its natural resources, goods, and services to meet peoples' needs and wants

2. Someone who puts money into a business

3. Someone who buys a product or uses a service

4. The money a business earns after it pays for costs

5. A large farm or ranch that is combined with other businesses

6. The business of growing crops or raising animals

7. A person who organizes and runs a business

8. The freedom of people to own and run their own businesses

9. Any way of turning raw food into different kinds of products

10. Making goods by the use of machinery

THINKING ABOUT FACTS

1. What are some of the first steps in starting a business?

2. What are some examples of service jobs? Think of one kind of service job that is not listed in the chapter.

3. How could Taking Care of Business tell their business was a success?

4. What are three factors that contribute to our state's successful economy?

5. What are some products that are made from our state's natural resources?

6. Why is Johnson Space Center important to our state?

7. What are the three biggest cities in Texas? What is each known for?

8. Why were there fewer family farms in our state after World War II?

9. What crop is grown more in our state than in any other state?

10. Which Texas ranch is one of the largest ranches in the world?

THINK AND WRITE

WRITING A LIST

Suppose you are a news reporter in July 1969. Bernard Harris has just returned from a space flight. Write three questions you would ask him in an interview.

WRITING A BUSINESS PLAN

Think of a product or service that people might buy. Write a business plan for your idea. Include the things you would need to get started—such as time, money, tools, and supplies. Name your company and plan your advertising.

WRITING A JOB DESCRIPTION

Choose an industry in our state that you might like to work in someday. Write a description of a job in that industry that you might enjoy doing.

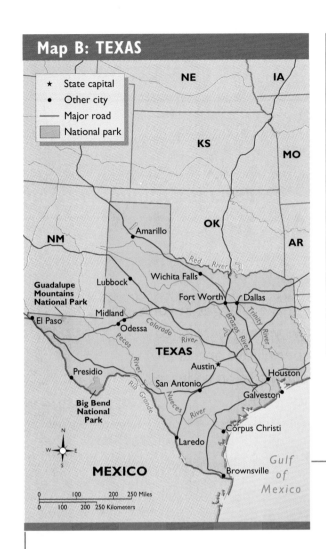

Map B: TEXAS

Legend:
- ★ State capital
- • Other city
- — Major road
- National park

NE
IA
KS
MO
OK
AR
NM
Amarillo
Red River
Guadalupe Mountains National Park
Lubbock
Wichita Falls
Fort Worth
Dallas
El Paso
Midland
Odessa
Colorado River
Pecos River
TEXAS
Brazos River
Trinity River
Presidio
Austin ★
Houston
San Antonio
Galveston
Rio Grande
Big Bend National Park
Nueces River
Córpus Christi
Laredo
MEXICO
Brownsville
Gulf of Mexico

0   100   200   250 Miles
0   100   200   250 Kilometers

N W E S

APPLYING GEOGRAPHY SKILLS

USING MAP SCALES

Refer to the map on this page to answer the following questions.

1. What is a map scale?

2. How does a scale strip help you to measure distances accurately?

3. Use a scale strip to measure the distance between Dallas and El Paso. Approximately how many miles is it from Amarillo to Brownsville?

4. Which cities are closer—Houston and Amarillo, or Dallas and El Paso?

5. Why is it useful to have maps drawn at different scales?

Summing Up the Chapter

Use the following word maps to organize information from the chapter. Copy the word maps on a sheet of paper. Then write at least one piece of information in each blank circle. When you have filled in the maps, use them to write a paragraph that answers the question "How do people in Texas make a living?"

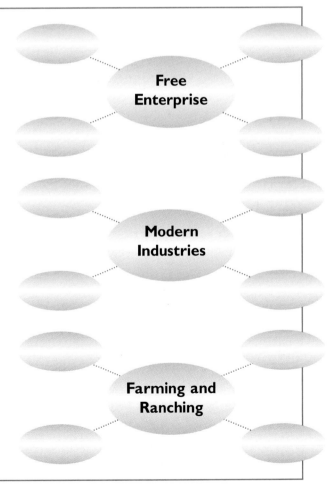

Free Enterprise

Modern Industries

Farming and Ranching

CHAPTER 11

Texas Government and You

THINKING ABOUT GEOGRAPHY AND CITIZENSHIP

Have you ever wondered how you could help make changes in your community? Have you ever thought about ways you would like to help our state? Do you know what your responsibilities are as an American? This chapter is all about government. Read on to learn how our local, state, and national governments work.

UNITED STATES

TEXAS

Austin

MEXICO

Gulf of Mexico

OUR LOCAL GOVERNMENT

READ ALOUD

Mayor Eva F. Medrano of Mathis wants people of all ages to take part in their community. In 1995 she said:

"We are the government. We all have the power to make our communities better places to live. We can make our voices heard when we vote."

THE BIG PICTURE

Texans are proud of being citizens of the United States. Citizens are people who are born in a country or who have earned the right to become members of that country. United States citizens have special rights, and also responsibilities and duties. In our country citizens elect their government leaders. To elect is to choose by voting. Leaders carry out the wishes of the people who elected them. Citizens have the important duty of paying taxes. Governments use tax money to pay for services such as fixing roads and building new schools.

In this lesson you will read about the ways in which our city, county, and other local governments affect our lives.

Focus Activity

READ TO LEARN
What role do citizens play in our cities and local government?

VOCABULARY
citizen
elect
municipal
mayor
city council
city manager
special district
county
commissioners court
sheriff

PEOPLE
Eva F. Medrano

PLACES
Mathis

328

GOVERNMENT IN YOUR COMMUNITY

Why is it important to have a government in your town or city? Local government is needed to make decisions. Of course, you—and your family—make decisions all the time. Some decisions affect only you. For example, you may decide where you want to play ball after school. But what if you thought that the playground you use should have new equipment? You could not make this decision alone. A new playground would affect your entire community. This decision would probably be made by your local government.

Local Government

The town or city where you live has a **municipal** government. Municipal, or city, governments provide many services. They build and care for sidewalks and street lights. Many municipal governments decide where new homes and businesses should be built. They run libraries, parks, and local police departments. When a public street needs to be repaired, a municipal department has it fixed. If there is a fire, the municipal fire department puts it out.

Look at the photographs on this page. They show some of the services that municipal governments provide. How are these services alike? How are they different? Do they protect us and improve our way of life? Helping people is what government is all about.

Government workers help us in many ways. A police officer (top) warns about drugs; a firefighter (center) battles a blaze; and a city worker (bottom) plants flowers.

MUNICIPAL GOVERNMENT

The chart shows that municipal governments are usually run by a mayor and a city council. Both are elected by the people who live in a city. The mayor is the head of the municipal government. The city council is a group of people that makes laws for and helps run a city or town. Traditionally, city councils in Texas have 5 to 9 members.

Mayors and city council members usually do not work for the government full-time. They often have other jobs. In cities such as Dallas and San Antonio, the mayor and city council hire a full-time city manager to run the city's daily business.

A Mayor's Job

In 1987 Eva F. Medrano was elected mayor of Mathis for two years. Mathis is near Corpus Christi. Since then she has been reelected four times. As mayor of Mathis she helps decide the goals that are important to the city. Mayor Medrano has been involved in rebuilding playgrounds and softball fields in Mathis. She has also taken actions to make sure that the city's drinking water is clean. And she has supported a program that brings students to work in city hall. This program helps students earn money and learn about their local government.

Special Districts

A special district is another kind of local government. It is formed for a special purpose. One kind of special district might oversee schools. A school district is run by a group of elected officials called school board members or trustees. They decide how to spend the district's money, help plan what students learn, and make other decisions about schools.

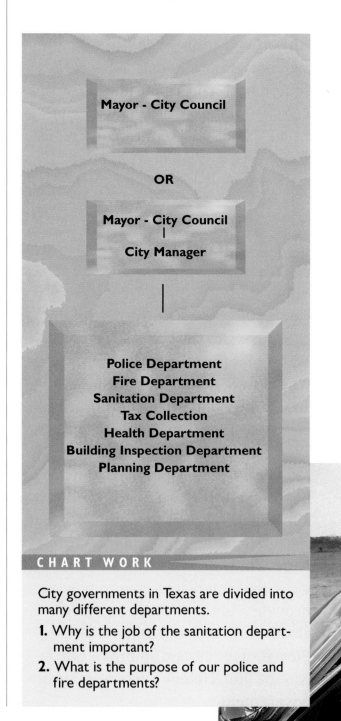

Mayor - City Council

OR

Mayor - City Council
|
City Manager

Police Department
Fire Department
Sanitation Department
Tax Collection
Health Department
Building Inspection Department
Planning Department

CHART WORK

City governments in Texas are divided into many different departments.

1. Why is the job of the sanitation department important?
2. What is the purpose of our police and fire departments?

COUNTY GOVERNMENT

County government is a third kind of local government. A county is one of the sections into which a state is divided. There are 254 counties in Texas—more than in any other state! Look at the county map in the atlas on page R18 and find the county in which you live.

County governments in Texas repair county roads and run the local courthouse and jail. Counties may also operate some hospitals, museums, and airports.

The commissioners court is a group of five elected leaders who make decisions about county issues. The head of the commissioners court is the county judge. Members of the court serve four-year terms.

Each county in Texas has a sheriff. The sheriff is the person in charge of the county's law-enforcement department. He or she makes sure that people obey the laws.

This officer in the Travis County Sheriff's Department helps enforce county laws.

WHY IT MATTERS

Government leaders make decisions that affect our health, safety, and education. Local government provides many services. But some problems cannot be solved entirely at the municipal or county level. Local government often works with state government to solve problems. In the next lesson, you will learn about the state government of Texas.

✓ Reviewing Facts and Ideas

SUM IT UP

- In the United States, citizens elect their government leaders to make laws and to provide services.
- Three kinds of local government are municipal, special district, and county governments.
- Municipal governments are run by a mayor and city council.
- The commissioners court is a group of five elected officials that makes decisions about county issues. The county judge is head of the commissioners court.

THINK ABOUT IT

1. What is a citizen?
2. What is a county?
3. **FOCUS** In what ways can citizens play a role in municipal and county government?
4. **THINKING SKILL** _Compare_ and _contrast_ the roles of municipal governments and special districts.
5. **WRITE** Write to the mayor of your town or city to find out more about what he or she does.

STUDYSKILLS

Reading Newspapers

VOCABULARY
news article
feature article
editorial
headline
byline
dateline

WHY THE SKILL MATTERS

You have just read that municipal governments are run by a mayor, a city council, and sometimes a city manager. What if you wanted to learn more about the decisions officials make? A good way to find out is to read a newspaper.

Reading a newspaper is often the best way to get information about what is happening today. Many newspapers cover events from all over our country and around the world. Some focus on events from a state, city, or town.

USING A NEWSPAPER

When you read a newspaper, it helps to know the different parts. Use the Helping Yourself box on page 333 to guide you in reading newspapers. The front section of a paper includes mostly news articles. These articles contain facts about recent events.

Another kind of article is a feature article. A feature article takes a detailed look at a specific person, subject, or event.

Newspapers also include sports articles, letters to the editor, and editorials. In an editorial, the editors—the people who run the paper—share their ideas about an issue. Unlike a news article, an editorial gives opinions rather than facts.

USING A NEWS ARTICLE

A news article usually begins with a headline—a title printed at the top of the story. The headline tells the main idea of the story in just a few words.

Look at the news article on the facing page. It is based on an article that appeared in the *Corpus Christi Caller-Times*. Find the headline "Portland Passes Skateboarding, Inline Skating Rules."

News articles often have a byline. The byline names the writer of the article. The writer of this story is Dan Parker.

Finally, many news articles include a dateline. This tells when and where the article was written. The dateline here tells you that this article was written on February 8, 1995, in Portland.

A well-written news article should answer five questions: (1) *Who* was involved in the event? (2) *What* took place? (3) *When* did the event happen? (4) *Where* did the event happen? (5) *Why* did the event happen?

Read this article. Does the article answer the five questions? The first answer, for example, might be "the Portland City Council." Can you explain *what* happened in your own words? Can you say *why* it happened?

TRYING THE SKILL

You just read a news article about a decision by the Portland City Council to make skateboarders and in-line skaters follow certain rules on public roads. Why do you think that reading a newspaper is a good way to learn about such an event? Can you think of any other sources for this kind of information?

Now suppose that your class is curious about a different topic: the construction of a new state highway. An article in the newspaper is called "Highway Opening Delayed." What kind of article do you think this is? Another is called "New

HELPING Yourself

- **Identify whether you are reading a news article, a feature article, or an editorial.**
- **Study the headline, byline, and dateline.**
- **Ask yourself the "five questions" about the story.**

Highway Is a Step in the Right Direction." What kind of article do you think this is? How do you know?

REVIEWING THE SKILL

1. Name three different kinds of articles that appear in newspapers.

2. How can you tell that the article printed below is a news article and not an editorial?

3. Why is it important for some news articles to have a dateline?

4. How would a newspaper help you learn more about Texas?

Portland Passes Skateboarding, Inline Skating Rules

By Dan Parker
PORTLAND, Texas, February 8—The Portland City Council on Tuesday passed a law limiting in-line skating and skateboarding after police reported complaints that skaters were darting into traffic and nearly causing accidents.

"We're going to address the situation before we have a tragedy that brings it home to all of us," said Portland Mayor Bill Webb.

"What I think the law says is that people on Rollerblades have to show good sense and follow the same kinds of rules a pedestrian or bicyclist would," Portland City Manager Rick Conner said.

But some parents opposed the law. They said children will be particularly hurt by it because many youngsters use skates and skateboards as a method of transportation around town.

OUR STATE'S GOVERNMENT

READ ALOUD

In 1995 Governor George W. Bush wrote this message to students reading this book:

"Your education is very important because you are the future of the Lone Star State. I want you to know that people love you and care about you and want you to succeed. You can be anything you want to be: a doctor, a lawyer, a teacher, even the Governor of Texas . . . if you study and work hard."

Focus Activity

READ TO LEARN
What are the jobs of the three branches of state government?

VOCABULARY
checks and balances
budget
executive branch
legislative branch
bill
veto
judicial branch

PEOPLE
George W. Bush
Ann Richards

PLACES
Austin

THE BIG PICTURE

The Texas Constitution we use today was modeled after the United States Constitution. It explains the three branches of state government and the duties of each one. A branch is a part of government. Our state constitution also describes the rights of our state's citizens.

The government has three branches so that no person or group of people will have too much power. Each branch of government keeps watch over the other two branches. This idea is called the principle of checks and balances.

OUR STATE AND YOU

Have you ever visited Austin, our state capital? Every day important decisions are made there. These decisions affect the daily lives of every Texan—including you!

Our state government provides services to people. For example, state workers take care of state parks and highways. Texans pay state taxes to provide for these services.

To decide how much to spend on services, our state government makes a plan for using taxes. This plan is called a budget. The circle graph shows how Texas spends taxes and other money.

The Executive Branch

You read the words of Governor George W. Bush in the Read Aloud. The governor is the head of the executive (eg ZEK yoo tihv) branch of our state's government. The job of the executive branch is to carry out the laws of the state.

The governor is elected by the people of our state to serve for a term of four years. The governor helps set goals for our state. He or she also chooses people to run state departments, such as the Department of Public Safety. The governor's office is in Austin. Many other state government offices are also located in Austin.

Ann Richards was governor of our state from 1991 to 1995. What does she say about government in this passage from her autobiography?

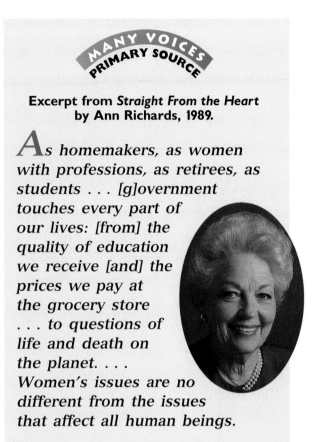

MANY VOICES PRIMARY SOURCE

Excerpt from *Straight From the Heart* by Ann Richards, 1989.

As homemakers, as women with professions, as retirees, as students . . . [g]overnment touches every part of our lives: [from] the quality of education we receive [and] the prices we pay at the grocery store . . . to questions of life and death on the planet. . . . Women's issues are no different from the issues that affect all human beings.

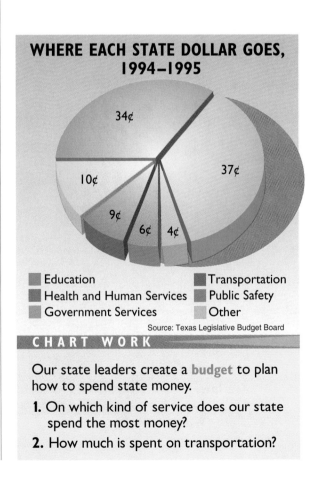

WHERE EACH STATE DOLLAR GOES, 1994–1995

34¢
10¢
37¢
9¢
6¢ 4¢

- Education
- Health and Human Services
- Government Services
- Transportation
- Public Safety
- Other

Source: Texas Legislative Budget Board

CHART WORK

Our state leaders create a budget to plan how to spend state money.

1. On which kind of service does our state spend the most money?
2. How much is spent on transportation?

335

THE LEGISLATIVE BRANCH

The **legislative** (LEJ is lay tiv) **branch** of our state makes the laws. The legislative branch has two parts—the Senate and the House of Representatives. The 31 senators and 150 representatives are elected by Texas voters. State senators serve four-year terms and representatives serve two-year terms. Senators and representatives work and vote on **bills**. Bills are proposals for laws.

How does a bill become a law? Let's follow the history of one bill. You know that James Hogg was governor of Texas from 1891 to 1895. Before he died, Governor Hogg told a friend he wanted a pecan tree planted on his grave. He said he wanted the nuts from this tree to be given to citizens "so that they may plant them and make Texas a land of trees."

In 1919 a member of the Texas legislative branch proposed a bill making the pecan tree our state tree. The Senate and the House of Representatives voted to pass the bill. Then it went to Governor William P. Hobby. If he had disagreed with the bill, he could have decided to **veto**, or reject it. Instead, he signed it. The pecan tree became and still is the state tree of Texas. Follow the steps in the chart below to see how a bill becomes law.

The Judicial Branch

The **judicial** (joo DISH uhl) **branch** of state government interprets, or

Follow the steps showing how a bill becomes a law.

HOW A BILL BECOMES A LAW

1 Citizens develop idea for a bill.

2 Members of the House of Representatives or the Senate propose the bill.

3 The House of Representatives and the Senate vote to approve the bill.

4 The governor signs the bill. OR The governor vetoes the bill.

5 If vetoed, more than 2/3 of the House of Representatives and the Senate vote for the bill again.

6 **Law** The bill becomes a law.

These high school students are learning about our state government by spending a day at the House of Representatives in Austin.

explains, our state's laws. This branch is made up of judges, who work in courts. The highest courts in Texas are the Court of Criminal Appeals and the Supreme Court. Texas voters elect nine judges to each of these courts. These judges serve six-year terms. The Court of Criminal Appeals handles important criminal cases. The Supreme Court handles cases involving such issues as property and disagreements over money.

Learn About Your Government

Every year about 1,500 high school students in Texas are selected to take part in programs called American Legion Auxiliary Bluebonnet Girls State and American Legion Boys State. These students go to Austin and the city of Seguin to experience what it is like to work in state government. When you are 18, you will be able to vote for our state's leaders. But don't wait until then to participate!

WHY IT MATTERS

A government works well when its citizens take an interest in what is happening. There are many ways to take part in government. What issues interest you? Write letters to your representatives. Elected officials need to hear from citizens in order to represent their views.

Reviewing Facts and Ideas

SUM IT UP

- The checks and balances system makes sure no one branch of government has too much power.
- Our state government provides services to the people of Texas.
- The state government is made of the executive, legislative, and judicial branches.

THINK ABOUT IT

1. What are checks and balances?

2. How does a bill become a law in our state?

3. **FOCUS** What is the job of each branch of our state government?

4. **THINKING SKILL** *Make a conclusion* about why it is important for citizens to communicate with their state leaders.

5. **GEOGRAPHY** Look in your local telephone book. Name any state offices located in or near your city.

OUR NATION'S GOVERNMENT

Focus Activity

READ TO LEARN
What are the rights and responsibilities we have as Americans?

VOCABULARY
democratic republic
elect
candidate
political party
United States Congress
United States Supreme Court
jury

PLACES
Washington, D.C.

READ ALOUD

"I pledge allegiance to the flag of the United States of America, and to the Republic for which it stands, one Nation under God, indivisible, with liberty and justice for all."

THE BIG PICTURE

These words are probably very familiar to you. When you say the Pledge of Allegiance, you make a promise. You are promising to be loyal to the United States and to support our country's government.

Running a government is not easy. After declaring the United States an independent country in 1776, our country's first leaders found just how tough the job is. In 1787 they wrote the Constitution, the plan for running our government.

The United States Constitution explains how the government is to be set up. The Constitution made our country a democratic republic. In our democratic republic, people pick representatives to run the government. Democracy means that the power to rule comes from the people.

THE UNITED STATES GOVERNMENT

In 1863 President Abraham Lincoln said that we have a "government of the people, by the people, for the people." His words remind us that democracy cannot work without its citizens. People in a democratic republic must care about choices that affect each other.

But the United States is a big country. Not every citizen can take part directly in every decision. They take part by voting. Voters elect, or choose, people to make decisions for them.

In an election, the people running for office are called candidates. Usually candidates are members of a political party. A political party is a group of citizens who share many of the same ideas about government. The Democratic and Republican parties are the largest political parties in the United States.

Like our local and state governments, the United States government provides services. One of these is defense. The United States government runs the Army and the rest of our armed forces. Our government pays for the building of ships, airplanes, and weapons to defend our country—as well as other countries.

Another service our government provides is disaster relief. The Federal Emergency Management Agency helps people recover from hurricanes, earthquakes, and other disasters. When Houston was flooded in 1994, this agency provided temporary shelter, replaced people's damaged belongings, and helped rebuild roads and homes.

Texans pay taxes on money earned to the national government. But unlike people in many other states, Texans do not pay this kind of tax, called an income tax, to our state government. Texans pay sales taxes to our state and local governments on things we buy. In addition, local governments in Texas collect taxes on houses, businesses, and other property. Without taxes the different levels of government could not provide the services we need.

When you are 18 you will be able to vote. Voting is a responsibility of all Americans.

REGISTER AND VOTE AMERI...

THE THREE BRANCHES

Our national government is located in Washington, D.C. Like our state government, our country's government has three branches. Each branch has different duties. Find these branches on the chart.

Congress

The legislative branch of our national government is called the United States Congress. Congress makes laws for the whole country. Congress has two parts, the Senate and the House of Representatives.

The voters of every state elect two senators to the United States Senate. The number of representatives voters elect depends on how many people live in their state. Texas, which has a large population, elects 30 people to the United States House of Representatives. The state of Vermont, on the other hand, elects only one representative. Senators serve for six years and representatives serve for two years.

The President

The President is elected every four years. This person is head of the executive branch of government. The President makes sure that laws passed by Congress are carried out. The President also meets with leaders of other countries and is Commander-in-Chief of our military forces. The President chooses people to head national departments in charge of areas such as transportation and defense.

NATIONAL GOVERNMENT: Three Branches

EXECUTIVE President	**LEGISLATIVE** Congress (100 Senators, 435 Representatives)	**JUDICIAL** Supreme Court (9 Judges)
● Carries out laws ● Meets with leaders of other countries ● Leads military	● Makes laws for our country ● Decides how much money to spend	● Makes sure our laws follow the Constitution

CHART WORK

Our national government, located in Washington, D.C., has three branches.

1. How many senators does Congress have? How many representatives?

2. Which branch does the President head?
3. What are the President's duties?
4. Who are the highest officials of the judicial branch of our government?

A Free People

The Congress, the President, and the Supreme Court all work hard to protect the rights of American citizens. So do state and local officials.

All Americans have the right to say what they believe about our country.

Americans also have the right to practice their own religions. The Constitution also promises that every American will be treated fairly under the law.

With rights come responsibilities. Citizens must pay taxes and obey our country's laws. As Americans, we are expected to learn about important issues and let our representatives know what we think. And at election time, it's important that we vote.

THE COURTS

The President also selects the judges of the United States Supreme Court. The Supreme Court is the highest court in our country. The courts make up the third branch of our national government. It is called the judicial branch.

Nine justices, or judges, serve on the United States Supreme Court. Once chosen and approved by the Senate, they serve for life. These judges hear cases that come from the lower courts. They also decide whether laws that are passed by Congress agree with the United States Constitution.

The lower courts decide whether laws have been obeyed. If a person is accused of breaking the law, the courts ask a jury to observe the trial. A jury is a group of citizens that decides whether the accused person is guilty under the law. United State citizens who are 18 or older may be called to serve on a jury.

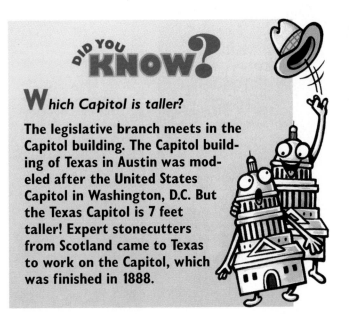

DID YOU KNOW?

Which Capitol is taller?

The legislative branch meets in the Capitol building. The Capitol building of Texas in Austin was modeled after the United States Capitol in Washington, D.C. But the Texas Capitol is 7 feet taller! Expert stonecutters from Scotland came to Texas to work on the Capitol, which was finished in 1888.

Infographic

Serving the Country in Washington D.C.

Many Texan men and women have played important parts in our country's government and history. In just the last 50 years, Texas has sent three Presidents to the White House. Other Texans have become known for their work in Congress or for heading important government departments.

KAY BAILEY HUTCHISON

Member of the United States Senate (first Texas woman to hold this post)

Took office in 1993

GEORGE BUSH

President of the United States

1989-1993

LYNDON B. JOHNSON

President of the United States

1963-1969

DWIGHT D. EISENHOWER

President of the United States

1953-1961

HENRY G. CISNEROS

United States Secretary of Housing and Urban Development

Took office in 1993

WHITE HOUSE

Lafayette Square

NEW YORK AVENUE

MASSA

17TH STREET

18TH STREET

14TH STREET

12TH STREET

9TH STREET

7TH STREET

D STREET

PENNSYLVANIA AVENUE

The Ellipse

CONSTITUTION AVENUE

NATIONAL MUSEUM OF AMERICAN HISTORY

NATIONAL MUSEUM OF NATURAL HISTORY

MADISON

DRIVE

The

National

Mall

NATIONAL GALLERY OF ART (WEST)

NATIONAL GALLERY OF AR (EAST)

CC

Constitution

Gardens

JEFFERSON

DRIVE

NATIONAL AIR AND SPACE MUSEUM

3RD STREET

WASHINGTON MONUMENT

SMITHSONIAN

IND

Tidal Basin

D STREET

VIRGINIA AVENUE

9TH STREET

7TH STREET

DEPARTMENT OF HOUSING AND URBAN DEVELOPMENT

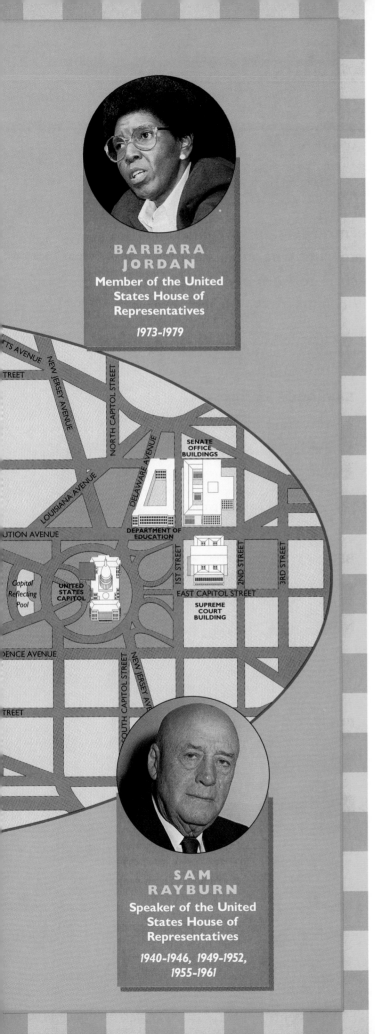

BARBARA JORDAN

Member of the United States House of Representatives

1973-1979

SAM RAYBURN

Speaker of the United States House of Representatives

1940-1946, 1949-1952, 1955-1961

WHY IT MATTERS

The United States is a democratic republic. Citizens elect leaders to serve in government. Texans are proud of the many people from our state who have served in our national government. You can see some of these leaders in the Infographic on these pages.

When you turn 18, you will be able to vote for national, state, and local leaders. Voting in elections will be your right and your responsibility.

✓ Reviewing Facts and Ideas

SUM IT UP

- The United States government uses taxes to pay for services such as defense and disaster relief.

- The three branches of our national government are headed by Congress, the President, and the Supreme Court.

- As Americans, Texans have the right to free speech, to practice their religion, to receive a fair trial, and to vote for their leaders.

THINK ABOUT IT

1. What is a democratic republic?

2. What is a political party?

3. **FOCUS** What rights and responsibilities do you have as an American citizen?

4. **THINKING SKILL** How can voters *make a decision* about which candidate to elect?

5. **WRITE** What qualities do you think are important in a citizen?

343

A NEW CENTURY IN THE WESTERN HEMISPHERE

Throughout this book you have been reading about connections with other places in the United States and with other countries of the Western Hemisphere. Use the chart to learn about each country of the Western Hemisphere. Which country is the largest in area? Which are the smallest?

ANTIGUA AND BARBUDA

CAPITAL★ St. John's

POPULATION 65,000

MAJOR LANGUAGE English

AREA 170 sq mi; 440 sq km

LEADING EXPORTS petroleum products, clothing, and household appliances

CONTINENT North America

ARGENTINA

CAPITAL★ Buenos Aires

POPULATION 33.9 million

MAJOR LANGUAGES Spanish, English, and Italian

AREA 1,068,299 sq mi; 2,766,890 sq km

LEADING EXPORTS meat, grain, hides, and wool

CONTINENT South America

THE BAHAMAS

CAPITAL★ Nassau

POPULATION: 0.3 million

MAJOR LANGUAGES: English and Creole

AREA: 5,382 sq mi; 13,940 sq km

LEADING EXPORTS: pharmaceuticals, cement, and crawfish

CONTINENT: North America

BARBADOS

CAPITAL★ Bridgetown

POPULATION: 0.3 million

MAJOR LANGUAGE: English

AREA: 166 sq mi; 430 sq km

LEADING EXPORTS: sugar, molasses, and electrical components

CONTINENT: North America

BELIZE

CAPITAL★ Belmopan

POPULATION: 0.2 million

MAJOR LANGUAGES: English and Spanish

AREA: 8,865 sq mi; 22,960 sq km

LEADING EXPORTS: sugar, citrus, clothing, and fish products

CONTINENT: North America

BOLIVIA

CAPITAL★ Sucre (judicial) and La Paz (administrative)

POPULATION: 7.7 million

MAJOR LANGUAGES: Spanish, Quechua, and Aymará

AREA: 424,163 sq mi; 1,098,580 sq km

LEADING EXPORTS: metals, natural gas, coffee, and soybeans

CONTINENT: South America

BRAZIL

CAPITAL★ Brasília

POPULATION: 158.7 million

MAJOR LANGUAGES: Portuguese, Spanish, French, and English

AREA: 3,286,488 sq mi; 8,511,965 sq km

LEADING EXPORTS: iron ore, coffee, orange juice, and footwear

CONTINENT: South America

CANADA

CAPITAL★ Ottawa

POPULATION: 28.1 million

MAJOR LANGUAGES: English and French

AREA: 3,851,798 sq mi; 9,976,140 sq km

LEADING EXPORTS: automotive products, timber, and natural gas

CONTINENT: North America

CHILE

CAPITAL★ Santiago

POPULATION: 14.0 million

MAJOR LANGUAGE: Spanish

AREA: 292,259 sq mi; 756,950 sq km

LEADING EXPORTS: copper, fish, metals, and minerals

CONTINENT: South America

COLOMBIA

CAPITAL★ Bogotá

POPULATION: 35.6 million

MAJOR LANGUAGE: Spanish

AREA: 439,734 sq mi; 1,138,910 sq km

LEADING EXPORTS: coffee, petroleum, coal, and bananas

CONTINENT: South America

COSTA RICA

CAPITAL★ San José

POPULATION: 3.3 million

MAJOR LANGUAGES: Spanish and English

AREA: 19,730 sq mi; 50,100 sq km

LEADING EXPORTS: coffee, bananas, textiles, and sugar

CONTINENT: North America

CUBA

CAPITAL★ Havana

POPULATION: 11.1 million

MAJOR LANGUAGE: Spanish

AREA: 42,803 sq mi; 110,860 sq km

LEADING EXPORTS: sugar, nickel, shellfish, and tobacco

CONTINENT: North America

DOMINICA

CAPITAL★ Roseau

POPULATION: 0.1 million

MAJOR LANGUAGES: English and Creole

AREA: 290 sq mi; 750 sq km

LEADING EXPORTS: bananas, soap, bay oil, and vegetables

CONTINENT: North America

DOMINICAN REPUBLIC

CAPITAL★ Santo Domingo

POPULATION: 7.8 million

MAJOR LANGUAGES: Spanish

AREA: 18,816 sq mi; 48,730 sq km

LEADING EXPORTS: sugar, coffee, ferronickel, cocoa, and gold

CONTINENT: North America

ECUADOR

CAPITAL★ Quito

POPULATION: 10.7 million

MAJOR LANGUAGES: Spanish and Quechua

AREA: 109,483 sq mi; 283,560 sq km

LEADING EXPORTS: oil, bananas, shrimp, and cocoa

CONTINENT: South America

EL SALVADOR

CAPITAL★ San Salvador

POPULATION: 5.8 million

MAJOR LANGUAGES: Spanish and Náhuatl

AREA: 8,124 sq mi; 21,040 sq km

LEADING EXPORTS: coffee, sugarcane, and shrimp

CONTINENT: North America

GRENADA

CAPITAL★ St. George's

POPULATION: 0.1 million

MAJOR LANGUAGES: English and French patois

AREA: 131 sq mi; 340 sq km

LEADING EXPORTS: nutmeg, mace, bananas, and cocoa

CONTINENT: North America

GUATEMALA

CAPITAL★ Guatemala City

POPULATION: 10.7 million

MAJOR LANGUAGES: Spanish and Mayan dialects

AREA: 42,042 sq mi; 108,890 sq km

LEADING EXPORTS: coffee, sugar, bananas, and cardamom

CONTINENT: North America

GUYANA

CAPITAL★ Georgetown

POPULATION: 0.7 million

MAJOR LANGUAGES: English, Hindi, and Urdu

AREA: 83,000 sq mi; 214,970 sq km

LEADING EXPORTS: sugar, bauxite, rice, shrimp, and molasses

CONTINENT: South America

HAITI

CAPITAL★ Port-au-Prince

POPULATION: 6.5 million

MAJOR LANGUAGES: French and French Creole

AREA: 10,714 sq mi; 27,750 sq km

LEADING EXPORTS: coffee and assembled lighting products

CONTINENT: North America

HONDURAS

CAPITAL★ Tegucigalpa

POPULATION: 5.3 million

MAJOR LANGUAGE: Spanish

AREA: 43,277 sq mi; 112,090 sq km

LEADING EXPORTS: coffee, bananas, shrimp, lobster, and minerals

CONTINENT: North America

JAMAICA

CAPITAL★ Kingston

POPULATION: 2.6 million

MAJOR LANGUAGES: English and Jamaican Creole

AREA: 4,243 sq mi; 10,990 sq km

LEADING EXPORTS: alumina, bauxite, sugar, and bananas

CONTINENT: North America

MEXICO

CAPITAL★ Mexico City

POPULATION: 92.2 million

MAJOR LANGUAGES: Spanish and Náhuatl

AREA: 761,604 sq mi; 1,972,550 sq km

LEADING EXPORTS: oil, cotton, coffee, silver, and consumer electronics

CONTINENT: North America

NICARAGUA

CAPITAL★ Managua

POPULATION: 4.1 million

MAJOR LANGUAGE: Spanish

AREA: 49,998 sq mi; 129,494 sq km

LEADING EXPORTS: cotton, coffee, chemicals, and foodstuffs

CONTINENT: North America

PANAMA

CAPITAL★ Panama City

POPULATION: 2.6 million

MAJOR LANGUAGES: Spanish and English

AREA: 30,193 sq mi; 78,200 sq km

LEADING EXPORTS: bananas, shrimp, clothing, and sugar

CONTINENT: North America

PARAGUAY

CAPITAL★ Asunción

POPULATION: 5.2 million

MAJOR LANGUAGES: Spanish and Guaraní

AREA: 157,047 sq mi; 406,750 sq km

LEADING EXPORTS: cotton, timber, coffee, and soybeans

CONTINENT: South America

PERU

CAPITAL★ Lima

POPULATION: 23.7 million

MAJOR LANGUAGES: Spanish, Quechua, and Aymará

AREA: 496,225 sq mi; 1,285,220 sq km

LEADING EXPORTS: oil, copper, zinc, lead, and coffee

CONTINENT: South America

ST. KITTS AND NEVIS

CAPITAL★ Basseterre

POPULATION: 40,671

MAJOR LANGUAGE: English

AREA: 139 sq mi; 360 sq km

LEADING EXPORTS: sugar, clothing, electronics, and stamps

CONTINENT: North America

ST. LUCIA

CAPITAL★ Castries

POPULATION: 145,090

MAJOR LANGUAGES: English and French patois

AREA: 239 sq mi; 620 sq km

LEADING EXPORTS: bananas, clothing, cocoa, and coconut oil

CONTINENT: North America

ST. VINCENT AND THE GRENADINES

CAPITAL★ Kingstown

POPULATION: 0.1 million

MAJOR LANGUAGE: English

AREA: 131 sq mi; 340 sq km

LEADING EXPORTS: bananas, taro, arrowroot starch, and tennis racquets

CONTINENT: North America

SURINAME

CAPITAL★ Paramaribo

POPULATION: 0.4 million

MAJOR LANGUAGES: Dutch, English, and Hindi

AREA: 63,039 sq mi; 163,270 sq km

LEADING EXPORTS: rice, bananas, aluminum, and fish

CONTINENT: South America

TRINIDAD AND TOBAGO

CAPITAL★ Port-of-Spain

POPULATION: 1.3 million

MAJOR LANGUAGES: English, Hindi, and French

AREA: 1,980 sq mi; 5,130 sq km

LEADING EXPORTS: oil, chemicals, and steel products

CONTINENT: North America

UNITED STATES

CAPITAL★ Washington, D.C.

POPULATION: 260.7 million

MAJOR LANGUAGE: English

AREA: 3,787,319 sq mi; 9,809,156 sq km

LEADING EXPORTS: automobiles, raw materials, and consumer goods

CONTINENT: North America

URUGUAY

CAPITAL★ Montevideo

POPULATION: 3.2 million

MAJOR LANGUAGES: Spanish and Brazilero

AREA: 68,039 sq mi; 176,220 sq km

LEADING EXPORTS: wool and meat

CONTINENT: South America

VENEZUELA

CAPITAL★ Caracas

POPULATION: 20.6 million

MAJOR LANGUAGES: Spanish and Indian dialects

AREA: 352,143 sq mi; 912,050 sq km

LEADING EXPORTS: oil, bauxite, aluminum, steel, and chemicals

CONTINENT: South America

Source: population, languages, area, exports—The CIA World Factbook, 1994; additional information on languages—The Europa World Book, 1995

CHAPTER 11 REVIEW

THINKING ABOUT VOCABULARY

A. Write a sentence for each pair of words below. Include details that give clues to the meaning of the first term in each pair.

1. citizen, elect
2. municipal, mayor
3. county, commissioners court
4. bill, veto
5. candidate, Congress

B. Number a sheet from 1 to 10. Next to each number write the word or term from the list above that best completes the sentence.

1. A _____ is one of the sections into which a state is divided.

2. A _____ is a proposal for a law.

3. A person who runs for office is called a _____.

4. A person who is born in a country or who has earned the right to become a member of that country is called a _____.

5. The town or city where you live has a _____ government.

6. A group of elected officials who make decisions about county issues is called the _____.

7. The elected head of the municipal government is the _____.

8. In our country, citizens _____ the government leaders.

9. The _____ is the legislative branch of government.

10. To _____ a bill is to reject it.

THINKING ABOUT FACTS

1. How do the citizens of the United States take part in the government?

2. Who is the head of the municipal government? What kinds of services do municipal governments provide?

3. What is the purpose of the Texas Constitution? What famous document was used as a model?

4. What are the three branches of our national and state governments? How does the system of checks and balances apply to them?

5. In which city is the office of our state's governor located? How is the governor chosen and how long does he or she serve?

6. What is the state tree of Texas? How was it chosen?

7. What services are provided by the United States government?

8. How many senators are elected by each state to the United States Senate? How many representatives to the United States House of Representatives are elected by Texas?

9. Who is the head of the executive branch of the United States government? Name two responsibilities that belong to this person.

10. What are the responsibilities of all Americans? What are the rights of all Americans?

348

THINK AND WRITE ◄≡)

WRITING A BILL
Suppose you are a senator from Texas. Write a bill proposing something that would make our state a better place to live.

WRITING A POSTER
Write a poster showing the three branches of our state government. Label the leaders and the responsibilities of each branch.

WRITING AN ARTICLE
Suppose you are the editor of a newspaper. Write an editorial encouraging people to vote in the next election. Explain why it is an important responsibility for each citizen to vote.

APPLYING STUDY SKILLS

READING NEWSPAPERS
1. What five questions should a well-written news article answer?
2. Look at the news article about skating on page 333. Identify the headline, the byline, and the dateline.
3. What is an editorial? How does it differ from a news article?
4. Look again at the news article on page 333. How would you change the article to an editiorial?
5. What can you learn from reading newspapers?

Summing Up the Chapter

Use the following table to organize information from the chapter. Copy the table on a sheet of paper. Then fill in the blank spaces on the table. When you have filled in the table, use it to write a paragraph that answers the question "What do the local, state, and national governments have in common? How are they different?"

	EXECUTIVE	LEGISLATIVE	JUDICIAL
Local			
State			
National			

UNIT 5 REVIEW

THINKING ABOUT VOCABULARY

Number a sheet of paper from 1 to 10. Next to each number write the word or term from the list below that best completes each sentence.

boom town
candidate
free enterprise system
high-tech industry
invention

judicial branch
sheriff
stock
suffrage
veto

1. After the discovery of petroleum in Beaumont, it became a _____ almost overnight.

2. One new _____ of the Roaring Twenties was the vacuum cleaner.

3. During the 1920s many people bought a share of ownership in a company, which is called _____.

4. The right to vote is called _____.

5. In a country with a _____, people are able to own and run their own businesses.

6. A company that makes computers or VCRs is a _____.

7. The _____ is in charge of a county's law-enforcement department.

8. A governor has the right to _____ a bill if he or she disagrees with it.

9. A person running for elected office is called a _____.

10. The courts are part of the _____ of government.

THINK AND WRITE ◄▬▬►

WRITING A LIST

Write a list of five vocabulary words from Unit 5. Then write a paragraph with five sentences, using each of the words.

WRITING A DESCRIPTION

Suppose you are living in the early 1900s. Your family buys a car for the first time. Describe how the car affects your family's daily life.

WRITING A SPEECH

Suppose that you are a candidate for mayor in the community in which you live. Write a speech explaining how you will try to make your town or city a better place to live.

BUILDING SKILLS

1. **Making generalizations** What is the first step in making a generalization?

2. **Making generalizations** List three inventions that you read about in Chapter 9. Then make a generalization about them.

3. **Using map scales** What does a map scale tell you about the map? When might it be helpful to use maps drawn to different scales?

4. **Reading newspapers** Why does a citizen need to read newspapers?

5. **Reading newspapers** If you wanted to learn the editor's opinion about an issue, what kind of news article would you read?

YESTERDAY, TODAY &

TOMORROW

You read in Chapter 9 about the importance of oil to our state economy. As you know, oil is a nonrenewable resource. Suppose that all our oil resources were used up in your lifetime. How would it affect your daily life? How would it affect the world?

READING ON YOUR OWN

Here are some books you might find at the library to help you learn more.

BARBARA JORDAN: CONGRESSWOMAN
by Linda Carlson Johnson
This book traces an African-American Texan's journey to excellence as a United States public figure.

SAM AND THE SPEAKER'S CHAIR
by Maurine Walpole Liles
Read about the life of Sam Rayburn, former speaker of the United States House of Representatives.

TWENTY TEXANS
by Betsy Warren
This book celebrates the contributions of 20 Texans, from the early 1800s to the present.

UNIT PROJECT

Make a Government Tree

1. With your group, review the unit and make a list of all the different branches of the national, state, and local governments. For example, the branches of state government include the judicial branch.

2. On a piece of oaktag, create a government tree. Start with the national government. Write each branch, its function, and an example of the types of decisions the government makes. Then do the same with the state and local governments.

3. Be sure to connect each major type of government with its branches. You may want to draw arrows with different colored markers.

4. Present your government tree to the class.

A GOVERNMENT TREE

OUR NATIONAL GOVERNMENT — EXECUTIVE BRANCH — JUDICIAL BRANCH — LEGISLATIVE BRANCH

OUR STATE GOVERNMENT — EXECUTIVE BRANCH — JUDICIAL BRANCH — LEGISLATIVE BRANCH

OUR LOCAL GOVERNMENT

GEORGIA O'KEEFFE PAINTING *RED MESA*; WILLIE NELSON; A MEXICAN FOLK DANCER

Texas Today and Tomorrow

" . . . whatever we want to be . . ."

from a statement by Texas Senator Mario Gallegos
See page 391.

WHY DOES IT MATTER?

What do you think Texas will be like in the next century? Do you think Texans will continue to work and play in the same ways they do now? What kinds of problems and opportunities do you think Texans will have in the future?

As Texas faces the twenty-first century, it has much to celebrate. We are lucky to live in a state where a blending of cultures gives us the opportunity to better understand the world we live in. In Unit 6 you will learn about the ways Texas is special both as a state and as part of the world community.

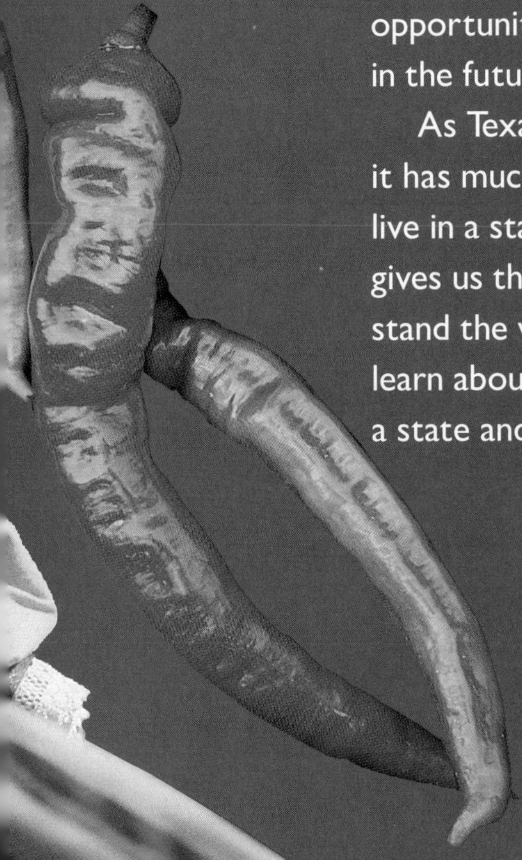

CHILI PEPPERS;
HAKEEM OLAJUWON OF
THE HOUSTON ROCKETS

353

Adventures
with
NATIONAL GEOGRAPHIC

The Place for Space

Welcome to Mission Control—the Lyndon B. Johnson Space Center, near Houston. Marvel at the enormous Saturn 5 rocket. Explore the hands-on museum. And if you dream of getting involved in space exploration, plan on spending a lot of time here someday. Spacecraft are designed at the center, astronauts are trained here, and space flights are controlled from here. You'll join a long line of explorers connected with the center: In 1969, the Apollo 11 moon landing was directed from here—just as space shuttle missions are today.

GEO JOURNAL

Write a letter explaining why you'd be a good candidate for the astronaut training program at Johnson Space Center.

CHAPTER 12

Our Special State

THINKING ABOUT GEOGRAPHY AND CULTURE

What is your favorite way to enjoy your free time? Maybe you like to play football, paint pictures, or go for long walks outdoors. We Texans have many ways to enjoy and celebrate our special state and our many cultures. Read Chapter 12 to find out more about the rich cultures of Texas.

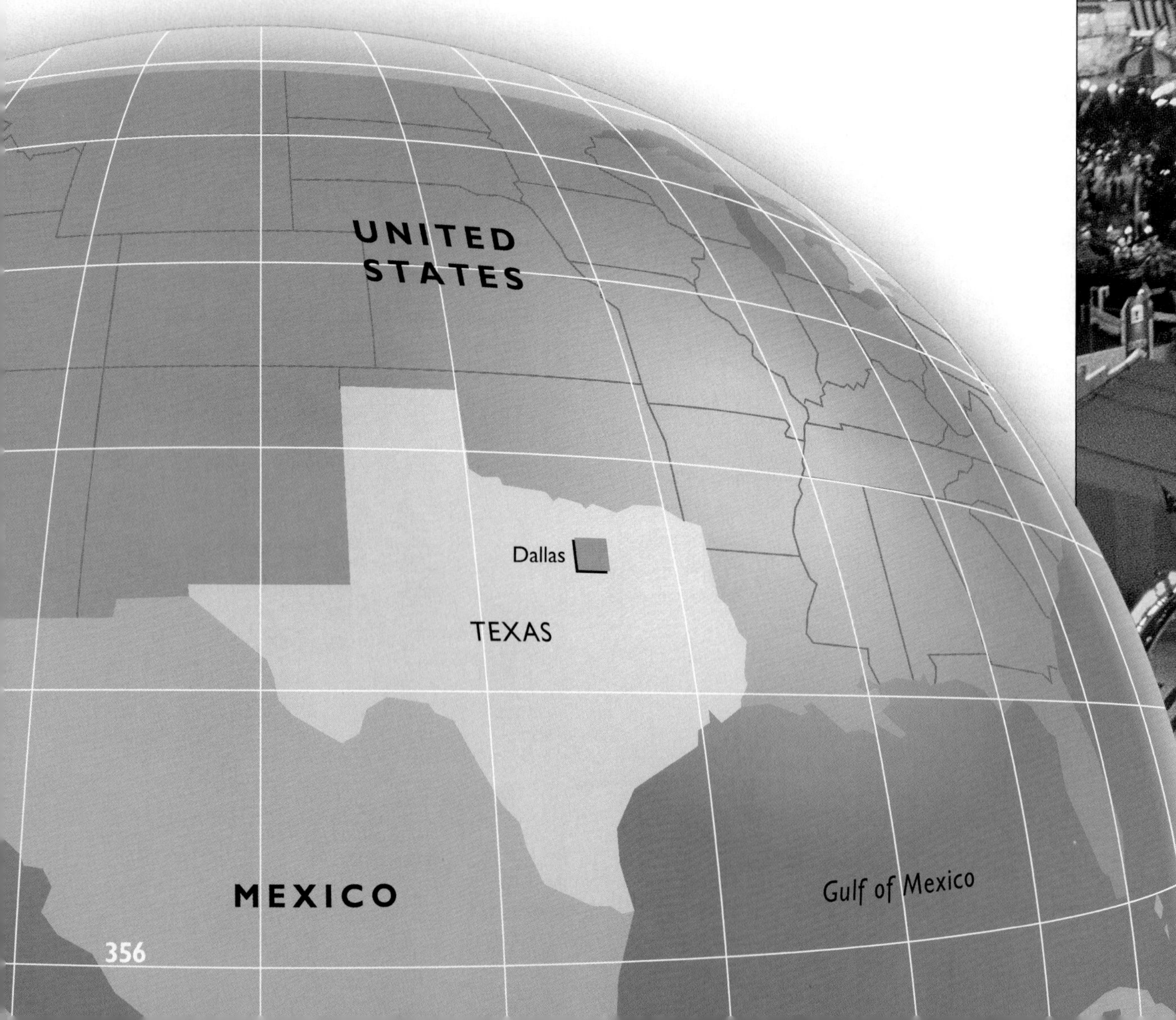
UNITED STATES
Dallas
TEXAS
MEXICO
Gulf of Mexico

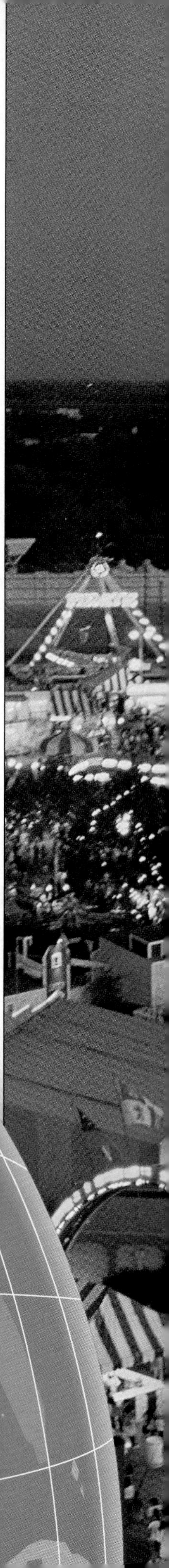

The State Fair of Texas is all about celebrating what it is like to be a Texan. We like to have fun in a BIG way. The Texas Star Ferris Wheel is the largest in the Western Hemisphere.

A BLEND OF CULTURES

Focus Activity

READ TO LEARN
How have different cultures contributed to making Texas a special state?

VOCABULARY
charro

PLACES
Panna Maria
Luling
Terlingua
Del Rio
Brownsville
Fredericksburg
Ennis

READ ALOUD

"We used to have what they called box suppers at school. We fixed boxes up real pretty. Crepe paper was used for covering them. All different colors were used. Tinsel was added to the crepe paper for additional decoration.

The boxes used for box suppers were many different shapes. Some of the shapes used were round, square, heart-shaped, diamond, or no particular shape at all. . . .

Box suppers were auctioned off [sold] to the highest bidder."

Omie Webb grew up in Texas. She remembers one way people in her community had a good time. People across our state have many ways of having fun.

THE BIG PICTURE

How people have fun is an important part of their culture. So, too, are the languages they speak and their beliefs about the world. Ways of having fun, languages, and beliefs vary from Texan to Texan. As you will read in this lesson, Texas is a blend of many cultures. We are lucky to live in a state where these differences in heritage come together. They create a special Texan way of life.

Wedding (below) and music (right) are important parts of religious heritage.

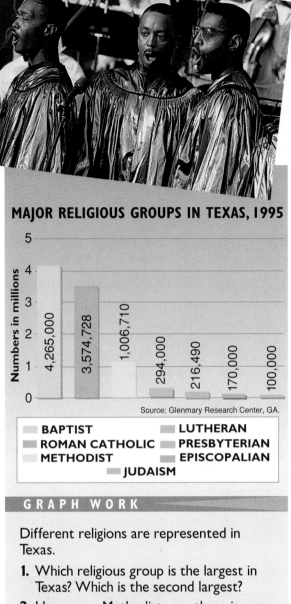

MAJOR RELIGIOUS GROUPS IN TEXAS, 1995

Numbers in millions

- 4,265,000
- 3,574,728
- 1,006,710
- 294,000
- 216,490
- 170,000
- 100,000

Source: Glenmary Research Center, GA.

■ BAPTIST   ■ LUTHERAN
■ ROMAN CATHOLIC   ■ PRESBYTERIAN
■ METHODIST   ■ EPISCOPALIAN
■ JUDAISM

GRAPH WORK

Different religions are represented in Texas.

1. Which religious group is the largest in Texas? Which is the second largest?
2. How many Methodists are there in our state as of 1995?

WHO WE ARE

Today Texans claim ties to over 80 countries around the world. Most of the nearly 20 million Texans speak English. However, about one out of four people speak a second language at home. More than three million of the people in this group speak Spanish. About 100,000 speak either German or Polish. About 110,000 Texans speak either Vietnamese or Chinese.

Many Religions

The Roman Catholic religion first came to Texas when the earliest Spanish explorers arrived in the 1500s. Most Mexican Americans in Texas are Roman Catholic. Many Roman Catholic immigrants began coming from countries in Europe in the 1800s. Panna Maria is said to have the oldest Polish Roman Catholic church in the United States. Today Roman Catholics make up the second-largest religious group in Texas. The largest group of Christians in Texas is Baptist. Look at the graph of religious groups in our state.

Many Jews were among the European immigrants who began arriving in the 1800s. Today about 100,000 Jews live throughout Texas. Muslims, Hindus, and Buddhists are among the other religious groups that live and worship in Texas.

A CELEBRATION OF CULTURES

Christmas and other Christian holidays are celebrated by many Texan families. Other important religious holidays include Passover among Jewish Texans and Ramadan among Muslim Texans.

Our state has many special celebrations. Texas hosts over 500 fairs and festivals each year. Along with events like the Watermelon Thump in Luling and the International Chili Cook-Off in Terlingua, Texas festivals celebrate the many cultures that make our state special.

Let's Celebrate!

Earlier in the book you read about how the Tigua celebrate their ancient heritage. You also learned about June 19, Emancipation Day, when African Americans celebrate freedom from slavery.

Mexican Americans celebrate their heritage, too. Each spring students in Del Rio and elsewhere in our state learn Mexican folk dances in time for Cinco de Mayo. This holiday honors Mexico's victory over the French in the 1800s. The Del Rio students' performance is the center of a two day event that packs the city's plaza with partygoers.

Brownsville students also learn Mexican dances and lead a parade during the Charro (CHAH roh) Days Festival. Named in honor of Mexican charros, or traditional

Texas celebrations include Emancipation Day (left), traditional dancing at Mexican festivals (above, right), and a traditional German band (top).

horsemen, this festival is filled with dancing and parades.

Fredericksburg is one of the oldest German American communities in our state. The sound of lively accordion music and the smell of spicy sausages signals that Oktoberfest has begun. People from all over Texas enjoy eating, dancing, and singing at this German festival. The polka is a popular dance here, but it's even bigger at the National Polka Festival in **Ennis**. Ennis is home of the largest Czech community in Texas. The city draws people from as far away as Europe for its weekend of dances, parades, and feasts.

What songs do you enjoy singing at festivals and celebrations? You can find the words and music to one famous Texas song, "Deep in the Heart of Texas," on the next page. What does this song celebrate?

DEEP IN THE HEART OF TEXAS

Music by Don Swander
Words by June Hershey

ANNUAL FESTIVALS IN TEXAS

MONTH	FESTIVAL	CITY
January	Citrus Festival	Mission
February	Fiesta Hidalgo	Edinburg
March	Texas Independence Day	Washington-on-the-Brazos
April	Bluebonnet Fair	Lampass
May	Western Heritage Classic	Abilene
June	National Cow Calling Contest	Miami
July	Great Texas Mosquito Festival	Clute
August	Cantaloupe Festival	Pecos
September	Comanche Country Pow-wow	Comanche
October	Turkeyfest	Cuero
November	Pecan Festival	San Saba
December	Fun Fiesta	Raymondville

RODEO CELEBRATIONS

Other favorite celebrations in Texas include the rodeo. It began as a way for cattle ranchers and cowboys to test their skills. At the Mesquite rodeo, just outside Dallas, contestants compete in events like bull riding, calf roping, and barrel racing. Look at the chart to see some other festivals that take place in our state.

WHY IT MATTERS

Texans have ancestors who were from all around the world. Many of us weren't even born in Texas. We celebrate different holidays and different traditions. Yet as Texans we also have a great deal in common. We believe in equal rights and opportunities for all. We also share the responsibility for taking care of our state, because its future is our future too.

✓ Reviewing Facts and Ideas

SUM IT UP

- Texans have ancestors from many different cultural backgrounds.
- The blend of cultures in our state is reflected in its many languages, religious beliefs, and celebrations.

THINK ABOUT IT

1. Name three languages spoken in our state.

2. What is the second-largest religious group in Texas? How can history help you understand why this group is so big in Texas?

3. **FOCUS** What can the festivals in Texas tell you about the people of our state?

4. **THINKING SKILL** *Make a generalization* about what makes a Texan a Texan.

5. **WRITE** Write a story describing a festival you've gone to.

SPORTS AND RECREATION

Focus Activity

READ TO LEARN
What do Texans do for recreation?

VOCABULARY
professional
Olympic games

PEOPLE
George Foreman
Nolan Ryan
Lee Trevino
Carl Lewis
Zina Garrison Jackson

READ ALOUD

"Between the seven of us [children], there was never enough [food]. . . . On Fridays, [my mother would] bring home a single hamburger and break it into eight pieces. Everybody got a taste. I remember thinking, 'Boy, that's rich man's food, a hamburger.' That mustard's tang is still in my mouth." While growing up in Houston, George Foreman dreamed of having enough to eat. In time he would win much more through his achievements in sports.

THE BIG PICTURE

In 1973 George Foreman became the world's heavyweight boxing champion. Even more amazingly, he regained that title in 1994 when he was 45 years old. He became the oldest heavyweight boxing champion in history. For Foreman and many other Texans, sports and recreation are some of the best parts of living in the Lone Star State. You will see some of the most famous people and places of Texas in the Infographic on pages 366–367. But you don't have to be famous to enjoy the many different sports Texas has to offer. Our state provides opportunities for recreation for everyone, no matter what your interests are.

ENJOYING OUR STATE

No matter where you live in Texas there is always something fun to do. Whether you like to swim, ride a bike, play football, or read a book, our state is the perfect place to be. As you know, activities which people do in their spare time are called recreation. We are lucky that we don't have far to go to enjoy recreation in Texas. All we have to do is step outside.

The Great Outdoors

Some of the best places for recreation in Texas are our state and national parks. We have about 90 of them to choose from. In West Texas you can hike through rugged Big Bend National Park. You can hike through huge stone canyons, walk along desert trails, climb mountains, and enjoy wildlife.

If water sports are more your style, you have lots of places you can go. Texas has about three million acres of freshwater lakes and rivers. Along the Gulf of Mexico, there are almost 400 miles of shore.

In North Texas, Eisenhower State Park is on Lake Texoma. The park is a perfect place to go bass fishing. If you like sun, sand and surf, then Padre Island National Seashore in South Texas is the place for you. Padre Island is also a good place to watch for rare sea turtles.

The Hill Country in Central Texas is an ideal place for horseback riding. You can also take a canoe trip or go tubing. Families camp and sleep under the stars at many state parks, from Galveston Island on the coast to Palo Duro Canyon State Park in the Panhandle. Campgrounds can fill up quickly, though, so it's a good idea to call before your family hits the road.

Texans like to canoe in the Hill Country and bicycle ride along Barton Creek in Austin.

Infographic

Famous People and Places

Our state is filled with places that people find interesting and fun to visit. You can see why many Texans spend their vacations right in our own state. How many of these places have you visited? The map also shows where some famous television and sports stars were born or have lived. These Texans are famous throughout our country.

Amarillo

Where else but at CADILLAC RANCH can you see 10 cars sticking out of the ground like huge fish out of water? This crazy car collection was built to honor Americans' love of automobiles.

El Paso

At the MUSEUM OF HISTORY you can see exciting exhibits about our state's first cowboys and how they lived.

The NATIONAL COWGIRL HALL OF FAME, based in Fort Worth, honors over 100 women who have made lasting marks on the American West.

Singer FREDDY FENDER was born here and now is the guest of honor at the city's annual HomeFest.

OTHER FAMOUS TEXANS	HOMETOWN
WAYLON JENNINGS, singer	LITTLEFIELD
SISSY SPACEK, actress	QUITMAN
WILLIE SHOEMAKER, jockey	FABENS
TOMMY LEE JONES, actor	SAN SABA
CAROL BURNETT, actress	SAN ANTONIO
BEN CRENSHAW, golfer	AUSTIN
TISH HINOJOSA, singer	SAN ANTONIO
STEVE MARTIN, actor	WACO
LYLE LOVETT, singer	KLEIN

TOMMY TUNE was born here and studied at the University of Texas and the University of Houston, before moving to New York City to become one of our country's leading musical theater directors.

JOBETH WILLIAMS graduated from Jesse H. Jones High School before moving on to become a famous actress.

In 1981 HAKEEM OLAJUWON moved here from Nigeria to study and play at the University of Houston. He is now one of the world's best basketball players.

CATHERINE CRIER was a judge here before becoming a national television reporter.

Wichita Falls

Did you ever wonder who invented the first hamburger? According to the "HOME OF THE HAMBURGER" **sign here, an Athens cook named Fletcher Davis achieved that honor back in 1895.**

Fort Worth

Dallas

Athens

Waco

Houston

Wharton

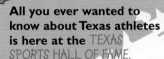

All you ever wanted to know about Texas athletes is here at the TEXAS SPORTS HALL OF FAME.

DAN RATHER was born here, then attended Sam Houston State College in Huntsville, before becoming one of our country's leading television reporters.

Corpus Christi

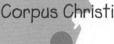

At the TEXAS STATE AQUARIUM you can see over 250 kinds of amazing sea creatures, including rare sea turtles that first came as injured "patients" and now call the aquarium home.

San Benito

367

SPORTS IN TEXAS

Texas is a great place to get involved in sports. From backyards to stadiums, Texans team up in almost every sport you can think of.

Touchdown!

Football fans across our state have a lot to cheer about. Two **professional** teams draw huge crowds every year. Professional teams are made up of athletes who play the sport as a job, not just for fun. The Houston Oilers play to eager fans in the Astrodome. The Dallas Cowboys make their home in Texas Stadium in Irving. The Cowboys have played in more Super Bowls than any other team in the United States.

Home teams are also very popular in Texas. Each fall Friday Night Football is a part of life all over our state. Crowds of 20,000 or more gather to watch their favorite high-school teams. Even bigger crowds pack stadiums to see college teams like the Texas A&M Aggies or the University of Texas Longhorns.

Hoops

After football season, Texas sport fans get caught up in another big game, basketball. Our state has three professional basketball teams—the Dallas Mavericks, the Houston Rockets, and the San Antonio Spurs. The Rockets won the National Basketball Association Championship in 1994 and 1995. Texas is also home to many college basketball teams, including the Texas Tech Lady Raiders. This team won the women's national championship in 1993.

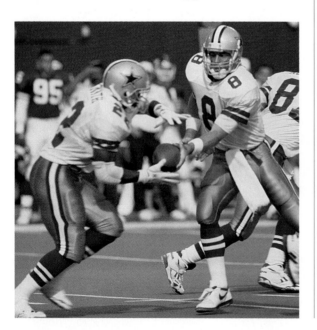

The Dallas Cowboys (left) and the Texas Tech Lady Raiders (above) are just two of the teams that keep us cheering all year long.

Many Sports, Many Stars

Baseball is also popular in Texas, from Little League to the pros. Texas has two professional baseball teams. The Houston Astros play in the Astrodome, and the Texas Rangers play in the Ballpark in Arlington. Golf and tennis are also popular.

Texans have become famous in all of these sports. Nolan Ryan of Alvin made history as one of the best baseball pitchers of all time. Lee Trevino of Dallas was a powerhouse in pro golf. In 1984 Houston's Carl Lewis became one of the only Americans in history to win four gold medals in the Olympic games.

Tennis star Zina Garrison Jackson, who has played all over the world, makes her home in Houston.

They are held every four years and involve athletes from all over the world.

Zina Garrison Jackson of Houston uses her world-class tennis skills and earnings to teach young people the game. You can learn more about these and other athletes at the Texas Sports Hall of Fame in Waco.

WHY IT MATTERS

From boxing to football, basketball, hiking, and canoeing, our state provides a variety of recreation. Thanks to our plentiful resources, we always have something fun to do in our great state.

✓✓ Reviewing Facts and Ideas

SUM IT UP

- Texas state and national parks offer outdoor recreation such as hiking, camping, and fishing.
- Football, basketball, and baseball are popular sports in Texas.

THINK ABOUT IT

1. Name two state parks in Texas.

2. What are two professional teams in Texas?

3. **FOCUS** How do Texans like to have fun?

4. **THINKING SKILL** *Predict* what life would be like if people did not take time for recreation.

5. **GEOGRAPHY** How does our state's geography affect the kind of recreation we can enjoy?

369

THE ARTS AND LITERATURE

Focus Activity

READ TO LEARN

How have artists and writers made Texas an interesting place to live?

VOCABULARY
ragtime
Norteño
Pulitzer Prize

PEOPLE
Elisabet Ney
Georgia O'Keeffe
Willie Nelson
Nanci Griffith
Scott Joplin
Flaco Jiménez
O. Henry
Katherine Anne Porter
Larry McMurtry
Ada Simond
Buck Ramsey

READ ALOUD

"I walked out past the last house . . . and sat on the fence for a long time. . . . There was nothing but sky and flat 'prairieland'—land that seems more like the ocean than anything else I know. . . . I love this country."

In 1916 artist Georgia O'Keeffe used these words to describe the land around her home in Canyon, Texas. O'Keeffe lived in the Panhandle for only about three years, but its big sky and big land would influence her work for years to come.

THE BIG PICTURE

The land and communities of Texas have helped shape an important part of our state's culture—its tradition of art. Art is made up of things like the pictures people paint, the songs they sing and the stories they write. No two works of art are exactly alike. Even so, artists often raise similar questions through their work. What is beautiful? What do we believe in? What makes life fun or difficult? As you will see, Texas artists have tried to answer such questions in many ways.

TEXAS ARTISTS

The tradition of art in Texas dates back to the earliest Native Americans living in our state. Their legends and rock paintings told about the making of the world.

Later arrivals in Texas brought their own art forms, adding to our old and rich tradition. Elisabet Ney moved here from Germany. She won fame for her sculptures of famous Texans such as Stephen F. Austin and Sam Houston. Today these statues stand in our state Capitol. Ney once said that making statues helped satisfy her wish "to meet the great people of the world."

Painter Georgia O'Keeffe had other goals in mind when she came to teach art in Amarillo and Canyon in the early 1900s. She taught her students to see beauty in everyday things. She saw beauty even in things like old cattle bones. O'Keeffe later said:

> I liked to [stress]. . . the idea that art is important in everyday life. I wanted them to learn the principle: that when you buy a pair of shoes or . . . address a letter or comb your hair, consider it carefully, so that it looks well.

Many of the statues created by Elisabet Ney (left) can be seen today at the Elisabet Ney Museum in Austin (below).

Archives Division, Texas State Library

This 1917 painting by Georgia O'Keeffe is called *Red Mesa*. Her art was influenced by the geography of the Southwest.

MUSIC AND MORE

Many Texan musicians have stressed the beauty and hardships of everyday life in their work. Country music star Willie Nelson, who grew up in Abbott, is famous for songs about life in Texas. Folk singer Nanci Griffith of Austin has written songs about farm families struggling to survive in the Panhandle.

Other Texan musicians have become famous for blending different styles of music to create new styles of their own. Scott Joplin, who was born in Texarkana in 1868, helped create ragtime. Ragtime was developed out of a mix of brassband, African American and other sounds and rhythms. Joplin wrote and co-wrote more than 60 pieces of music. Pehaps his most famous is "Maple Leaf Rag." Ragtime helped give birth to jazz.

While Joplin was making ragtime music famous, the grandfather of Flaco Jiménez was learning how to play the accordion from German musicians in San Antonio. As a result, the use of accordions and polka beats became popular in Mexican American dance music. Today Flaco Jiménez's own accordion playing has made this special style of *Norteño* (nawr TAY nyoh), or northern, music famous throughout the world.

Willie Nelson (top), Nanci Griffith (center), and Scott Joplin (bottom) are three of the Texans who have made our state's music famous.

Texan Writers

Storytelling is a well-loved tradition throughout Texas. O. Henry, whose real name was William Sydney Porter, lived in Austin during the late 1800s. He wrote short stories that ended with a surprise twist. One of his most famous short stories is "The Ransom of Red Chief." Katherine Anne Porter, who grew up in Indian Creek, also became well known for her short stories. In 1966 she won a Pulitzer Prize for her work, *Collected Stories*. Pulitzer Prizes are awarded every year for the best work in literature and newspaper writing.

In 1986 Archer City's Larry McMurtry also won a Pulitzer Prize. His award-winning book, *Lonesome Dove*, told the story of a cattle drive from Texas to Montana in the 1800s.

Ada Simond, born in Texas in the early 1900s, wrote many stories about growing up as an African American in Texas.

Links to **READING**

About the Author

You can read more about Ada Simond's life in her own words. Although all her books are about a girl named Mae Dee, they're really about Simond's own life. One of her most famous books is *Mae Dee and Her Family Join the Juneteenth Celebration*. In your school library, try to find a book by Ada Simond, or a book by a different author about his or her own life. Discuss the book you read with your class.

Texan authors Katherine Anne Porter (left) and O. Henry (above) gained great popularity for their stories.

POETRY

Poet **Buck Ramsey** of Amarillo worked as a cowboy until his legs were seriously hurt in an accident. He then began writing poems that describe life and work on the range. In his poem, "And As I Rode Out on the Morning", how does Ramsey describe how cowhands viewed the land they worked on?

**Excerpt from the poem
"And As I Rode Out on the Morning" by
Buck Ramsey, 1993.**

W̲e were the native strangers
   there
Among the things the land was
   growing—
To know this gave us more the
   care
To let the grass keep at its
   growing
And let the streams keep at
   their flowing.
We knew the land would not be
   ours,
That no one has the awful
   pow'rs
To claim the vast and common
   nesting,
To own the life that gave him
   birth.

WHY IT MATTERS

You don't have to be a star to create art in Texas. You can write songs, paint, or write stories at home or in school. Read the Making a Difference on the next page to see how students in one Texas school learned to create art out of their own school building. Whenever you choose to make art yourself, you are adding to the rich heritage of our state.

✔ Reviewing Facts and Ideas

SUM IT UP

- Painting, writing, and acting are all art forms.
- Painter Georgia O'Keeffe and musicians Willie Nelson and Nanci Griffith have made art out of ordinary lives and objects.
- Musicians Scott Joplin and Flaco Jiménez helped blend different styles of music together to create ragtime and *Norteño* music.

THINK ABOUT IT

1. Name two writers who have lived in Texas and one work written by each of them.

2. Why can painters, writers, sculptors, poets, and musicians all be called artists?

3. FOCUS How do artists make Texas an interesting place to live?

4. THINKING SKILL Identify one _fact_ and one _opinion_ in this lesson. Explain your choices.

5. WRITE Choose an event from your life. Write a poem or story that tells about it.

Opening Doors

HOUSTON, TEXAS—The paintings of artist Fidencio Durán appear in art galleries and museums throughout our state. Durán usually paints his pictures on canvas. But in the summer of 1995, he painted on a brick wall two stories high and as long as three classrooms side by side. This brick wall was on the outside of Crockett Elementary School in Houston. Durán turned the wall's red brick into a rainbow-colored mural called "Our House." A mural is a picture painted on a wall or ceiling. Durán's mural shows the many achievements of Crockett students and the rich multicultural heritage of the surrounding community.

"Before the mural project began," says Crockett Elementary School principal Elida Troutman, "many of my students did not even know what the word 'mural' meant." Durán and other artists visited every classroom and talked with the students about what they wanted on the mural.

Because the mural was so large, many people helped Durán complete it. Art students from a nearby college and volunteers from Crockett School came to paint.

Crockett student Norma Garcia helped paint flowers in the mural. She was surprised at the difference the mural made in the look of the school. "Before," she says, "the wall was nothing but a stack of bricks. Now it makes the whole school seem brighter."

Durán says that he took part in the project because he wanted to work with students. "Growing up," he says, "I was always exposed to the arts. Just think of not having had that doorway into the life of the imagination." Now he is opening that doorway for others.

"Just think of not having had that doorway . . ."

Fidencio Durán

STUDYSKILLS

Reading Road Maps

VOCABULARY
road map
interstate highway

WHY THE SKILL MATTERS

In the last lesson you read about Texas artists Elisabet Ney and O. Henry. Both are honored with museums in Austin. Suppose you and your family wanted to drive to Austin to visit those museums.

How could you figure out how to get to these museums from your community?

One way would be to use a road map to find your route. Road maps show the roads you can use to get from one place to another. Use the Helping Yourself box to guide you in reading the road map of Texas that is shown in this lesson.

USING THE SKILL

Look at the road map of Texas on this page. It shows some of our state's cities. It also shows some of the major roads that connect them.

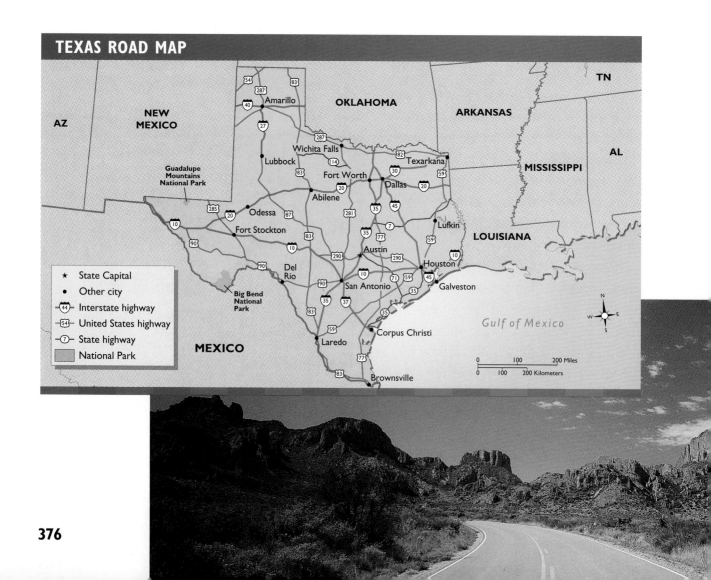

TEXAS ROAD MAP

Legend:
★ State Capital
• Other city
Interstate highway
United States highway
State highway
National Park

The map shows several kinds of roads. Look at the map key. As you can see, a heavy green line shows that a road is an **interstate highway**. An interstate highway connects two or more states. Usually these roads have at least two lanes in each direction. Look again at the map key. You can see that a red line stands for a United States highway.

You probably noticed that most roads on the map have numbers on them that appear inside a special symbol. Those numbers are the "names" of the roads. The number of the road that connects San Antonio and Houston is 10. What kind of road is it?

If you follow some roads with your finger, you will see that they have more than one number. That's because more than one road may "share" a certain route. Follow the road from Amarillo to Lubbock, for example.

You may have noticed something else too. Most even-numbered roads usually run east and west. Odd-numbered roads usually run north and south. For example, 83 runs north-south, but 40 runs east-west. This fact can help lost drivers figure out in which direction they're going.

This road map also shows some parks, historic sites, and other places of interest. How can you find a park?

TRYING THE SKILL

Suppose you want to plan a trip from Wichita Falls to Corpus Christi. Along the way you want to visit the Elisabet Ney Museum in Austin. Which route will you take? What kind of roads are on the route? How can you tell?

Now suppose you want to return to Wichita Falls on a different route. Which route is most direct? Which kinds of roads are on this route?

REVIEWING THE SKILL

1. What does a road map show?
2. According to the map, which interstate highways connect Texas with New Mexico? With Louisiana? What did you do to find your answer?
3. What other kinds of roads do road maps show?
4. How can the skill of reading road maps help you in your own life?

MUSIC FROM MANY CULTURES

You have read about many ethnic groups living in our state. Many of these groups have contributed to the development of musical styles we hear throughout Texas today.

Our state is best known for its country sound—cowboy songs and country-and-western music.

Tejano music has been influenced by Mexican music and traditions. Mariachi music is from Mexico.

The musical style known as blues often expresses loneliness or hard times. The blues combines African American music and music brought by Europeans.

Today the music from many cultures is not only heard in Texas. It is a legacy enjoyed all over the world.

Institute of Texan Cultures

The Center for American History, The University of Texas at Austin

Blind Lemon Jefferson (left) was a well-known Texas blues singer. The Baca's Family Orchestra (above pictured in 1907) was the first Czechoslovakian band in Texas. Mariachi players (right) carry on their tradition making Mexican music.

Selena Quintanilla (left) was a popular Tejano singer. Her music combined Texan and Mexican influences. Willie Nelson (below) continues the country-music tradition.

379

CHAPTER 12 REVIEW

THINKING ABOUT VOCABULARY

Number a sheet of paper from 1 to 5. Next to each number write the word or phrase from the list that best completes the sentence.

Charro   Pulitzer Prize
Olympic   ragtime
professional

1. The _____ is awarded each year for the best work in literature and newspaper writing.

2. The Dallas Cowboys and the Houston Rockets play _____ ball for Texas.

3. A _____ is a traditional Mexican horseman.

4. Every four years athletes from all over the world compete in the _____ Games.

5. _____ music developed out of a mix of brass-band and African American rhythms.

THINKING ABOUT FACTS

1. Name three languages that are spoken in our state.

2. What is the village of Panna Maria known for?

3. Name five festivals that are celebrated in Texas.

4. Who was Georgia O'Keeffe? What is she known for?

5. Name three professional sports teams from Texas. Which sports do they play?

6. Who are the Texas Tech Lady Raiders?

7. Who is Carl Lewis? What achievement is he known for?

8. What famous sculptor said that making statues helped satisfy her wish "to meet the great persons of the world"?

9. What instrument is commonly used to play *Norteño* music?

10. Name two Texas authors who have won the Pulitzer Prize.

THINK AND WRITE

WRITING AN ARTICLE

Suppose you are a sports reporter for the local newspaper. You have been assigned to one of the sports events mentioned in Lesson 2. Write an article covering the event. Include a headline, a dateline, and a byline.

WRITING A RESEARCH REPORT

Choose an artist or a writer you read about in Lesson 3. Do some research to learn more about the person and his or her work. Then write a report about the person and share it with the class.

WRITING A DESCRIPTION

Suppose you have just attended one of the festivals described in Lesson 1. Write a description of the event. Include as many details as you can think of.

APPLYING GEOGRAPHY SKILLS

READING ROAD MAPS

To answer the following questions, use this road map of Texas.

1. What does a road map show?

2. How does the map show which roads are interstate highways?

3. On which interstate(s) would someone travel from Corpus Christi to Dallas?

4. Which interstate connects Houston with Fort Stockton?

5. Why is it important to know how to read a road map?

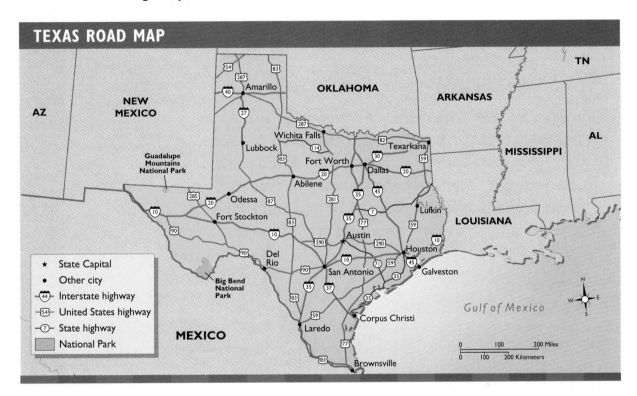

TEXAS ROAD MAP

Legend:
- ★ State Capital
- • Other city
- 44 Interstate highway
- 54 United States highway
- 7 State highway
- National Park

Summing Up the Chapter

Use the following main-idea chart to organize information from the chapter. Copy the chart on a sheet of paper. Then fill in the blank spaces on the chart. When you have filled in the chart, use it to write a paragraph answering the question "How have art, recreation, and culture contributed to making Texas a special state?"

CULTURE	SPORTS AND RECREATION	THE ARTS

CHAPTER
13

Texas, the Western Hemisphere, and the World

THINKING ABOUT
GEOGRAPHY AND CITIZENSHIP

You already know that there are many things that make Texas special. Now you'll find out about the special contributions our state makes to the world around us. As you read Chapter 13, think about the role that you would like to play in Texas, the United States, the Western Hemisphere, and the world in the future.

UNITED
STATES

Dallas

TEXAS

Houston

Laredo

MEXICO

Gulf of Mexico

Dallas/Fort Worth International Airport
DALLAS

Texas is a growing state. Many people from around the United States move here every day. Newcomers are welcomed at one of our nation's busiest airports in Dallas/Fort Worth.

ONE FOR ALL, ALL FOR ONE

ERECTED BY THE
REGIONAL DIRECTORS
OF THE
PAN AMERICAN
ROUND TABLES
OF TEXAS.
APRIL 14ᵀᴴ, 1935.

ERIGIDO POR LAS
DIRECTORAS REGIONALES
DE LAS
MESAS REDONDAS
PAN AMERICANAS
DE TEXAS.
14 DE ABRIL DE 1935.

Texas/Mexico Border
LAREDO

Because Mexico is so close to Texas, it is our number one trading partner. But our state also trades with other countries in the Western Hemisphere.

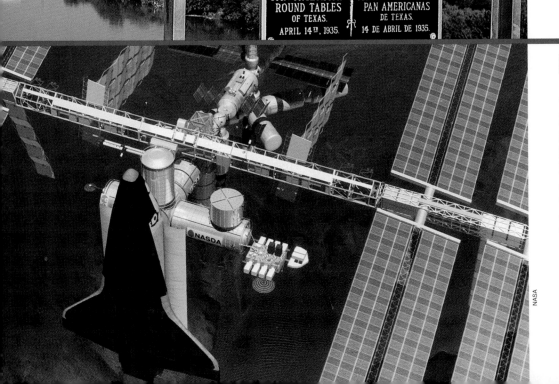

International Space Station near
HOUSTON

This picture was made by a computer to show how the International Space Station might look in the year 2002. Anything is possible when Texans and others from around the world work together.

NASA

383

OUR GROWING STATE

Focus Activity

READ TO LEARN
What are some of the ways in which Texas is changing?

VOCABULARY
Sun Belt
census
endangered

READ ALOUD

"We're in a great central location. We're in the middle of the United States, the Western Hemisphere, and the world."

Krista Sherwood at the Texas Department of Commerce knows that our state's central location is an important reason for its growth.

THE BIG PICTURE

Texas is growing every day. In addition to our central location, Texas is located in the Sun Belt. This part of the United States has a warm climate all year. The states in the Sun Belt are the fastest growing in our country. Many people are moving to Texas because they want to enjoy the quality of life that our state offers. Even more people come here for the jobs that our strong and growing free-enterprise economy provides.

Population growth in our state means exciting changes. New people bring new businesses and customs. Growth also brings challenges. New businesses create jobs for people, but they can also make it harder to keep our air, water, and soil clean. People in Texas are working together to meet these challenges.

TEXAS POPULATION TODAY

In 1990 the United States government sent a letter and a list of questions to every home in our country. The letter was part of a **census** (SEN sus), a count of the people who live in a place. The United States census takes place every ten years. The census of 1990 asked people across the nation to give information about themselves. When Texans returned their letters, the government had learned a great deal about our state.

The census showed that 16,986,510 people were living in Texas in 1990. That's enough people to fill the Houston Astrodome 309 times! Population estimates since then show that Texas is now the second most populated state in the nation, after California. In the year 2000 the government will carry out another census. By then the population of Texas is predicted to be about 20 million.

Links to LANGUAGE ARTS

Names with Meaning!

Have you ever been to Fredericksburg? What you might not know is that *burg* means "town" in German. You also read that Castroville was begun by Henri Castro. But did you know that *ville* means "town" in French?

Arroyo City got its name from a Spanish word. Look up the meaning of *arroyo* in the dictionary.

VILLE=TOWN BURG=TOWN ARROYO=?

FREDERIKSBURG
CASTROVILLE
ARROYO CITY

Learning About Texans

The 1990 census told us that only two out of every three Texans were born in our state. Every day, more than 400 newcomers move here from around the world. The census also told us that four out of five Texans live in cities.

GREETINGS
From the Houston Astrodome

Hello! from Fort Stockton Texas

FORT STOCKTON TEXAS
PAISANO PETE
WORLD'S LARGEST ROADRUNNER

Texas is full of special places, such as the Houston Astrodome (left), built in 1965. Fort Stockton is known for its huge roadrunner statue (above).

AS TEXAS GROWS

New technology has helped industries such as electronics to grow in Texas cities. High-tech products made in our state range from hand-held calculators to computers to spacecraft. There are about 25,000 high-tech businesses in Texas.

Growth can be tough on our state's environment, however. Greater numbers of people need more homes, schools, roads, and stores. As a result, animals and plants have fewer natural places in which to live.

Our Special Environment

The environment of Texas is special because it is so varied. You have learned that Texas includes forests, beaches, prairies, mountains, and deserts. Each of these areas has its own kinds of plants and animals.

Today about 70 kinds of animals in Texas are endangered. This word means that they are close to disappearing forever. Endangered animals in Texas include the black bear, the loggerhead sea turtle, and Attwater's prairie chicken.

Pollution is another problem that can come with growth. Some factories dump poisonous chemicals in the ground or waterways. For example, people in Texas are concerned about water pollution in the Rio Grande caused by some industries. Our local, state, and national governments are spending millions of dollars to clean up polluted areas.

People in communities can also cause pollution. Too many cars and trucks sometimes pollute the air we breathe. In cities such as Dallas, Fort Worth, and San Antonio, air pollution is sometimes so bad that people are asked not to drive their cars as much. Even the chemicals we use on our lawns can be harmful to the environment.

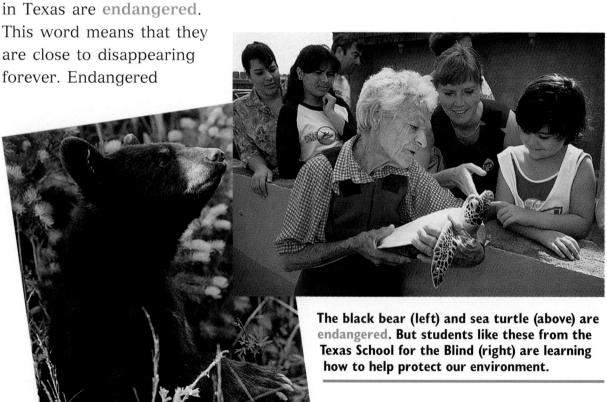

The black bear (left) and sea turtle (above) are endangered. But students like these from the Texas School for the Blind (right) are learning how to help protect our environment.

Helping the Environment

But Texans are working together to solve these problems. The Texas Natural Resource Conservation Commission has developed a program called "Clean Texas 2000." Cities and businesses around our state have joined this program. The goal is to reduce pollution and garbage in Texas by half by the year 2000. Each year, businesses that cut their pollution receive awards from the governor.

You too can learn about and help improve the environment of Texas. Each summer in Austin, for example, 400 students go to a special camp called Earth Camp Austin. Some of them are students at the Texas School for the Blind. At this camp, students visit the places where their garbage is dumped. They also take trips to nature centers and learn about ways to recycle paper, glass, and metal.

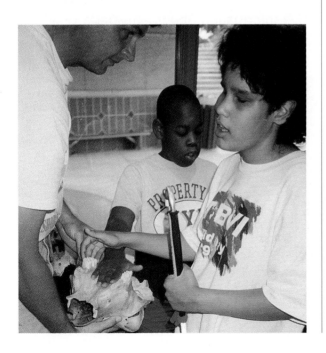

WHY IT MATTERS

Texas has a growing population. This growth has brought new opportunities and new challenges for our state. People in Texas want to keep a balance between meeting the needs of Texans and preserving our environment. If we can keep this balance, our natural resources will be available for generations to come.

Reviewing Facts and Ideas

SUM IT UP

- Texas is located in the Sun Belt.
- The census of 1990 showed that four out of five Texans live in urban areas.
- There are about 70 kinds of endangered animals in Texas including the black bear.
- "Clean Texas 2000" is a state program that aims to cut pollution by half by the year 2000.

THINK ABOUT IT

1. What kind of information did the 1990 census give us about the people who live in our state?
2. What does *endangered* mean?
3. **FOCUS** How is Texas changing?
4. **THINKING SKILL** Describe the *cause*-and-*effect* relationship between population growth and pollution of the environment.
5. **WRITE** Make a list of your ideas about how your class or school could help protect an endangered animal or the environment. Discuss your list with your teacher and classmates.

STUDY SKILLS

Using Primary and Secondary Sources

VOCABULARY

primary source
secondary source

WHY THE SKILL MATTERS

In the last lesson you read that some kinds of animals in Texas have become endangered. Suppose you wanted to learn more about a particular endangered animal, such as Attwater's prairie chicken. You could get your information from two different kinds of sources.

One is a primary source. A primary source is information that comes from someone who observed or took part in what he or she is describing. A primary source might be a diary, a letter, or an autobiography. Another type of primary source is a government document. In this textbook, you have read several primary sources. For example, in Chapter 5 you read a "Many Voices" in which Mary Crownover Rabb described her difficult journey to Texas in 1823.

Most of the information in this textbook, however, is from a secondary source. This kind of source is written by people who were not present at the events they describe. Encyclopedias and history textbooks are secondary sources. The writers of secondary sources get their information "secondhand."

Both kinds of information are important. A primary source can make us feel as though "we were there." A secondary source may help us to see a broader view of events.

USING THE SKILL

Read the two excerpts shown. Both give information about Attwater's prairie chicken. The speaker in Excerpt A is a

Attwater's prairie chicken is an endangered animal.

scientist who studies these birds. He refers to himself as *I*. Excerpt B is from a book about endangered animals. The writer of this excerpt does not refer to himself or herself at all.

Excerpt A

I'm not really a morning person, but it's not hard to get up early to observe prairie chickens. It's a big privilege to have the opportunity to work with them. It's also a huge responsibility. If the prairie chicken disappears, to me the prairie is going to be a lonelier place.

Excerpt B

Attwater's prairie chicken is a medium-sized grouse [kind of bird] with a barred, brown and buff [tan] pattern . . . Males have . . . an area of yellow skin on either side of the neck, which is [sometimes] inflated . . . Prairie chickens feed on plants and insects . . . Nesting sites are usually located in tall grasses.

HELPING Yourself

- **A primary source** is an account of an event by an eyewitness who saw or experienced it.

- **A secondary source** is written by someone who was not present at the events he or she describes.

TRYING THE SKILL

Use the Helping Yourself box to guide you in using primary and secondary sources. You have read the two excerpts about Attwater's prairie chicken. Excerpt A was a primary source. Excerpt B was a secondary source. Now think about the differences between them. Which gives you a broader range of information about this bird?

Suppose you wanted to find out more about how scientists and concerned people are trying to save Attwater's prairie chicken. Would you read the words of a person who was working to protect Attwater's prairie chicken, or would you read an encyclopedia article about this bird? If you wanted to learn more about the birds of our state, would you read an article written by a scientist studying one particular bird or a secondary source about the birds of Texas?

REVIEWING THE SKILL

1. What is the difference between a primary source and a secondary source?

2. If you wrote an article about your vacation, would it be a primary or a secondary source? Why?

3. Is a biography a primary or a secondary source? How is an autobiography different from a biography?

4. How do both primary and secondary sources help us to understand history?

389

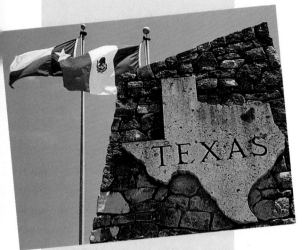

TEXAS AND THE WESTERN HEMISPHERE

READ ALOUD

In the summer of 1995, David and Mary Ann Mitchell of San Antonio welcomed two Mexican students to their home. Angel Llavot, who was 21, and Armando Solarez, who was 23, stayed with the Mitchells for a month while studying in Texas. "We really enjoyed getting to know them," David Mitchell said. "When they left, at the airport there were tears everywhere."

THE BIG PICTURE

Throughout this book you have explored some of the ways the United States and the nations of the Western Hemisphere are linked. Our state's location has made it an important part of these links.

As you read in Chapter 1, the United States and other countries are interdependent. In this lesson you will learn about some of the products that our state trades with other countries. You will also learn how the people of Texas and other people in the Western Hemisphere cooperate to reach shared goals and to solve shared problems.

WORKING TOGETHER

David and Mary Ann Mitchell enjoyed having Mexican students stay with them. They took Angel and Armando to the Texas Hill Country. They strolled along San Antonio's River Walk. They had such a good time, in fact, that the Mitchells made a plan to visit Angel and Armando in Mexico!

You too can meet people from other countries. For example, you could become pen pals with a student in another country. Exchanging letters helps you to learn about other ways of life.

Some Sister City programs, such as the one you read about in Chapter 1, have "exchange programs." Young people from Texas go to a Sister City in another country. They live there with a family for several days or weeks. They attend local schools and give presentations about Texas and the United States. At the same time, students from the other country visit and stay with a family in Texas. "Exchange students" from many countries have learned about our state and country by visiting Texas and speaking with Texans.

Mario Gallegos is the first Mexican American from Harris County to serve in the Texas Senate. What do you think a student might learn by speaking with Mario Gallegos?

Excerpt from an Interview with Mario Gallegos, 1995.

The more education you have, the better living standard [way of life] you and your family will have. We have the freedom of choice to be whatever we want to be. I would never have dreamed that I would one day be sitting in the state Senate. If I can do it from a poor neighborhood, then others can as well. The road to reaching your goals is through education.

Before going home, Angel and Armando left the Mitchells this note (far right). Later they sent a postcard (right).

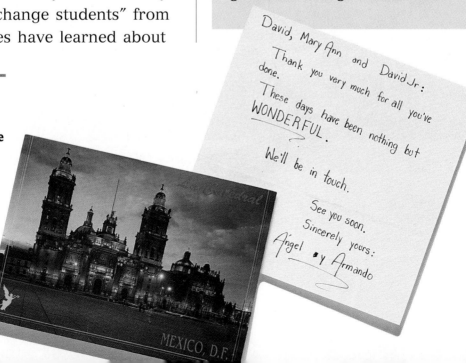

David, Mary Ann and David Jr:

Thank you very much for all you've done.

These days have been nothing but WONDERFUL.

We'll be in touch.

See you soon.
Sincerely yours:
Angel y Armando

MEXICO, D.F.

INTERDEPENDENT COUNTRIES

Texans trade with most of the countries in the Western Hemisphere. Look at the chart to see some of the goods Texas sells to other countries.

Trade Agreements

Trade agreements allow goods and services to be exchanged between people in different countries. In 1993 an important trade agreement called NAFTA was signed. NAFTA stands for North American Free Trade Agreement. The goal of NAFTA was to build closer trading ties between the United States, Mexico, and Canada.

Now it is easier to send exports from one of these three countries to another. An export is something that is sold or traded to another country.

All three governments have agreed to lower their taxes on the imports they receive from one another. An import is something that is brought in from another country for sale or use. By the year 2002 there will be no taxes on most imports between these countries.

NAFTA has made it easier for Mexico to export fruits and vegetables to the United States and Canada. NAFTA has also made it easier for our country to export electronic equipment and automobiles to Mexico and Canada.

People in the United States have disagreed about NAFTA. Some believe that NAFTA will cause Americans to lose jobs because factories will move to Mexico, where workers are

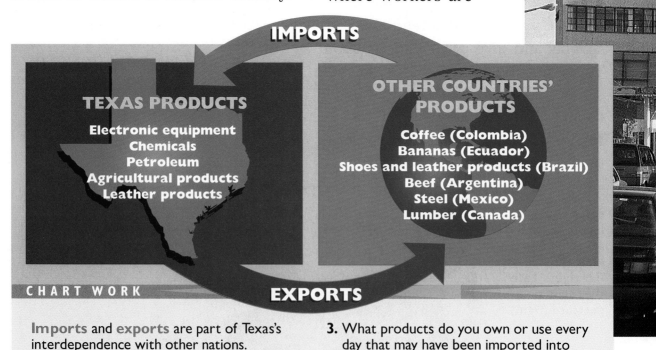

IMPORTS

TEXAS PRODUCTS

Electronic equipment
Chemicals
Petroleum
Agricultural products
Leather products

OTHER COUNTRIES' PRODUCTS

Coffee (Colombia)
Bananas (Ecuador)
Shoes and leather products (Brazil)
Beef (Argentina)
Steel (Mexico)
Lumber (Canada)

EXPORTS

CHART WORK

Imports and exports are part of Texas's interdependence with other nations.

1. Name three products that Texas exports.
2. What does Texas import from Canada?

3. What products do you own or use every day that may have been imported into Texas?

paid less. Others believe NAFTA will improve the economies of all three countries.

Partners with Mexico

Mexico is Texas's largest trading partner. There are two main reasons. One is that we are neighbors. Also, we share history and culture. The governments of the United States and Mexico have passed laws to make it easier for people to travel and trade across the Texas-Mexico border. In cities near the border, people cross over daily for shopping, entertainment, and work. Maquiladoras (mah KEE lah dawr us), or "twin factories," are often built in Texan

In cities like Laredo near the border, bridges make it easy for people to go shopping in the United States or Mexico.

and Mexican cities that are close to one another such as Laredo and Nuevo Laredo. Both of these cities are part of one economy.

WHY IT MATTERS

The United States and other countries in the Western Hemisphere cooperate to bring economic success to all. In the next lesson you will read about ties between Texas and the rest of the world.

✓ Reviewing Facts and Ideas

SUM IT UP

- The United States and other countries in the Western Hemisphere are interdependent.
- NAFTA makes it easier for Mexico, the United States, and Canada to import and export products.

THINK ABOUT IT

1. Name some goods that Texas imports and exports.

2. What are the reasons that some people in the United States support NAFTA but others do not?

3. **FOCUS** What are some of the ties Texas has with the rest of the Western Hemisphere?

4. **THINKING SKILL** _Make a generalization_ about why Texans are interested in writing to or meeting people from other countries.

5. **GEOGRAPHY** Which city would you choose as a Sister City for your school? What country is this city in?

TEXAS AND THE WORLD

READ ALOUD

In the summer of 1995, Ray and Caryl Yosko of Woodville spent three weeks in the European country of Poland teaching children to speak English. Caryl Yosko said the Polish students were "very interesting, very open, very curious about America," and that she learned from them too. "We are living in a shrinking world," she said. "We all need to be able to relate to each other."

THE BIG PICTURE

Some scientists forecast, or predict, what life will be like in the next century. Within ten years, for example, some scientists forecast that cars may be made mostly of plastic. New kinds of airplanes may fly from the United States to Europe in under two hours. They also forecast that more people will live in urban areas, more people will work on computers at home, and more people will hold jobs than ever before. These and other changes will be partly the result of links between our country and the rest of the world. Texans and other Americans will change and grow as they travel, trade, share knowledge, and exchange ideas.

PART OF THE WORLD

Texas is not just part of the United States, North America, and the Western Hemisphere. It is also part of the world community. Tourism brings visitors to our state from all over the world. Through industry and trade, Texas also is connected to Europe, Africa, and Asia.

Many of Texas's major trading partners are countries on the Pacific Rim of Asia. These countries all have ports on the Pacific Ocean. Look at the Atlas map on page R14. Find the Pacific Rim countries of Japan, South Korea, and China. Texas exports many products—such as oil, chemicals, and packaged food—to these countries on the Pacific Rim. Texas imports such goods as automobiles from Japan, electronics from South Korea, and clothing from China.

Scientific Cooperation

Trade is just one connection Texas has to other countries. Scientists from Texas team up with scientists from around the world. Texan Dr. Wah Chiu (WAH CHYOO) works at Baylor College of Medicine in Houston. He studies viruses that cause diseases. Understanding viruses can help us fight many diseases.

In his work, Dr. Chiu often cooperates with an expert in Scotland, Dr. Frazer Rixon. Because they live and work so far away from each other, they often discuss their work through computer messages.

Dr. Chiu and Dr. Rixon hope to find a way to keep viruses from harming people and animals. When scientists from many countries cooperate to fight disease, the chances for success are greater.

Dr. Chiu (below right) looks at photographs of viruses (right). Dr. Rixon (below) uses special glasses to see viruses in three dimensions.

Dr. Mitch Porias, far left, is one Texan volunteer who brings good medical care to El Salvador and other countries.

SHARING KNOWLEDGE

As the countries of the world become more interdependent, people are sharing their knowledge. Texans in business, agriculture, medicine, and other fields have become part of this global sharing.

Helping Around the World

Benevolent Missions International, for example, is an organization based in Conroe. This organization has sent nurses and eye doctors from Texas to do volunteer work in Bolivia, Belize, and El Salvador. These volunteers help poor people. They give out medicine and eyeglasses. They also do operations. One patient was a 10-year-old boy in El Salvador who was blind in one eye. In 1994 Dr. Mitch Porias of Houston performed surgery that helped him see better. "Sometimes you've got to reach out and help somebody else," said Dr. Porias. "It's a good feeling."

Joint Space Programs

NASA's programs are another example of how Texans are working with people around the world. In 1995 the United States space shuttle Atlantis docked in space at a Russian space station named Mir (mihr). "This flight heralds [signals] a new era of friendship and cooperation between our two countries," said Daniel S. Goldin, the administrator of NASA. Goldin said that the United States and other countries around the world will cooperate to build an international space station. It is expected to be completed by 2002.

You Are the Future

Students like you in Texas, in other states, and in other countries are the future of our world. As Texas and the world grow and change, education is the key to preparing for the future. Years ago young Texans who did not work on farms or ranches had few choices for other jobs. Now the job choices in Texas are practically endless.

The future of Texas depends on you and all students. You can contribute right now by learning about your community and taking an active part in it.

This computer image shows how the completed international space station will look with a docked shuttle. The station is being built by the United States, Canada, and Japan, as well as Russia and other European countries.

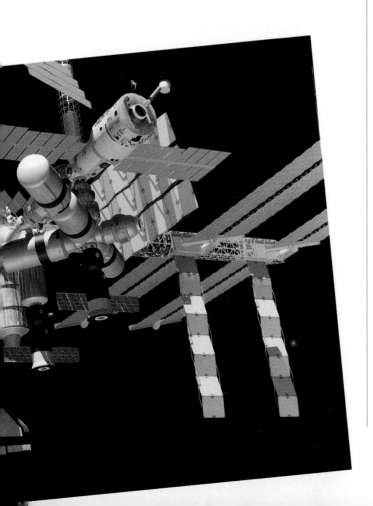

WHY IT MATTERS

The role of Texas in the world is growing. At the same time, the ties Texas has to many other countries make the world seem smaller. It is important for people around the world to work together toward a better future for everyone.

✓✓ Reviewing Facts and Ideas

SUM IT UP

- As Texas grows, our state develops more ties to other countries around the world.

- Many of our state's major trading partners are countries on the Pacific Rim.

- Doctors and scientists in Texas cooperate with other experts around the world to increase knowledge and help people.

THINK ABOUT IT

1. What are some of the changes scientists forecast for the 21st century?

2. Name an import and export that travels between Texas and the countries on the Pacific Rim.

3. **FOCUS** What are some of the ties that Texans have to people around the world?

4. **THINKING SKILL** *Make a conclusion* about why doctors and nurses from Texas would volunteer their time in another country.

5. **WRITE** Think about the kind of job you would like to have. Write a list of questions that would help you learn about the education and skills you will need.

TODAY AND TOMORROW IN THE WESTERN HEMISPHERE

Focus Activity

READ TO LEARN

How has the economy of Mexico changed since World War II?

VOCABULARY

commercial farmer
dam
industrialization
assembly line

READ ALOUD

"We have made extraordinary progress in our country," said Mexico's President Ernesto Zedillo in 1994. Like Texas, Mexico has experienced great changes in the 1900s. Many of these changes have resulted from the growth of Mexico's population and its economy.

THE BIG PICTURE

In the early 1900s most Mexicans were farmers. Farming was hard because much of the land is filled with deserts, mountains, and volcanoes. Those who dreamed of making better lives for themselves had few opportunities in Mexico. Then World War II began, and Mexico started to change. Factories sprang up to make clothes, food, and building supplies. Before the war Mexico had imported most of these products from the United States. Thousands of farmers looking for work began moving to the growing cities. By the 1960s more Mexicans lived in urban areas than rural areas. Today Mexico City is the world's second-largest urban area after Tokyo, Japan.

FARMING ON A DIFFICULT LAND

Although more Mexicans today live in cities than in rural areas, farming is still an important way of life for millions of people. This is true even though only one out of every eight acres in Mexico is fit for farming.

The Two Faces of Farming

Many farmers in Mexico are subsistence farmers—that is, they work to grow enough food to feed themselves and their families. Survival, not sale of crops, is their goal. Survival is not easy for the many families whose land is poor.

Life is very different for Mexico's big commercial farmers, who raise crops or livestock for sale. New technology has changed the way they work. It has also increased the size of harvests they can get from the land.

Oscar Sanchez Lopez grows vegetables on 200 acres of land in northern Mexico. Lopez produces bumper crops each year. He does this with the help of 400 workers, some big machines, and a computer. In one year, in fact, his farm can send over 300,000 boxes of squash, peppers, radishes, zucchini, and green onions to market! Because of trade agreements like NAFTA, Lopez's crops can appear in United States supermarkets just three days after they are picked.

Amazingly enough, Lopez grows his crops on land that was once desert. He can do this because the government has built dams. Dams are walls built across rivers to hold back the water and form lakes. Farmers rely on this water to irrigate their land. The dams also provide power for Mexico's industrialization, or its development of manufacturing industries.

Industrialization has provided different kinds of jobs for subsistence farmers who are seeking better lives in the cities. Power created by the dams helps keep cities and factories running. However, building the dams also caused some problems for many people. In order to build the dams, some nearby areas had to be flooded. This flooding damaged the farms of some families.

This Mexican farmer is harvesting prickly pear cactus. The fruit of this plant can be eaten. The plant can also be used to make medicine.

GREAT CHANGES

The electricity produced by dams has been just one source of power for Mexico's industrialization. An even bigger source has been oil. In 1974 scientists discovered some of the world's biggest reserves of oil in southeastern Mexico. Since then that oil has created great changes in Mexico's economy.

The price of oil was very high in the 1970s because it was in short supply on world markets. Then Mexico's new oil fields were discovered, and suddenly the country seemed to be very rich. Banks from other countries started lending billions of dollars to Mexico because they believed the country was now very wealthy. Some of this money was spent to create new factories, homes, and office buildings.

During the 1980s, however, oil prices dropped. Mexico's "black gold" was suddenly worth less. And the country did not have money to pay off its large debt to the banks.

Today Mexico is still struggling to recover from borrowing money in the 1970s.

Factories

Today fewer than 100,000 people work in Mexico's oil industry. Their labor produces about one-third of Mexico's entire wealth. That wealth has helped to create new factories that make everything from cars to clothes to televisions. About one out of every five Mexicans now works in a factory.

Not all the factories are owned by Mexicans. Dozens of United States companies have built manufacturing plants in Mexico, where wages are lower. Some people in the United States think this is unfair because it takes jobs out of our country. Others say that it allows United States companies to cut costs and pass the savings on to buyers in the United States. You read about this kind of link between businesses in Mexico and Texas in Lesson 2 of this chapter.

Workers in a clothing factory in Mexico are sewing together pieces of fabric. Much of the finished product will be exported.

A Bicycle Helmet Assembly Line

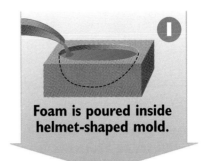

1 Foam is poured inside helmet-shaped mold.

2 Plastic shell is fitted over mold.

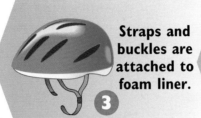

3 Straps and buckles are attached to foam liner.

4 Plastic shell is attached to foam liner.

5 Decals and reflectors are attached.

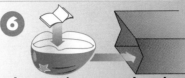

6 Instructions are placed inside helmet. Helmet is placed inside plastic bag.

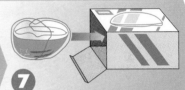

7 Bagged helmet is placed into carton.

Each step is necessary to make a helmet correctly. When are reflectors attached?

An Assembly Line

Like their counterparts in Texas and the rest of the United States, factory workers in Mexico often work along **assembly lines**. On an assembly line, the work of making a product is divided into many different steps. Each worker specializes in performing a single task.

In Tijuana, Mexico, for example, about 400 people work on an assembly line to make bicycle helmets. As the chart above shows, it takes many steps to put a bicycle helmet together. It would take a long time for one person to complete all these tasks. Working together, though, the women and men in the factory can make over 10,000 helmets in a single day!

Work at this factory doesn't only affect people in Mexico. Because of trade agreements like NAFTA, the helmets affect jobs all over the world. Workers in the United States design how the helmets are made. Others make the foam and plastic parts. Truckers, ship workers, and store clerks help to get the helmets into stores in the Western Hemisphere, Europe, Asia and Africa. As a result, people can be protected when riding a bicycle.

Infographic

The Economy of the Western Hemisphere

Bike helmets are just one kind of product made in the Western Hemisphere. What other goods and services are important to the economies of this part of the world?

Dig It!

Canada mines one-fourth of the world's nickel, which is used not only in coins but also in stainless steel products.

Oil's Well

Mexico is the world's fourth-largest producer of oil. Scientists believe Mexico's oil reserves are bigger than those in the oil-rich country of Saudi Arabia.

Dessert, Anyone?

Costa Rica makes more money from coffee, bananas, and sugar than from any other products. That's why it is said to have a "dessert economy."

Fruit of their Labors

Chile's commercial farmers make over a billion dollars each year exporting fruit. Summer harvests in Chile take place when the United States is experiencing winter. This geographic fact allows people in the United States to enjoy Chile's grapes and other fruit in the middle of winter.

Supermarket to the World

The United States is home of the world's biggest car, computer, soft-drink, and software companies. It also produces three-fourths of the world's corn exports, and one-third of its wheat exports.

Southern Exposure

Brazil produces some of the most-watched television shows in the world. Most popular are Brazil-style "soap operas" whose plots often address real-life problems in the country today.

Where's the Beef?

Argentina is a leading producer of beef. Cowhands there tend over 50 million cattle. That is more than the country's population!

WHY IT MATTERS

The Infographic on these two pages tells about the economy of some countries in the Western Hemisphere. More economic changes lie ahead for Mexico and the rest of the Western Hemisphere. Technology will con–tinue to change how people live and work. There will be new challenges in the future. We can only guess at the challenges ahead. Perhaps you will be part of the solutions.

✓✓ Reviewing Facts and Ideas

SUM IT UP

- The shortage of goods during World War II helped start industri-alization in Mexico.

- Though most people live in cities, farming is still a big industry in Mexico. Commercial farmers use modern technology to increase their crops.

- Mexico's oil reserves helped pay for the country's industrialization. Overspending of oil money left Mexico with huge debts.

THINK ABOUT IT

1. What is an assembly line? Why does it save time?

2. How has technology helped Mexi-co's commercial farmers?

3. **FOCUS** How has Mexico's economy changed since World War II?

4. **THINKING SKILL** _Make a generaliza-tion_ about how oil has affected Mexico's economy.

5. **GEOGRAPHY** How has industrializa-tion affected the movement of peo-ple in Mexico?

CHAPTER 13 REVIEW

THINKING ABOUT VOCABULARY

Number a sheet of paper from 1 to 5. Next to each number write the letter of the definition that best matches each word.

1. endangered

a. common throughout the state

b. close to taking over

c. causing danger to people

d. close to disappearing forever

2. NAFTA

a. Native American Free Trade Agreement

b. North American Free Trade Agreement

c. North Atlantic Free Trade Association

d. New Americans Free Trees Association

3. export

a. something sold or traded to another country

b. a tax on goods or services

c. something that is brought in from another country for sale or use

d. a place from which ships leave

4. industrialization

a. development of rural areas

b. development of urban areas

c. development of agriculture

d. development of manufacturing industries

5. forecast

a. to cast a fishing line

b. to know the future

c. to communicate with other countries

d. to predict

THINKING ABOUT FACTS

1. Why are people moving to our state in great numbers?

2. What information did the United States government learn about Texas from the 1990 census? What is the predicted population for Texas in the year 2000?

3. Name one positive effect of population growth in our state. Name one problem caused by population growth in Texas.

4. Name three endangered animals in our state. About how many kinds of animals are endangered in Texas?

5. What is "Clean Texas 2000"? What is its goal? How does the governor encourage businesses to cooperate with the program?

6. List three ways that Texas is connected with other countries.

7. What is NAFTA? How has NAFTA affected Mexico and the United States?

8. Name two Pacific Rim countries. Name two examples of goods that Texas exports to the Pacific Rim countries.

9. Why do scientists from Texas work with scientists in other parts of the world? How do these scientists communicate with each other?

10. What is the purpose of Benevolent Missions International?

THINK AND WRITE

WRITING A PROPOSAL

Suppose an exchange student will visit you for one week. Write a plan of activities that will help the student to learn about the history, culture, and customs of Texas.

WRITING A PLAN

You have read about the program, "Clean Texas 2000." Write a plan that supports the program and might be used in your school.

WRITING A PARAGRAPH OF DESCRIPTION

In Lesson 3 you read about forecasts for the future. Write a paragraph about forecasts that might affect your life twenty years from now.

BUILDING STUDY SKILLS

USING PRIMARY AND SECONDARY SOURCES

1. Explain the difference between a primary source and a secondary source.
2. Find two primary sources in Unit 6.
3. Name two examples of secondary sources.
4. How are primary sources useful in studying history?
5. Why is it helpful to understand the difference between primary and secondary sources?

Summing Up the Chapter

Use the chart below to organize information in the chapter. Copy the chart on a sheet of paper. Then write at least three pieces of information under each topic. When you have filled in the chart, use it to write a paragraph that answers the question "How do Texas and Mexico continue to change and grow in today's world?"

TEXAS TODAY	TEXAS AND THE WESTERN HEMISPHERE	TEXAS AND THE WORLD	MEXICO TODAY

UNIT 6 REVIEW

THINKING ABOUT VOCABULARY

Number a sheet of paper from 1 to 10. Next to each number write the word or term from the list below that best completes the sentence.

census   NAFTA
charro   Olympic
endangered   Pulitzer Prize
export   ragtime
forecast   Sun Belt

1. Each year in Brownsville, a festival is held to celebrate the special heritage of the _____.

2. An _____ is something that is sold or traded with another country.

3. Carl Lewis won four gold medals in the 1984 _____ Games.

4. Scott Joplin helped to create _____ music from a mix of brass-band, African American, and other sounds.

5. Texan Larry McMurtry won a _____ for his book, *Lonesome Dove*.

6. Texas is located in the _____, the part of the United States that has a warm climate all year.

7. In 1990 the national government conducted a _____, or count, of the people in our country.

8. Today there are about 70 kinds of animals in our state that are _____.

9. _____ is an important trade agreement among three countries in North America.

10. Scientists _____ that more people will work at home on computers in the next century.

THINK AND WRITE

WRITING A LIST
Choose an athlete you read about in Lesson 2 of Chapter 12. Write a list of questions you would like to ask him or her.

WRITING A REPORT
Choose a cultural group from Lesson 1 that you know little about. Do some research about the group. Then write a report and share it with the class.

WRITING A LETTER
Suppose you have a new pen pal in Canada. Write a letter describing "Clean Texas 2000" and other ways that Texans are cleaning up the environment.

BUILDING SKILLS

1. **Reading road maps** How is a road map different from an elevation map?

2. **Reading road maps** Look at the map of Texas on page 376. Suppose your family wants to drive the shortest route between Amarillo and Dallas. Which route would you take?

3. **Reading road maps** Look at the map of Texas on page 376. How can you tell the difference between state and interstate highways?

4. **Using primary and secondary sources** Read the section about poetry in Lesson 3 of Chapter 12. Is a primary or a secondary source used to show the example?

5. **Using primary and secondary sources** Suppose you read an article in an encyclopedia about a famous artist in our state. Would the article be a primary or a secondary source?

YESTERDAY, TODAY &
TOMORROW

You have read that the population of Texas is growing. Suppose the population of Texas doubles during your lifetime. What effect do you think the population would have on the natural resources in our state? How can we protect our natural resources for the future and still continue to grow?

READING ON YOUR OWN

Here are some books you might find at the library to help you learn more.

EATS: A FOLK HISTORY OF TEXAS FOOD
by Joyce Gibson Roach and Ernestine Sewell Linck
You will enjoy this entertaining collection of Texan recipes with stories.

TEXANS: A STORY OF TEXAS CULTURE FOR YOUNG PEOPLE
by Barbara Evans Stanush
Read about Texan ethnic groups.

TEXAS TRADITIONS: THE CULTURE OF THE LONE STAR STATE
by Robyn Montana Turner
You'll find interesting facts about the land, people, traditions, and history of Texas.

UNIT PROJECT

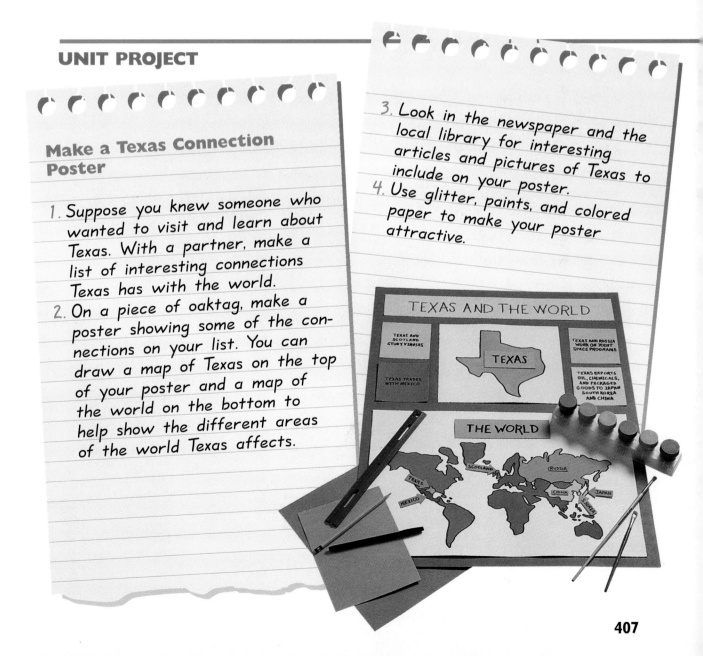

Make a Texas Connection Poster

1. Suppose you knew someone who wanted to visit and learn about Texas. With a partner, make a list of interesting connections Texas has with the world.

2. On a piece of oaktag, make a poster showing some of the connections on your list. You can draw a map of Texas on the top of your poster and a map of the world on the bottom to help show the different areas of the world Texas affects.

3. Look in the newspaper and the local library for interesting articles and pictures of Texas to include on your poster.

4. Use glitter, paints, and colored paper to make your poster attractive.

REFERENCE SECTION

The Reference Section has many parts,

each with a different type of information.

Use this section to look up people,

places, and events as you study.

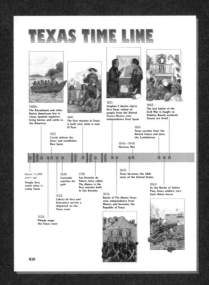

Atlas

An atlas is a collection of maps. An atlas
can be a book or a separate section within a
book. This Atlas is a separate section with
maps to help you study the history and
geography presented in this book.

MAP BUILDER
The United States: Land Use

The map on the facing page is a special kind of map.
Each transparent overlay shows a particular use of
land in our country. You can build a map that gives you
a larger picture of land use in the United States. Start
by lifting all of the transparent overlays to see the
base map, which shows the land and states of our
country. Then cover the base map with the first overlay and see where the land is covered mostly with
forests. Bring the second overlay down to see where
the land is covered mostly with grazing land and crop-
land. When you bring the third overlay down to cover
the rest, you will see major urban areas in our country. Compare the locations and amounts of land used
for growing crops and for urban development. Which
kind of land use is shown for the area where you live?

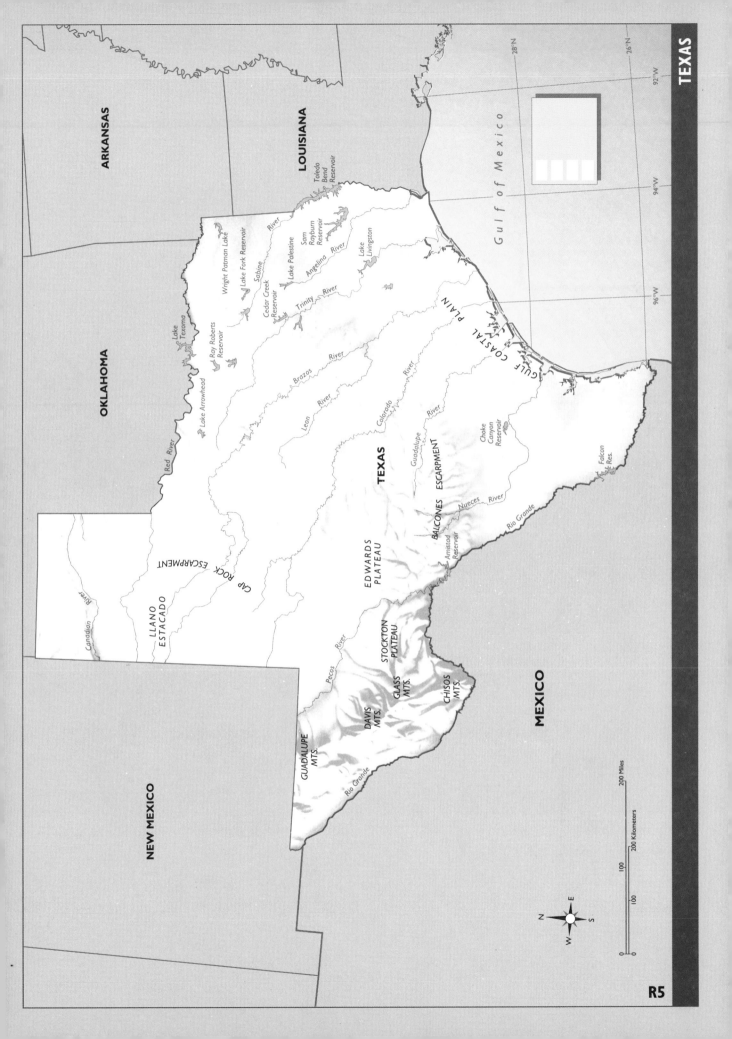

ARKANSAS

OKLAHOMA

NEW MEXICO

LOUISIANA

Gulf of Mexico

28°N

26°N

92°W

94°W

96°W

Toledo Bend Reservoir

Wright Patman Lake

Lake Fork Reservoir

Sabine River

Cedar Creek Reservoir

Lake Palestine

Sam Rayburn Reservoir

Angelina River

Lake Livingston

Trinity River

Lake Texoma

Ray Roberts Reservoir

Lake Arrowhead

Red River

Brazos River

Leon River

Colorado River

GULF COASTAL PLAIN

Choke Canyon Reservoir

Falcon Res.

Guadalupe River

TEXAS

BALCONES ESCARPMENT

Nueces River

Rio Grande

Amistad Reservoir

EDWARDS PLATEAU

CAP ROCK ESCARPMENT

LLANO ESTACADO

Canadian River

Pecos River

STOCKTON PLATEAU

GLASS MTS.

DAVIS MTS.

CHISOS MTS.

GUADALUPE MTS.

Rio Grande

MEXICO

N
W   E
S

200 Miles

200 Kilometers

100

100

0

0

R5

ALASKA
★Juneau

WEST

MIDDLE WEST

NORTHEAST

Olympia ★
WASHINGTON

MONTANA
★Helena

NORTH DAKOTA
★Bismarck

MINNESOTA

NEW HAMPSHIRE
VERMONT
MAINE
Augusta ★
★Concord

Montpelier ★

OREGON
★Salem

Boise ★

IDAHO

WYOMING

SOUTH DAKOTA
Pierre ★

St. Paul ★

WISCONSIN

Madison ★

MICHIGAN

Lansing ★

Albany ★
NEW YORK
Hartford ★

MASSACHUSETTS
★Boston
Providence

RHODE ISLAND
CONNECTICUT

NEVADA
★Carson City

Salt Lake City ★

Cheyenne ★

NEBRASKA

Lincoln ★

IOWA
★Des Moines

INDIANA

OHIO
Columbus ★

PENNSYLVANIA
Harrisburg ★

Trenton ★

Dover ★
NEW JERSEY

Sacramento ★

UTAH

★Denver

COLORADO

Topeka ★

ILLINOIS
Springfield ★

Indianapolis ★

WEST VIRGINIA
Charleston ★

Annapolis ★

DELAWARE
MARYLAND
Washington, D.C.

CALIFORNIA

KANSAS

MISSOURI
Jefferson City ★

Frankfort ★

Richmond ★
VIRGINIA

ARIZONA

Santa Fe ★

NEW MEXICO

★Phoenix

OKLAHOMA
★Oklahoma City

ARKANSAS
Little Rock ★

KENTUCKY

Nashville ★
TENNESSEE

NORTH CAROLINA
Raleigh ★

Columbia ★

SOUTH CAROLINA

MISSISSIPPI

★Atlanta

GEORGIA

TEXAS

★Austin

LOUISIANA

Baton Rouge ★

Jackson ★

Montgomery ★
ALABAMA

★Tallahassee

FLORIDA

SOUTHWEST

SOUTHEAST

Honolulu

HAWAII

ARCTIC OCEAN

Beaufort Sea

GREENLAND
(DENMARK)

Baffin Bay

ALASKA
(U.S.)

Arctic Circle

Arctic Circle

Yukon River

Fairbanks

• Anchorage

Mackenzie River

• Yellowknife

• Iqaluit

• Nuuk

Davis Strait

60°N

60°N

Hudson Bay

NORTH AMERICA

CANADA

Labrador Sea

• Edmonton

• Winnipeg

Great Lakes

Quebec •

Gulf of St. Lawrence

Vancouver

• Seattle

Missouri River

Ottawa ⊛

• Portland

Minneapolis •

Toronto •

• Boston

UNITED

Detroit •

Great Salt Lake

Salt Lake City •

Chicago •

• New York City

• Denver

St. Louis •

⊛ Washington, D.C.

Colorado River

San Francisco •

STATES

ATLANTIC OCEAN

• Los Angeles

Phoenix •

• Atlanta

BERMUDA
(U.K.)

30°N

Rio Grande

Houston •

Mississippi River

New Orleans •

30°N

Gulf of California

MEXICO

Gulf of Mexico

THE BAHAMAS

Tropic of Cancer

Monterrey •

Miami •

⊛ Nassau

HAWAII
(U.S.)

Havana ⊛

CUBA

HAITI

DOMINICAN REPUBLIC

PACIFIC OCEAN

Guadalajara •

Santo Domingo ⊛

ST. KITTS AND NEVIS

Mexico City ⊛

BELIZE

Port-au-Prince ⊛

San Juan •

ANTIGUA AND BARBUDA

Belmopan ⊛

JAMAICA

PUERTO RICO
(U.S.)

DOMINICA

Guatemala City ⊛

HONDURAS

Kingston ⊛

ST. LUCIA

GUATEMALA

Tegucigalpa ⊛

Caribbean Sea

GRENADA

BARBADOS

San Salvador ⊛

NICARAGUA

ST. VINCENT AND THE GRENADINES

EL SALVADOR

Managua ⊛

Maracaibo •

TRINIDAD AND TOBAGO

San José ⊛

Panamá City ⊛

Caracas ⊛

SURINAME

COSTA RICA

PANAMA

VENEZUELA

Georgetown ⊛

Paramaribo ⊛

• Cayenne

Bogotá ⊛

GUYANA

FRENCH GUIANA
(FRANCE)

COLOMBIA

0°

Equator

Quito ⊛

0°

GALAPAGOS ISLANDS
(ECUADOR)

ECUADOR

Guayaquil •

Manaus •

• Belém

Amazon River

SOUTH AMERICA

Recife •

PERU

BRAZIL

Lima ⊛

Bahia •

Callao •

BOLIVIA

Brasília ⊛

La Paz ⊛

• Santa Cruz

Rio de Janeiro •

Sucre ⊛

PARAGUAY

São Paulo •

Tropic of Capricorn

Antofagasta •

São Paulo •

Tucumán •

Asunción ⊛

Porto Alegre •

30°S

CHILE

URUGUAY

30°S

Valparaíso •

Rosario •

Santiago ⊛

Buenos Aires ⊛

Montevideo ⊛

La Plata •

Concepción •

ARGENTINA

Mar del Plata •

Comodoro Rivadavia •

N
W   E
S

⊛ National capital   • Other city

| 0 | 1,000 | 2,000 Miles |

| 0 | 1,000 | 2,000 Kilometers |

FALKLAND ISLANDS
(U.K.)

Punta Arenas •

Strait of Magellan

SOUTH GEORGIA
(U.K.)

R7

RUSSIA

ARCTIC OCEAN

70°N

Arctic Circle

ALASKA

● Nome

Yukon

● Fairbanks

60°N

180°

CANADA

● Anchorage

River

Juneau ★

PACIFIC
OCEAN

170°W

160°W

150°W

140°W

0   250   500 Miles

0   250   500 Kilometers

CANADA

River

● Seattle

Spokane ●

WASHINGTON

Olympia ★

Great Falls ●

Missouri River

40°N

Columbia

● Portland

Helena ★

MONTANA

★ Salem

● Eugene

IDAHO

● Billings

OREGON

★ Boise

WYOMING

Snake River

● Pocatello

Casper ●

NEVADA

Great
Salt
Lake

● Ogden

● Reno

★ Salt Lake City

Cheyenne ★

● Carson City

San Francisco ●

★ Sacramento

● Oakland

● Provo

COLORADO

● San Jose

UTAH

Denver ★

Colorado
Springs ●

PACIFIC OCEAN

CALIFORNIA

Las
Vegas ●

Pueblo ●

● Los Angeles

River

● Long Beach

30°N

Colorado

ARIZONA

Santa
Fe ★

● San Diego

Albuquerque ●

★ Phoenix

NEW MEXICO

Tucson ●

130°W

El Paso ●

Rio Grande

160°W

PACIFIC
OCEAN

155°W

Kauai

Niihau

Oahu

Honolulu ★

Molokai

HAWAII

Lanai

Maui

Kahoolawe

20°N

MEXICO

Hawaii

Hilo ●

0   100   200 Miles

0   100   200 Kilometers

120°W

110°W

20°N

CANADA

Lake Superior

NORTH DAKOTA
Grand Forks
★ Bismarck • Fargo

SOUTH DAKOTA
• Pierre
Sioux Falls

MINNESOTA
• Duluth
Minneapolis • ★ St. Paul

Missouri River

NEBRASKA
Omaha •
★ Lincoln
Platte River

WISCONSIN
Green Bay •
Madison ★ • Milwaukee

MICHIGAN
Grand Rapids •
• Lansing ★
Detroit •

Lake Michigan
Lake Huron
Lake Ontario

IOWA
Cedar Rapids •
• Rockford
Davenport •
★ Des Moines

Mississippi River

Chicago •
• Gary
Fort Wayne •

INDIANA
★ Indianapolis

ILLINOIS
★ Springfield

Peoria •

Toledo •

Lake Erie

Cleveland •

OHIO
• Columbus ★

Cincinnati •

NEW YORK
Buffalo •
Albany ★

MAINE
★ Augusta

Burlington • ★ Montpelier
VERMONT **NEW HAMPSHIRE**
★ Concord
• Portland

Hartford ★
CONNECTICUT
MASSACHUSETTS
★ Boston
Providence ★
RHODE ISLAND

Newark •
★ • New York
Trenton ★
NEW JERSEY

PENNSYLVANIA
Pittsburgh •
Harrisburg ★
Philadelphia •

• Wheeling

WEST VIRGINIA
Charleston ★

VIRGINIA
Richmond ★ •

Baltimore •
Annapolis ★
Washington, D.C. ⊛
DELAWARE
Dover ★
MARYLAND

Norfolk •

MISSOURI
Kansas City •
★ Jefferson City
St. Louis •

KANSAS
Topeka ★ • Kansas City
• Wichita
Arkansas River

KENTUCKY
Frankfort ★
Louisville •
Evansville •

TENNESSEE
Nashville ★
Knoxville •
Memphis •
Tennessee River

NORTH CAROLINA
★ Raleigh
• Charlotte

SOUTH CAROLINA
Columbia ★
• Charleston

OKLAHOMA
★ Oklahoma City
Tulsa •
Fort Smith ★

ARKANSAS
Little Rock ★

Red River

TEXAS
Fort Worth • • Dallas
★ Austin
Houston •
• San Antonio
• Laredo
Corpus Christi •

LOUISIANA
• Shreveport
★ Jackson
Baton Rouge ★
New Orleans •

MISSISSIPPI
Mississippi River

ALABAMA
Birmingham •
★ Montgomery

GEORGIA
• Atlanta ★
Columbus •
Savannah •

• Charleston

Biloxi • Mobile •
★ Tallahassee • Jacksonville

FLORIDA
Tampa •
Miami •

Gulf of Mexico

ATLANTIC OCEAN

THE BAHAMAS

CUBA

⊛ National capital   ★ State capital   • Other city

0   150   300 Miles
0   150   300 Kilometers

50°N
40°N
30°N
70°W
100°W   90°W   80°W

R9

RUSSIA

ARCTIC OCEAN

70°N

BROOKS RANGE

ALASKA

CANADA

Bering Strait

Yukon River

ALASKA RANGE

▲ Mt. McKinley
20,320 ft.
(6,194 m)

60°N

Bering Sea

170°W

160°W   150°W   140°W

0   250   500 Miles
0   250   500 Kilometers

CANADA

Missouri   River

Yellowstone River

Puget Sound

Mt. Rainier
14,410 ft.
(4,391 m)
▲
Mt. St. Helens
8,366 ft.
(2,550 m)

Columbia River

Mt. Hood
11,235 ft.
(3,424 m)

CASCADE RANGE

COAST RANGES

COLUMBIA PLATEAU

Snake River

ROCKY MOUNTAINS

Granite Peak
12,799 ft.
(3,900 m) ▲

TETON RANGE

BLACK HILLS

40°N

130°W

Cape Mendocino

▲ Mt. Shasta
14,162 ft.
(4,316 m)

Sacramento River

Great Salt Lake

GREAT SALT LAKE DESERT

RANGE

WASATCH

Kings Peak
13,528 ft.
(4,123 m) ▲

GREAT

GREAT BASIN

San Francisco Bay

COAST

SIERRA NEVADA

CENTRAL VALLEY

Lake Tahoe

San Joaquin River

Mt. Elbert
14,433 ft.
(4,398 m) ▲

Pikes Peak
14,107 ft.
(4,301 m) ▲

PLAINS

▲ Mt. Whitney
14,491 ft.
(4,418 m)

PACIFIC OCEAN

RANGES

Lake Mead

River

COLORADO PLATEAU

DEATH VALLEY

MOJAVE DESERT

Wheeler Peak
13,065 ft.
(3,982 m) ▲

Humphreys Peak
12,633 ft.
(3,850 m) ▲

Colorado

Salton Sea

SONORA DESERT

Gila   River

Pecos River

30°N

Guadalupe Peak
8,751 ft.
(2,667 m) ▲

EDWARDS PLATEAU

160°W   PACIFIC OCEAN   155°W

Kauai

Oahu

N
W   E
S

Maui

HAWAII

Hawaii

Mauna Kea
13,796 ft.
(4,205 m) ▲

20°N

0   100   200 Miles
0   100   200 Kilometers

Rio Grande

MEXICO

Gulf of California

120°W

110°W

CANADA

Lake of
the Woods

Lake Superior

GREAT

LAKES

MESABI RANGE

Lake Michigan

Lake Huron

Lake Ontario

ADIRONDACK
MTS.

St. Lawrence River

GREEN MTS.

WHITE MTS.

▲ Mt. Washington
6,288 ft.
(1,917 m)

Cape Cod

CENTRAL PLAINS

Mississippi

River

Lake Erie

ALLEGHENY
PLATEAU

Hudson River

Long Island

40° N

70° W

Platte   River

Missouri

River

Wabash

River

Ohio

River

ALLEGHENY MOUNTAINS

APPALACHIAN MOUNTAINS

Susquehanna
River

Potomac
River

Delaware Bay

ATLANTIC COASTAL PLAIN

Chesapeake Bay

INTERIOR   PLAINS

Arkansas

River

OZARK
PLATEAU

River

Tennessee

River

ALLEGHENY MOUNTAINS

▲ Mt. Mitchell
6,684 ft.
(2,037 m)

PIEDMONT

Cape Hatteras

OUACHITA
MOUNTAINS

Red

River

Mississippi

River

Alabama

River

Chattahoochee

River

Savannah   River

ATLANTIC COASTAL PLAIN

ATLANTIC OCEAN

Brazos

River

Colorado   River

GULF   COASTAL   PLAIN

Mobile Bay

30° N

Galveston Bay

Mississippi Delta

Lake
Okeechobee

Bahama Islands

Gulf of Mexico

N
W   E
S

0   150   300 Miles

0   150   300 Kilometers

Florida Keys

Straits of Florida

80° W

90° W

CUBA

R11

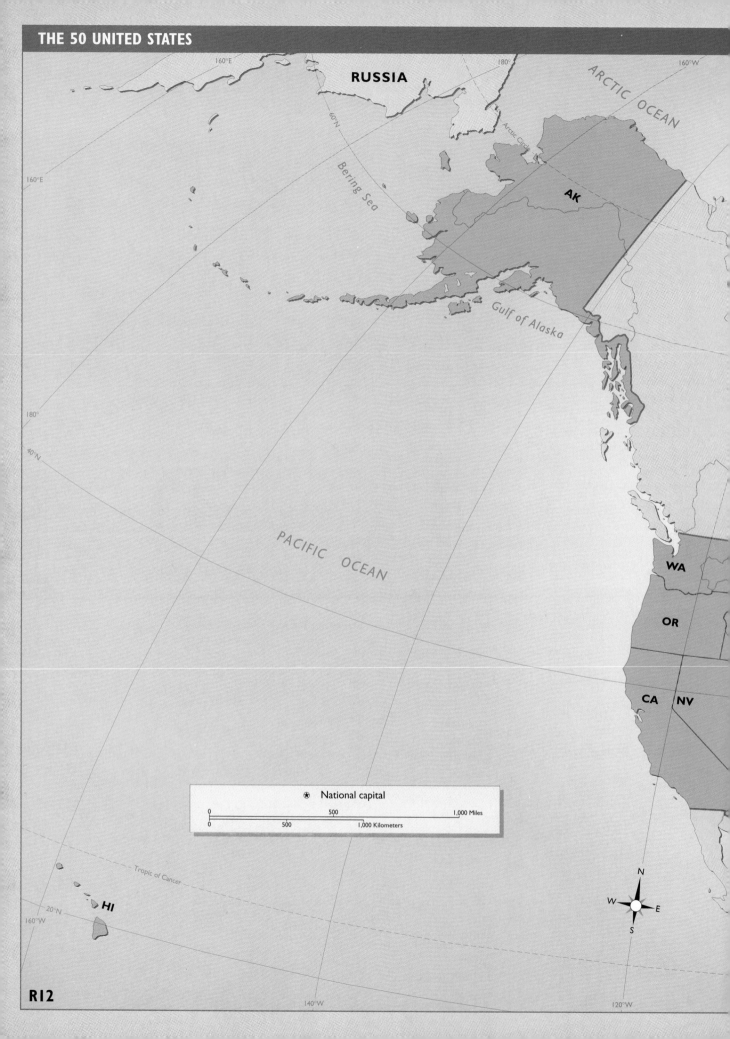

160°E   160°E   180°   160°W

RUSSIA

ARCTIC OCEAN

60°N

Arctic Circle

Bering Sea

AK

180°

Gulf of Alaska

40°N

PACIFIC   OCEAN

WA

OR

⊛ National capital

| 0 | | 500 | | 1,000 Miles |
| 0 | 500 | | 1,000 Kilometers | |

CA   NV

Tropic of Cancer

N

W   E

HI

20°N

160°W

S

140°W   120°W

MEXICO

140°W   80°N   120°W   100°W   80°W   60°W   40°W   20°W

Greenland
(DENMARK)

40°W
60°N

Hudson Bay

CANADA

Great Lakes

60°W

MT   ND   MN   MI   ME
                   WI   MI   VT
ID   SD   NY   NH
   WY   IA   MI   MA
         NE   PA   CT
UT   IL   IN   OH   RI
   CO   KS   KY   WV   NJ   40°N
         MO   VA   Washington, D.C.
                   TN   MD   DE
AZ   NM   OK   AR   NC   ATLANTIC OCEAN
         TX   MS   AL   GA   SC
              LA   FL

NC

Gulf of Mexico

MEXICO   80°W

100°W   CUBA

R13

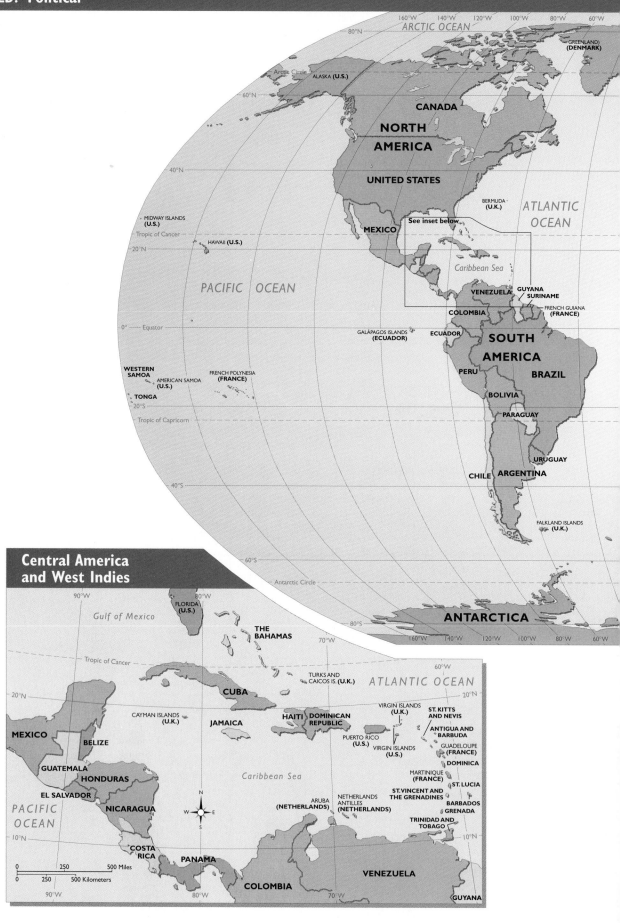

ARCTIC OCEAN

160°W 140°W 120°W 100°W 80°W 60°W

80°N

GREENLAND)
(DENMARK)

Arctic Circle

ALASKA (U.S.)

60°N

CANADA

NORTH
AMERICA

40°N

UNITED STATES

BERMUDA
(U.K.)

ATLANTIC
OCEAN

Midway Islands
(U.S.)

MEXICO

See inset below

Tropic of Cancer

20°N

HAWAII (U.S.)

Caribbean Sea

VENEZUELA GUYANA
SURINAME

PACIFIC   OCEAN

COLOMBIA

FRENCH GUIANA
(FRANCE)

0° Equator

GALÁPAGOS ISLANDS
(ECUADOR)

ECUADOR

SOUTH
AMERICA

WESTERN
SAMOA

AMERICAN SAMOA
(U.S.)

FRENCH POLYNESIA
(FRANCE)

PERU

BRAZIL

BOLIVIA

TONGA

20°S

PARAGUAY

Tropic of Capricorn

URUGUAY

40°S

CHILE ARGENTINA

FALKLAND ISLANDS
(U.K.)

60°S

Antarctic Circle

80°S

ANTARCTICA

160°W 140°W 120°W 100°W 80°W 60°W

Central America and West Indies

90°W 80°W

Gulf of Mexico

FLORIDA
(U.S.)

THE
BAHAMAS

70°W

Tropic of Cancer

TURKS AND
CAICOS IS. (U.K.)

ATLANTIC OCEAN

60°W

20°N

CUBA

20°N

CAYMAN ISLANDS
(U.K.)

JAMAICA

HAITI DOMINICAN
REPUBLIC

VIRGIN ISLANDS
(U.K.)

ST. KITTS
AND NEVIS

MEXICO

BELIZE

PUERTO RICO
(U.S.)

VIRGIN ISLANDS
(U.S.)

ANTIGUA AND
BARBUDA

GUADELOUPE
(FRANCE)

GUATEMALA

DOMINICA

HONDURAS

Caribbean Sea

MARTINIQUE
(FRANCE)

ST. LUCIA

EL SALVADOR

N

ST.VINCENT AND
THE GRENADINES

PACIFIC
OCEAN

NICARAGUA

W E

ARUBA
(NETHERLANDS)

NETHERLANDS
ANTILLES
(NETHERLANDS)

BARBADOS

GRENADA

S

TRINIDAD AND
TOBAGO

10°N

COSTA
RICA

PANAMA

10°N

0   250   500 Miles

0   250   500 Kilometers

COLOMBIA

VENEZUELA

GUYANA

90°W 80°W 70°W

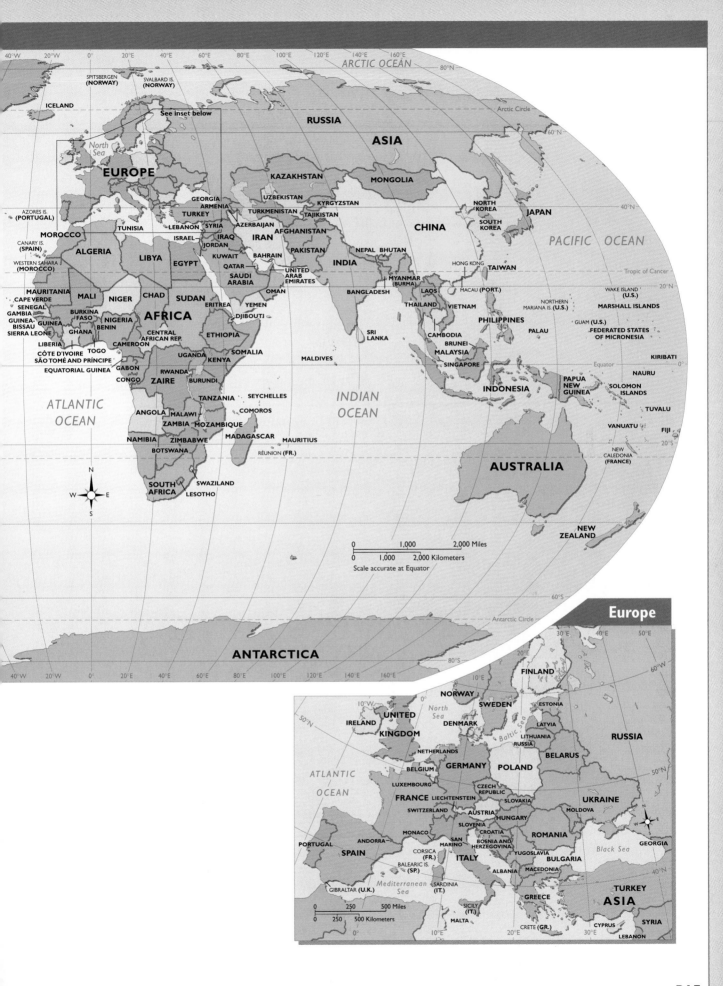

ARCTIC OCEAN

80°N

Arctic Circle

60°N

RUSSIA

ASIA

40°N

SPITSBERGEN
(NORWAY)

SVALBARD IS.
(NORWAY)

ICELAND

See inset below

North
Sea

EUROPE

AZORES IS.
(PORTUGAL)

GEORGIA
ARMENIA
TURKEY

KAZAKHSTAN

MONGOLIA

NORTH
KOREA

SOUTH
KOREA

JAPAN

PACIFIC OCEAN

UZBEKISTAN
TURKMENISTAN

KYRGYZSTAN
TAJIKISTAN

MOROCCO

TUNISIA

LEBANON
ISRAEL
JORDAN

SYRIA

AZERBAIJAN

AFGHANISTAN

CHINA

CANARY IS.
(SPAIN)

IRAQ

KUWAIT

IRAN

PAKISTAN

NEPAL BHUTAN

Tropic of Cancer

WESTERN SAHARA
(MOROCCO)

ALGERIA

LIBYA

EGYPT

QATAR
SAUDI
ARABIA

BAHRAIN
UNITED
ARAB
EMIRATES

INDIA

HONG KONG

MACAU (PORT.)

TAIWAN

20°N

MAURITANIA

CAPE VERDE
SENEGAL
GAMBIA
GUINEA-
BISSOU
SIERRA LEONE

MALI

BURKINA
FASO

GUINEA

NIGER

NIGERIA
BENIN

CHAD

SUDAN

OMAN

ERITREA

YEMEN

DJIBOUTI

MYANMAR
(BURMA)

LAOS

WAKE ISLAND
(U.S.)

MARSHALL ISLANDS

NORTHERN
MARIANA IS. (U.S.)

BANGLADESH

AFRICA

GHANA

CENTRAL
AFRICAN REP.

ETHIOPIA

THAILAND

VIETNAM

PHILIPPINES

GUAM (U.S.)
FEDERATED STATES
OF MICRONESIA

PALAU

KIRIBATI

LIBERIA
CÔTE D'IVOIRE
SÃO TOMÉ AND PRÍNCIPE

TOGO
CAMEROON

UGANDA

SOMALIA

KENYA

SRI
LANKA

MALDIVES

CAMBODIA
BRUNEI
MALAYSIA

SINGAPORE

Equator

NAURU

EQUATORIAL GUINEA

GABON
CONGO

ZAIRE

RWANDA

BURUNDI

INDONESIA

PAPUA
NEW
GUINEA

SOLOMON
ISLANDS

**ATLANTIC
OCEAN**

TANZANIA

SEYCHELLES

**INDIAN
OCEAN**

TUVALU

ANGOLA

MALAWI

COMOROS

ZAMBIA MOZAMBIQUE

VANUATU

FIJI

20°S

NAMIBIA

ZIMBABWE

MADAGASCAR

MAURITIUS

NEW
CALEDONIA
(FRANCE)

BOTSWANA

RÉUNION (FR.)

AUSTRALIA

N

W   E

S

SOUTH
AFRICA

SWAZILAND

LESOTHO

| 0 | 1,000 | 2,000 Miles |
| 0 | 1,000 | 2,000 Kilometers |

Scale accurate at Equator

**NEW
ZEALAND**

60°S

Antarctic Circle

80°S

ANTARCTICA

40°W   20°W   0°   20°E   40°E   60°E   80°E   100°E   120°E   140°E   160°E

Europe

FINLAND

NORWAY

SWEDEN

ESTONIA

IRELAND

UNITED
KINGDOM

North
Sea

DENMARK

LATVIA

Baltic Sea

LITHUANIA

RUSSIA

RUSSIA

NETHERLANDS

**ATLANTIC

OCEAN**

BELGIUM

LUXEMBOURG

GERMANY

POLAND

BELARUS

CZECH
REPUBLIC

UKRAINE

FRANCE

LIECHTENSTEIN

SLOVAKIA

MOLDOVA

SWITZERLAND

AUSTRIA

HUNGARY

SLOVENIA

CROATIA

ROMANIA

MONACO

SAN
MARINO

BOSNIA AND
HERZEGOVINA

YUGOSLAVIA

BULGARIA

Black Sea

GEORGIA

PORTUGAL

ANDORRA

SPAIN

CORSICA
(FR.)

ITALY

ALBANIA

MACEDONIA

GIBRALTAR (U.K.)

BALEARIC IS.
(SP.)

Mediterranean
Sea

SARDINIA
(IT.)

GREECE

TURKEY

ASIA

| 0 | 250 | 500 Miles |
| 0 | 250 | 500 Kilometers |

SICILY
(IT.)

MALTA

CRETE (GR.)

CYPRUS

SYRIA

LEBANON

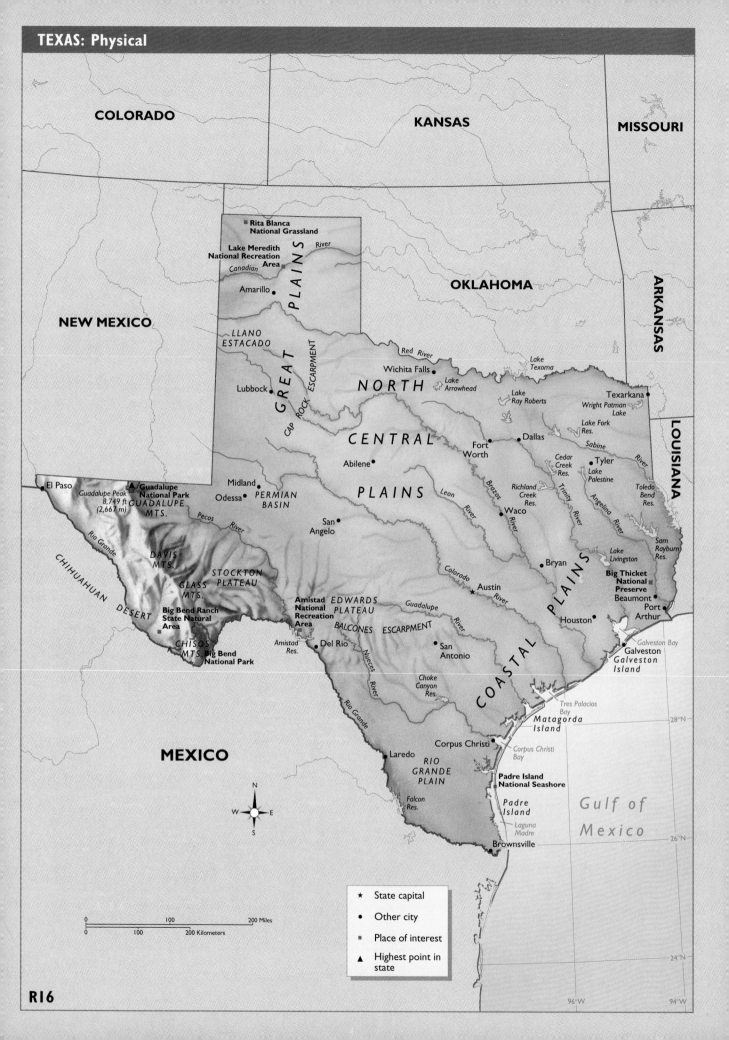

TEXAS: Physical

COLORADO

KANSAS

MISSOURI

NEW MEXICO

OKLAHOMA

ARKANSAS

LOUISIANA

**Rita Blanca
National Grassland**

**Lake Meredith
National Recreation
Area**

Canadian River

Amarillo

*LLANO
ESTACADO*

GREAT PLAINS

CAP ROCK ESCARPMENT

Lubbock

NORTH

Red River

Wichita Falls

*Lake
Texoma*

Lake
Arrowhead

*Lake
Ray Roberts*

Texarkana

*Wright Patman
Lake*

CENTRAL

Fort
Worth

Dallas

Sabine

*Lake Fork
Res.*

Tyler

*Lake
Palestine*

Abilene

*Cedar
Creek
Res.*

PLAINS

*Richland
Creek
Res.*

Trinity River

Angelina River

*Toledo
Bend
Res.*

El Paso

*Guadalupe Peak
8,749 ft
(2,667 m)*

▲ **Guadalupe
National Park**
*GUADALUPE
MTS.*

Midland

Odessa

*PERMIAN
BASIN*

Pecos River

San
Angelo

*Leon
River*

*Brazos
River*

Waco

*Sam
Rayburn
Res.*

Rio Grande

*DAVIS
MTS.*

*STOCKTON
PLATEAU*

*GLASS
MTS.*

**Big Bend Ranch
State Natural
Area**

*CHISOS
MTS.* **Big Bend
National Park**

CHIHUAHUAN DESERT

**Amistad
National
Recreation
Area**

*EDWARDS
PLATEAU*

BALCONES ESCARPMENT

*Guadalupe
River*

*Colorado
River*

Austin ★

Bryan

Houston

*Lake
Livingston*

**Big Thicket
National
Preserve**

Beaumont

Port
Arthur

*Amistad
Res.*

Del Rio

San
Antonio

*Nueces
River*

*Choke
Canyon
Res.*

COASTAL

PLAINS

Galveston Bay

Galveston
*Galveston
Island*

*Tres Palacios
Bay*

*Matagorda
Island*

28°N

MEXICO

Corpus Christi

Laredo

*RIO
GRANDE
PLAIN*

*Falcon
Res.*

*Corpus Christi
Bay*

**Padre Island
National Seashore**

*Padre
Island*

*Laguna
Madre*

Brownsville

*Gulf of
Mexico*

26°N

★	State capital
●	Other city
■	Place of interest
▲	Highest point in state

0   100   200 Miles
0   100   200 Kilometers

N
W — E
S

24°N

96°W   94°W

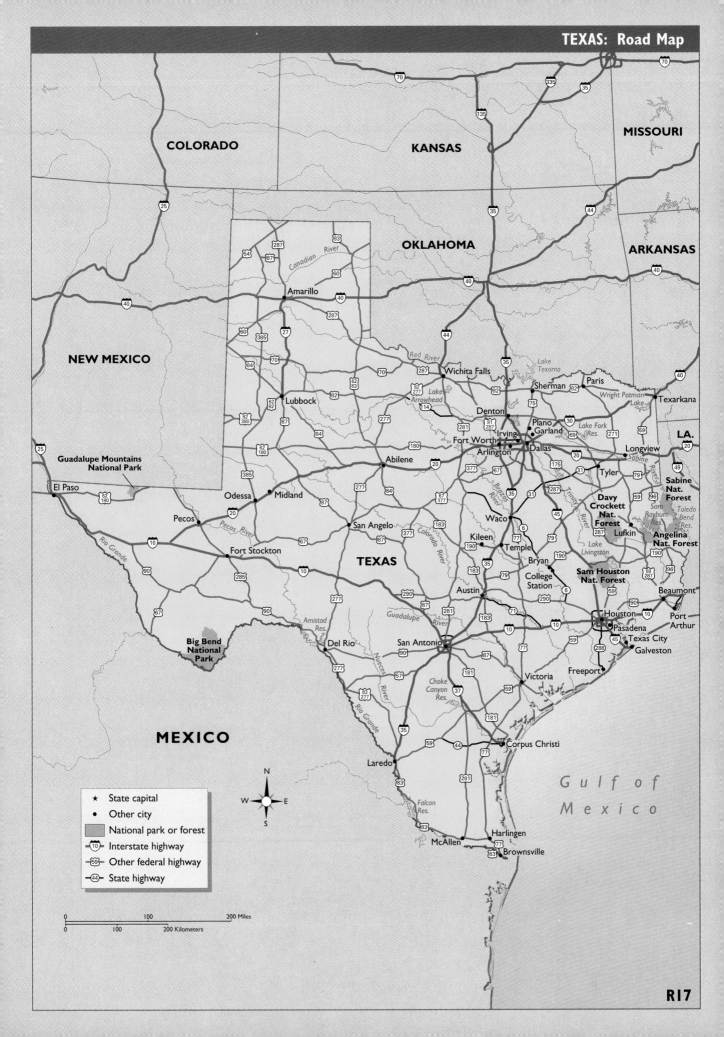

See table for key to numbers

0   50   100 Miles
0   50   100 Kilometers

TEXAS COUNTIES

County	No.	County	No.	County	No.
Anderson	133	Culberson	116	Hill	131
Andrews	97	Dallam	1	Hockley	46
Angelina	158	Dallas	86	Hood	106
Aransas	240	Dawson	76	Hopkins	69
Archer	53	Deaf Smith	16	Houston	156
Armstrong	18	Delta	68	Howard	99
Atascosa	227	Denton	65	Hudspeth	115
Austin	208	De Witt	219	Hunt	67
Bailey	27	Dickens	49	Hutchinson	8
Bandera	198	Dimmit	33	Irion	142
Bastrop	205	Donley	19	Jack	63
Baylor	52	Duval	242	Jackson	231
Bee	237	Eastland	104	Jasper	177
Bell	150	Ector	120	Jeff Davis	161
Bexar	200	Edwards	195	Jefferson	213
Blanco	185	Ellis	109	Jim Hogg	248
Borden	77	El Paso	114	Jim Wells	243
Bosque	130	Erath	105	Johnson	108
Bowie	44	Falls	152	Jones	80
Brazoria	222	Fannin	41	Karnes	228
Brazos	170	Fayette	206	Kaufman	88
Brewster	180	Fisher	79	Kendall	199
Briscoe	24	Floyd	30	Kenedy	250
Brooks	249	Foard	34	Kent	58
Brown	127	Fort Bend	210	Kerr	197
Burleson	188	Franklin	70	Kimble	183
Burnet	167	Freestone	132	King	50
Caldwell	204	Frio	226	Kinney	214
Calhoun	239	Gaines	75	Kleberg	246
Callahan	103	Galveston	223	Knox	51
Cameron	254	Garza	57	Lamar	42
Camp	72	Gillespie	184	Lamb	28
Carson	13	Glasscock	122	Lampasas	148
Cass	74	Goliad	229	La Salle	234
Castro	22	Gonzales	218	Lavaca	220
Chambers	212	Gray	14	Lee	187
Cherokee	134	Grayson	40	Leon	155
Childress	26	Gregg	94	Liberty	191
Clay	37	Grimes	172	Limestone	153
Cochran	45	Guadalupe	203	Lipscomb	5
Coke	124	Hale	29	Live Oak	236
Coleman	126	Hall	25	Llano	166
Collin	66	Hamilton	129	Loving	118
Collingsworth	20	Hansford	3	Lubbock	47
Colorado	207	Hardeman	33	Lynn	56
Comal	201	Hardin	192	McCulloch	145
Comanche	128	Harris	211	McLennan	151
Concho	144	Harrison	96	McMullen	235
Cooke	39	Hartley	6	Madison	171
Coryell	149	Haskell	60	Marion	95
Cottle	32	Hays	202	Martin	98
Crane	139	Hamphill	10	Mason	165
Crockett	162	Henderson	111	Matagorda	232
Crosby	48	Hidalgo	252	Maverick	224

County	No.	County	No.	County	No.
Medina	216	Red River	43	Titus	71
Menard	164	Reeves	117	Tom Green	143
Midland	121	Refugio	238	Travis	186
Milam	169	Roberts	9	Trinity	157
Mills	147	Robertson	154	Tyler	176
Mitchell	100	Rockwall	87	Upshur	93
Montague	38	Runnels	125	Upton	140
Montgomery	190	Rusk	112	Uvalde	215
Moore	7	Sabine	160	Val Verde	194
Morris	73	San Augustine	159	Van Zandt	89
Motley	31	San Jacinto	174	Victoria	230
Nacogdoches	135	San Patricio	244	Walker	173
Navarro	110	San Saba	146	Waller	209
Newton	178	Schleicher	163	Ward	137
Nolan	101	Scurry	78	Washington	189
Nueces	245	Shackelford	81	Webb	241
Ochiltree	4	Shelby	136	Wharton	221
Oldham	11	Sherman	2	Wheeler	15
Orange	193	Smith	92	Wichita	36
Palo Pinto	83	Somervell	107	Wilbarger	35
Panola	113	Starr	251	Willacy	253
Parker	84	Stephens	82	Williamson	168
Parmer	21	Sterling	123	Wilson	217
Pecos	138	Stonewall	59	Winkler	119
Polk	175	Sutton	182	Wise	64
Potter	12	Swisher	23	Wood	91
Presidio	179	Tarrant	85	Yoakum	54
Rains	90	Taylor	102	Young	62
Randall	17	Terrell	181	Zapata	247
Reagan	141	Terry	55	Zavala	225
Real	196	Throckmorton	61		

GOVERNORS *of* TEXAS

State Capitol Building, Austin

PRESIDENTS OF THE REPUBLIC OF TEXAS	TERM
David G. Burnet	1836
Sam Houston	1836–1838
Mirabeau B. Lamar	1838–1841
Sam Houston	1841–1844
Anson Jones	1844–1846

GOVERNORS OF THE STATE OF TEXAS	TERM
J. Pinckney Henderson	1846–1847
George T. Wood	1847–1849
P. Hansborough Bell	1849–1853
J.W. Henderson	1853
Elisha M. Pease	1853–1857
Hardin R. Runnels	1857–1859
Sam Houston	1859–1861
Edward Clark	1861
Francis R. Lubbock	1861–1863
Pendleton Murrah	1863–1865
Andrew J. Hamilton	1865–1866
James W. Throckmorton	1866–1867
Elisha M. Pease	1867–1869
Edmund J. Davis	1870–1874
Richard Coke	1874–1876
Richard B. Hubbard	1876–1879
Oran M. Roberts	1879–1883
John Ireland	1883–1887
Lawrence S. Ross	1887–1891
James S. Hogg	1891–1895
Charles A. Culberson	1895–1899
Joseph D. Sayers	1899–1903
S.W.T. Lanham	1903–1907
Thomas M. Campbell	1907–1911
Oscar B. Colquitt	1911–1915
James E. Ferguson	1915–1917
William P. Hobby	1917–1921
Pat M. Neff	1921–1925
Miriam A. Ferguson	1925–1927
Dan Moody	1927–1931
Ross S. Sterling	1931–1933
Miriam A. Ferguson	1933–1935
James V. Allred	1935–1939
W. Lee O'Daniel	1939–1941
Coke R. Stevenson	1941–1947
Beauford H. Jester	1947–1949
Allan Shivers	1949–1957
Price Daniel	1957–1963
John B. Connally	1963–1969
Preston Smith	1969–1973
Dolph Briscoe	1973–1979
William P. Clements	1979–1983
Mark White	1983–1987
William P. Clements	1987–1991
Ann W. Richards	1991–1995
George W. Bush	1995–

TEXAS TIME LINE

1500s
The Karankawa and other Native Americans live in Texas; Spanish explorers bring horses and cattle to the Americas

1681
The first mission in Texas is built near what is now El Paso

1521
Cortés defeats the Aztec and establishes New Spain

1821
Stephen F. Austin starts first Texas colony of people from the United States; Mexico wins independence from Spain

1865
The last battle of the Civil War is fought at Palmito Ranch; enslaved Texans are freed

1861
Texas secedes from the United States and joins the Confederacy

1846–1848
Mexican War

1500s · 1600s · 1700s · 1800s

About 12,000 years ago
People first reach what is today Texas

1540
Coronado searches for gold

1718
San Antonio de Valero, later called The Alamo, is the first mission built in San Antonio

1845
Texas becomes the 28th state of the United States

1863
At the Battle of Sabine Pass, Texas soldiers turn back Union forces

1528
Cabeza de Vaca and Estevanico survive a shipwreck on the Texas coast

1836
Battle of The Alamo; Texas wins independence from Mexico and becomes the Republic of Texas

1520
Piñeda maps the Texas coast

1866–1880s
Cattle drives take Texas longhorn cattle north to railroads

1901
Oil is discovered at Spindletop

1995
Mission Control helps United States shuttle *Atlantis* dock at Russian space station Mir

1876
New state Constitution is adopted

1929
Stock market crashes and Great Depression begins

1969
Johnson Space Center directs the first landing of astronauts on the moon

1870
Texas is readmitted to the United States

1881
Railroads reach El Paso

1914–1918
World War I

1900s

1874
The Battle of Palo Duro Canyon forces Native Americans to move to reservations

1939–1945
World War II

1924
Miriam A. Ferguson becomes first woman governor of Texas

1993
NAFTA makes trade between the United States, Canada, and Mexico easier

1869
Chinese and other laborers help build first railroads through Texas; African Americans first elected to state government

1920
American women gain the right to vote; first radio broadcast in Texas

OUR FIFTY STATES

ALABAMA
★
Montgomery

DATE OF STATEHOOD 1819

NICKNAME **Heart of Dixie**

POPULATION 4,040,587

AREA 52,423 sq mi;
135,776 sq km

REGION **Southeast**

ALASKA
Juneau ★

DATE OF STATEHOOD 1959

NICKNAME **The Last Frontier**

POPULATION 550,043

AREA 656,424 sq mi;
1,700,138 sq km

REGION **West**

ARIZONA
★
Phoenix

DATE OF STATEHOOD 1912

NICKNAME **Grand Canyon State**

POPULATION 3,665,228

AREA 114,006 sq mi;
295,276 sq km

REGION **Southwest**

ARKANSAS
★
Little Rock

DATE OF STATEHOOD 1836

NICKNAME **Land of Opportunity**

POPULATION 2,350,725

AREA 53,182 sq mi;
137,741 sq km

REGION **Southeast**

CALIFORNIA
★
Sacramento

DATE OF STATEHOOD 1850

NICKNAME **Golden State**

POPULATION 29,760,021

AREA 163,707 sq mi;
424,001 sq km

REGION **West**

Denver ★
COLORADO

DATE OF STATEHOOD 1876

NICKNAME **Centennial State**

POPULATION 3,294,394

AREA 104,100 sq mi;
269,619 sq km

REGION **West**

★
Hartford
CONNECTICUT

DATE OF STATEHOOD 1788

NICKNAME **Constitution State**

POPULATION 3,287,116

AREA 5,544 sq mi;
14,359 sq km

REGION **Northeast**

★
Dover
DELAWARE

DATE OF STATEHOOD 1787

NICKNAME **First State**

POPULATION 666,168

AREA 2,489 sq mi;
6,447 sq km

REGION **Northeast**

★
Tallahassee
FLORIDA

DATE OF STATEHOOD 1845

NICKNAME **Sunshine State**

POPULATION 12,937,926

AREA 65,758 sq mi;
170,313 sq km

REGION **Southeast**

★
Atlanta
GEORGIA

DATE OF STATEHOOD 1788

NICKNAME **Peach State**

POPULATION 6,478,216

AREA 59,441 sq mi;
153,952 sq km

REGION **Southeast**

HAWAII
★
Honolulu

DATE OF STATEHOOD 1959

NICKNAME **The Aloha State**

POPULATION 1,108,229

AREA 10,932 sq mi;
28,314 sq km

REGION **West**

★ Boise
IDAHO

DATE OF STATEHOOD 1890

NICKNAME **Gem State**

POPULATION 1,006,749

AREA 83,574 sq mi;
216,457 sq km

REGION **West**

ILLINOIS
★
Springfield

DATE OF STATEHOOD 1818

NICKNAME The Prairie State

POPULATION 11,430,602

AREA 57,918 sq mi;
150,008 sq km

REGION Middle West

INDIANA
★
Indianapolis

DATE OF STATEHOOD 1816

NICKNAME Hoosier State

POPULATION 5,544,159

AREA 36,420 sq mi;
94,328 sq km

REGION Middle West

IOWA
★
Des Moines

DATE OF STATEHOOD 1846

NICKNAME Hawkeye State

POPULATION 2,776,755

AREA 56,276 sq mi;
145,755 sq km

REGION Middle West

Topeka ★

KANSAS

DATE OF STATEHOOD 1861

NICKNAME Sunflower State

POPULATION 2,477,574

AREA 82,282 sq mi;
213,110 sq km

REGION Middle West

KENTUCKY
★
Frankfort

DATE OF STATEHOOD 1792

NICKNAME Bluegrass State

POPULATION 3,685,296

AREA 40,411 sq mi;
104,664 sq km

REGION Southeast

LOUISIANA

Baton Rouge ★

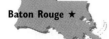

DATE OF STATEHOOD 1812

NICKNAME Pelican State

POPULATION 4,219,973

AREA 51,843 sq mi;
134,273 sq km

REGION Southeast

MAINE
Augusta
★

DATE OF STATEHOOD 1820

NICKNAME Pine Tree State

POPULATION 1,227,928

AREA 35,387 sq mi;
91,652 sq km

REGION Northeast

MARYLAND

Annapolis ★
★

DATE OF STATEHOOD 1788

NICKNAME Free State

POPULATION 4,781,468

AREA 12,407 sq mi;
32,134 sq km

REGION Northeast

Boston ★

MASSACHUSETTS

DATE OF STATEHOOD 1788

NICKNAME Bay State

POPULATION 6,016,425

AREA 10,555 sq mi;
27,337 sq km

REGION Northeast

MICHIGAN

★
Lansing

DATE OF STATEHOOD 1837

NICKNAME Wolverine State

POPULATION 9,295,297

AREA 96,810 sq mi;
250,738 sq km

REGION Middle West

MINNESOTA

St. Paul ★

DATE OF STATEHOOD 1858

NICKNAME North Star State

POPULATION 4,375,099

AREA 86,943 sq mi;
225,182 sq km

REGION Middle West

MISSISSIPPI

★
Jackson

DATE OF STATEHOOD 1817

NICKNAME Magnolia State

POPULATION 2,573,216

AREA 48,434 sq mi;
125,444 sq km

REGION Southeast

MISSOURI
★ Jefferson City

DATE OF STATEHOOD 1821

NICKNAME Show Me State

POPULATION 5,117,073

AREA 69,709 sq mi; 180,546 sq km

REGION Middle West

MONTANA
★ Helena

DATE OF STATEHOOD 1889

NICKNAME Treasure State

POPULATION 799,065

AREA 147,046 sq mi; 380,849 sq km

REGION West

NEBRASKA
Lincoln ★

DATE OF STATEHOOD 1867

NICKNAME Cornhusker State

POPULATION 1,578,385

AREA 77,358 sq mi; 200,357 sq km

REGION Middle West

NEVADA
★ Carson City

DATE OF STATEHOOD 1864

NICKNAME Silver State

POPULATION 1,201,833

AREA 110,567 sq mi; 286,369 sq km

REGION West

NEW HAMPSHIRE
Concord ★

DATE OF STATEHOOD 1788

NICKNAME Granite State

POPULATION 1,109,252

AREA 9,351 sq mi; 24,219 sq km

REGION Northeast

NEW JERSEY
★ Trenton

DATE OF STATEHOOD 1787

NICKNAME Garden State

POPULATION 7,730,188

AREA 8,722 sq mi; 22,590 sq km

REGION Northeast

NEW MEXICO
★ Santa Fe

DATE OF STATEHOOD 1912

NICKNAME Land of Enchantment

POPULATION 1,515,069

AREA 121,598 sq mi; 314,939 sq km

REGION Southwest

NEW YORK
Albany ★

DATE OF STATEHOOD 1788

NICKNAME Empire State

POPULATION 17,990,455

AREA 54,475 sq mi; 141,090 sq km

REGION Northeast

NORTH CAROLINA
Raleigh ★

DATE OF STATEHOOD 1789

NICKNAME Tar Heel State

POPULATION 6,628,637

AREA 53,821 sq mi; 139,396 sq km

REGION Southeast

NORTH DAKOTA
Bismarck ★

DATE OF STATEHOOD 1889

NICKNAME Peace Garden State

POPULATION 638,800

AREA 70,704 sq mi; 183,123 sq km

REGION Middle West

OHIO
★ Columbus

DATE OF STATEHOOD 1803

NICKNAME Buckeye State

POPULATION 10,847,115

AREA 44,828 sq mi; 116,105 sq km

REGION Middle West

OKLAHOMA
★ Oklahoma City

DATE OF STATEHOOD 1907

NICKNAME Sooner State

POPULATION 3,145,585

AREA 69,903 sq mi; 181,049 sq km

REGION Southwest

OREGON
★ Salem

DATE OF STATEHOOD 1859

NICKNAME Beaver State

POPULATION 2,842,321

AREA 98,386 sq mi; 254,820 sq km

REGION West

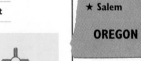

PENNSYLVANIA
Harrisburg ★

DATE OF STATEHOOD 1787

NICKNAME Keystone State

POPULATION 11,881,643

AREA 46,058 sq mi;
119,290 sq km

REGION Northeast

RHODE ISLAND
Providence ★

DATE OF STATEHOOD 1790

NICKNAME Ocean State

POPULATION 1,003,464

AREA 1,545 sq mi;
4,002 sq km

REGION Northeast

SOUTH CAROLINA
★
Columbia

DATE OF STATEHOOD 1788

NICKNAME Palmetto State

POPULATION 3,486,703

AREA 32,007 sq mi;
82,898 sq km

REGION Southeast

SOUTH DAKOTA
Pierre ★

DATE OF STATEHOOD 1889

NICKNAME Mount Rushmore State

POPULATION 696,004

AREA 77,121 sq mi;
199,743 sq km

REGION Middle West

TENNESSEE
★Nashville

DATE OF STATEHOOD 1796

NICKNAME Volunteer State

POPULATION 4,877,185

AREA 42,146 sq mi;
109,158 sq km

REGION Southeast

TEXAS
Austin ★

DATE OF STATEHOOD 1845

NICKNAME Lone Star State

POPULATION 16,986,510

AREA 268,601 sq mi;
695,677 sq km

REGION Southwest

UTAH
★
Salt Lake City

DATE OF STATEHOOD 1896

NICKNAME Beehive State

POPULATION 1,722,850

AREA 84,904 sq mi;
219,901 sq km

REGION West

VERMONT
★
Montpelier

DATE OF STATEHOOD 1791

NICKNAME Green Mountain State

POPULATION 562,758

AREA 9,615 sq mi;
24,903 sq km

REGION Northeast

VIRGINIA
Richmond ★

DATE OF STATEHOOD 1788

NICKNAME Old Dominion

POPULATION 6,187,358

AREA 42,769 sq mi;
110,772 sq km

REGION Southeast

WASHINGTON
★ Olympia

DATE OF STATEHOOD 1889

NICKNAME Evergreen State

POPULATION 4,866,692

AREA 71,303 sq mi;
184,675 sq km

REGION West

WEST VIRGINIA
★ Charleston

DATE OF STATEHOOD 1863

NICKNAME Mountain State

POPULATION 1,793,477

AREA 24,231 sq mi;
62,758 sq km

REGION Southeast

WISCONSIN
Madison ★

DATE OF STATEHOOD 1848

NICKNAME Badger State

POPULATION 4,891,769

AREA 65,503 sq mi;
169,653 sq km

REGION Middle West

WYOMING
Cheyenne ★

DATE OF STATEHOOD 1890

NICKNAME Equality State

POPULATION 453,588

AREA 97,818 sq mi;
253,349 sq km

REGION West

Sources: population—U.S. Bureau of Census, 1990; area—U.S. Bureau of Census, 1991; capital—World Almanac, 1995.

Dictionary of GEOGRAPHIC TERMS

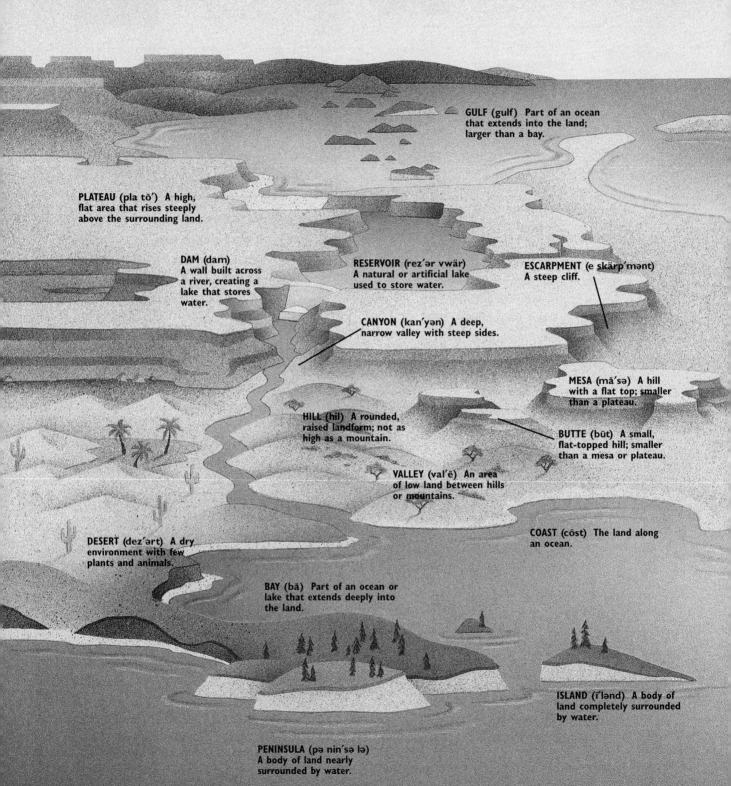

GULF (gulf) Part of an ocean that extends into the land; larger than a bay.

PLATEAU (pla tō′) A high, flat area that rises steeply above the surrounding land.

DAM (dam) A wall built across a river, creating a lake that stores water.

RESERVOIR (rez′ər vwär) A natural or artificial lake used to store water.

ESCARPMENT (e skärp′mənt) A steep cliff.

CANYON (kan′yən) A deep, narrow valley with steep sides.

MESA (mā′sə) A hill with a flat top; smaller than a plateau.

HILL (hil) A rounded, raised landform; not as high as a mountain.

BUTTE (būt) A small, flat-topped hill; smaller than a mesa or plateau.

VALLEY (val′ē) An area of low land between hills or mountains.

DESERT (dez′ərt) A dry environment with few plants and animals.

COAST (cōst) The land along an ocean.

BAY (bā) Part of an ocean or lake that extends deeply into the land.

ISLAND (ī′lənd) A body of land completely surrounded by water.

PENINSULA (pə nin′sə lə) A body of land nearly surrounded by water.

VOLCANO (vol kā′nō) An opening in Earth's surface through which hot rock and ash are forced out.

MOUNTAIN (moun′tən) A high landform with steep sides; higher than a hill.

PEAK (pēk) The top of a mountain.

HARBOR (här′bər) A sheltered place along a coast where boats dock safely.

GLACIER (glā′shər) A huge sheet of ice that moves slowly across the land.

CANAL (kə nal′) A channel built to carry water for irrigation or transportation.

LAKE (lāk) A body of water completely surrounded by land.

PORT (pôrt) A place where ships load and unload their goods.

TRIBUTARY (trib′yə ter ē) A smaller river that flows into a larger river.

SOURCE (sôrs) The starting point of a river.

TIMBERLINE (tim′bər lin) A line beyond which trees do not grow.

RIVER BASIN (riv′ər bā′sin) All the land that is drained by a river and its tributaries.

WATERFALL (wô′tər fôl) A flow of water falling vertically.

MOUNTAIN RANGE (moun′tən rānj) A row or chain of mountains.

RIVER (riv′ər) A stream of water that flows across the land and empties into another body of water.

PLAIN (plān) A large area of nearly flat land.

BASIN (bā′sin) A bowl-shaped landform surrounded by higher land.

DELTA (del′tə) Land made of soil left behind as a river drains into a larger body of water.

MOUTH (mouth) The place where a river empties into a larger body of water.

BARRIER ISLAND (bar′ē ər i′lənd) A narrow island between the mainland and the ocean.

OCEAN (ō′shən) A large body of salt water; oceans cover much of Earth's surface.

Gazetteer

This Gazetteer is a geographical dictionary that will help you to pronounce and locate the places discussed in this book. Latitude and longitude are given for cities and some other places. The page numbers tell you where each place appears on a map or in the text.

A

Abilene (ab′ə lēn) City located in northwestern Texas; 32°N, 100°W. (m. 57, t. 58)

Africa (af′ri kə) Continent located in the Eastern and Southern hemispheres. (m. G5, t. G4)

Alamo (al′ə mō) Also known as the San Antonio de Valero mission. In 1836 it was the site of the most famous battle in Texas history. (m. 131, t. 166)

Amarillo (am ə ril′ō) City in northwestern Texas; 35°N, 102°W. (m. 29, t. 30)

Amazon River (am′ə zôn riv′ər) The longest river in South America. (m. 78, t. 74)

Andes Mountains (an′dēz moun′tənz) Large mountain range in South America (m. 78, t. 74)

Antarctica (ant ärk′ti kə) Continent located in the Southern Hemisphere. (m. G5, t. G4)

Appalachian Mountains (ap ə lā′chē ən moun′tənz) Chain of mountains in the eastern United States. (m. 45, t. 45)

Arctic Ocean (ärk′tik ō′shən) Ocean surrounding the North Pole. (m. G5, t. G4)

Argentina (är jən tē′nə) Country in South America. (m. R7, t. 208)

Asia (ā′zhə) The largest continent, located in the Eastern and Northern hemispheres. (m. G5, t. G4)

B

Balcones Escarpment (bal kō′nəs e skärp′mənt) Steep cliff that cuts across part of Texas from north to south. (m. 22, t. 21)

Beaumont (bō′mänt) City in southeastern Texas, that was the site of an early oil boom; 30°N, 94°W. (t. 283)

Bering Strait (bə′ring strāt) Body of water that separates North America from Asia. (t. 91)

Beringia (bə rin′jē ə) A land bridge believed to have connected Asia with North America for about 2,000 years during the Ice Age. (m. 91, t. 91)

Big Bend National Park (big bend nash′ən əl pärk) National park in western Texas on a bend of the Rio Grande. (m. G8, t. 71)

Brazil (bra sil′) Country along the northeast coast of South America. (m. 138, t. 139)

Brownsville (brownz′vil) Port city in southern Texas; 26°N, 98°W. (m. 22, t. 360)

Atlantic Ocean, Austin, Australia, Austria-Hungary

Atlantic Ocean (at lan′tik ō′shən) Ocean that borders eastern North and South America and western Europe and Africa. (m. G5, t. G4)

Austin (ôs′tən) Capital of Texas, located in the south-central part of the state; 30°N, 98°W. (m. G7, t. 54)

Australia (ôs trāl′yə) Continent and country located in the Eastern and Southern hemispheres. (m. G5, t. G4)

Austria-Hungary (ôs′trē yə hung′ə rē) Large empire that once combined several countries in central Europe. (t. 288)

---

pronunciation key

a	at	ī	ice	u	up	th	thin	
ā	ape	îr	pierce	ū	use	th	this	
ä	far	o	hot	ü	rule	zh	measure	
âr	care	ō	old	ù	pull	ə	about, taken,
e	end	ô	fork	ûr	turn		pencil, lemon,
ē	me	oi	oil	hw	white		circus
i	it	ou	out	ng	song		

C

Canada (kan′ə də) Country bordering the United States to the north. (m. 11, t. 11)

Cap Rock Escarpment (kap rôk e skärp′mənt) Steep cliff in Texas that divides the Great Plains from the North Central Plains. (m. 65, t. 66)

Castroville (kas′ trō vil) A town settled by French immigrants to Texas in the 1800s; 29°N, 99°W. (t. 203).

Central America (sen′trəl ə mer′i kə) Part of North America between Mexico and South America made up of a number of countries. (m. 11, t. 11)

Central Plains (sen′trəl plānz) Part of the Interior Plains of the Middle West, an area of gently rolling hills where much corn is grown. (m. 45, t. 47)

Chapultepec (chə pul′tə pek) A rocky hill in Mexico City, Mexico. Site of a fortress captured by United States forces during the Mexican War; 19°N, 99°W. (t. 198)

Chihuahuan Desert (chə wä′wun dez′ərt) Flat dry area stretching from western Texas to northern Mexico. (m. 69, t. 69)

Chisholm Trail (chiz′əm trāl) Cattle drive route in 1880s stretching about 800 miles from San Antonio, Texas, to Abilene, Kansas. (m. 248, t. 248)

Chisos Mountains (chē′sôs moun′tənz) Mountain range in western Texas. (m. 69, t. 68)

Ciudad Juarez (sē′ü dad hwär′əs) Mexican city across the Rio Grande from El Paso; 32°N, 106°W. (m. 69, t. 70)

Coastal Plain (kōs′təl plān) Low plain along the Atlantic Coast from Massachusetts to Texas. The Coastal Plain forms the easternmost region of Texas. (m. 53, t. 52)

Colorado River (kôl ə rad′ō riv′ər) River that flows from the Rocky Mountains to the Gulf of Mexico. (t. 151)

Columbia (kə lum′ bē ə) Town on the Brazos River that was the first capital of the Republic of Texas; 29°N, 96°W. (t. 185)

Corpus Christi (kôr′ pəs kris′ tē) Port city in southern Texas; 28°N, 98°W. (m. 53, t. 30)

Corpus Christi Bay (kôr′ pəs kris′ tē bā) Narrow body of water leading to the Gulf of Mexico, located in southern Texas. (m. 53, t. 53)

Cross Timbers (krôs tim′ bərz) One of three geographical areas in the North Central Plains of Texas. (m. 57, t. 56)

D

Dallas (dal′əs) City in northeastern Texas; 33°N, 97°W. (m. 22, t. 9)

Davis Mountains (dā′vəs moun′tənz) One of three groups of mountains located in western Texas. (m. 69, t. 68)

Del Rio (del rē′ō) Port city in southwestern Texas; 29°N, 101°W. (t. 360)

E

Eastern Hemisphere (ēs′tərn hem′i sfîr) The half of Earth east of the prime meridian. (m. G5, t. G5)

Edwards Plateau (ed′wərdz pla tō′) One of three geographical areas on the Great Plains of Texas. (m. 65, t. 64)

El Capitan (el kap ə tan′) One of the Guadalupe Mountains of western Texas; 32°N, 105°W. (m. 69, t. 69)

El Paso (el pas′ ō) City in westernmost Texas on the Rio Grande; 32° N, 106° W. (m. 69, t. 29)

England (ing′ lənd) Island country in Europe which began establishing colonies in North America in the 1500s. England is part of the United Kingdom of Great Britain. The United States fought against Great Britain in the American Revolution. (m. R15, t. 122)

Ennis (en′əs) City in north central Texas and home of the largest Czech community in Texas; 32°N, 97°W. (t. 361)

Europe (yûr′əp) Continent located in the Eastern and Northern hemispheres. (m. G5, t. G4)

Gazetteer

F

Fort Sumter (fôrt sum'tûr) Union fort in South Carolina where the first Civil War battle took place; 33°N, 80°W. (m. 235, t. 229)

Fort Worth (fôrt wərth) City located in the North Central Plains of Texas; 33°N, 98°W. (m. 57, t. 58)

France (frans) Country in western Europe which began establishing colonies in North America in the 1500s. (m. R15, t. 122)

Fredericksburg (fre' dər iks bûrg) Town in the Texas Hill Country founded by German immigrants; 30°N, 99°W. (t. 203)

G

Galveston (gal' və stən) Port city in southeastern Texas; 29°N, 94°W. (m. 22, t. 31)

Goliad (gō'lē ad) Southern Texas town that was the site of a massacre of 300 Texans in 1836; 29°N, 97°W. (m. 165, t. 164)

Gonzales (gôn sa'ləs) Southern Texas town near San Antonio. Site of the first battle in the Texas Revolution; 29°N, 97°W. (m. 165, t. 164)

Grand Canyon (grand kan'yən) Large canyon on the Colorado River in northwestern Arizona. (t. 48)

Great Lakes (grāt lāks) Chain of five large freshwater lakes between the northern United States and Canada. (m. R7, t. 74)

Great Plains (grāt plānz) Part of the Interior Plains of the Middle West, an area of dry grassland where much wheat is grown. The Great Plains form one of the regions of Texas. (m. 45, t. 47)

Guadalupe Mountains (gwäd a lüp'ā moun'tənz) Mountain range in southern New Mexico and southwestern Texas. (m. 22, t. 20)

Guadalupe Mountains National Park (gwäd a lüp'ā moun'tənz na'shə nəl pärk) National park in southwestern Texas. (m. 69, t. 71)

Guadalupe Peak (gwäd a lüp'ā pēk) Highest mountain in Texas and a peak of the Guadalupe Mountains. (m. 69, t. 21)

Gulf of Mexico

Gulf of Mexico (gulf əv mek'si kō) A gulf of the Atlantic Ocean bordering Mexico and five states of the United States, including Texas. (m. 22, t. 8)

H

High Plains (hī plānz) One of three geographical areas on the Great Plains of Texas, located in the Panhandle. (m. 65, t. 64)

Houston (hūs'tən) Port city in southeastern Texas and a major oil-refining center; 30°N, 95°W. (m. 320, t. 308)

Houston Ship Channel (hūs'tən ship chan'əl) A 50-mile-long body of water that connects Houston with the Gulf of Mexico. (m. 53, t. 55)

I

Indian Ocean (in'dē ən ō'shən) An ocean between Africa, southern Asia, and Australia. (m. G5, t. G4)

Indian Territory (in'dē ən ter'ə tôr ē) Area set aside for Native Americans in what is now the state of Oklahoma. (t. 263)

Interior Plains (in tir'ē ər plānz) The large plain in the central part of the United States that includes the Central Plains and the Great Plains. (m. 45, t. 47)

J

Jamestown (jāmz'toun) The first permanent English settlement in America, established in the colony of Virginia in 1607; 37°N, 77°W. (m. 137, t. 137)

Japan (jə pán) Country of eastern Asia made up of islands in the Pacific Ocean. (m. R15, t. 395)

Johnson Space Center (jon'sən) An important center for the United States space program. It is located in Clear Lake, a suburb of Houston. (t. 310)

K

Kilgore (kil'gôr) A city in southeastern Texas, site of early oil boom; 30°N, 94°W. (t. 283)

L

Louisiana Territory (lü ē'sē an ə ter'ə tôr ē) The area stretching from the Mississippi River to the Rocky Mountains claimed by French explorer La Salle and purchased in 1803 by the United States for $15 million. (t. 150)

Lubbock (lub'ək) City in northwestern Texas; 34°N, 102°W. (m. 65, t. 66)

Luling (lü'ling) City in south central Texas; 30°N, 98°W. (t. 360)

M

Massachusetts colony (mas ə chü'sits kol'ə nē) One of the 13 English colonies, founded in 1620; later became the state of Massachusetts. (m. 137, t. 137)

Mathis (ma'this) City in Texas near Corpus Christi; 28°N, 98°W. (t. 330)

Metroplex (met'rō pleks) Metropolitan area made up of two large Texas cities, Dallas and Fort Worth. (t. 59)

Mexico (mek'si kō) Country bordering the United States to the south. (m. 11, t. 9)

Mexico City (mek'si kō sit'ē) Capital and largest city of Mexico, built as a Spanish settlement on the ruins of Tenochtitlán; 19°N, 99°W. (m. 138, t. 121)

Middle West (mid'əl west) A region of the United States made up of the Great Lakes states of Illinois, Indiana, Michigan, Minnesota, Ohio, and Wisconsin, and the Plains states of Iowa, Kansas, Missouri, Nebraska, North Dakota, and South Dakota. (m. R6, t. 44)

Midland (mid'lənd) City on the Great Plains of Texas; 32°N, 102°W. (m. 65, t. 65)

Millsap (mil'sap) Town in north-central Texas; 33°N, 98°W. (m. 57, t. 58)

Mississippi River (mis ə sip'ē riv'ər) The longest river in the United States. (m. 45, t. 46)

Mountains and Basins (moun'tənz and bā'sinz) Westernmost region of Texas. (m. 69, t. 68)

N

Nacogdoches (nakə do'chez) City in East Texas; 32°N, 95°W. (t. 223)

New Braunfels (nü brôn'felz) Town in the Texas Hill Country founded by German immigrants; 30°N, 98°W. (t. 203)

New Spain (nü spān) Area of the Aztec empire renamed by its conqueror, Hernando Cortés. New Spain included Mexico and what is now Texas. (m. 138, t. 121)

North America (nôrth ə mer'i kə) Continent in the Western hemisphere. (m. G5, t. G4)

North Central Plains (nôrth sentral plānz) Region of Texas that is part of the Interior Plains of the United States. (m. 57, t. 56)

Northeast (nôrth ēst') A region of the United States made up of the New England states of Connecticut, Maine, Massachusetts, New Hampshire, Rhode Island, and Vermont, and the Middle Atlantic states of Delaware, Maryland, New Jersey, New York, and Pennsylvania. (m. R6, t. 44)

Northern Hemisphere (nôr'thərn hem'i sfîr) The half of Earth north of the equator. (m. G5, t. G5)

North Pole (nôrth pōl) The most northern place on Earth. (m. G5, t. G5)

Nueces River (nwā'sāz ri'ver) River in southeastern Texas involved in border dispute during the Mexican War. (m. 197, t. 197)

O

Odessa (ō des'ə) City on the Great Plains of western Texas; 32°N, 102°W. (m. 65, t. 65)

P

Pacific Ocean (pə sif'ik ō'shən) Ocean that borders western North and South America and eastern Asia. (m. G4, t. G4)

---

pronunciation key

a **at**; ā **ape**; ä **far**; âr **care**; e **end**; ē **me**; i **it**; ī **ice**; îr **pierce**; o **hot**; ō **old**; ô **fork**; oi **oil**; ou **out**; u **up**; ū **use**; ü **rule**; u̇ **pull**; ûr **turn**; hw **white**; ng **song**; th **thin**; th **this**; zh **measure**; ə **about, taken, pencil, lemon, circus**

Padre Island (päd'rā ī'lənd) Barrier island in the Gulf of Mexico off the south Texas coast. (m. 53, t. 53)

Palmito Ranch (pal mēt'ō ranch) Site of the final battle of the Civil War. (m. 234, t. 233)

Palo Duro Canyon (pal'ô dùr'ô kan'yən) Canyon along the Red River in northwestern Texas. (m. 245, t. 265)

Panama Canal (pan'ə ma kə nal') Canal through the country of Panama that links the Atlantic and Pacific oceans; 9°N, 80°W. (t. 75)

Panhandle (pan' han dəl) An arm of land that extends like the handle of a pan in northwestern Texas. (m. 65, t. 8)

Panna Maria (pa'na ma rē'ə) Village in Texas that is believed to have the oldest Polish Roman Catholic church in the United States. (t. 203)

Permian Basin (pər'mē ən bā sin) One of the world's largest oil-producing areas, located in the Great Plains of Texas. (m. 65, t. 65)

Piney Woods (pī'nē wùdz) The wettest of the five areas that make up the Coastal Plain of Texas. (m. 53, t. 52)

Plymouth (pli'məth) Settlement in what is now Massachusetts, established by Pilgrims sailing from England on the Mayflower in 1620; 42°N, 71°W. (m. 137, t. 137)

Portugal (pôr'chə gəl) Country in southwestern Europe which began establishing colonies in South America in the 1500s. (m. R15, t. 122)

Prince Edward Island (prins ed'wərd ī'lənd) One of Canada's provinces. (t. 77)

R

Rio Grande (rē'ō grän'dē) The longest river in Texas, it forms part of the border between the United States and Mexico. (m. 22, t. 22)

Rio de Janeiro (rē'ō dā zhə nā'rō) Port city in southeastern Brazil; 23°S, 43°W. (m R7, t. 269)

Rocky Mountains (rok'ē moun'tənz) Mountain range that stretches from Canada through the western United States into Mexico. (m. 45, t. 48)

S

Sabine Pass (sə bēn' pas) Where Sabine Lake opens into the Gulf of Mexico in eastern Texas. It was the site of an important battle during the Civil War; 30°N, 94°W. (m. 243, t. 231)

Sabine River (sə bēn' riv'ər) River in eastern Texas. (m. 197, t. 197)

San Antonio (san an tō'nē ō) Third largest city in Texas; 29°N, 99°W. (m. 53, t. 9)

San Antonio de Béxar (san an tō'nē ō dā bā'här) Fort built to protect the San Antonio de Valero mission. (t. 133)

San Antonio de Valero (san an tō'nē ō dā va lär'ō) Mission on the San Antonio River whose church later became known as the Alamo; 29°N, 99°W. (m. 131, t. 133)

San Felipe de Austin (san fə lē' pā də ô'stin) Town chosen by Stephen F. Austin as the capital for his colony; 30°N, 96°W. (m. 165, t. 152)

San Jacinto River (san jə sin'tō riv'ər) River in southeastern Texas. The battle that won independence for Texas was fought at the mouth of this river. (t. 175)

South America (south ə mer'i kə) Continent in the Western Hemisphere. (m. 11, t. 11)

Southern Hemisphere (suth'ərn hem'i sfîr) The half of Earth south of the equator. (m. G5, t. G5)

Southeast (south ēst') A region of the United States made up of Alabama, Arkansas, Florida, Georgia, Kentucky, Louisiana, Mississippi, North Carolina, South Carolina, Tennessee, Virginia, and West Virginia. (m. 45, t. 44)

South Pole (south pōl) The southernmost place on Earth. (m. G5, t. G5)

Southwest (south west') A region of the United States made up of Arizona, New Mexico, Oklahoma, and Texas. (m. 10, t. 10)

Spain (spān) Country in southwestern Europe which began establishing colonies in North and South America in the 1500s. (m. R15, t. 118)

St. Lawrence Seaway (sānt lôr′əns sē′wā) Series of canals built by the United States and Canada to allow ships to travel from the Great Lakes to the Atlantic Ocean. (t. 76)

St. Lawrence River (sānt lôr′əns riv′ər) River in eastern North America that flows from Lake Ontario into the Atlantic Ocean. (t. 76)

T

Tenochtitlán (te nōch tē tlän′) Capital of the ancient Aztec empire, on the site of present-day Mexico City; 19°N, 99°W. (m. 99, t. 99)

Terlingua (tûr ling′ə) Town in far western Texas; 29°N, 104°W. (t. 360)

Texas (tek′səs) A state of the Southwest region. (m. 10, t. 8)

Tomball (tom′bôl) Town in southeastern Texas; 30°N, 96°W. (t. 305)

U

United States (ū nī′tid stātz) Country in North America, made up of 50 states. (m. 10, t. 10)

V

Valley of Mexico (val′ē əv mek′si kō) Area of low-lying land in central Mexico where the Aztec established their capital, Tenochtitlán. (m. 99, t. 99)

Venezuela (ven ə zwā′lə) Country in northern South America. (m. R7, t. 209)

Victoria (vic tôrē ə) Town founded by Don Martín and Patricia de la Garza de León; 29°N, 97°W. (t. 153)

W

Washington, D.C. (wô′shing tən dē sē) Capital of the United States; 39°N, 77°W. (t. 340)

Washington-on-the-Brazos (wō′shing tən on thə braz′əs) Town where the Texas Declaration of Independence was signed; 30°N, 96°W. (m. 165, t. 170)

West (west) A region of the United States made up of the Mountain states of Colorado, Idaho, Montana, Nevada, Utah, and Wyoming, and the Pacific states of Alaska, California, Hawaii, Oregon, and Washington. (m. R6, t. 44)

Western Hemisphere (wes′tərn hem′i sfîr) The half of Earth west of the prime meridian. (m. G5, t. G5)

Wichita Falls (wich′ə ta falz) City in north central Texas; 34°N, 98°W. (m. 57, t. 58)

Y

Ysleta Mission (ē slā′tə) First Spanish mission in Texas, built in 1681 near what is now El Paso; 32° N, 106° W. (m. 131, t. 131)

---

pronunciation key

a **a**t; ā **a**pe; ä **f**ar; âr **c**are; e **e**nd; ē **m**e; i **i**t; ī **i**ce; îr **pie**rce; o h**o**t; ō **o**ld; ô **f**ork; oi **o**il; ou **ou**t; u **u**p; ū **u**se; ü r**u**le; u̇ p**u**ll; ûr t**ur**n; hw **wh**ite; ng so**ng**; th **th**in; th **th**is; zh mea**s**ure; ə **a**bout, tak**e**n, penc**i**l, lem**o**n, circ**u**s

Biographical Dictionary

Biographical Dictionary

The Biographical Dictionary tells you about the people you have learned about in this book. The Pronunciation Key tells you how to say their names. The page numbers tell you where each person first appears in the text.

A

Adair, Christia (a dâre′), 1893-1990 Fought segregation during the 1950s and 1960s. (p. 298)

Arnold, Hendrick (ärn′əld, hen′drik), ?-1849 Free African American who acted as a scout and soldier during the Texas Revolution. (p. 175)

Austin, Moses (au′stin), 1761-1821 Planned the first colony of United States settlers in Texas. (p. 150)

Austin, Stephen F. (au′stin), 1793-1836 Established the first colony of United States settlers in Texas. (p. 150)

B

Borginnis, Sarah (bôr gin′nis), ?-1866 Helped the United States army during the Mexican War. (p. 198)

Bolívar, Simón (bō lē′vär, sē mōn′), 1783-1830 Venezuelan leader who helped South American countries fight for independence. (p. 209)

Bowie, Jim (bü′ē, bō′ē), 1796-1836 Led a group of volunteers who fought at the Alamo. (p. 167)

Bowles, Philip (bōlz′), ?-1839 Cherokee chief who signed a peace treaty with Sam Houston. (p. 186)

Brackenridge, Eleanor (brak′ən rij), 1837-1924 Worked for women's suffrage. (p. 296)

Burnet, David G. (bûr net′), 1788-1870 The first president of the Republic of Texas. (p. 170)

Bush, George (bùsh), 1924- Texan President of the United States from 1989 to 1993. (p. 342)

Bush, George W. (bùsh), 1946- Elected governor of Texas in 1994. (p. 335)

C

Cabeza de Vaca, Alvar Núñez (ka bā′sa də va′ka, al′vär nün′yāz), 1490?-1560? Spanish explorer who was shipwrecked and enslaved by the Karankawa in Texas. (p. 124)

Cabral, Pedro Alvares (kə bräl′, pä′dro äl′vä räs) 1460?-1526? First Portuguese explorer to land in area that is now Brazil. (p. 139)

Cisneros, Henry (sis ne′rōs), 1947- In 1993, he became United States Secretary of Housing and Urban Development. (p. 343)

Clark, Edward (clärk), 1815-1880 Governor of Texas under the Confederacy. (p. 229)

Cockrell, Sarah (kok′rəl), 1819-1892 Dallas businesswoman. (p. 257)

Columbus, Christopher (kə lum′bəs), 1451-1506 Italian explorer working on behalf of Spain who arrived in the Americas in 1492. (p. 118)

Coronado, Francisco Vásquez de (kôr ô nä′dô, fran sēs′kô vas kās də), 1510-1554 Spanish explorer who led an army into Texas in search of the Seven Cities of Gold. (p. 125)

Cortés, Hernando (kôr tes′, er nän′dô), 1485-1547 Spanish conquistador who defeated the Aztec empire. (p. 120)

Cos, Martín Perfecto de (kôs, mär′tēn pär fek′tô də), 1800-1854 Mexican general during the Texas Revolution. (p. 164)

Crockett, David (kro′kət), 1786-1836 Led a group of volunteers from Tennessee who fought at the Alamo. (p. 167)

Cuney, Norris Wright (kyü′nē), 1846-1897 African American businessman who served in Texas and national governments. (p. 255)

D

Davis, Edmund J. (dā′vis), 1827-1883 Governor of Texas during Reconstruction. (p. 240)

pronunciation key

a	at	ī	ice	u	up	th	thin
ā	ape	îr	pierce	ū	use	th	this
ä	far	o	hot	ü	rule	zh	measure
âr	care	ō	old	ù	pull	ə	about, taken,
e	end	ô	fork	ûr	turn		pencil, lemon,
ē	me	oi	oil	hw	white		circus
i	it	ou	out	ng	song		

Davis, Jefferson (dā′vis), 1808-1889 President of the Confederate States of America. (p. 228)

de León, Don Martín (də lə ôn′, dôn mär tēn′), 1765-1833 A Tejano empresario who brought 200 families to Victoria in 1824. (p. 153)

de León, Patricia de la Garza (də lə ōn′, pa trē′sya də la gär′sa), 1760s-1849 Tejano who helped found Victoria. (p. 153)

de Narváez, Pánfilo (när vā′es, pan′fi lô də), 1478-1528 Spanish explorer who died in a shipwreck off the Texas coast. (p. 123)

de Soto, Hernando (dā sô′tô, er nän′dô), 1500?-1542 Spanish explorer of what is now the southeastern United States. (p. 127)

Dickenson, Suzanna (dik′ən sən), 1820-1883 Alamo survivor who helped spread word of the battle throughout Texas. (p. 170)

E

Eisenhower, Dwight D. (ī′zən how ər), 1890-1969 Texan who was Allied commander in Europe during World War II and President of the United States from 1953 to 1961. (p. 294)

Estevanico (es tə va nē′kô), ?-1539 Enslaved Moroccan scout for Fray Marcos. (p. 124)

F

Fannin, James W. (fan′ən), 1804-1836 Texan commander who was killed with 300 soldiers in the Goliad Massacre. (p. 171)

Ferguson, Miriam (fûrg′ə sən), 1875-1961 First woman governor of Texas. (p. 297)

Flipper, Henry O. (flip′ər), 1856-1940 African American who served in the Texas Cavalry. (p. 266)

Foreman, George (fôr′mən), 1949- Boxing champion in 1973 and 1994. (p. 364)

G

Gallegos, Mario (go yā′gôs), 1950- Elected to Texas Senate in 1994. (p. 298)

Garrison Jackson, Zina (gär′ə sən jak′sən, zē′nə), 1963- World-class tennis player from Houston. (p. 369)

Glidden, Joseph F. (glid′ən), 1813-1906 Iowa farmer who invented barbed wire. (p. 251)

González, Henry B. (gon so′ləs), 1916- United States Representative from Texas. (p. 299)

Goyens, William (goi′əns), 1794-1856 Free African American businessman and interpreter for Sam Houston. (p. 223)

Grant, Ulysses S. (grant, ūlis′ēz), 1822-1885 Union general during the Civil War. (p. 233)

Griffith, Nanci (grif′əth), 1953- Texan folk singer and songwriter. (p. 372)

H

Henderson, James Pinckney (hen′dər sən, jāmz pink′nē), 1808-1858 First governor of Texas. (p. 191)

Henry, O. (hen′rē, ō), 1862-1910 Pen name of short-story writer William S. Porter, who lived in Austin during the late 1800s. (p. 373)

Hidalgo, Miguel (ē dal′gô, mē gel′), 1753-1811 Mexican priest who helped Mexico begin to fight for independence. (p. 207)

Higgins, Pattillo (hig′ənz, pa til′yô), 1863-1955 Texas mechanic who discovered oil at Spindletop in 1901. (p. 283)

Hobby, Oveta Culp (ho′bē, ō vēt′ə kulp), 1905-1995 Organized and commanded the Women's Army Corps during World War II. (p. 294)

Hogg, James S. (hog), 1851-1906 Texas governor from 1891 to 1895. (p. 259)

Houston, Sam (hū′stən), 1793-1863 A general during the Texas Revolution, he later served as president of the Republic of Texas and governor of Texas. (p. 162)

Hutchison, Kay Bailey (huch′ə sən), 1943- First Texan woman to serve in United States Senate. (p. 342)

I

Idar, Jovita (ē′där, hô′vē ta), 1885-1946 Formed the League of Mexican Women. (p. 298)

Iturbide, Agustín de (ē tür′bē də, a güs tēn′ də), 1783-1824 Mestizo leader who won Mexico's independence from Spain. (p. 207)

J

Jefferson, Thomas (jef′ər sən), 1743-1826 President of the United States from 1801 to 1809. (p. 150)

Jiménez, Flaco (hē men′ez, fla′kô), 1939- Accordionist and popularizer of Norteño music. (p. 372)

João, Dom (jô ow′, dôm), 1769-1826 Ruler of Portugal who put his son, Prince Pedro, in charge of Brazil. (p. 269)

Johnson, Andrew (jon'sən), 1808-1875 President of the United States from 1865 to 1869. (p. 236)

Johnson, Lady Bird or Claudia Taylor (jon'sən), 1912- First Lady from 1963-1969. Worked to protect Texas wildlife. (p. 25)

Johnson, Lyndon B. (jon'sən), 1908-1973 Texan who was President of the United States from 1963 to 1969. (p. 298)

Jones, Anson (jōnz, an'sən), 1798-1858 Last president of the Republic of Texas. (p. 190)

Joplin, Scott (jop'lən), 1868-1917 Ragtime composer born in Texarkana. (p. 291)

Jordan, Barbara (jôr'dən), 1936-1996 Texan who served in the United States House of Representatives from 1973 to 1979. (p. 343)

K

King, Martin Luther, Jr. (king), 1929-1968 Civil-rights leader who worked to gain equal rights for African Americans. (p. 298)

L

Lamar, Mirabeau B. (lə mär', mir'ə bō), 1798-1859 President of the Republic of Texas from 1838 to 1840. (p. 186)

La Salle, René Robert Cavelier, Sieur de (lə sal', re nā' rō bâre' ka vəl yā', sir de), 1643-1687 French explorer who helped establish Fort St. Louis in Texas. (p. 127)

Lee, Robert E. (lē), 1807-1870 Confederate general during the Civil War. (p. 233)

Lewis, Carl (lü'is), 1961- Houston runner who won 4 gold medals at 1984 Olympics. (p. 369)

Lincoln, Abraham (ling'kən), 1809-1865 President of the United States from 1861 to 1865. (p. 228)

Long, Jane (long), 1798-1880 One of the old Three Hundred. Often called the "Mother of Texas." (p. 150)

Lucchese, Josephine (lü ka'zē), 1901-1974 Opera singer from San Antonio. (p. 291)

M

MacKenzie, Ranald S. (mə ken'zē), 1840-1889 United States Army colonel in the Battle of Palo Duro Canyon. (p. 265)

McMurtry, Larry (mək mûr'trē), 1936- Texan writer who won a Pulitzer Prize. (p. 373)

Medrano, Eva F. (mə dra'nō), 1950- Became mayor of Mathis in 1987. (p. 328)

Moctezuma II (mok tə zü'mə), 1480?-1520 Last ruler of the Aztec empire. (p. 120)

Morelos, José María (mô rə'lôs, hô sə' ma rē'a), 1765-1815 Priest who helped lead the struggle for Mexico's independence. (p. 207)

Moscoso de Alvarado, Luis de (môs kôs' ô də al va ra'dô, lü ēs' də), 1505-1551 Spanish explorer who led Southeast expedition after the death of de Soto. (p. 127)

Murphy, Audie (mûr'fē, ô'dē), 1924-1971 Most decorated American soldier during World War II. (p. 294)

N

Navarro, José Antonio (nä vär'rō, hô sə' an tō'nē ō), 1795-1870 Signer of the Texan Declaration of Independence. (p. 170)

Nelson, Willie (nel'sən), 1933- Country music star from Abbott. (p. 372)

Ney, Elisabet (nā, ə lis'a bet), 1833-1907 Sculptor of Sam Houston and Stephen F. Austin statues in the Texas Capitol. (p. 371)

Niza, Fray Marcos de (ni'sa, frī mär'kôs də), 1500s-1558 Spanish priest and explorer who searched for the Seven Cities of Gold. (p. 125)

O

O'Keeffe, Georgia (ō kēf', jôr'jə), 1887-1986 Painter who taught briefly in Texas and was influenced by the prairie landscape. (p. 371)

Osterman, Rosanna (ös'tər min, rō zan'na), 1818-1866 Created Galveston army hospital during the Civil War. (p. 232)

P

Parker, Cynthia Ann (pär'kər), 1827-1864 Daughter of white settlers who was captured and adopted by Comanche. Mother of Quanah Parker. (p. 263)

Parker, Quanah (pär'kər, kwän'ə), 1845-1911 Comanche chief who led his people against the Texas Rangers in the Red River Campaign. (p. 263)

Pedro I, Dom (pä'drô, dôm), 1798-1834 Declared Brazil's independence and became King in 1821. (p. 269)

Pedro II, Dom (pä'drô, dôm), 1825-1891 Ruler of Brazil who ended slavery there in 1888. (p. 270)

Piñeda, Alonso Alvarez de (pin yə′da, a lôn′zô al′va rəs də), late 1400s-early 1500s Spanish explorer who may have been the first European to see present-day Texas. (p. 123)

Polk, James K. (pōlk), 1795-1849 President of the United States who helped make Texas the 28th state in 1845. (p. 190)

Porter, Katherine Anne (pôr′ter), 1890-1980 Pulitzer Prize-winning writer who grew up in Indian Creek. (p. 373)

R

Rabb, Mary Crownover (rab), 1805-1882 One of the Old Three Hundred. (p. 155)

Ramsey, Buck (ram′zē), 1937- Cowboy poet from Amarillo. (p. 374)

Rankin, Melinda (rang′kən), 1811-1888 Christian missionary, writer, and abolitionist. (p. 227)

Rayburn, Sam (rā′bərn), 1882-1961 Texan who served in the United States House of Representatives for almost 50 years. (p. 343)

Richards, Ann (ri′chərdz), 1933- Governor of Texas from 1991 to 1995. (p. 335)

Roosevelt, Franklin Delano (rōz′velt, frang′klən del′ə nō), 1882-1945 President of the United States from 1933 to 1945. (p. 293)

Ruby, George T. (rü′bē), 1841-? African American elected to 1869 Texas Senate. (p. 240)

Ruíz, Francisco (rü îs′; fran sîs′ kō), 1783-1840 Signer of the Texan Declaration of Independence. (p. 170)

Ryan, Nolan (rī′ən, nō′lən), 1947- Baseball player from Alvin. (p. 369)

S

Santa Anna, Antonio López de (san′ta an′a, an tô′nē ô lô′pəs də), 1795-1876 President of Mexico and general who led attack on the Alamo. He was defeated at San Jacinto. (p. 162)

Satanta (sə tan′te), 1807?-1878 Kiowa chief who fought the relocation of Native Americans to reservations. (p. 262)

Scott, Winfield (skot, win′fēld), 1786-1866 United States general who captured Mexico City during the Mexican War. (p. 198)

Seguín, Juan (sə gēn′, hwan), 1806-1889 Tejano leader who fought for Texas at the Battle of San Jacinto. (p. 167)

Sherman, William Tecumseh (tə küm′sə), 1820-1891 Civil War general sent to Texas in 1871. (p. 264)

Simond, Ada (sī′mənd), 1903-1989 Writer of short stories that tell of growing up as an African American in Texas. (p. 373)

Smith, Erastus Deaf (smith, ə ras′təs def), 1787-1837 Army scout during the Texas Revolution. (p. 175)

Stinson, Marjorie (stin′sən), 1896-1975 and **Katherine** 1891-1977 Sisters who were pioneers of aviation. (p. 289)

T

Taylor, Zachary (tā′lər, zak′ə rē), 1784-1850 United States general during the Mexican War and President of the United States from 1849 to 1850. (p. 197)

Travis, William B. (tra′vəs), 1809-1836 Commander of the Texans at The Alamo. (p. 163)

Trevino, Lee (trə vē′nō), 1939- Golf champion from Dallas. (p. 369)

W

Washington, George (wô′shing tən), 1732-1799 Commander of the American army during the American Revolution and first President of the United States. (p. 206)

Williams, Lizzie Johnson (wil′yəmz), 1843-1924 Known as the "Cattle Queen of Texas." (p. 248)

Williamson, Clara McDonald (wil′yəm sən), 1875-1970s Artist who captured Texas history. (p. 257)

Z

Zavala, Lorenzo de (sa va′la, lô rən′sô də), 1788-1836 Mexican who established a colony in eastern Texas and became the first vice president of the Republic of Texas. (p. 170)

pronunciation key

a at; ā ape; ä far; âr care; e end; ē me; i it; ī ice; îr pierce; o hot; ō old; ô fork; oi oil; ou out; u up; ū use; ü rule; ů pull; ûr turn; hw white; ng song; th thin; th this; zh measure; ə about, taken, pencil, lemon, circus

Glossary

This Glossary will help you to pronounce and understand the meanings of the vocabulary in this book. The page number at the end of the definition tells where the word first appears.

A

abolition (ab ə lish′ən) Ending or doing away with completely; often used in reference to slavery. (p. 227)

adobe (ə dō bē) Brick made from clay and straw that has been dried in the sun. (p. 109)

agribusiness (ag′rə biz nis) A large farm or ranch which is combined with other businesses. (p. 318)

agriculture (ag′ri kul chər) The business of growing crops and raising animals. (p. 319)

Allied Powers (al′īd pow′ərz) Countries who fought in World War I on the side led by England, France, Russia, and the United States. (p. 289)

Allies (al′īz) Countries who fought in World War II on the side led by England, France, Russia, and the United States. (p. 294)

amendment (a mend′mənt) Addition to the United States Constitution. (p. 238)

American Revolution (ə mer′i kən rev ə lü′shən) The war fought by the American colonies to end British rule, 1775-1783. (p. 206)

ancestor (an′ses tər) A person in your family, starting with your parents, who was born before you. (p. 16)

annexation (an ek sā′shən) Incorporating a territory into a country. (p. 189)

aquifer (ak′wə fər) A layer of rock or gravel that absorbs rainfall and keeps it flowing underground. (p. 23)

archaeology (ar kē ol′ə jē) The study of the way people lived in the past, including prehistoric times. (p. 92)

artifact (ar′tə fakt) Object made by people who lived in the past, often found and studied by archaeologists. (p. 92)

assembly line (ə sem′blē līn′) A line of workers and machines along which a product is moved to be put together. (p. 401)

atlatl (at′la təl) A throwing stick used by early peoples who attached it to a spear to make the spear go faster and farther. (p. 93)

Axis Powers (ak′sis pow′ərz) Countries who fought in World War II on the side led by Germany, Italy, and Japan. (p. 294)

B

band (band) Small family group to which some Native Americans belonged. (p. 105)

barbed wire (bärbd wīr) Wire with sharp metal points that is used to fence off areas of land. (p. 251)

barrier island (bar′ē ər ī′lənd) A narrow island between the mainland and the ocean. (p. 53)

barter (bärt′ər) To trade things for other things without using money. (p. 157)

basin (bā′sin) A low, bowl-shaped landform surrounded by higher land. (p. 21)

Battle of The Alamo (al′ə mō) One of the most important battles of the Texas Revolution. (p. 167)

Battle of San Jacinto (san jə sint′ō) Last battle on the Texas Revolution. Santa Anna's troops were defeated. (p. 176)

bilingual (bī ling′gwəl) People who are able to speak two languages. (p. 161)

bill (bil) A proposal for a law. (p. 336)

Black Codes (blak kōdz) Laws passed by Southern states, including Texas, that restricted the rights of African Americans. (p. 238)

blockade (blo kād′) Shutting off of an area to prevent supplies from entering or leaving. (p. 232)

boom town (büm′town) A community that grows at a rapid rate. (p. 283)

border (bôr′dər) A line that people agree on to separate two places. (p. 68)

brand (brand) A design that cowboys burned into an animal's hide to identify the ranch to which it belonged. (p. 247)

pronunciation key

a	at	ī	ice	u	up	th	thin
ā	ape	îr	pierce	ū	use	th	this
ä	far	o	hot	ü	rule	zh	measure
âr	care	ō	old	u̇	pull	ə	about, taken,
e	end	ô	fork	ûr	turn		pencil, lemon,
ē	me	oi	oil	hw	white		circus
i	it	ou	out	ng	song		

budget (buj′it) Plan for using an amount of money for specific purposes. (p. 335)

butte (būt) A flat-topped hill, smaller than a mesa. (p. 57)

byline (bī′līn) A line at the beginning of a newspaper article that names the writer. (p.332)

C

canal (kə nal′) A waterway dug across land for transportation or irrigation. (p. 75)

candidate (can′di dāt) A person running for office in an election. (p. 339)

canyon (can′yən) A deep valley with steep sides. (p. 22)

cardinal direction (kär′də nəl di rek′shən) One of the main directions of the globe; north, south, east, and west. (p. G6)

cash crop (kash krop) A crop that is grown to be sold for money rather than to be used on the farm where it is grown. (p. 157)

cattle drive (cat′əl drīv) A journey in which cowboys herded cattle north to railroad depots in the late 1800s. (p. 248)

cause (kôz) An event that makes something else happen. (p. 172)

cavalry (ka′vəl rē) A group of soldiers who fight on horseback. (p. 231)

CD-ROM (sē dē rom′) A reference source used with a computer that may include writing, pictures, sounds, or short movies. (p. 201)

census (sen′səs) A count of the people who live in a place. (p. 385)

Central Powers (sen′trəl pow′ərz) Countries that fought in World War I on the side which included Germany, Austria-Hungary, and Italy. (p. 289)

charro (chä′ rō) A traditional Mexican horseman. (p. 361)

checks and balances (cheks and bal′ən səs) The idea that each branch of government keeps watch over the others. (p. 334)

circle graph (sûr′kəl graf) A graph in the shape of a circle that shows the sizes of different parts of a whole; also called a pie graph. (p. 158)

citizen (sit′ə zən) A person who is born in a country or who has earned the right to become a member of that country by law. (p. 328)

city council (sit′ē kown′səl) Group of people elected to make laws for and help run a city or town. (p. 330)

city manager (sit′ē man′ə jər) Person hired by the mayor and city council of a large city to run its daily business. (p. 330)

civilization (siv əl ə zā′shən) A developed culture or society. (p. 98)

civil rights (siv′əl rīts) The rights of people to be treated equally under the law. (p. 298)

Civil War (siv′əl wôr) The war in the United States between the Union states of the North and the Confederate states of the South, 1861-1865. (p. 229)

climate (klī′mit) The pattern of weather of a certain place over many years. (p. 28)

coast (kōst) The land next to an ocean. (p. 9)

colony (kol′ə nē) A place that is ruled by another country. (p. 119)

commercial farmer (kə mūr′shəl fär′mər) Farmer who grows crops or raises livestock for sale. (p. 399)

compass rose (kum′pəs rōz) A small drawing on a map that shows directions. (p. G6)

commissioners court (ko mish′ə nərz kōrt) Group of five elected leaders, headed by the county judge, who makes decisions about county issues. (p. 331)

communications (kə mū ni kā′shənz) The exchange of information between people, often using the latest technology. (p. 291)

conclusion (kən klū′zhən) A statement that pulls together several pieces of information and gives them a meaning. (p. 96)

Confederacy (kən fed′ər ə sē) The government formed by 11 Southern states that seceded from the United States, 1861-1865. (p. 229)

congress (kong′ris) The legislative, or law-making, branch of a state or national government. (p. 184)

conquistador (kon kēs′tə dôr) The Spanish word for a conqueror; one who takes ownership by force. (p. 120)

conservation (kon sər vā′shən) The careful use of a natural resource. (p. 35)

constitution (kon sti tü′shən) A document that has the basic rules to govern a state or country. (p. 170)

consumer (kon sü′mər) Person who buys a product or uses a service. (p. 306)

continent (kon′tə nənt) One of Earth's seven great bodies of land—Africa, Antarctica, Asia, Australia, Europe, North America, and South America. (p. G4)

convention (kən ven′shən) A formal meeting held for a special purpose. (p. 162)

county (kown′tē) One of the sections into which a state is divided. (p. 331)

crop rotation (krop rō tā′shən) Method of planting a different crop each year on the same soil. (p. 111)

crude oil (krüd oil) Petroleum that lies near the surface of the ground. (p. 284)

culture (kul′chər) The way of life shared by a group of people, including language, beliefs, music, foods, and holidays. (p. 14)

custom (kus′təm) The special way a group of people does something. (p. 15)

D

dam (dam) A wall built across a river to control the flow of water. (p. 399)

dateline (dāt′lin) The lead-in to a newspaper article, telling when and where the story was written. (p. 332)

Davis Guards (dā′vis gärdz) Texas Confederate soldiers stationed at Fort Griffin. They turned back the Union Army at the Battle of the Sabine Pass. (p. 331)

debt (det) Amount of money owed. (p. 185)

decision (di sizh′ən) A choice that helps you reach a goal. (p. 72)

degree (di grē′) A unit for measuring distance on Earth's surface; also a unit for measuring temperature represented by the symbol °. (p. 60)

delegate (del′i git) A person who is chosen to speak for a group. (p. 162)

democratic republic (dem ə krat′ik ri pub′lik) A government in which citizens elect representatives to run the government. (p. 338)

desert (dez′ərt) A dry area that gets less than 10 inches of precipitation each year. (p. 48)

dictator (dik′tā tər) A leader with complete control of the gevernment. (p. 163)

dictionary (dik′shə ner ē) A book that explains the meanings of words and shows how to pronounce and spell them. (p. 200)

discrimination (dis kri mi nā′shən) Unfair difference in the treatment of people. (p. 296)

dugout (dug′out) A home dug out of the side of a hill. (p. 156)

E

economy (i kon′ə mē) The way a country or other place produces and uses natural resources, goods, and services. (p. 304)

editorial (ed i tôr′ē əl) A newspaper article that gives opinions, rather than facts. (p. 332)

effect (i fekt′) An event that happens as a result of another event. (p. 172)

elect (i lekt′) Choose by voting. (p. 328)

elevation (el ə vā′shən) The height of land above sea level. (p. 26)

Emancipation Proclamation (i man sə pā′shən prok lə mā′shən) Announcement by President Lincoln in 1863 that all enslaved people living in Confederate states were free. (p. 233)

empire (em′pi ər) A large area of different groups of peoples ruled by one country or leader. (p. 98)

empresario (em prəs är′ē ō) A person given a large piece of land by a government and allowed to sell the land to settlers. (p. 153)

encyclopedia (en sī klə pē′dē ə) A book or set of books that gives facts about people, places, things, and events. (p. 201)

endangered (en dān′jərd) Close to disappearing forever, especially a species of animal. (p. 386)

entrepreneur (än trə prə nûr′) Person who organizes and runs a business. (p. 305)

environment (en vī′rən mənt) The surroundings in which people, plants, or animals live. (p. 32)

equator (i kwā′tər) An imaginary line that lies halfway between the North Pole and the South Pole, at 0° latitude. (p. G5)

ethnic group (eth′nik grüp) A group of people whose ancestors are from the same country or area. (p. 17)

executive branch (eg zek′yə tiv branch) The branch of government that carries out laws. (p. 335)

expedition (eg spə dish′ ən) A journey of exploration. (p. 123)

explore (ek splôr′) To travel in unfamiliar places in order to find out and learn about them. (p. 119)

export (ek′spôrt) Something sold or traded to another country. (p. 392)

F

fact (fakt) A statement that can be checked and proven true. (p. 252)

feature article (fē′chər är′ti kəl) A newspaper story that takes a detailed look at a person, subject, or event. (p. 332)

food processing (füd pros′es ing) Any of hundreds of ways of turning crops and livestock into different food products. (p. 309)

forecast (fôr′kast) To predict what may or will happen. (p. 394)

Freedmen's Bureau (frēd′menz byü′rō) Organization which helped former slaves build new lives for themselves, established by the government during Reconstruction. (p. 237)

free-enterprise system (frē en′tər priz sis′təm) The economic system that allows people to own and run their own businesses. (p. 304)

frontier (frun tîr′) The edge of a settled area. (p. 151)

fuel (fū əl) A substance burned as a source of heat and power, such as coal, wood, or oil. (p. 34)

G

generalization (jen ər ə lə zā′shən) A statement that ties together several different examples, showing how they are connected by a single concept or idea. (p. 286)

geography (jē og′rə fē) The study of Earth and the way people, plants, and animals live on and use it. (p. 20)

glacier (glā′shər) A huge sheet of ice that moves slowly across the land. (p. 91)

global grid (glō′bəl grid) The crisscrossing lines of latitude and longitude found on a map or globe. (p. 62)

Goliad Massacre (gō′lē ad mas′ə ker) A brutal event of the Texas Revolution in which surrendering Texans were murdered by Santa Anna. (p. 171)

Grange (grānj) An association formed by farmers in the late 1800s. Grange members worked to make life better for farmers by sharing information about crops, prices, and supplies. (p. 258)

graph (graf) A diagram that shows information in a picture. (p. 158)

Great Depression (grāt di presh′ən) Period of widespread economic hardship in the 1930s. (p. 292)

guide word (gīd wûrd) One of the words at the top of each page of a reference book that shows the first and last entries on that page. (p. 200)

gusher (gush′ər) An oil well that gives forth a lot of oil without being pumped. (p. 283)

H

hailstorm (hāl′stôrm) Shower of small rounded chunks of ice. (p. 58)

headline (hed′līn) A title printed in large letters at the beginning of a newspaper article. (p. 332)

helium (hē′lē əm) A very light, colorless, odorless gas. (p. 66)

hemisphere (hem′i sfîr) Half a sphere; one of the four hemispheres of Earth—Northern, Southern, Eastern, and Western hemispheres. (p. G5)

heritage (her′i tij) The history and traditions that a group of people share. (p. 17)

high-tech industry (hī tek in′dus trē) The use of advanced scientific ideas and special skills and tools to meet people's needs. (p. 309)

historical map (his tor′i kəl map) A map that shows information about past events and where they occurred. (p. G11)

history (his′tə rē) The story of what happened in the past, usually as preserved in written records. (p. 92)

Hood's Texas Brigade (hudz tek′səs bri gād′) A brigade of Texas Confederate soldiers led by General John Bell Hood. (p. 231)

hurricane (hûr′i kān) A storm with very strong winds and heavy rains. (p. 31)

I

Ice Age (īs āj) A period of time when glaciers covered much of Earth's surface. (p. 91)

immigrant (im′i grənt) A person who comes to a new country to live. (p. 16)

import (im′pôrt) Something brought in from another country for sale or use. (p. 392)

industrialization (in dus trē əl ə zā′shən) Development of manufacturing industries. (p. 399)

industry (in′də strē) All the businesses that make one kind of product or provide one kind of service. (p. 54)

interdependent (in tər di pen′dənt) Relying on one another to meet needs and wants. (p. 13)

intermediate direction (in tər mē′dē it di rek′shən) Any direction in between two cardinal directions—northeast, southeast, southwest, northwest. (p. G6)

interstate highway (in′tər stāt hī′wā) A road that connects cities in two or more states with at least two lanes of traffic in each direction. (p. 376)

invention (in ven′shən) A newly created product. (p. 290)

investor (in ves′tər) Someone who puts money into a business and expects a share of the profit. (p. 306)

irrigation (ir i gā′shən) The use of ditches or pipes to bring water to fields. (p. 64)

J

judicial branch (jü dish′əl branch) The branch of government that interprets, or explains, laws. (p. 336)

jury (jùr′ē) A group of citizens in a court of law who must decide if someone accused of a crime is innocent or guilty. (p. 341)

K

kerosene (ker′ ə sēn) A colorless liquid made from petroleum that is used as a fuel. (p. 282)

L

landform (land′fôrm) Any of the shapes that make up Earth's surface. (p. 21)

---

pronunciation key

a **at**; ā **ape**; ä **far**; âr **care**; e **end**; ē **me**; i **it**; ī **ice**; îr **pierce**; o **hot**; ō **old**; ô **fork**; oi **oil**; ou **out**; u **up**; ū **use**; ü **rule**; ù **pull**; ûr **turn**; hw **white**; ng **song**; th **thin**; <u>th</u> **this**; zh **measure**; ə **about, taken, pencil, lemon, circus**

landform map (land´fôrm map) A map that shows the landforms of an area. (p. G10)

latitude (lat´i tüd) A measure of distance on Earth north or south of the equator. (p. 60)

legacy (leg´ə sē) A tradition that is handed down from one generation to the next and is a valued part of peoples lives today. (p. 38)

legislative branch (lej´is lā tiv branch) The branch of government that makes laws. (p. 336)

line graph (līn graf) A graph that shows how a piece of information changes over time. (p. 158)

locator (lō´kāt ər) A small map or globe set onto another map that shows where the main map is located. (p. G8)

longhorn (lông´hôrn) One of a breed of cattle having very long horns. (p. 246)

longitude (lon´ji tüd) A measure of distance on Earth east or west of the prime meridian. (p. 61)

Louisiana Purchase (lü ē zē an´ə pûr´chəs) The purchase of the Louisiana Territory in 1803 by President Thomas Jefferson. (p. 150)

Louisiana Territory (lü ē zē an´ə ter´itôrē) The land that stretched from the Mississippi River west to the Rocky Mountains. (p. 150)

lowland (lō´land) Land with an elevation just above sea level. (p. 53)

M

Manifest Destiny (man´ə fest des´tə nē) Idea popular around the 1840s that the United States would grow as far west as the Pacific and as far south as the Rio Grande. (p. 188)

manufacturing (man yə fak´chər ing) The making of goods by machinery. (p. 309)

map key (map kē) An explanation of what the symbols on a map represent. (p. G7)

marsh (märsh) An area of low wet land covered mostly with tall grasses. (p. 95)

massacre (mas´ə kər) The brutal killing of many people. (p. 171)

mayor (mā´ər) Elected head of the government of a city. (p. 330)

meridian (mə rid´ē ən) A line of longitude. (p. 61)

mesa (mā´sə) A flat landform that rises steeply above the surrounding land; smaller than a plateau. (p. 57)

mesquite (mes kēt´) A small thorny tree with long roots that dig deep to find water. (p. 57)

mestizo (me stē´zō) Person who is part Spanish and part Mexican Indian. (p. 131)

metropolitan area (met rə pol´i tən âr´ē ə) A city and its suburbs together. (p. 54)

Mexican War (mek´sə kən wôr) The war fought between Mexico and the United States between 1846 and 1848 over Texas. (p. 198)

mineral (min´ər əl) A nonrenewable natural resource that is found in the ground and does not come from plants or animals. (p. 34)

mission (mish´ən) A settlement where Europeans taught Native Americans the Christian religion. (p. 130)

missionaries (mish´ən âr ēz) People who teach their religion to others who have different beliefs. (p. 131)

mohair (mo´hār) Hair of the angora goat. (p. 65)

monarchy (mon´är kē) Nation or state that is led by a king, queen, or other ruler. (p. 269)

mouth (mouth) The place where a river empties into an ocean or another large body of water. (p. 46)

municipal (mū nis´ə pəl) Having to do with the running of a city. (p. 329)

N

NAFTA (naf´tə) North American Free Trade Agreement, which has made import and export easier between the United States, Mexico, and Canada. (p. 392)

natural feature (nach´ər əl fē´chər) Any part of Earths surface formed by nature. (p. 9)

natural resource (nach´ər əl rē´sôrs) Something found in the environment that people can use. (p. 32)

New Deal (nü dēl) Government programs introduced during the Depression by President Franklin D. Roosevelt. (p. 293)

news article (nüz är´ti kəl) A newspaper story that contains facts about recent events. (p. 332)

nonrenewable resources (non ri nü´ə bel rē sôr´sez) Resources that are available in a limited supply. When used they are gone forever. (p. 34)

Norteño (nôr tā´ nyō) Mexican American dance music. (p. 372)

O

ocean (ō´shən) One of Earths four largest bodies of water—the Atlantic, Arctic, Indian, and Pacific oceans. (p. G4)

Old Three Hundred, The (ōld thrē hun´drid) The first three hundred families to settle in San Felipe de Austin in 1825. (p. 152)

Olympics (ō lim´piks) International athletic contests held every four years. (p. 369)

opinion (ə pin´yən) A personal feeling or belief. (p. 252)

outline (out´līn) A plan for organizing written information about a subject. (p. 224)

P

parallel (par'ə lel) A line of latitude. (p. 60)

petrochemical (pet rō kem'i kəl) One of various substances produced in refineries from petroleum. (p. 284)

petroleum (pə trō'lē əm) A thick, black liquid found underground, commonly called oil. (p. 34)

physical map (fiz'i kəl map) A map that shows natural features of Earth. (p. G10)

pilgrim (pil'grəm) A person who travels to a place for religious reasons. (p. 137)

pioneer (pī ə nîr') A person who leads the way. (p. 150)

plain (plān) A large area of flat or nearly flat land. (p. 21)

Plan of Iguala (i gwä'lə) Agustín de Iturbide's plan for Mexican independence from Spain in 1821. (p. 207)

plantation (plan tā'shən) A large farm where cash crops such as cotton or corn were grown. (p. 220)

plateau (pla tō') A high, flat area that rises steeply above the surrounding land. (p. 21)

political map (pə lit'i kəl map) A map that shows information such as cities, capitals, states, and countries. (p. G9)

political party (pə lit'i kəl pär'tē) Group of people who share similar ideas about government. (p. 339)

pollution (pə lü'shən) Result of carelessly using resources, such as chemicals, that make air, water, or soil dirty. (p. 35)

population (pop yə lā'shən) The number of people who live in a place or area. (p. 158)

port (pôrt) A place where ships load and unload their goods. (p. 55)

prairie (prâr'ē) Flat or gently rolling land thickly covered with grasses and wildflowers. (p. 53)

precipitation (pri sip i tā'shən) The moisture that falls to the ground as rain, snow, sleet, or hail. (p. 29)

presidio (pri sid'e o) A fort where soldiers lived to protect nearby Spanish settlements. (p. 130)

prehistory (prē his'tə rē) The time before written records. (p. 92)

primary source (prī'mer ē sôrs) Information that comes from someone who observed or took part in what he or she is describing. (p. 388)

prime meridian (prīm mə rid'ē ən) The line of longitude, marked 0°, from which other meridians are numbered. (p. 61)

professional (prə fesh'ə nəl) A person who gets paid for an activity usually done for fun, like sports. (p. 368)

profit (prof'it) The money a business earns after it pays for tools, salaries, and other costs. (p. 305)

province (prov'ins) A smaller part of some countries, such as Canada. (p. 76)

Pueblo (pweb'lō) "Village" in Spanish; any of several Native American groups that live in adobe and stone houses. (p. 109)

Pulitzer Prize (pül'it sər prīz) Award given every year for the best work in literature and news reporting. (p. 373)

R

ragtime (rag'tīm) A type of music which mixes brass band, African American, and other sounds and rhythms. (p. 372)

rain shadow (rān shad'ō) The side of a mountain that is usually dry because precipitation falls on the other side. (p. 49)

ranch (ranch) A large area of land used to raise cattle, sheep, or horses. (p. 57)

Reconstruction (re kon struk'shən) Time period following the Civil War in which the Southern states were brought back into the Union. (p. 236)

recreation (rek rē ā'shən) What people do for relaxation or enjoyment. (p. 22)

recycle (rē sī'kəl) To use something again instead of discarding it. (p. 35)

reference source (ref'ər əns sôrs) A book or any form of information that contains facts about many different subjects. (p. 200)

refinery (ri fī'nə rē) A place where a raw substance such as crude oil or sugar is separated into parts to be used. (p. 284)

reform (rē fôrm') A change designed to make things better. (p. 259)

region (rē'jən) An area with common features that set it apart from other areas. (p. 10)

religion (rē lij'ən) The way people worship God, a god, or gods they believe in. (p. 101)

---

pronunciation key

a **at**; ā **ape**; ä **far**; âr **care**; e **end**; ē **me**; i **it**; ī **ice**; îr **pierce**; o **hot**; ō **old**; ô **fork**; oi **oil**; ou **out**; u **up**; ū **use**; ü **rule**; u̇ **pull**; ûr **turn**; hw **white**; ng **song**; th **thin**; <u>th</u> **this**; zh **measure**; ə **about, taken, pencil, lemon, circus**

renewable resource (ri nü′ə bəl rē′sôrs) A natural resource that can be replaced for later use, such as a forest. (p. 33)

republic (ri pub′ lik) A form of government in which people choose leaders to represent them. (p. 177)

reservation (rez ər vā′shən) Land set aside by the United States government for a purpose, such as for Native Americans to live on. (p. 263)

reservoir (rez′ər vwär) A natural or artificial lake used to store water. (p. 70)

resolution (rez ə lü′shən) Decision stated in a formal way. (p. 190)

revolution (rev ə lü′shən) A sudden change of government. (p. 164)

road map (rōd map) A map that shows travelers which roads to use to get from one place to another. (p. 376)

Roaring Twenties (rôr′ing twen′tēz) What people often call the 1920s, a decade of many exciting changes. (p. 290)

rodeo (rō′dē ō) Contest of cowhand skills. (p. 57)

Runaway Scrape (run′ə wā skrāp) The flight of Texans from the advance of Mexican troops during the Texas Revolution. (p. 174)

rural (rür′əl) Of the countryside. (p. 9)

S

scale (skāl) The relationship between the distance shown on a map and the real distance on Earth. (p. G8, 316)

secede (sə sēd′) To withdraw or formally leave an organization such as a government. (p. 228)

secondary source (sek′ən der ē sôrs) Information written by someone who was not present at the events described. (p. 388)

segregation (seg ri gā′shən) The practice of keeping two groups separate. (p. 298)

service industry (sûr′vis in′də strē) Businesses or jobs in which people help others. (p. 54)

sharecropper (shâr′krop ər) A person who grows crops on someone else's land, then pays a part of that crop to the owner. (p. 239)

sheriff (she′rif) Person in charge of law-enforcement for a county. (p. 331)

slavery (slā′və rē) The practice of making one person the property of another. (p. 17)

source (sôrs) The place where a river begins. (p. 46)

special district (spe′shəl dis′trikt) Group of people elected for a special purpose, such as overseeing schools. (p. 330)

spring (spring) A place where underground water comes to the surface. (p. 24)

stampede (stam pēd′) Herd of cattle running wild. (p. 249)

states' rights (stāts rīts) Belief that the people of each state have the right to decide laws for themselves. (p. 226)

stock (stok) A share, or part, of ownership in a company. (p. 292)

subsistence farming (səb sis′təns fär′məng) Growing only enough food to live, not to sell. (p. 156)

suffrage (suf′rij) The right to vote. (p. 296)

Sun Belt (sun belt) Those parts of the United States that have a warm, sunny climate all or most of the year. (p. 384)

symbol (sim′bəl) Anything that stands for something else. (p. G7)

T

tax (taks) Money people pay to a government (p. 163)

technology (tek nol′ə jē) The use of skills, ideas, and tools to meet people's needs. (p. 308)

teepee (tē′pē) A cone-shaped tent that can be put up and taken down quickly. (p. 104)

Tejano (te hän′ō) Mexican people who live in Texas. (p. 153)

temperature (tem′per ə chər) A measurement of how hot or cold something is. (p. 29)

territory (ter′i tôr ē) Land owned by a country that does not have the full rights of a state. (p. 189)

Terry's Texas Rangers (ter′ēz tek′ses rān′jerz) A group of cavalry soldiers, led by Colonel Benjamin Franklin Terry, who fought for the Confederacy. (p. 231)

Texas Declaration of Independence (tek′səs dek lə rā′shən uv in di pen′dəns) A document declaring Texas's separation from Mexico. (p. 170)

Texas Rangers (tek′ses rān′jerz) A group of volunteers formed to defend the Republic of Texas in 1835. Today they are part of the state police force. (p. 185)

Texas Revolution (tek′ses rev ə lü′shən) The fight for Texas' independence from Mexico. (p. 164)

Texas Railroad Commission (tek′səs rāl′rōd ko mi′shən) Organization created to stop the railroad companies' unfair practices. (p. 259)

time line (tīm līn) A diagram that shows a series of events in the order in which they happened. (p. 128)

time zone (tīm zōn) A region in which all the clocks are set to the same time. (p. 70)

tornado (tôr nā′dō) A destructive, swirling funnel of wind that moves over the ground at high speeds. (p. 31)

tourist (tür′əst) A person who travels for the fun of seeing new sights. (p. 71)

trade (trād) Buy and sell goods. (p. 12)

transportation map (trans pər tā′shən map) A map that shows how to travel from one place to another. (p. G10)

treaty (trē′tē) A formal agreement between countries. (p. 177)

Treaty of Guadalupe Hidalgo (trē′tē uv gwa də lü′pə hi dol′gō) Agreement signed by the United States and Mexico in 1848 ending the Mexican War. (p. 198)

Treaty of Medicine Lodge Creek (trē′tē uv med′ə sin loj crēk) Treaty of 1867 that said that some Native Americans would move their people to reservations in what is today Oklahoma. (p. 263)

Treaty of Velasco (trē′tē uv vəl as′ kō) The agreement of 1836 which ended the Texas Revolution. (p. 177)

tributary (trib′yə ter ē) Any river that flows into another, larger river. (p. 46)

tribute (trib′yūt) Payment in the form of valuable goods and services, usually demanded by a foreign ruler. The Aztecs demanded tribute from the people they conquered. (p. 100)

trotline (trot′līn) A long heavy fishing line that has several baited hooks on it. (p. 110)

tundra (tun′dra) A huge plain that is frozen for most of the year. (p. 75)

U

Union (ūn′yən) The states that make up the United States. Used during the Civil War to refer to the government of the Northern States. (p. 227)

United States Congress (kong′ris) The legislative branch of our national government. (p. 340)

United States Supreme Court (sə prēm′ kôrt) The highest court of the United States. (p. 341)

urban (ûr′bən) Of a city. (p. 9)

V

vaquero (vä kâr′ō) Ranch workers from Mexico who became the first cowboys. (p. 153)

vegetation (vej ə tā′shən) The plant life of an area. (p. 52)

veto (vē′tō) The power of the executive branch to reject a bill passed by the legislative branch. (p. 336)

W

World War I (wûrld wôr wun) The first war between countries from around the world, fought mostly in Europe from 1914 to 1918. The Allied Powers fought against the Central Powers. (p. 288)

World War II (wûrld wôr tü) War fought mostly in Europe, North Africa, and the Pacific from 1939 to 1945. The Allies fought against the Axis Powers. (p. 294)

---

pronunciation key

a **at**; ā **ape**; ä **far**; âr **care**; e **end**; ē **me**; i **it**; ī **ice**; îr **pierce**; o **hot**; ō **old**; ô **fork**; oi **oil**; ou **out**; u **up**; ū **use**; ü **rule**; ú **pull**; ûr **turn**; hw **white**; ng **song**; th **thin**; <u>th</u> **this**; zh **measure**; ə **about**, tak**e**n, penc**i**l, lem**o**n, circ**u**s

index

This Index lists many topics that appear in the book, along with the pages on which they are found. Page numbers after an *m* refer you to a map. Page numbers after a *p* indicate photographs, artwork, or charts.

nonrenewable, 34
renewable, 33, *p33*
of Texas, 32–37, 282–285
Navarro, José Antonio, 170
Nebraska, 248
Nelson, Willie, 372, 378, *p372, p379*
Nevada, 198
New Braunfels, Texas, 203
New Deal, 293, 295, *p293*
New Mexico, 9–10, 48, 70, 105, 199, *m10*
News article, 332–333, *p333*
New Spain, 121, 137, *m138*
Newspapers, reading, 332–333, *p333*
Ney, Elisabet, 371, *p371*
Nicaragua, 208, 346
Nocona, Peta, 263
Nonrenewable resource, 34
North America, 11, 91, *m11*
North Central Plains region, 52–53, 56–59, 66–67, *m57*
North Dakota, 47
Northeast, 44–45
Northers, 58
North Pole, 61, 75, *m60, m61*
Notes, writing, 224–225, *p224*
Nuclear power, 34
Nueces River, 197, 246, *m197*

O

Oceans, G4
Odessa, Texas, 65, *m65*
Ogallala Aquifer, 23–24, 66–67, *p303*
O. Henry, 373, *p373*
Oil, 34, 54–55, 59, 65, 282–285, 288–289, 309, 400, *p282, p284*
O'Keeffe, Georgia, 21, 370–371, *p370–371*
Oklahoma, 9–10, 48, 50, 105, 112, 187, 263, *m10*
Oktoberfest, 361
Old Three Hundred, The, 150, 152, 155
Olympic games, 369
Opinion, 252–253
Orange, Texas, 258
Osterman, Rosanna, 232
Outlines, writing, 224–225, *p224*

P

Pacific Ocean, 49, 188, 196, 199, 395, *m45*
Pacific Rim countries, 395
Padre Island, 53, 73, *m53*
Padre Island National Seashore, 38–39, 73, 365, *p39*
Palmito Ranch, 233, *p234*

Palo Duro Canyon, 265, *p265*
Palo Duro Canyon State Park, 365
Pampas, 75, *p78–79*
Panama, *p208, p346*
Panama Canal, 75, *p75*
Panhandle, 8, 21, 64–67, 125, 266, 365, 370, *m65*
Panna Maria, Texas, 203, 359, *p183*
Paraguay, *p208, p346*
Parallels, 60–61, *m60*
Parker, Cynthia Ann, 263, *p263*
Parker, Quanah, 263–265, *p263*
Passover, 360
Pearl Harbor, Hawaii, 294
Pedro I, Dom, 269, 271
Pedro II, Dom, 271
Peer mediation, 241
Permian Basin, 65, *m65*
Peru, 74, *p208, p347*
Petrochemicals, 284, 285, *p284*
Petroleum, 34, 284–285. See also Oil
Pickett, Bill, 253, *p253*
Pilgrims, 137
Piñeda, Alonso Alvarez de, 123, *m123, m126, p123, p129*
Piney Woods, 52–53, 73, 110, *m53*
Pioneer, 150, 202–205, *p154–157, p202, p205*
Plain, 21
Plains Indians, 104–107, *m103*
Plan of Iguala, 207
Plantation, 220–221, 224–225, 239, 269, 271
Plateau, 21
Pledge of Allegiance, 338
Plymouth, Massachusetts, 137, *m137*
Poland, 203
Polish Americans, 15, 203, 359
Political party, 339
Polk, James K., 190–191, 196–197, *p190*
Poll tax, 255
Pollution, 35, 386–387
Population, 158–159, 384–385, 387, *p158–159*
Port, 55
Port Arthur, Texas, 29, *m29*
Porter, Katherine Anne, 373, *p273*
Portugal, 122, 136, 139, 269–270, *p208*
Post Oak Belt, 52, *m53*
Prairie, 53
Prairie dog, 36, *p36*
Precipitation, 29, *m29*
Prehistory, 92
President, 340, *p340*
of Confederacy
Davis, Jefferson 229, *p229*

of Mexico
Santa Anna, Antonio Lopez de, 162–168, 171, 174–177, 198, *p162*
of Texas
Burnet, David G., 170, 175
Houston, Sam, 185–190, 195, *p186, p195*
Jones, Anson, 190–191, *p190*
Lamar, Mirabeau B., 186, 189, 195, *p187, p195*
of United States
Bush, George, 342, *p342*
Eisenhower, Dwight D., 342, *p342*
Johnson, Andrew, 236, 238
Johnson, Lyndon B., 298, 343, *p298, p343*
Lincoln, Abraham, 226, 228–229, 233, 236, 339
Polk, James K., 190–191, 196–197, *p190*
Roosevelt, Franklin D., 293, *p293*
Presidio, 130, *p179*
Primary sources, 388–389
Prime meridian, 61, *m61*
Prince Edward Island, 77
Prisoner of war camps, 295
Professional teams, 368–369
Profit, 305
Protestants, 359, *p359*
Province, 76
Pueblo, 109, *p116*
Pulitzer Prize, 373

Q

Quilts, 260–261, *p260–261*
Quintanilla, Selena, 378–379, *p379*

R

Rabb, Mary Crownover, 155–156, *p148, p155*
Radio, 290–291, *p280*
Railroads, 205, 248, 251, 254, 256–259, *m256, p254, p256–258*
Rain forest, Amazon, 75, *p79*
Rain shadow, 49, *p49*
Ramadan, 360
Ramsey, Buck, 374, *p374*
Ranch, 57
Ranching, 320–321, *p320–321*
Rancho, 130
Rankin, Melinda, 227, *p227*
Rattlesnake, 36, *p36*
Rayburn, Sam, 342–343, *p343*
Reconstruction, 236–240, 255–256
Recreation, 22, 364–369, *p365*
Recycle, 35, 387, *p35*
Red Cross, 289, *p289*
Red River Campaign, 264–265, 267, *p265*

CREDITS

Cover Design: Pentagram

Maps: Geosystems

Chapter Opener Globes: Greg Wakabayashi

Illustrations: Michael Adams: pp 88-89, 116-117, 148-149, 182-183, 195, 218-219, 244-245, 280-281; Hugh Biber: pp 366-367; pp Randy Chewning: pp 23, 36-37, 49; David Clar: pp 18; Joseph Forte: pp 168-169; Lary Greiner: pp 342-343; Rodica Prato: pp 132; Den Schofield: pp 100, 106-107; Steven Stankiewicz: pp 336, 392, 401; Oliver Williams: pp 126; Jerry Zimmerman: pp 13, 24, 34, 50-51, 57, 78-79, 94, 170, 204, 233, 249, 321, 341, 385, 402-403

PHOTOGRAPHY CREDITS: All photographs are by the Macmillan/McGraw-Hill School Division (MMSD) except as noted below.

Cover: Stephen Seeger, © 1996. i: Jack Hollingsworth. iii: b. David R. Frazier. iv: t. Cecil Carter Caddo Indian Tribe; b.l. Vanni Genova/Art Resource; b.r. Bob Sacha/National Geographic Society. v: t. Sam C. Pierson Jr.; b.r. Laurence Parent; b.l. Star of the Republic Museum. vi: t. The Granger Collection; b.r. Library of Congress; b.l. Sam C. Pierson, Jr. vii: t. Center for American History/University of Texas, Austin; b. Peter Pearson/Tony Stone Images. viii: t., b.r. Bob Daemmrich; b.l. Bill Frakes/Sports Illustrated Picture Collection. ix: Dave Wilhelm/The Stock Market. x: t. Star of The Republic Museum; b. Bob Daemmrich. G2: t. Dan Dry; b.l., b.r. Will Van Overbeek. G3: t. Zigy Kaluzny; b. Charles O'Reer. G4: Monica Stevenson for MMSD. **Chapter 1** 2 b.l. M.H. Sharp/Photo Researchers; m. Bob Daemmrich; t.r. Kevin Stillman, Texas Department of Trasportation; t.l. John Yurka/The Picture Cube. 2–3: b. Lindsay Hebberd/Woodfin Camp; b.r. Dr. Gary P. Garrett/Texas Parks and Wildlife Department. 4: t. Wyman Meinzer; b.l. Michael Melford; b.r. Bob Daemmrich. 4–5: Phyllis Greenburg/Comstock. 5: t. Bob Daemmrich; b. Laurence Parent. 6: t. Freeman/Brishaber/Photo Edit; m., b. David R. Frazier Photo Library. 7: t.l., m.l. Bob Daemmrich; m.r. Ray Hendley/ProFiles West; b.r. Andy Sacks/Tony Stone; t.r. David R. Frazier Photo Library. 8–9: Thaine Manske/The Stock Market. 12: b. David R. Frazier Photo Library. 15: t. Bob Daemmrich; b. Zigy Kaluzny. 16: t.r., t.m., b.r. Scott Harvey for MMSD; t.r. Western History Collections, University of Oklahoma Library; t.l. The Institute of Texan Cultures, San Antonio, Texas/courtesy of Onishi family; t.m. The Institute of Texan Cultures, San Antonio, Texas/courtesy of Ida Trevino; b.l. The Institute of Texan Cultures, San Antonio, Texas/courtesy of Mrs. Otto Schulze; b.r. The Institute of Texan Cultures, San Antonio, Texas/courtesy of Mrs. Annie Lee. 19: b., t. Bob Daemmrich. 20: t. Tom Bean/The Stock Market; b. David R. Frazier. 21: m. Stephen J. Krasemann/DRK Photo. 23: t.r. Billy E. Barnes/Stock Boston. 25: Dennis Fagan/National Wildflower Research Center. 28: t. Donna West Mulder/Stock Options. 30: l. Freeman Photography. 30–31: r. Stephan Myers/TexStockPhotoInc. 31: r. A. & J. Verkaik/The Stock Market. 32: t. Owen Franken/Stock Boston. 33: b.l. Bob Daemmrich; b.r. Bob Daemmrich/Stock Boston; t. Don Klumpp/The Image Bank. 34: Steve Allen/The Image Bank. 35: b.l. Karen Warren/Austin American Statesman; b.r. David W. Hamilton/The Image Bank; m. Bob Daemmrich/Stock Boston. 36: t.l. G.C. Kelley/Photo Researchers, Inc.; m.l. David J. Sams/Stock Boston; b.l. Charles Krebs/The Stock Market; t.r. Renee Lynn/Photo Researchers, Inc.; b.r. Stephen J. Krasemann/Photo Researchers, Inc.; m.r. David R. Frazier Photography. 37: b. Jeff Foott/DRK Photo; b.m. Dr. M. Tuttle/Bat Conservation International, Inc.; t.m. Dr. Randall E. Moss; t.r. Pat & Tom Leeson/Photo Researchers, Inc. 38–39: Odyssey/Frerck/Chicago. 39: t. Jeff Gnass Photography/West Stock; b. David R. Frazier Photo Library. **Chapter 2** 42: t. Steve Chenn/Westlight; m.t. Bob Daemmrich/The Image Works; m.b. George Hall/Woodfin Camp and Associates; b. Thomas Dimock/The Stock Market. 44: Thomas Kitchin/Tom Stack & Associates. 45: Kevin Schafer/Tony Stone Images. 46: t. Library of Congress; b. Larry Fisher Photog./Masterfile. 47: t. Roy Morsch/The Stock Market; b. W. Geiersperger/The Stock Market. 48: b. C.C. Lockwood/DRK Photo; t. Bill Ross/First Light. 49: Superstock. 52: Odyssey/Frerck/Chicago. 53: b. Robert Redding for MMSD. 54: Hank Morgan/Photo Researchers, Inc. 55: J.S. Covington/Stock Options. 56: Buddy Mays/Travel Stock. 58: l., r. Ray Hand for MMSD. 59: Jack Hollingsworth/Stock Options. 64: t. Jack Lewis/TXDOT. 64–65: William Johnson/Stock Boston. 66: b. Grant Heilman/Grant Heilman Photography, Inc. 66–67: t. Joe Viesti/Viesti Associates, Inc.; b. Grant Heilman/Grant Heilman Photography, Inc. 68: Tom Till/DRK Photo. 69: b. Odyssey/Frerck/Chicago; t. Tom McHugh/Photo Researchers, Inc. 70: b. Bob Daemmrich Photo; t. Courtesy of Tony Lama Boot Company. 70–71: Grant Heilman Photography, Inc. 72: t. Richard Stockton/The Stockhouse, Inc.; b. Jeff Gnass/The Stock Market. 74: David Ball/The Picture Cube. 75: l. Masterfile; r. Match 2 Stock Exchange, Ltd. 76: b. Bill Brooks/Masterfile; t. Mark Tomalty/Masterfile. 77: J. Sylvester/First Light. 78: t. Wolfgang Kaehler; b. Crandall/The Image Works. 79: b. Wayne Lynch/DRK; t. Frans Lanting/Minden Pictures. m. Ellen Halloran. 84: t. Sam C. Pierson Jr.; m. David R. Frazier Photo Library/Institute of Texan Cultures, San Antonio, TX. 84–85: b. Robert and Linda Mitchell. 85: Vanni Genova/Art Resource. 86: m. Informedia; t. Bob Daemmrich/Tony Stone Worldwide; b. Zigy Kaluzny. 86–87: Will Van Overbeek. **Chapter 3** 90: t., b. Robert & Linda Mitchell. 92: l., r. Caddoan Mounds State Historical Park. 93: t. Panhandle-Plains Historical Museum; b. Institute of Texan Cultures, San Antonio Light Collection. 94–95: Texas Archeological Research Laboratory, The University of Texas at Austin. 96: l. Texas Archeological Research Laboratory, The University of Texas at Austin; m. Laurence Parent; r. Institute of Texan Cultures, San Antonio, Texas. 97: l., r. Texas Archeological Research Laboratory, The University of Texas at Austin. 98: Sam C. Pierson, Jr. 101: Bodleian Library, Oxford, U.K. 102: Gilcrease Museum, Tulsa, OK. 103: Courtesy of the Witte Museum, San Antonio, TX. 105: t. Institute of Texan Cultures, San Antonio, TX; b. The Heard Museum, Phoenix, AZ. 108: Caddoan Mounds State Historical Park. 110: David R. Frazier Photo Library/Institute of Texan Cultures, San Antonio, TX. 112: Cecil Carter, Caddo Indian Tribe, 1972. 113: Courtesy of Nancy Hisa. 115: Caddoan Mounds State Historical Park. **Chapter 4** 118: t. Vanni Genova/Art Resource. 118–119: Bob Sacha/National Geographic Society. 119: t. Ronald Sheridan/Ancient Art & Architecture Collection. 120–121: The Granger Collection. 122: b. Sam C. Pierson, Jr. 122–123: The Granger Collection. 123: Ronald Sheridan/Ancient Art & Architecture Collection. 124: t. University of Texas/American History Center. 124–125: Spencer Swanger/Tom Stack & Associates. 125: r. courtesy of Panhandle Plains Historical Museum, Canyon, TX. 130: Laurence Parent. 132–133: Mission San Lorenzo de la Santa Cruz. 134: L. Kolvoord/ The Image Works. 135: t. Brian Seed/Tony Stone Images; b. Bob Daemmrich; m. Laurence Parent. 136: Brownie Harris/ The Stock Market. 139: Missouri Historical Society. 144: t.l. Archives Division-Texas State Library; t.r. Laurence Parent; m. Star of the Republic Museum; b. The Bettmann Archive. 145: t. Sam C. Pierson, Jr.; b. Archives Division/Texas State Library. 146–147: Michael O'Brien. 146: b. Laurence Parent. 147: t. New York Public Library; b. Archives Division-Texas State Library. **Chapter 5** 150: Sam C. Pierson, Jr. 151: Archives Division, Texas State Library, Austin. 152: Laurence Parent. 153–154: The Institute of Texan Cultures, San Antonio, Texas. 155: b. Jan Butchofsky-Houser '94; t. Barker Texas Historical Center, UT-Austin/Courtesy of John & Mary Rabb. 156: t. The Institute of Texan Cultures, San Antonio, Texas; b. Robert & Linda Mitchell. 157: Star of The Republic Museum, TX, Lynn A. Hermann. 160: Sam C. Pierson, Jr. 161: Archives Division-Texas State Library. 162: b. Benson Latin American Collection, University of Texas at Austin; t. The Granger Collection. 162–163: Benson Latin American Collection, University of Texas at Austin. 163: r. Robert & Linda Mitchell. 164: l. Illusions Studio; r. The Institute of Texan Cultures, San Antonio, Texas. 166: t. Laurence Parent. 166–167:b. The Institute of Texan Cultures, San Antonio, Texas. 167: l. The Granger Collection; r. The Institute of Texan Cultures, San Antonio, Texas. 170: r. Archives Division-Texas State Library. 171: l. Sam C. Pierson, Jr. 172–173: Robert Frerck/Woodfin Camp & Associates. 174: Byron Augustin/D.D.B. Stock Photo. 175: The Bettmann Archive. 176: t. Sam C. Pierson, Jr. for MMSD; b. Archives Division-Texas State Library, Photo by Eric Beggs. 178: Bob Daemmrich. 178–179: b. James P. Rowan/Tony Stone Images. 179: m. UPI/Bettmann; t. Daemmrich/Stock Boston. **Chapter 6** 184: The Granger Collection. 184–185: The Granger Collection. 185: b. Culver Pictures, Inc.; t. Archives Division-Texas State Library. 186: t. Sam C. Pierson, Jr.; b. Texas State Archives/Archives Division-Texas State Library. 187: b. Sam C. Pierson, Jr.; t.m. Archives Division-Texas State Library. 188: Star of the Republic Museum. 190: l. Brown Brothers; r. The Granger Collection. 190–191: Star of the Republic Museum, Texas/Lynn A. Herrmann. 191: The Institute of Texan Cultures, San Antonio, Texas. 192: t.l., t.r., b.l. Gallery of the Republic; b.r. Star of the Republic Museum. 193: t. Gallery of the Republic; b. Michael Shay/Photogroup/FPG. 194: Photographs Collection, The Center for American History, The University of Texas at Austin. 195: b. Sam C. Pierson, Jr.; t. The Granger Collection. 196: The Granger Collection. 198: Sam C. Pierson, Jr. 201: Sunlight Images for MMSD. 202: Laurence Parent. 203: Star of the Republic Museum, TX/Lynn A. Hermann. 204: Byron Augustin/DDB Stock Photo. 205: r. North Wind Picture Archives; l. Keystone View Co./FPG International. 206: Peter Gridley/FPG International. 207: t. Sam C. Pierson, Jr.; b. Allan Barnes, 1995/D.D.B. Stock Photo. 214: t.l. Library of Congress; t.r. Thomas Gilcrease Institute of American History and Art; b. High Impact Photography/Time-Life Books, Inc.; m. The Granger Collection. 215: b.l. The Institute of Texan Cultures, San Antonio, TX/Courtesy Emmett Shelton; t.r. The Granger Collection; b.r. High Impact Photography/Time Life Books, Inc. 216–217: Laurence Parent. 216: b. Archives Division/Texas State Library. 217: b. Mike Murphy; t. Union Pacific Railroad Museum Collection. **Chapter 7** 220: D. Donne Bryant/D.D.B. Stock Photography. 222: Dallas Museum of Art, The Karl and Esther Hoblitzelle Collection, gift of the Hoblitzelle Foundation. 223: Institute of Texan Cultures. 225: Woodfin Camp/Hulton Deutsch. 226: North Wind Picture Archives. 227: General Libraries, University of Texas, Austin. 229: t. The Granger Collection; b. North Wind Picture Archives. 230: t. The Granger Collection; b. High Impact Photography/Time Life Books, Inc. 231: l. High Impact Photography/ Time Life Books, Inc.; r. Archives Division, Texas State Library. 232: t.l., b.l., r. High Impact Photography/Time Life Books, Inc.; m. Brown Brothers. 234: t.l., t.r. The Institute of Texan Cultures, San Antonio, Texas; b.r. Texas Southmost College, Brownsville, Texas. 235: The Granger Collection. 237: l. Brazoria County Historical Museum; r. Archives Division, Texas State Library. 239: Brown Brothers. 240: Archives Division, Texas State Library. 241: Courtesy; E. Fritrell/J.C. Austin. **Chapter 8** 246: Lara Hartley/Hartley Photography. 247: l. Henry Nelson © Wichita Art Museum; r. Sam C. Pierson, Jr. 248: The Institute of Texan Cultures, San Antonio, Texas/courtesy: Emmett Shelton. 251: t. Fort Worth Star-Telegram; m. North Wind Picture Archives. 252: Sam C. Pierson, Jr. 253: Library of Congress. 254: Hulton Deutsch/Woodfin Camp and Assoc. 255: Archives Division, Texas State Library. 256: t. Southwestern Pacific Lines; m., b. Earl Nottingham. 257: A. H. Belo Corporation Foundation. 258: l. Library of Congress; r. Houston Public Library. 259: The Institute of Texan Cultures, San Antonio, Texas. 260–261: "String Scrap Quilt", by Gazzie Hill, from LONE STARS: A LEGACY OF TEXAS QUILTS, 1836–1936, by Karoline Patterson Bresenhan and Nancy O'Bryant Puentes, copyright © 1986. By permission of the authors and the University of Texas Press. 262: Thomas Gilcrease Institute of American History and Art, Tulsa, OK. 263: t. The Institute of Texan Cultures, San Antonio, Texas; m. The Texas Collection of Baylor University; b. Wyman Meinzer. 264: Wyman Meinzer. 265: t. The Institute of Texan Cultures, San Antonio, Texas; b. Smithsonian Institution. 266: Lieb Image Archives. 267: Public Affairs Office/Department of Army. 268: Hulton Deutsch/Woodfin Camp and Assoc. 269: m., b. NorthWind Picture Archives; t. Holt Studios International/Photo Researchers, Inc. 276: t. The Institute of Texan Cultures, San Antonio, TX/Courtesy A.Ike Idar; b. Peter Pearson/Tony Stone Worldwide; m.r. Library of Congress. 277: t. UPI/Bettman; b. Sullivan/TexaStock. 278–279: Don Smetzer/Tony Stone Worldwide. 278: Gladys City Boomtown Museum, Lamar University, Beaumont, TX. 279: t. Mieko Mahi; b. Fred A. Schell, Courtesy: American Petroleum Institute. **Chapter 9** 282: The Center for American History, University of Texas at Austin. 283: r. Memorial Art Gallery/Univerisity of Rochester; Marion Stratton Gould Fund; l. Woodfin Camp & Associates, Inc. 285: Mike Nelson/FPG International. 286–287: Courtesy of Panhandle-Plains Historical Museum, Canyon, Texas. 287: r. Lynn Ivory. 288–289: Frank Whitney 1990/ The Image Bank. 289: t. American Red Cross-Tarrant County Chapter; m. The Institute of Texan Cultures, The San Antonio Light Collection. 290: Library of Congress. 291: t. The Institute of Texan Cultures; b. The Bettmann Archive. 292: The Institute of Texan Cultures, The San Antonio Light Collection. 293: b. Keystone View Co./FPG International; t. The Institute of Texan Cultures/The San Antonio Light Collection. 294: t. U.S. Dept. of the Army, Office of The Chief of Information, Washington, D.C. 20310 (National Archives Negative); m. Woodfin Camp & Associates, Inc./Y. Karsh. 295: The San Antonio Light Collection, The Institute of Texan Cultures. 296: The Texas Collection of Baylor Univesity. 297: l., r. The Institute of Texan Cultures, The San Antonio Light Collection. 298: Cecil Stoughton/Lyndon B. Johnson Library Collection. 299: The Institute of Texan Cultures, San Antonio, Texas, Courtesy A. Ike Idar. **Chapter 10** 303: m.t. David Stoecklein/The Stock Market; m.b. Greg Smith/SABA; b. Bob Daemmrich. 303: t. Bob Gomel/The Stock Market. 304–307: Courtesy of Debbie Redding/Southwestern Bell Telephone. 308: B. Mahoney/The Image Works. 309: l. David R. Frazier Photo Library. 310: l. NASA. 310–311: Peter Pearson/Tony Stone Images, Inc. 314: Phillip Boyer/Photo Researchers, Inc. 315: t. Deanna Appell; m. King Fisher Marine Service, Inc.; b. Texas Parks & Wildlife Department. 318: Tom Bean/DRK Photo. 319: Bob Redding for MMSD. 320: Zigy Kaluzny. 322–323: Bob Daemmrich/Stock Boston. 323: t., m. Robert E. Daemmrich/Tony Stone Images; b. Kolvoord/The Image Works. **Chapter 11** 326–327: Dave Wilhelm/The Stock Market. 328: Bob Redding for MMSD. 329: t. Larry Kolvoord/Viesti Assoc. Inc.; m. Bob Daemmrich/The Image Works; b. Ralph Barrera/TexaStock. 330–331: Bob Daemmrich/Stock Boston. 333: David Young-Wolff/Photo Edit. 334: t. Bob Daemmrich; b. Sally Cassidy/The Picture Cube. 335: Zigy Kaluzny/Gamma Liaison. 337: Bob Daemmrich/The Image Works. 338: t. Uniphoto; m., b. Culver Pictures. 339: B.Mahoney/The Image Works. 341: Sygma. 342: l. David A. Rodgers/Sygma. 343: t.l. Najlah Feanny/SABA; t.m. Kolvoord/TexaStock; t.r. Morton Tadder/Archive Photos; b.l. Bernard Gotfryd/Woodfin Camp & Assoc.; b.r. Larry Downing/Sygma. 352: b. Jack Hollingsworth/Stock Options; t. © Malcolm Varon, 1987; m. Ken Nahoum/Sygma. 353: r. John McDonough/Sports Illustrated, © Time, Inc.; b.l. D.Cavagnaro/DRK Photo. 354: t. m. Larry Lee/Westlight; b. Carter Smith/Sygma. 354–355: William James Warren/Westlight. **Chapter 12** 357: Robert E. Daemmrich/Tony Stone Images. 358: Bob Daemmrich. 359: l. Chuck Savage/The Stock Market; r. Bob Daemmrich/Stock Boston. 360: l. Bob Daemmrich. 360–361: Robert E. Daemmrich/Tony Stone Images. 361: t. Bob Daemmrich Photos/Stock Boston; b. Lindsay Hebberd/Woodfin Camp & Assoc., Inc. 362: David Parker/SPL/Photo Researchers, Inc. 363: Bob Daemmrich Photo, Inc. 364: Haviv/SABA. 365: t. Bob Daemmrich Photos, Inc.; b. L. Kolvoord/The Image Works. 366: Dan Golden/Shooting Star. 367: m.r. Snap Photo/Outline; b.r., b.l. Pam Francis; t.l. Jack Mitchell/Outline; m.l. Douglas Kirkland/Sygma. 368: l. Scott Halleran/Allsport USA; r. Texas Tech Student Publications. 369: Bill Frakes/Sports Illustrated Picture Collection. 370: The Bettmann Archive. 371: t. Archives Division-Texas State Library; m. Bob Daemmrich; b. © Malcolm Varon, 1987. 372: t. Bob Daemmrich; m. Chiasson/Liaison; b. The Bettmann Archive. 373: r. Culver Pictures, Inc.; l. The Bettmann Archive. 374: © Wyatt McSpadden. 375: t. Ben De Soto; b.l. Fidencio Duran. 376–377: Lindsay Hebberd/Woodfin Camp & Assoc., Inc. 378: b. The Center for American History/The University of Texas at Austin; t. The Institute of Texan Cultures, San Antonio, TX. 379: t. Sung Park/Austin American Statesman/Sygma; m. Ken Nahoum/Sygma; b. Huntly Hersch/The Picture Cube. 382–383: t. Poulides Thatcher/Tony Stone; m. David R. Frazier PhotoLibrary; b. NASA. **Chapter 13** 384: Odyssey/Frerck/Chicago. 385: l. Ron Litt/Stock Options; r. J. Messerschmidt/The Stock Market. 386: l. Robert Winslow/Viesti Associates, Inc.; r. Daemmrich/Stock Boston. 387: Earth Camp Austin '95/Green Piece/Environmental & Conservation Services Dept., City of Austin, TX. 388: Ray Sasser. 390: © Wernher Krutein/Liaison International. 391: t. Courtesy of State Senator Mario Gallegos. 392–393: David J. Sams/Texas Imprint/Stock Boston. 394: Nigel Press/Tony Stone Images. 395: t. courtesy of Dr. B.W. Prasad, Dept. of Biochemistry, Baylor College of Medicine, Houston, TX 77030; l., r. E. Joseph Deering/ Houston Chronicle. 396: t. courtesy of Lori Whited, L.P.N., C.O.T./The Eye Clinic, Lake Charles, LA. 396–397: NASA. 398: Viviane Moos/SABA. 399: Cameramann/The Image Works. 400: Michael Newman/PhotoEdit. R19: Dave Wilhelm/the Sock Market. R21: r. NASA. Endpapers: Bridgeman Art Library.